LINGUISTICS

LINGUISTICS

AN INTRODUCTION TO LANGUAGE AND COMMUNICATION

Adrian Akmajian
Richard A. Demers
Ann K. Farmer
Robert M. Harnish

Third Edition

The MIT Press
Cambridge, Massachusetts
London, England

Third printing, 1992

© 1990 Massachusetts Institute of Technology

This book was set in Times Roman by Asco Trade Typesetting Ltd., Hong Kong and printed and bound by Halliday Lithograph in the United States of America.

Library of Congress Cataloging-in-Publication Data

Linguistics, an introduction to language and communication / Adrian
  Akmajian ... [et al.].—3rd ed.

    p.   cm.
  Rev. ed. of: Linguistics, an introduction to language and communication /
Adrian Akmajian, Richard A. Demers, Robert M. Harnish. 2nd ed. © 1984.
Includes bibliographical references.
ISBN 0-262-01109-3.—ISBN 0-262-51042-1 (pbk.)
  1. Linguistics. I. Akmajian, Adrian.
P121.A4384   1990
410—dc20

CONTENTS

Appendix
THE WRITTEN REPRESENTA-
TION OF LANGUAGE   467

ACKNOWLEDGMENTS

For the evolution of this third edition we would like to thank the many students we have taught and from whom we have learned, and our colleagues in the Departments of Linguistics at the University of Arizona and SUNY Albany. We would especially like to mention Keith Allan, Ken Forster, Francine Frank, Merrill Garrett, Eloise Jelinek, Adrienne Lehrer, Nancy Levin, Paul Saka, Ernest Scatton, and Louisa M. Slowiaczek. We would also like to thank all our colleagues and friends who took the time to fill out questionnaires assessing the second edition. These comments were taken seriously in completing the third edition. Finally, thanks to Larry Hagberg for help on the glossary and to Ellen Livingston for help on the index.

NOTE TO THE TEACHER

This third edition of our text evolved from our continuing collaboration in teaching introductory linguistics at the University of Arizona. Classroom experience, as well as valuable feedback from students and colleagues around the country, revealed ways in which the material of the second edition could be revised and improved. The text is divided into two parts. The first part deals with the *structural* and *interpretive* parts of language: morphology, phonetics, phonology, syntax, semantics, variation, and change. The second part is cognitively oriented and includes chapters on pragmatics, psychology of language, language acquisition, and language and the brain.

In this edition all chapters have been revised and updated. Many of them include sections on special topics of particular interest, which are set off at the end of the chapter so that the flow of discussion is not disturbed. The earlier phonology chapter has been split into two chapters: the phonetics chapter contains a detailed description of several features of American English, and the phonology chapter includes a motivation for distinctive feature theory and an introduction to metrical structures associated with words. Finally, topics in anaphora are discussed from the perspective of morphology, syntax, semantics, pragmatics, and language acquisition.

Despite the changes we have made, certain aspects of the text remain unchanged. In particular, we must emphasize once again our concern with imparting basic conceptual foundations of linguistics and the method of argumentation, justification, and hypothesis testing within the field. In no way is this edition intended to be a complete survey of the facts or putative results that have occupied linguists in recent years. On the contrary, we have chosen a small set of linguistic concepts that we understand to be among the most fundamental within the field at this time, and in presenting these concepts we have attempted to show how to argue for linguistic hypotheses. By dealing with a relatively small number of topics in detail, students can get a feeling for how work in different areas of linguistics is done. If an introductory course can impart this feeling for the field, it will have largely succeeded.

Although we have added a small number of linguistic examples from other languages (such as Japanese), we have drawn the examples in this edition, as in the previous ones, almost exclusively from English. Once again we should note that we recognize the great importance of studying language universals and the increasingly significant role that comparative studies will play in linguistic research. In presenting conceptual foundations of linguistics to students who have never been exposed to the subject before, however, we feel it is crucial that they should be able to draw upon their linguistic intuitions when required to make subtle judgments about language, both in following the text and in doing exercises. This is not merely for convenience, to set up as few obstacles as possible in an introductory course; rather, we feel that it is essential that students be able to evaluate critically our factual claims at each step, for this encourages a healthy skepticism and an active approach toward the subject matter. Given that the majority of our readers are native speakers of English, our focus on English examples provides benefits that we feel far outweigh the lack of data from other languages. Obviously, the general principles we discuss must be applicable to all languages, and some teachers may wish to emphasize universals and cross-language data in their lectures. Such material can be found in *A Linguistics Workbook*, by Richard A. Demers and Ann K. Farmer, also published by The MIT Press.

Lesson Plans

We have organized this edition to give teachers maximum flexibility in designing a linguistics course for their own (and their students' own) special needs. The book has been designed specifically so that teachers can skip over entire sections or chapters not relevant for their own pedagogical purposes (see the special sections); thus, it can be used in a modular fashion. We will take up some specific examples.

For teachers working in the quarter system, this edition can be used easily for a one-quarter course. For a course oriented toward more traditional topics in linguistics, the following is a possible format (with variations depending on the teacher):

Chapter 2: Morphology
Chapter 3: Phonetics

Chapter 4: Phonology
Chapter 5: Syntax
Chapter 7: Language Variation
Chapter 8: Language Change

The chapters cited do not depend crucially on the ones that have been skipped over; thus, we have ensured that a traditional core exists within this edition.

For a one-quarter course with an emphasis on psycholinguistics, cognitive science, or human communication, the following is a possible format:

Chapter 2: Morphology
Chapter 5: Syntax
Chapter 6: Semantics
Chapter 9: Pragmatics
Chapter 10: Psychology of Language
Chapter 12: Language and the Brain

The individual chapters are designed with numerous subsections and in such a way that core material is often presented first, with additional material following as special topics. In this way, teachers who can spend only a week on a certain chapter are able to choose various subsections, so that students are exposed to the material most relevant for that particular course.

Teachers working within the semester system (or teaching courses that run two quarters in the quarter system) will find that this edition can be used quite comfortably within a 14- or 15-week term. For example, for a one-semester linguistics course oriented toward more traditional topics, the following is a possible format:

Chapter 2: Morphology
Chapter 3: Phonetics
Chapter 4: Phonology
Chapter 5: Syntax
Chapter 6: Semantics
Chapter 7: Language Variation
Chapter 8: Language Change
Chapter 9: Pragmatics

Obviously, teachers with other interests will pick different modules for a course. For example, given a course with a psycholinguistic, cognitive science, or human communication orientation, the following choice of topics seems reasonable:

Chapter 2: Morphology
Chapter 5: Syntax
Chapter 6: Semantics
Chapter 9: Pragmatics
Chapter 10: Psychology of Language
Chapter 11: Language Acquisition
Chapter 12: Language and the Brain

In short, by varying the selection of chapters, subsections, and special topics, teachers from diverse backgrounds and in diverse academic departments will be able to design an introduction to linguistics that is custommade for their purposes.

Part I

THE STRUCTURE OF HUMAN LANGUAGE

INTRODUCTION

In this section we will examine the structure of human language, and in doing so we will discover a system that is highly complex. Beginning students of linguistics are often surprised to find that linguists spend considerable time formulating theories to represent an account for the structure (as well as functioning) of human language. What is there, after all, to explain? Speaking one's native language is a natural and effortless task, carried out with great speed and ease. Even young children can do it with little conscious effort. From this, it is commonly concluded that aside from a few rules of grammar and pronunciation there is nothing else to explain about human language.

But it turns out that there is a great deal to explain. If we "step outside" language and look at it as an object to be consciously studied and described and not merely used, we discover an exciting sphere of human knowledge previously hidden from us.

In beginning the study of the structural properties of human language, it is useful to note a common theme that runs throughout part I: the structural analysis of human language can be stated in terms of (1) discrete units of various sorts and (2) rules and principles that govern the way these discrete units can be combined and ordered. In the sections on morphology (chapter 2), phonetics (chapter 3), phonology (chapter 4), and syntax (chapter 5), we will discuss the significant discrete units that linguists have postulated in the study of these subareas of linguistics. In addition to isolating discrete units such as morphemes, phonetic features, and syntactic phrases, we will examine the rules and principles by which words are formed, sounds are combined and varied, and syntactic units are structured and ordered into larger phrases.

In addition to discussing the core areas of morphology, phonology, syntax, and semantics (chapter 6), we will discuss two subfields of linguistics that draw heavily on those core areas, namely, language variation (chapter 7) and language change (chapter 8). In these chapters we will consider the ways in which language varies across individual speakers and dialect groups (regionally, socially, and ethnically) and how languages vary and relate to each other historically. Thus, having isolated important structural units and rules for combination in chapters 2–5, we will then examine how such units and rules can vary along a number of dimensions.

The subfields represented in chapters 2–6 form the core of what has classically been known as *structural linguistics* (as practiced in the United States from the 1930s to the 1950s), and they continue to form a central part of *transformational/generative linguistics*, the theoretical perspective we adopt here. The latter dates from the publication of Noam Chomsky's 1957 work *Syntactic Structures* and has been the dominant school of linguistics in the United States since that time. It has also come to be a dominant school in Western Europe and Japan and has increasing influence in several Eastern European countries as well.

Assuming that the majority of our readers are native speakers of English, we have drawn the language data used in this book almost exclusively from English (see *A Linguistics Workbook*, by Richard A. Demers and Ann K. Farmer, also published by The MIT Press, for exercises based on over 20 languages). We encourage you to use your native linguistic judgments in evaluating our arguments and hypotheses. It is important that you test hypotheses, since this is an important aspect of doing scientific investigations. We should also stress that the general aspects of the linguistic framework we describe here are supposed to hold for all languages, or at least for a large subset of languages, and we encourage you to think about other languages you may know as you study the English examples.

Chapter 1

WHAT IS LINGUISTICS?

The field of linguistics, the scientific study of human natural language, is a growing and exciting area of study, with an important impact on fields as diverse as education, anthropology, sociology, language teaching, cognitive psychology, philosophy, computer science, and artificial intelligence, among others. Indeed, the last four fields cited, along with linguistics, are the key components of the newly emerging field of cognitive science, the study of the structure and functioning of human cognitive processes.

In spite of the importance of the field of linguistics, many people, even highly educated people, will tell you that they have only a vague idea of what the field is about. Some believe that a linguist is a person who speaks several languages fluently. Others believe that linguists are language experts who can help you decide whether it is better to say "It is I" or "It's me." Yet it is quite possible to be a professional linguist (and an excellent one at that) without having taught a single language class, without having interpreted at the UN, and without speaking any more than one language.

What is linguistics, then? Fundamentally, the field is concerned with the nature of language and communication. It is apparent that people have been fascinated with language and communication for thousands of years, yet in many ways we are only beginning to understand the complex nature of this aspect of human life. If we ask, What is the nature of language? or How does communication work? we quickly realize that these questions have no simple answers and are much too broad to be answered in a direct way. Similarly, questions such as What is energy? or What is matter? cannot be answered in a simple fashion, and indeed the entire field of physics is an attempt to answer them. Linguistics is no different: the field as a whole represents an attempt to break down the broad questions about the nature of language and communication into smaller, more manageable questions that we can hope to answer, and in so doing establish reasonable results that we can build on in moving closer to answers to the larger questions. Unless we limit our sights in this way and restrict ourselves to particular frameworks for examining different aspects of language and communication, we cannot hope to make progress in answering the broad questions that have fascinated people for so long. As we will see, the field covers a surprisingly broad range of topics related to language and communication.

The first part of the text contains chapters dealing primarily with the structural components of language. Chapter 2, "Morphology," is concerned with the properties of words and word-building rules. Chapter 3, "Phonetics," introduces the physiology involved in the production of speech sounds as well as phonemic and phonetic transcription systems that are used to represent the sounds of English. Chapter 4, "Phonology," surveys the organizational principles that determine the patterns the speech sounds are subject to. Chapter 5, "Syntax," presents a study of the structure of sentences and phrases. Chapter 6, "Semantics," surveys the properties of meaning and denotation. Chapter 7, "Language Variation," deals with the ways speakers and groups of speakers can differ from each other in terms of the various forms of language that they use. Chapter 8, "Language Change," examines how languages change over time and how languages can be historically related.

Having examined certain structural properties of human language in part I, we turn to functional properties in part II. Chapter 9, "Pragmatics," explores some of the issues involved in describing human communication and proposes certain communication strategies that people use when they talk to each other. Chapter 10, "Psychology of Language," examines how language is cognitively processed and perceived; chapter 11, "Language Acquisition in Child and Chimp," studies the stages involved in language acquisition by normal humans; and chapter 12, "Language and the Brain," deals with how language is stored and processed in the brain.

To turn now from the particular to the general, what are some of the background assumptions that linguists make when they study language? Perhaps the most important fundamental assumption is that human language at all levels is rule- (or principle-) governed. Every known language has systematic rules governing pronunciation, word formation, and grammatical construction. Further, the way in which meanings are associated with phrases of a language is characterized by regular rules. Finally, the *use* of language to communicate is governed by important generalizations that can be expressed in rules. The ultimate aim in each chapter, therefore, is to formulate linguistic rules to describe and explain the phenomena under consideration. Indeed, chapter 7 shows that even so-called casual speech is governed by systematic regularities expressible in rules.

At this point we must add an important qualification to what we have just said. That is, we are using the terms *rule* and *rule-governed* in the special way that linguists use them. This usage is very different from the layperson's understanding of the terms. In school most of us were taught so-called rules of grammar, which we were told to follow in order to speak and write "correctly"—rules such as "Do not end a sentence with a preposition," or "Don't say 'ain't'," or "Never split an infinitive." Rules of this sort are called *prescriptive rules*; that is to say, they prescribe, or dictate to the speaker, the way the language supposedly should be written or spoken in order for the speaker to appear correct or educated. Prescriptive rules are really rules of style rather than rules of grammar.

In sharp contrast, when linguists speak of rules, they are not referring to prescriptive rules from grammar books. Rather, linguists try to formulate *descriptive rules* when they analyze language, rules that describe the actual language of some group of speakers and not some hypothetical language that speakers "should" use. Descriptive rules express generalizations and regularities about various aspects of language. Thus, when we say that language is rule-governed, we are really saying that the study of human language has revealed numerous generalizations about and regularities in the structure and function of language. In spite of the fact that language is governed by strict principles, speakers nonetheless control a system that is *unbounded in scope*, which is to say that there is no limit to the kinds of things that can be talked about. How language achieves this property of *effability* (unboundedness in scope) is addressed in chapters 2 and 5, "Morphology" and "Syntax."

Another important background assumption that linguists make is that the various human languages constitute a *unified phenomenon*: linguists assume that it is possible to study human language in general and that the study of particular languages will reveal features of language that are universal. What do we mean by universal features of language?

So far we have used the terms *language* and *human language* without referring to any specific language, such as English or Chinese. Students are sometimes puzzled by this general use of the term *language*; it would seem that this use is rarely found outside of linguistics-related courses. Foreign language courses, after all, deal with specific languages such as French or Russian. Further, specific human languages appear on the surface to be so different from each other that it is often difficult to understand how linguists can speak of language as though it were a single thing.

Although it is obvious that specific languages differ from each other on the surface, if we look closer we find that human languages are surprisingly similar. For instance, all known languages are at a similar level of complexity and detail—there is no such thing as a primitive human language. All languages provide a means for asking questions, making requests, giving orders, making assertions, and so on. And there is nothing that can be expressed in one language that cannot be expressed in any other. Obviously, one language may have terms not found in another language, but it is always possible to invent new terms to express what we mean: anything we can imagine or think, we can express in any human language.

Turning to more abstract properties, even the formal structures of language are similar: all languages have sentences made up of smaller phrasal units, these units in turn being made up of words, which are themselves made up of sequences of sounds. All of these features of human language are so obvious to us that we may fail to see how surprising it is that languages share them. When linguists use the term *language*, or *natural human language*, they are revealing their belief that at an abstract level, beneath the surface variation, languages are remarkably similar in form and function and conform to certain universal principles.

In relation to what we have just said about universal principles, we should observe once again that most of the illustrative examples in this book are drawn from the English language. This should not mislead you into supposing that what we say is relevant only to English. We will be introducing fundamental concepts of linguistics, and we believe that these have to be applicable to all languages. We have chosen English examples so that you can continually check our factual claims and decide whether they are empirically well founded. Linguistics, perhaps more than any other science, provides an opportunity for the student to participate in the research process. Especially in Chapter 5, "Syntax," you will be able to assess the accuracy of the evidence that bears on hypothesis formation, and after having followed the argumentation in that chapter, you will be in a position to carry out similar reasoning processes in the exercises at the end.

Finally, we offer a brief observation about the general nature of linguistics. To many linguists the ultimate aim of linguistics is not simply to understand how language itself is structured and how it functions. We hope that as we come to understand more about human language, we will correspondingly understand more about the processes of human thought. In this view the study of language is ultimately the study of the human mind. This goal is perhaps best expressed by Noam Chomsky in his book *Reflections on Language* (1975, 3–4):

Why study language? There are many possible answers, and by focusing on some I do not, of course, mean to disparage others or question their legitimacy. One may, for example, simply be fascinated by the elements of language in themselves and want to discover their order and arrangement, their origin in history or in the individual, or the ways in which they are used in thought, in science or in art, or in normal social interchange. One reason for studying language—and for me personally the most compelling reason—is that it is tempting to regard language, in the traditional phrase, as "a mirror of mind." I do not mean by this simply that the concepts expressed and distinctions developed in normal language use give us insight into the patterns of thought and the world of "common sense" constructed by the human mind. More intriguing, to me at least, is the possibility that by studying language we may discover abstract principles that govern its structure and use, principles that are universal by biological necessity and not mere historical accident, that derive from mental characteristics of the species. A human language is a system of remarkable complexity. To come to know a human language would be an extraordinary intellectual achievement for a creature not specifically designed to accomplish this task. A normal child acquires this knowledge on relatively slight exposure and without specific training. He can then quite effortlessly make use of an intricate structure of specific rules and guiding principles to convey his thoughts and feelings to others, arousing in them novel ideas and subtle perceptions and judgments. For the conscious mind, not specifically designed for the purpose, it remains a distant goal to reconstruct and comprehend what the child has done intuitively and with minimal effort. Thus language is a mirror of mind in a deep and significant sense. It is a product of human intelligence, created anew in each individual by operations that lie far beyond the reach of will or consciousness.

Bibliography

Chomsky, N. (1975). *Reflections on language*. New York: Pantheon Books.

Chapter 2

MORPHOLOGY:
THE STUDY OF THE
STRUCTURE OF WORDS

2.1 WORDS: SOME BACKGROUND CONCEPTS

We begin our study of human language by examining one of the most fundamental units of linguistic structure: the word. In early stages of learning our native language as children, we utter single words ("No!" "More!" "Mommy!"), and we must learn thousands more in order to become fluent native speakers. Indeed, according to Miller and Gildea (1987, 198), we know approximately 80,000 words by age 17. Anyone who has mastered a language has mastered an astonishingly long list of facts encoded in the form of words. The list of words for any language, though not a complete list, as we will see, is referred to as its *lexicon*.

When we think about our native language, the existence of words seems obvious. After all, when we hear others speaking our native language, we hear them uttering words. In reading a printed passage, we see words on the page, neatly separated by spaces. But now imagine yourself in a situation where everyone around you is speaking a foreign language that you have just started to study. Suddenly the existence of words no longer seems obvious. While listening to a native speaker of French, or Navajo, or Japanese, all you hear is a blur of sound, as you strain to recognize words you have learned. If only the native speaker would slow down a little (the eternal complaint of the foreigner!), you would be able to divide that blur of sound into individual words. The ability to analyze a continuous stream of sound (spoken language) into discrete units (for example, individual words) is far from trivial, and it constitutes a central part of language comprehension. When you have "mastered" a language, you have learned to recognize individual words without effort, as well as many other things you know when you know a word.

What *do* we know when we know a word? To put it another way, what kinds of information have we learned when we learn a word? It turns out that the information encoded in a word is fairly complex, and we will see that a word is associated with different kinds of information. In discussing these types of information, we will in fact be referring to each of the subfields of linguistics that will be dealt with in this book:

1. *Phonological information.* For every word we know, we have learned a pronunciation. Part of knowing the word *tree* is knowing a certain sound—more precisely, a certain sequence of sounds. *Phonology* is the subfield of linguistics that studies the structure and systematic patterning of sounds in human language (see chapter 4).

2. *Morphological information.* For every word we have learned, we intuitively know something about its internal structure. For example, our intuitions tell us that the word *tree* cannot be broken down into any meaningful parts. In contrast, the word *trees* seems to be made up of two parts: the word *tree* plus an additional element, *-s* (known as the "plural" ending). *Morphology* is the subfield of linguistics that studies the internal structure of words and the relationships among words.

3. *Syntactic information.* For every word we learn, we learn how it fits into the overall structure of sentences in which it can be used. For example, we know that the word *reads* can be used in a sentence like *Mary reads the book*, and the word *readable* (related to the word *read*) can be used in a sentence like *The book is readable*. We may not know that *reads* is called a verb or that *readable* is called an adjective; but we intuitively know, as native speakers, how to use those words in different kinds of sentences. *Syntax* is the subfield of linguistics that studies the internal structure of sentences and the relationships among the internal parts (see chapter 5).

4. *Semantic information.* For virtually every word we know, we have learned a meaning or several meanings. For example, to know the word *brother* is to know that it has a certain meaning (the equivalent of "male sibling"). In addition, we may or may not know certain extended meanings of the word, as in *John is so friendly and helpful, he's a regular brother to me*. *Semantics* is the subfield of linguistics that studies the nature of the meaning of individual words, and the meaning of words grouped into phrases and sentences (see chapter 6).

5. *Pragmatic information.* For every word we learn, we know not only its meaning or meanings but also how to use it in the context of discourse or conversation. For instance, the word *brother* can be used not only to refer to a male sibling but also as a conversational exclamation, as in "Oh brother! What a mess!" In some cases, words seem to have a use but no

meaning as such. For example, the word *hello* is used to greet, but it seems to have no meaning beyond that particular use. *Pragmatics* is the subfield of linguistics that studies the use of words (and phrases and sentences) in the actual context of discourse (see chapter 9).

In addition to the types of information outlined here—information that we assume any native speaker must have learned about a word in order to know it—there are additional aspects of words that linguists study, which may or may not be known to native speakers. For example, words and their uses are subject to variation across groups of speakers. In American English the word *bonnet* can be used to refer to a type of hat; in British English it can be used to refer to the hood of a car.

Words and their uses are also subject to variation over time. For example, the English word *deer* at one time was the general word meaning "animal," but now it is used to refer only to a particular species of animal. These facts about word variation and historical changes may not be known to most native speakers—even for highly educated speakers, the history and dialectal variation of most words remain obscure—but such facts form the subject matter of other important subfields of linguistics, which we will explore in chapters 7 and 8.

In addition to being concerned with what we know when we know a word, linguists are interested in developing hypotheses that constitute plausible representations of this knowledge. As a starting point, one could ask if Webster's II New Revised Dictionary is a good representation of a speaker's knowledge of words? Do the dictionary entries represent what we know about words? For example, is the entry for the word *baker* a good representation of what we know about that word? Consider the following dictionary entry for *bake*:

bake (bāk) *v.* **baked, bak·ing. 1.** to cook, esp. in an oven, with dry heat. **2.** to harden and dry in or as if in an oven ⟨*bake* pottery⟩ —*n.* A social gathering at which baked food is served. —**bak'er** *n.*

Baker is a subentry for the verb *bake*. Let us assume that when a word is a subentry, it is related to the main entry. The only information given for *baker* is that it is a noun. No definition is provided. The meaning of the noun is somehow related to the meaning of the verb, but what exactly is the nature of this relatedness? The dictionary does not specify. Intuitively we know that a baker is someone who bakes and not, for example, the thing that gets baked. We know this, and yet the dictionary does not represent how or why we pick one option rather than the other. Would adding a definition for the word *baker* resolve this inadequacy? The answer turns out to be no. The problem runs deeper than this one example. To see this, imagine that we coin a new verb, *fleeb*. From this we can make up yet another word, *fleeber*. Hearing this word, any native speaker of English will know that a *fleeber* is one who fleebs and *not* one who gets fleebed. The latter is impossible.

This example highlights several fundamental problems with the dictionary. First, the dictionary provides no basis for producing *fleeber* and assigning it a meaning. Second, it fails to capture the similarity between the pairs *bake/baker* and *fleeb/fleeber*. Third, the dictionary constitutes a finite list of words, and yet speakers are capable of producing unlimited numbers of novel words like *fleeber*. That is, in principle there is an infinite number of possible words.

We have seen that words are associated with a wide range of information and that each type of information forms an important area of study for a subfield of linguistics. In this chapter we will be concerned with the subfield known as morphology. First we will consider certain basic concepts of morphology. Then we will discuss how new words are created, and finally we will motivate the postulation of rules and principles of word formation that will address the inadequacies of the dictionary as a representation of a speaker's knowledge of words.

Some Basic Concepts of Morphology

Within the field of morphology, it is possible to pose many questions about the nature of words, but among the more persistent questions have been the following:

What are words and how are they formed?
How are more complex words built up from simpler parts?
What are the basic building blocks in the formation of complex words?
How is the meaning of a complex word related to the meaning of its parts?
How are individual words of a language related to other words of the language?

These are all difficult questions, and linguists studying morphology have not yet arrived at completely satisfactory answers to any of them. Once we begin to construct plausible answers, we quickly discover that interesting and subtle new problems arise, which leads us to revise those answers.

Let us start with the following rather basic observation. A word is an *arbitrary pairing of sound and meaning*. For example, the word *brother* is a complex pattern of sounds associated with a certain meaning ("male sibling"). There is no necessary reason why the particular combination of sounds represented by the written word *brother* should mean what it does. In French, Papago, and Japanese the sounds represented by the written words *frère, we:nag,* and *otooto,* respectively, share the meaning "male sibling." Clearly, it is not the nature of the sound that dictates what the meaning ought to be; hence, the pairing of sound and meaning is said to be *arbitrary*. It is true that every language contains *onomatopoeic* words (that is, words whose sounds imitate or mimic sounds in the world about us: *meow, bow-wow, splash, bang, hoot, crash,* and so on). But such words form a very limited subset of the words of any given language; for the vast majority of words the sound-meaning pairing is arbitrary.

Morphemes and Complex Words

It has long been recognized that words must be classed into at least two categories: *simple* and *complex*. A simple word such as *tree* seems to be a minimal unit; there seems to be no way to analyze it, or break it down further, into meaningful parts. On the other hand, the word *trees* is made up of two parts: the noun *tree* and the plural ending, spelled *-s* in this case. The following lists of English words reveal that the plural *-s* (or *-es*) can be attached to nouns quite generally:

(1)

Noun	Plural form (+ s)
boy	boys
rake	rakes
lip	lips
dog	dogs
bush	bushes
brother	brothers

Not every noun in English forms its plural in this fashion; for example, the plural of *child* is *children,* not *childs*. However, for nouns such as those in (1), and others of this large class, we can say that complex plural forms (such as *trees*) are made up of simple nouns (such as *tree*) followed by the plural ending *-s*. The basic parts of a complex word—that is, the different building blocks that make it up—are called *morphemes*. Each of the plural nouns listed in (1) is made up of two morphemes: a *base morpheme* such as *boy* or *rake,* and a *plural morpheme, -s,* which is attached to the base morpheme. The meaning of the plural forms listed in (1) is a combination, in some intuitive sense, of the meaning of the base morphemes and the meaning of the plural morpheme -*s*. In short, we will say that morphemes are the *minimal units of word building* in a language: they cannot be broken down any further into recognizable or meaningful parts.

Morphemes are further categorized into two classes: *free* morphemes and *bound* morphemes. A free morpheme can stand alone as an independent word in a phrase, such as the word *tree* in *John sat in the tree*. A bound morpheme cannot stand alone but must be *attached* to another morpheme—as, for example, the plural morpheme -*s*, which can only occur attached to nouns. Certain bound morphemes are known as *affixes* (reflecting the fact that they must be attached, or "affixed," to other morphemes). Affixes are referred to as *prefixes* when they are attached to the beginning of another morpheme (like the prefix *re-* in words such as *redo, rewrite, rethink*) and *suffixes* when they are attached to the end of another morpheme (like -*ize* in words such as *modernize, equalize, centralize*). The morpheme to which an affix is attached is the *base* (or *stem*) morpheme. A basic classification of morphemes is summarized in figure 2.1.

Certain languages also have affixes known as *infixes*, which are attached *within* another morpheme. For example, in Bonto Igorot, a language of the Philippines, the infix -*in*- is used to indicate the product of a completed action (Sapir 1921). Taking the word *kayu*, meaning "wood," one can insert the infix -*in*- immediately after the first consonant *k* to form the word *kinayu*, meaning "gathered wood." In this way, the infix -*in*- fits into the base morpheme *kayu* in the internal "slot" *k*- -*ayu* (hence, *kinayu*). In addition, the infix -*um*- is used in certain verb forms to indicate future tense; for example, -*um*- can be added within a morpheme such as *tengao*, meaning "to celebrate a holiday," to create a verb form such as *tumengao-ak*, meaning "I will have a holiday" (the suffix -*ak* indicates the first person "I"). Here, the infix -*um*- fits into the base morpheme *tengao* in the internal

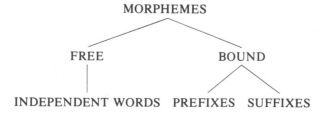

Figure 2.1
A basic classification of morphemes

"slot" immediately following the first consonant (*t- -engao*). Infixation is common in languages of Southeast Asia and the Philippines, and it is also found in some Native American languages.

It must be noted, in regard to figure 2.1, that not all bound morphemes are affixes. For example, in English certain words have *contracted* ("shortened") forms. The word *will* can occur either as *will*, in sentences such as *They will go*, or in a contracted form, spelled *'ll*, in sentences such as *They'll go*. The form *'ll* is a bound morpheme in that it cannot occur as an independent word and must be attached to the preceding word or phrase (as in *they'll* or *The birds who flew away'll return soon*, respectively). Other contractions in English include *'s* (the contracted form of *is*, as in *The old car's not running anymore*); *'ve* (the contracted form of *have*, as in *They've gone jogging*); and *'d* (the contracted form of *would*, as in *I'd like to be rich*); and several other contracted forms of auxiliary verbs. These contracted forms are all bound morphemes in the same sense as *'ll*.

Still another type of bound morpheme is illustrated by the morpheme *cran-*, which occurs in words such as *cranberry, cranapple,* and *cranprune*. The form *cran-* cannot stand alone as a free morpheme but must occur within words such as those just cited. For this reason, we say that *cran-* is a bound morpheme or *bound base*.

To sum up, then, we have seen that words fall into two general classes: simple and complex. Simple words are single free morphemes that cannot be broken down further into recognizable or meaningful parts. Complex words consist of two or more morphemes in combination.

Categories (Parts of Speech)

Each word belongs to a category. For example, *dog* is a noun, *run* is a verb, *famous* is an adjective, *up* is a preposition, and *quickly* is an adverb. A word such as *dog* shares various properties with the word *chair*. For example, the inflectional suffix *-s* can be attached to each of these words, forming the plural nouns *dogs* and *chairs*. This *inflectional* suffix attaches to words classified as *nouns* and produces plural nouns. Though there are exceptions—for instance, irregular plurals (*children* and not *childs*) and mass nouns (*rice* and not *rices*)—most nouns can be pluralized in this fashion, whereas a word such as *famous* cannot be. Thus, there exists *morphological* evidence for distinguishing nouns from words belonging to other categories.

Morphological evidence also exists that differentiates the other categories from one another.

Verbs take the suffix *-s* (as in *bake–bakes, walk–walks, hit–hits*) in the present tense. This is known as the "third person singular" form, because this is the form of the verb that occurs when the subject of the sentence is third person singular. The following present tense verb forms illustrate this:

	Singular	*Plural*
1st Person	I walk.	We walk.
2nd Person	You walk.	You walk.
3rd Person	She *walks*.	They walk.
	He *walks*.	
	It *walks*.	

Notice that the verb form remains the same in all cases, except when the subject is third person singular.

Verbs can also take the suffix *-ing*, as in *bake–baking, walk–walking, hit–hitting, sing–singing*, illustrated in sentences such as *They are baking, She is singing*.

Adjectives can usually take the suffixes *-er* and *-est* (as in *big–bigger–biggest, red–redder–reddest, wise–wiser–wisest*). Some adjectives occur not with *-er* or *-est* but with the comparative words *more* and *most* (*beautiful–more beautiful–most beautiful*).

Adverbs share many of the properties of adjectives and are often formed from adjectives by the addition of the suffix *-ly*. For example, the adjective *quick* can be converted into an adverb by adding *-ly*, to form *quickly* (and similarly for pairs such as *easy–easily, ferocious–ferociously, obvious–obviously*). (But note that adverbs are not the only class of words in English that can end in *-ly*. Adjectives can too: witness *lonely man, loneliest man*.)

Prepositions are invariant. No affixes can be attached to them. Therefore, there is no positive morphological evidence for the class of prepositions.

The question now arises, Are these categories (part-of-speech classes) found in all languages, or just in English? The answer is by no means simple. However, linguists generally assume that certain "major" categories—in particular, nouns and verbs—are "universal"; that is, they exist in most, if not all, languages.

By and large, the grammatical properties of a given part-of-speech class are quite specific to a given language or small group of languages. For example, the property of taking a plural suffix (*-s*), which defines English nouns, obviously cannot be used as a general defining property for nouns across languages. Although some other languages have a plural suffix for nouns (note, for example, German *Frau* "woman" versus *Frau<u>en</u>* "women"), other languages have no special affix for indicating a plural form for nouns. For example, in Japanese a noun like *hon* "book, books" can be used with either singular or plural meaning. In other languages the plural form for nouns is formed by a process known as *reduplication*, in which a specific part of the singular form is *reduplicated* (repeated) to construct the plural form. For example, in Tohono O'odham, a Native American language of southern Arizona and northern Mexico, we find pairs such as *daikuḍ* "chair"–*dadaikuḍ* "chairs," *kawyu* "horse"–*kakawyu* "horses," *gogs* "dog"–*gogogs* "dogs," in which the first consonant + vowel sequence of the singular form is repeated at the beginning of the word to construct the plural form. Hence, there is no single affix to indicate plurality in these cases. We see, then, that in some languages there is no morphological indication of plural form for nouns; in other languages the plural is morphologically indicated by an affix or by reduplication (among other ways). In short, in terms of our intuitive notions we can probably say that nouns exist in many (if not all) languages; but it must be kept in mind that the specific grammatical properties associated with nouns can vary across languages.

Though it may be true that most, if not all, languages share the categories noun and verb (and possibly a few others), it is also clear that other categories are found in some languages but not others. For example, Japanese has a class of bound morphemes known as *particles*, which are attached to noun phrases to indicate grammatical function. In a Japanese sentence such as *John-ga hon-o yonda* "John read the book," the particle *-ga* indicates that *John* functions as the subject of the sentence (the "doer" of the action), and the particle *-o* indicates that *hon* "book, books" functions as the object (that which "undergoes" the action) of the verb *yonda* "read." English has no such particles to indicate subject or object; instead, such grammatical functions are indicated most often by word order. The subject of an English sentence typically precedes the verb and the object typically follows it, as in *John read the book*.

Conversely, English has grammatical categories not found in Japanese. For example, English has a class of words known as *articles*, including *the* (the so-called definite article) and *a* (the so-called indefinite article), as in *the book* or *a book*. Articles are not found in Japanese, as the example sentence *John-ga hon-o yonda* illustrates. The noun *hon* is followed by the particle *-o* (indicating its object function), but it is accompanied by no morphemes equivalent to the English articles. This is not to say that Japanese speakers cannot express the difference in meaning between *the* *book* (definite and specific) and *a book* (indefinite and nonspecific). Instead, this difference is determined by the context (both linguistic and nonlinguistic) of the sentence. For example, if a certain book has been mentioned in previous discourse, speakers of Japanese interpret *John-ga hon-o yonda* as meaning "John read *the* book" rather than "John read *a* book."

To sum up, whether or not all languages share certain part-of-speech categories, we nevertheless expect to find groups of words within any given language that share significant grammatical properties. To account for these similarities, we hypothesize that words sharing significant properties all belong to the same category. Such categories are traditionally labeled *noun*, *verb*, and so on, but we must remain open to the possibility that a given language may have a grammatical category not found in others. The existence of part-of-speech categories shows that the lexicon of a language is not simply a long, random list. Rather, it is structured into special subgroups of words (the various grammatical categories).

Open versus Closed Class Words

In discussions about words, a distinction is sometimes made between *open class words* and *closed class words* (sometimes referred to as *content words* and *function words*, respectively). Examples of open class words include the English words *brother*, *run*, *tall*, and *quickly*. The open class words are those belonging to the major part-of-speech classes (nouns, verbs, adjectives, and adverbs), which in any language tend to be quite large and "open-ended." That is, an unlimited number of new words can be created and added to these classes (recall *fleeb/fleeber*).

In contrast, closed class words are those belonging to grammatical, or function, classes (such as articles, demonstratives, conjunctions, and prepositions), which in any language tend to include a small number of fixed elements. Function words in English include conjunctions (*and*, *or*), articles and demonstratives (*the*, *a*, *this*, *that*), and prepositions (*to*, *from*, *at*, *with*). To take one specific case, consider the word *and*. The essential feature of the word *and* is that it functions grammatically to *conjoin* noun phrases (for instance, *the woman and the man*). Any change in membership of such a class happens only very slowly (over centuries) and in small increments. Thus, a speaker of English may well encounter dozens of new nouns and verbs during the coming year; but it is extremely unlikely that the English language will acquire a new definite article (or lose the current one) in the coming year (or even in the speaker's lifetime).

One familiar variety of language in which the distinction between open class words and closed class words is important is known as *telegraphic speech* (or *telegraphic language*). The term *telegraphic* derives from the kind of language used in telegrams, where considerations of space (and money) force one to be as terse as possible: HAVING WONDERFUL TIME; HOTEL GREAT; RETURNING FLIGHT 256; SEND MONEY; STOP. Generally speaking, in telegraphic forms of language the open class words are retained, whereas the closed class words are omitted wherever possible. Telegraphic forms of language are not limited to telegrams and postcards but can also be observed in early stages of child language; in the speech of people with certain brain disorders known as aphasic brain syndromes (see Bradley, Garrett, and Zurif 1980); in classified advertising; in certain styles of poetry; and generally in any use of language where messages must be reduced to the absolute essentials.

The morpheme classifications discussed in this section are summarized in figure 2.2. Note, incidentally, that affixes could also be classified as belonging to "closed classes." For example, the classes of prefixes and suffixes also consist of a small number of fixed elements, augmented or changed only very slowly over time. It has been customary to use the term "closed class" to refer to function words (rather than to bound affixes), however, and we adopt that usage in figure 2.2. Both are sometimes grouped together and referred to as *grammatical morphemes*.

2.2 HOW ARE NEW WORDS CREATED?

One of the more interesting ways to approach the questions and problems of morphology is to explore the question, How are new words created? By examining the process involved in the creation of new words, we may be able to discover basic and general principles of word formation.

Coining New Words

Entirely new, previously nonexistent words keep entering a language. This often happens when speakers invent (or *coin*) new words to name previously nonexistent objects that result from technological change. For example, coined words such as *radar*, *laser*, *kleenex*, and *xerox* are very recent additions to the English language.

The words *radar* and *laser* are *acronyms*: each of the letters that spell the word is the first (or second) letter of some other complete word. For example, *radar* derives from <u>ra</u>dio <u>d</u>etecting <u>a</u>nd <u>r</u>anging, and *laser* derives

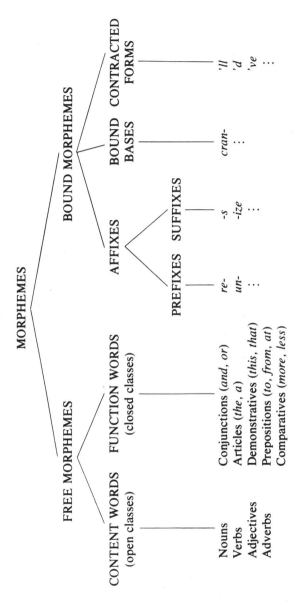

Figure 2.2
Summary of the classification of morphemes

from *light amplification (by) stimulated emission (of) radiation*. It is important to note that even though such words are originally created as acronyms, speakers quickly forget such origins and the acronyms become new independent words.

The process of forming acronyms is just one of the processes of abbreviation, or shortening, that is becoming increasingly more common in American society (and perhaps internationally) as a means of word formation. For many Americans, one-time abbreviations such as *TV* have come to replace longer words, such as *television*, in most styles of casual speech—a new, previously nonexistent word has come into use. Various forms of identity cards are now simply called *ID*; venereal disease is widely referred to as *VD*; and although it was once a joke to use *OJ* to refer to orange juice, the word is beginning to come into wider use. Abbreviations such as *prof* for *professor*, *math* for *mathematics*, and *gas* for *gasoline* are in common use now (such shortenings are sometimes called *clippings*, since the words have been "clipped" short).

No account of coined words would be complete, of course, without reference to possibly the most famous word in the English language, one that has become an international vocabulary item: *OK*. Dozens of theories have been advanced to explain the origin of this word. According to one theory, *OK* stands for *Old Kinderhook*, the name of a Democratic Party organization, abbreviated as the O.K. Club, which supported President Van Buren for reelection in 1840 (Kinderhook being Van Buren's birthplacc in New York State). According to another theory, *OK* stands for *oll korrect*, a parody spelling of *all correct*. The word *OK* is attested in American English as early as the 1830s, and there is some speculation that it may have been connected with another abbreviation, *D.K.*, for *don't know*. In any event, all of the theories seem equally dubious. The important point is that words such as *OK* and *TV* are felt to be complete words and not merely abbreviations, as evidenced by the fact that in casual styles of writing we now see spellings like *okay* and *teevee*.

The words *kleenex* and *xerox* represent another technique of coining previously nonexistent words, namely, using specific brand names of products as names for the products in general. Hence, *kleenex*, a brand name for facial tissue, has come to denote facial tissue in general. *Xerox* is the name of the corporation that produces a well-known photocopying machine, and much to the dismay of the company, the term *xerox* has lost its specific brand-name connotation and has come to be used to describe the process of photocopying in general (*I xeroxed a letter*). Hence, in casual speech we can commit the grave sin of talking about buying an IBM *xerox* machine.

New words can also be formed from existing ones by various *blending* processes, for example creating blends such as *motel* (from *motor hotel*), *selectric* (from *select* and *electric*), *brunch* (from *breakfast* and *lunch*), *Reaganomics* (from *Reagan* and *economics*), and *Irangate* (from *Iran* and *Watergate*).

Compounds and Compounding

In English (as in many other languages) new words can be formed from already existing words by a process known as *compounding*, in which individual words can be "joined together" to form a *compound* word, as illustrated in table 2.1. For example, the noun *ape* can be joined with the noun *man* to form the compound noun *ape-man*; the adjective *sick* can be joined with the noun *room* to form the compound noun *sickroom*; the adjective *red* can be joined with the adjective *hot* to form the compound adjective *red-hot*; and so on, for other examples shown in table 2.1, which lists some other types of compounds found in English (following Selkirk 1982).

Generally speaking, the part of speech of the whole compound is the same as the part of speech of the *rightmost* member of the compound, which is termed the *head* of the compound (Selkirk 1982). For example, the rightmost member (the "head") of the compound *high chair* is a noun (the noun *chair*); hence, the whole compound *high chair* is also a noun. The rightmost member of the compound *overdo* is a verb (the verb *do*); hence, the whole compound is also a verb.

Compounds are not limited to two words, as shown by examples such as *bathroom towel-rack* and *community center finance committee*. Indeed,

Table 2.1
Some types of compounds in English

Noun + Noun	Adjective + Noun	Preposition + Noun	Verb + Noun
landlord	high chair	overdose	hit-man
bathroom	blackboard	underdog	swearword
fire truck	wildfire	underarm	scarecrow

Adjective + Adjective	Noun + Adjective	Preposition + Verb
red-hot	sky-blue	oversee
icy-cold	earthbound	overstuff
bittersweet	skin-deep	underfeed

the process of compounding seems unlimited in English: starting with a word like *sailboat*, we can easily construct the compound *sailboat rigging*, from which we can in turn create *sailboat rigging design, sailboat rigging design training, sailboat rigging design training institute*, and so on.

You may wonder when compound words are to be written as single words (that is, as long words with no spaces between the individual words), as hyphenated words, and as sequences of words separated by spaces. For instance, *bathroom, ape-man*, and *high jump* are all compounds. The conventions of writing compounds in English are simply inconsistent. The hyphen is used when a compound has been newly created or is not widely used; when a compound has gained a certain currency or permanence, it is often spelled closed up, without the hyphen. The word *blackboard*, when it was first created, was written *black-board*, a spelling found in texts from the first part of this century. The rule in English for spelling multiword compounds, such as *community center finance committee*, is not to write them as a single word. In contrast, the conventions for writing German are much more consistent. Both two-word and multiword compounds are written as a single word: *Versicherungsgesellschaft* "insurance company," *Feuerundlebensversicherungsgesellschaft* "fire and life insurance company."

Certain compounds have a characteristic stress pattern (accent pattern). For example, in compound nouns consisting of two words the main stress (position of heaviest accent) comes on the *leftmost* member of the compound. The compound *movie star* is pronounced *MOVIEstar* (where capital letters indicate the location of the heaviest accent), not *movieSTAR*; the compound noun *bathroom* is pronounced *BATHroom*, not *bathROOM*. The stress pattern can sometimes be a clue to whether a sequence of two words is a compound noun or not. For example, the sequence *high* and *chair* can be pronounced either *HIGHchair*, in which case it is a compound noun denoting a special kind of chair that babies sit in; or it can be pronounced *highCHAIR*, in which case it is simply the noun *chair* modified by the adjective *high*, denoting some chair that happens to be high (not necessarily a baby's high chair).

Although the meaning of a complex word such as *trees* is a combination of the meaning of its parts, the meaning of compounds cannot always be predicted in this way. For example, consider the contrast between the compounds *alligator shoes* and *horseshoes*: alligator shoes are shoes made from alligator hide; yet horseshoes are not shoes made from horsehide, but rather are iron "shoes" for horses' hooves. Similarly, a *salt pile* is a pile made of salt, but a *saltshaker* is not a shaker made of salt. The compound

Bigfoot refers to a mythical creature with large feet; but the compound *bigwig* does not refer to a large wig. Nevertheless, certain generalizations can be made about the meaning of compounds. For example, an *apron string* is a kind of string, whereas a *string apron* is a kind of apron; in other words, the meaning of the head of the compound seems to be central in the meaning of the whole compound, at least for certain kinds of compounds (Selkirk 1982).

Compounding is a rich source of new words in English, and many compounds are numbered among recent additions to the language, such as *spaceman, moon-walk, hot tub, pothead*, and many others.

Word Formation Rules

A very important means of word formation involves building up complex words from base morphemes and affixes. Let us return to such words as *baker*. *Agentive nouns* are formed by adding the suffix *-er* to verbs:

(2)

Verb	*Agentive noun (V + -er)*
(to) write	writer
(to) kill	killer
(to) play	player
(to) win	winner
(to) run	runner
(to) farm	farmer
(to) open	opener
(to) scrape	scraper
(to) roll	roller
(to) level	leveler

The derived noun form means roughly "one who does *X*" or "an instrument that does *X*," where *X* is the meaning of the verb. Suppose that a new verb enters the English language, such as the verb *to xerox* (recall that *xerox* was originally a trademark for a photocopying process). Native speakers of English automatically know that this verb can be converted into an agentive noun, *xeroxer*. This word would be perfectly natural in a sentence such as *If you want to get that copied, you'll have to see John, because he's our xeroxer around here.* Hence, the process of agentive noun formation (using the suffix *-er*) establishes a relationship between verbs and nouns. The study of how affixes combine with stems to *derive* new words is known as *derivational morphology*, and affixes such as the *-er* agentive suffix are known as *derivational affixes*.

There is evidence from many languages of the world that word formation follows systematic morphological principles. That is, there are rules by which complex words are built up from simpler words and morphemes and, conversely, these same rules permit complex words to be analyzed into simpler ones. We will examine the general process of word formation by examining in detail one such process in English, namely, the word formation rule for the derivational suffix *-able*. Consider the following sets of words:

(3)

(to) read	readable
(to) wash	washable
(to) break	breakable
(to) drink	drinkable
(to) pay	payable
(to) move	movable
(to) excuse	excusable

In the left-hand column is a set of verbs; in the right-hand column those same verbs have the derivational suffix *-able* attached to them. There is an obvious systematic relation between the words in the two columns. To native speakers of English who know the words listed in the left-hand column, many features of the words in the right-hand column are completely predictable. That is, the relation between *read* and *readable* is not arbitrary—rather, the suffix *-able* is a morpheme that is used in a highly systematic way. What are the various effects of the *-able* suffix? In what basic ways are the verbs changed when *-able* is added?

Obviously, there is a phonological change, which in this case is quite straightforward: when the *-able* suffix is added, the pronunciation of the verb must be augmented by a certain sequence of sounds that we can transcribe with the symbols *-əbl* (where the phonetic symbol *ə* stands for the vowel sound, spelled as *a*, in the suffix *-able*). With other derivational suffixes the phonological changes that are triggered by the attachment of these suffixes are not so trivial. For example, when *-ion* is added to verbs, it triggers sound changes in the verb stem itself:

(4)

rel<u>a</u>te	rel<u>a</u>tion
d<u>i</u>ctate	d<u>i</u>ctation
inv<u>e</u>stigate	investig<u>a</u>tion

correlate   correlation
appreciate   appreciation

Two changes are taking place. The *t*-sound in the *-ate* words is pronounced as a *sh*-sound in the corresponding *-ion* words and, no matter where the main stress (emphasis) is located in the *-ate* words, it always occurs on the vowel just before *-ion* in the *-ion* words.

The suffix *-able* introduces another obvious change when it is added to a word. Note that when *-able* attaches to verbs, the resulting words are adjectives (and hence can modify nouns):

(5)
a. This book is readable. (Compare: This book is blue.)
b. a readable book (Compare: a blue book)

The suffix *-able* introduces a new element of meaning, roughly "able to be *X*'d," where *X* is the meaning of the verb. For example, *breakable* means roughly "able to be broken," *movable* means "able to be moved," and so on. Thus, at least three changes are associated with this suffix:

(6)
a. a phonological change (sound change)
b. a category change (part-of-speech change)
c. a semantic change (meaning change)

Other facts reveal that there are certain restrictions on the use of *-able*. For example, if we wish to express the idea that man is mortal, we cannot say *Man is dieable*. If a car is able to go, we nevertheless cannot say that it is *goable*; if John and Mary are able to cry, they are still not *cryable*. It is all too tempting to suppose that these cases are somehow exceptions or that no rule or principle governs the data in question. But if we compare the columns in (7), a generalization emerges:

(7)

Verbs taking -able	*Verbs not taking* -able
read	die
break	go
wash	cry
play	sleep
mend	rest
debate	weep
use	sit
drive	run
spray	walk

The verbs on the left are *transitive*—they occur with object noun phrases—whereas the verbs on the right are *intransitive*—they do not occur with objects. For example:

(8)

a. Pat read the book. (*read + the book = transitive verb + object*)

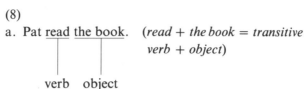

verb   object

b. Terry broke the dish.

verb   object

c. John washed his clothes.

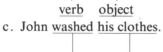

verb   object

(9)

a. Pat died. (*died = intransitive verb* with no following object)

b. Terry went.

c. John cried.

It seems to be the case that *-able* attaches only to transitive verbs, not to intransitive verbs. Nevertheless, just based on the list in (7), there appear to be some counterexamples. What about *walkable* and *runnable*?

(10)

a. The dog is walkable.

b. The race is runnable.

It will turn out that these are only apparent counterexamples, not real ones. Note that the verbs *walk* and *run* have both a transitive and an intransitive use:

(11)

a. John will walk.

b. John will walk the dog.

(12)

a. Mary runs fast.

b. Mary will run the race.

The (a) examples exhibit the intransitive use of *walk* and *run*; the (b) examples illustrate the transitive use. In a moment we will see that it is the transitive version of these verbs that is available for the attachment of *-able*.

An interesting relation emerges between sentences with transitive verbs and sentences with corresponding *-able* words. A comparison of the following examples reveals what is going on:

(13)

a. We can read <u>these books.</u>   (*these books* = object of the verb *read*)

b. <u>These books</u> are readable.   (*these books* = subject of *are readable*)

(14)

a. We can wash <u>these clothes.</u>

b. <u>These clothes</u> are washable.

(15)

a. We can drive <u>this car</u>.

b. <u>This car</u> is drivable.

The relation that emerges is this: the subject of each (b) sentence corresponds to the object in the corresponding (a) sentence. In other words, the subject of V + *able* is always understood as the object (that which "undergoes" the action) of V. For this reason, if (at a tennis match) we say *Kim isn't beatable*, we mean that no other player can beat Kim (*Kim* is understood as the object of *beat*); we do not mean that Kim is unable to beat other players.

Returning to our "counterexamples," we can now see that they in fact accord with the generalization just noted:

(16)

a. John walked <u>the dog</u>.

b. <u>The dog</u> is walkable.

(17)

a. Mary ran <u>the race</u>.

b. <u>The race</u> is runnable.

We can now state the *-able* word formation rule as follows:

(18)
a. *Phonological change*: When *-able* is attached to a base, the pronunciation of the base is augmented by the phonetic sequence *-əbl*.
b. *Category change*: *-able* is attached to transitive verbs and converts them into adjectives.
c. *Semantic change*: If *X* is the meaning of the verb, then *-able* adds the meaning "able to be *X*'d."

In general, then, whenever we postulate a systematic morphological relation between sets of words, we will describe (1) the systematic phonological changes, if any, (2) the category changes, and (3) the semantic changes, if any, that characterize the relationship.

Not all affixes cause the sorts of changes we have observed with the *-able* suffix. For example, English has a so-called diminutive suffix, usually spelled *-y* (or *-ie*), which is added to nouns such as those in the following pairs: *dad–daddy*, *mom–mommy*, *dog–doggy*, *horse–horsie*. The suffix *-y* causes no phonological changes in the base word to which it is attached; it does not change the part of speech of the base (both *dad* and *daddy* are nouns); and finally, it causes no obvious semantic change (in the sense that both *dad* and *daddy* denote the same persons, except that the form *daddy* is used in baby-talk or intimate family contexts). In other words, although affixes *may* cause the types of changes we have discussed in connection with *-able*, it is not generally the case that affixes *must* cause such changes, and indeed affixes vary in the types of changes they cause in the stem to which they are attached.

Given these remarks, we can observe that word formation rules state *predictable* information about complex words. We can see this very clearly from a different point of view. Suppose someone invents a nonsense word, such as *fleeb*. Even though we know nothing about the meaning of this word, if we are told that *-able* can be added to *fleeb* to form *fleebable*, we can in turn make a claim about another property of *fleeb*, namely, that it is a transitive verb. As for *fleebable*, we know that it means "able to be fleebed" and that it is an adjective.

Problematic Aspects of Morphological Analysis

Productivity and Isolating the Base

Now we must face one of the hard facts of life in doing morphological analysis, namely, the exceptions or apparent exceptions to many aspects of a given analysis. For example, we have claimed that the suffix *-able* is attached only to transitive verbs. Yet English does have a small set of *nouns* that seem to occur with the same suffix *-able*:

(19)

peaceable	companionable
marriageable	impressionable
knowledgeable	actionable
saleable	reasonable
fashionable	

Does this mean that word formation rule (18) is wrong? The answer seems to be no. The nouns listed in (19) form a small, closed set, and as far as anyone can tell, few words, if any, are entering English that consist of *-able* attached to a noun. Using more technical terminology, we say that the attachment of *-able* to transitive verbs is *productive*—that is, it happens quite freely—but its attachment to nouns is *not productive*. New V + *able* forms continually enter the language, but the nouns in (19) are now fixed, or dead, expressions that are learned by rote, not formed, or analyzable, by a productive rule.

Another general problem we must be sensitive to is the possibility of *false analysis*. Consider the following words:

(20)
hospitable
sizeable

Even though these words end in the phonetic sequence *əbl*, it is unlikely that we would want to analyze this sequence as the suffix *-able*. For one thing, *able* in these words does not seem to have the meaning "to be able," which is certainly a feature of regular (productive) *-able* words. For another thing, the *-able* suffix can itself regularly take the suffix *-ity* to form a noun:

(21)

readable	readability
provable	provability
breakable	breakability

But this is not possible with the words listed in (20): *hospitability* and *sizeability* are not possible English words. We do not speak of the hospitability of our host or the sizeability of the crowd. In two respects, then, *able* in the words of (20) differs significantly from the productive suffix *-able*; hence, it would seem to be a false analysis to claim that the words of (20) contain the productive suffix *-able*. These words simply happen to end in a sequence spelled *able*, and they bear only an accidental resemblance to words with the real suffix *-able*.

Returning to the words in (19), we might try to make the case that these words end accidentally in the phonetic sequence ǝbl and that it would be a false analysis to claim that it is the *-able* suffix. Against this idea we note that some of the words do seem to include the meaning "be able" (for example, *marriageable* "eligible to marry"), and the *-ity* noun form *marriageability* does seem possible (although some speakers of English might well reject it). Other words of (19), however, are not so regular. In any event, in carrying out a morphological analysis we must always be careful to determine whether the processes in question are productive and whether a certain analysis might be a false analysis.

Closely related to these issues is another classic problem of morphology, namely, the case of a complex word with a recognizable suffix or prefix, attached to a base that is not an existing word of the language. For example, among the *-able* words are words such as *malleable* and *feasible*. In both cases the suffix *-able* (spelled *ible* in the second case because of a different historical origin for the suffix) has the regular meaning "be able," and in both cases the *-ity* form is possible, as in *malleability* and *feasibility*. We have no reason to suspect that *able/ible* here is not the real suffix *-able*. Yet if it is, then *malleable* must be broken down as *malle + able* and *feasible* as *feas + ible*; but there are no existing words (free morphemes) in English such as *malle* or *feas*, or even *malley* or *fease*. We thus have to allow for the existence of a complex word whose base exists only in that complex word (recall the earlier discussion of the bound base *cran-*, which occurs only in *cranberry* and a few other words).

The problems discussed so far are problems in isolating the *base* of a complex word: (1) sometimes the base (the form to which the affix is attached) comes from a closed set of forms no longer productive as the base for the word formation rule; (2) sometimes one must be alert to the possibility of a completely false analysis of the base; and (3) sometimes the base may not be an existing word. All of these problems have to do with correctly analyzing how the complex word is structured.

The Meaning of Complex Words

Another difficulty in morphological analysis is how to analyze the meaning of complex words and how to determine the relation between the meaning of an entire complex word and the meanings of its parts.

First, consider some complex words that appear to have a predictable meaning. For example, *fixable* seems to mean nothing more than "able to be fixed," *mendable* means "able to be mended," and *inflatable* means "able to be inflated." The meaning of these *-able* words seems to be a regular combination of the meaning of the verb stem and the simplest meaning of the *-able* suffix.

However, in other cases certain complications arise. Take, for example, the words *readable, payable, questionable,* and *washable.* The word *readable* does not mean simply "able to be read." When we say that a book is readable, we usually mean that it is well written, has a good style, and in general is a good example of some type of literature. A banker who says that a bill is payable on October 1 does not mean simply that the bill "can be paid" on that date—normally, we would understand *payable* as meaning "should be paid." If a theory or an explanation is *questionable*, it is not merely the case that it can be questioned. After all, any statement can be questioned, even very well established theories. Rather, a questionable theory or account is one that is, in fact, dubious and suspect. Finally, the word *washable* does not mean merely "able to be washed"; we in fact use the word in a very specialized way, to refer to certain types of objects, notably fabrics. Hence, though we can talk about washing a car, it would be somewhat odd to say that the car is washable (even if this is, strictly speaking, true). It is perfectly natural, however, to say that a shirt is washable or that the plastic parts of a table are washable (whereas the wooden parts are not).

These facts illustrate in a particularly clear way that the meanings of many complex words are not merely composites of the meanings of their parts. The word *washable* is more than a composite of *wash* and *-able*; rather, it has its own additional elements of meaning. When a word accrues some additional feature of meaning independent from its morphological origin, as *washable* has, we say that the word has undergone *semantic drift.* At least for the cases given here, the additional meaning, over and above the basic meaning of the complex word, involves a narrowing or restricting of the more general meaning of the complex word.

Inflectional versus Derivational Morphology

In the study of word formation, a distinction has often been drawn between *inflectional* and *derivational* morphology. The basis for the distinction has never been made entirely precise, but we can begin by listing the affixes of English that are referred to as *inflectional affixes* or *inflectional endings* (classified according to the part of speech each affix occurs with):

(22)
Noun inflectional suffixes
a. Plural marker *-s*
   girl–girl<u>s</u>
   (*The girls are here*)
b. Possessive marker *'s*
   Mary–Mary'<u>s</u>
   (*Mary's book*)

Verb inflectional suffixes
c. Third person present singular marker *-s*
   bake–bake<u>s</u>
   (*He bakes well*)
d. Past tense marker *-ed*
   wait–wait<u>ed</u>
   (*They waited*)
e. Progressive marker *-ing*
   sing–sing<u>ing</u>
   (*They are singing*)
f. Past participle markers *-en* or *-ed*
   eat–eat<u>en</u>
   (*She has eaten dinner*)
   bake–bak<u>ed</u>
   (*He has baked a cake*)

Adjective inflectional suffixes
g. Comparative marker *-er*
   fast–fast<u>er</u>
   (*She is faster than you*)
h. Superlative marker *-est*
   fast–fast<u>est</u>
   (*She is fastest*)

English has only the inflectional affixes listed above, and all inflectional affixes in English are suffixes (none are prefixes, unlike the situation with derivational affixes, which include both suffixes and prefixes).

The distinction between inflectional and derivational affixes in English is based on a number of factors.

First, inflectional affixes never change the category (part of speech) of the base morpheme (the morpheme to which they are attached). For example, both *eat* and *eats* are verbs; both *girl* and *girls* are nouns. In contrast, derivational affixes often change the category of the base morpheme. Thus, *read* is a verb, but *readable* is an adjective. (As noted earlier, though, some derivational affixes do not change category: for example, derivational prefixes in English generally do not change the part of speech of the base morpheme to which they are attached, so that both *charge* and *recharge*, for instance, are verbs.)

Second, inflectional and derivational suffixes occur in a certain relative order within words: namely, inflectional suffixes *follow* derivational suffixes. Thus, in *modernize–modernizes* the inflectional *-s* follows derivational *-ize*. If an inflectional suffix is added to a verb, as with *modernizes*, then no further derivational suffixes can be added. English has no form *modernizesable*, with inflectional *-s* followed by derivational *-able*. For these reasons it is often noted that inflectional affixes mark the "outer" layer of words, whereas derivational affixes mark the "inner" layer. These properties of derivational and inflectional affixes are summarized in table 2.2, which provides a morphological analysis of sample words containing selected English suffixes. (In the table we have ignored certain features of spelling; for example, *read + able + ity* is spelled *readability*.)

Intuitively, the function of certain derivational affixes is to create new base forms (new *stems*) that other derivational or inflectional affixes can attach to. Thus, the suffix *-ize* creates verbs from adjectives, and such *-ize* verbs, like other verbs, can have the inflectional ending *-s* attached to them.

Table 2.2
Relative order of derivational and inflectional suffixes, with morphological analysis of sample words

Sample Word	Base ("Stem")	Derivational Suffixes ("Inner Layer")	Inflectional Suffixes ("Outer Layer")
modern	modern		
modernize	modern	ize	
modernizes	modern	ize	s (3rd person)
modernizers	modern	ize + er	s (plural)
write	write		
writer	write	er	
writer's	write	er	's (possessive)
readability	read	able + ity	
reading	read		ing (progressive)
big	big		
bigger	big		er (comparative)
biggest	big		est (superlative)
friend	friend		
friendly	friend	ly	
friendlier	friend	ly	er (comparative)

In this sense, then, certain derivational affixes create new members for a given part-of-speech class, whereas inflectional affixes always attach to already existing members of a given part-of-speech class. This intuitive distinction is reflected in the scheme shown in table 2.2.

Finally, inflectional and derivational affixes can be distinguished in terms of semantic relations. In the case of inflectional affixes, the relation between the meaning of the base morpheme and the meaning of the base + affix is quite regular. Hence, the meaning difference between *tree* and *trees* (singular versus plural) is paralleled quite regularly in other similar pairs consisting of a noun and a noun + plural affix combination. In contrast, in the case of derivational affixes the relation between the meaning of the base morpheme and the meaning of the base + affix is sometimes unpredictable, as we have seen. For example, the pair *fix* and *fixable* shows a simple meaning relation ("*X*" and "able to be *X*'d"); but recall pairs such as *read–readable* and *wash–washable*, where the -*able* form has undergone semantic drift and has accrued new elements of meaning beyond the simple combination of the meaning of the base and the meaning of -*able*. Such semantic drift is generally not found in cases of a base + inflectional affix, so that a word such as *trees* is simply the plural of *tree* and has not accrued any additional meaning.

Note that derivational and inflectional affixes can sometimes be identical in form. For example, -*ing* is an inflectional suffix that is attached to verbs. Thus, -*ing* can be attached to the verb *write* to form the verb *writing*, as in the sentence *I am writing*. However, there is also a derivational suffix -*ing*, which is attached to verbs to form a corresponding noun. For example, the verb *write* can be changed into a noun, *writing*, as in the sentence *Her writings are brilliant*. In this case the suffix -*ing* changes a verb into a noun, and this category change leads us to classify -*ing* as a derivational suffix.

To sum up, then, inflectional affixes indicate certain grammatical functions of words (such as plurality or tense); they occur in a certain order relative to derivational affixes; and they are not associated with certain changes that are associated with derivational affixes (such as category changes or unpredictable meaning changes). Inflectional affixes are often discussed in terms of word sets called *paradigms*. For example, the various forms that verbs can take (*bake–bakes–baking*) form a set of words known as a *verb paradigm*. Verb paradigms in English are rather simple compared to such paradigms in, say, the Romance languages (Italian, French, Spanish, Portuguese, and others) or Latin (in which, for example, a verb such as *amare* "to love" is said to have at least 100 inflectional forms, including *amō* "I love," *amās* "thou lovest," *amat* "he loves," *amāmus* "we love," *amem* "I may love," *amāverint* "they will have loved," *amābāmur* "we were being loved," and so on).

Backformation

As we have seen, given a newly created verb such as *to xerox*, we can create another new word, *xeroxable*, based on the word formation rule for *-able*. In this way, word formation rules are not merely artificial creations of linguists; they correspond to processes used by speakers to create new words.

A particularly interesting case illustrating the "psychological reality" of morphological rules is a phenomenon known as *backformation*, in which word formation processes are "reversed." We can illustrate backformation with the following examples, taken from Williams 1975. It is a historical fact about English that the nouns *pedlar, beggar, hawker, stoker, scavenger, swindler, editor, burglar*, and *sculptor* all existed in the language before the corresponding verbs *to peddle, to beg, to hawk, to stoke, to scavenge, to swindle, to edit, to burgle*, and *to sculpt*. Each of these nouns denoted a general profession or activity, and speakers simply assumed that the sound at the end of each one was the agentive suffix *-er*. Having made this (mistaken) assumption, speakers could then subtract the final *-er* and arrive at a new verb—just as we can subtract the *-er* affix on *writer* and arrive at the verb *write*. In short, backformation is the process of using a word formation rule to analyze a morphologically simple word as if it were a complex word in order to arrive at a new, simpler form.

An interesting contemporary example of backformation also involves the agentive suffix *-er*. Consider the acronym *laser*. *Laser* ends in *er* only because *e* stands for *emission* and *r* stands for *radiation* (*light amplification (by) stimulated emission (of) radiation*). Speakers quickly forget such origins, though, and before long physicists had invented the verb *to lase*, used in sentences such as *This dye, under the appropriate laboratory conditions, will lase*, where *to lase* refers to emitting radiation of a certain sort. The *er* on *laser* accidentally resembles the agentive suffix *-er*, and the word itself denotes an instrument; hence, physicists took this *er* sequence to be the agentive suffix and subtracted it to form a new verb.

Another recent example of backformation involves the plural suffix *-s*. The word in question is *kudos*, which is a synonym for "praise." The final *s* in this word is not a plural morpheme. However, some speakers now use the word *kudo*, having mistakenly analyzed the *s* as a plural morpheme and removed it to derive a singular. In other words, they use the originally singular noun *kudos* as a plural, "praises," and their new backformation *kudo* as a singular, "praise." In the original pronunciation of *kudos*, the final *s* sounded like the *s* in *mouse*. Interestingly, the speakers who use both *kudos* and the backformation *kudo* pronounce the *s* in *kudos* like *z*, as in *dogs*, *please*. It turns out that this is no accident. Once the *s* in *kudos* has been analyzed as being the plural *-s*, then it *must* be pronounced like *z* in this word. We will see the reason for this in chapter 3 when we discuss certain phonological properties associated with the English plural.

Other examples of backformation cited in Williams 1975 are as follows:

(23)

Existed earlier	*Formed later by backformation*
resurrection	to resurrect
preemption	to preempt
vivisection	to vivisect
electrocution	to electrocute
television	to televise
emotion	to emote
donation	to donate

It is ironic that even the word *backformation* is undergoing backformation. The technical linguistic term *backformation* existed in English first, and now one hears linguists saying *Speakers backformed word X from word Y*, creating a new verb in English, *to backform*. What is happening in all these cases is that speakers recognize that the ending *-ion* is used to create abstract nouns from verbs (for example, *to instruct–instruction*). Hence, they can take nouns ending in *-ion*, factor out the ending, and arrive back at a verb, which has a simpler morphological shape (that is, it lacks the ending).

Finally, a slightly different sort of backformation has applied to the word *cranberry*. Until very recently in American English, the *cran-* of *cranberry* existed in that word alone. In fact, linguists coined the term *cranberry morph* for bound bases, such as *cran-*, that occur in only one word of a language. Currently, however, even though the morpheme *cran-* is not yet an independent word, speakers of English have begun using it in other words besides *cranberry*. In particular, the fruit juice section of any supermarket reveals new linguistic blends such as *cranapple*, *cranicot*, and *cran-prune*. By subtracting the recognizable morpheme *berry* from *cranberry*, speakers have extended the use of the morpheme *cran-* by backformation, using it in various new blends.

In sum, these cases show that morphological rules and analyses are not simply abstract aspects of morphological theory. In actuality, speakers produce (and hearers understand) new words using procedures corresponding to these rules and analyses.

Meaning Extensions: Metaphorical Extension, Broadening, and Narrowing

In this chapter we have discussed various ways in which new words can be created and added to a language. Thus far, we have focused on morphological processes by which new words can be created. In closing the chapter, we will examine processes that do not involve morphological mechanisms (such as affixation) but instead involve modification (or extension) of the meaning of already existing words, thereby creating new uses for old words.

When a language does not seem to have just the right expression for certain purposes, speakers often take an existing one and extend its meaning in a recognizable way. The language does not gain a new word as such, but since a word is being used in a new way, the language has been augmented, as though a new word had been added. Let us consider an example. Even though space exploration is a relatively recent phenomenon in human history, it is interesting to note that speakers of English have adopted many existing terms from the realm of ocean navigation to use in speaking of space exploration. For example, we use the word *ship* to refer to space vehicles as well as to ocean-going vessels; we speak of a spaceship *docking* with another in a way related to the way an ocean-going ship docks; we speak of *navigation* in both types of transportation; we could certainly speak of a spaceship *sailing* through space, even though no wind or sails are involved; we speak of certain objects as *floating* in space and of ships as floating on water; we speak of a *captain* and a *crew* for both kinds of ships; and we have carried over the names of ship parts, such as *hull*, *cabin*, *hatch*, and (at least on television shows) *deck*. It is striking that terms that basically derive from the historical epoch of wind-powered ocean navigation have with great ease been *extended* into the realm of space navigation. The technology in the two realms is radically different, yet we apparently perceive enough similarities to use already existing terms, in new ways, to describe the new phenomena. This is an important fact, for it shows that technological changes in a society do not necessarily result in the addition of previously nonexistent words to its language. Indeed, speakers of all human languages show great creativity and imaginative power in extending the existent language into new realms of experience.

The example just given is a case of *metaphorical extension*, in which certain objects, ideas, or events from one realm are described with words from a different realm of objects, ideas, and events. The metaphorical extension, if successful, becomes part of the conventional linguistic meaning of the word(s) in question. Another interesting case is the metaphorical extension of words from the physical realm of food and digestion into the mental realm of ideas and interpersonal exchange of ideas. For example, consider the following sentences:

(24)

a. Let me *chew on* these ideas for a while.

b. They just wouldn't *swallow* that idea.

c. She'll give us time to *digest* that idea.

d. On the exam, please don't merely *regurgitate* what I've told you.

e. He *bit off* more than he could chew. (speaking of someone's research project)

f. Will you stop *feeding* me that old line!

In these examples, one realm (roughly, a realm involving ideas) is described in terms of words form another realm (food and digestion). A feature of this particular case is that words from a physical realm are being extended into a mental realm, perhaps because the physical vocabulary provides a familiar and public frame of reference for discussing our private mental life.

Metaphorical extension is not the only mechanism by which already existing words can be put to new uses. Sometimes the use of existing words can become *broader*. For example, the slang word *cool* was originally part of the professional jargon of jazz musicians and referred to a specific artistic style of jazz (a use that was itself an extension). With the passage of time, the word has come to be applied to almost anything conceivable, not just music; and it no longer refers just to a certain genre or style, but is a general term indicating approval of the thing in question.

Conversely, the use of a word can *narrow*. A typical example is the word *meat*. At one time in English it meant any solid consumable food (a meaning that persists in the word *nutmeat*), but now it is used to refer only to the edible solid flesh of animals.

Finally, *reversals* of meanings can occur. In certain varieties of American slang the word *bad* has come to have positive connotations, with roughly the meaning "emphatically good." Hollywood movies of the '30s and '40s reveal that the words *square* and *straight* had positive connotations, meaning "honest" and "upright," meanings that survive in the phrases *square deal* and *play it straight*. During the late '50s and into the '60s, the word *square* came to have a negative connotation, referring to anyone or any-thing hopelessly conventional and uncomprehending of "in" things. By the late '60s this use of *square* had itself come to be regarded as old-fashioned and the word dropped out of favor (which, incidentally, illustrates the rapid rate at which so-called slang terms enter and leave a language). In the same period the word *straight* came to be used in a wide range of areas, always with the general meaning of adhering to conventional norms: for example, a straight person is one who doesn't take drugs; who is hetero-sexual rather than homosexual; who is generally "out of it"; and so on.

We have discussed various kinds of extensions and modifications of meaning as a way to create new uses for already existing words. Although this is one of the most interesting areas of word meaning, we unfortunately have very little understanding of the exact mechanisms of meaning change and extension. For one thing, we have very little idea *what* the meaning of a word is: Is the meaning an abstract idea, a concept? Is it an image? When we describe the meaning of the word, are we describing the thing that the word denotes? Or is meaning best described neither as an idea nor as a referent, but rather as the *use* of a word in some context? We will discuss these possibilities in more detail in chapter 6, which deals with semantics. Suffice it to say here that because we do not know precisely *what* the meaning of a word is and because theories of psychology of human thought are still at a rudimentary level, we can currently say very little about the exact nature of metaphorical extension or other meaning shifts. However, this area, especially the study of so-called slang, will be extremely impor-tant for future research because it provides fundamental evidence about speakers' linguistic creativity.

2.3 SPECIAL TOPICS

More on Compounds

In section 2.2 we briefly discussed a way to create new words, namely, compounding. Creating complex words by way of combining simpler ones provides a very rich source of new words. Compounding is extremely productive. Consider the following Noun + Noun compounds: *lynx-brush, gin-life, lettuce-dog, house-roach, goat-ghost*. Probably, you have never encountered any of these compounds before. More than likely, they won't be found in any dictionary. Though you may be uncertain about their meanings (indeed, each has a range of reasonable meanings), you will certainly judge them as being plausible words. That is, they are *possible* though not necessarily *occurring* words. As mentioned earlier, there is no limit to the number of compounds that can be produced—more evidence that the dictionary is not a very good representation of our knowledge of words.

Table 2.1 listed several types of compounds in English. Among these are Noun + Noun (*landlord, fire truck*), Adjective + Adjective (*icy-cold, red-hot*), Adjective + Noun (*blackboard, high chair*), and Noun + Adjective (*earthbound, sky-blue*). All of the examples involve *primary compounds*; that is, each word that makes up the compound is itself morphologically simple. Speakers create new compounds of this type relatively easily (to use the technical term, such compounding is quite *productive*).

There are compounds that involve combining morphologically complex words. In particular, we will look at *synthetic* (or *verbal*) compounds: those two-word English compounds in which the second word is *deverbal* (derived from a verb). An example of a deverbal noun is our now familiar example *baker*, a noun derived from a verb by attaching the agentive suffix *-er*. Verbal compounds exhibit some rather interesting properties. Consider the examples in table 2.3. Why are some of these combinations of adjective (noun, or adverb) + deverbal noun good, whereas others are clearly odd? That is, why is *good-looker* well formed, but not *grim-wanting*? In order to tease out the relevant differences, let us turn to the original verbs. Consider the sentences in table 2.4. In groups I–III a certain pattern

Table 2.3
Verbal compounds. (Adapted from Roeper and Siegel 1978.)

	Possible	Impossible
I	good-looker odd-seeming clever-sounding	*grim-wanting *clever-supporting
II	fast-mover late-bloomer rapidly-rising	*quick-owner *fast-finding *rapidly-raising
III	wage-earner trend-setter profit-sharing	*child-bloomer *cat-seeming *cake-riser
IV	church-goer cave-dweller opera singer apartment-living	*shortstop-thrower (= throw something to shortstop) *doctor-grafting (= grafting of skin by a doctor)

Table 2.4
Base verbs in a syntactic context

	Possible	Impossible
I	Sarah *looks good*.	*Sam *wants grim*.
	John *seems odd*.	*John *supports clever*.
	Jill *sounds clever*.	
II	The cat *moves fast*.	*The man *owns quick*.
	John *bloomed late*.	*John *found fast*.
	The water is *rising rapidly*.	*Bob is *raising rapidly*.
III	Everyone *earns a wage*.	*The mother *blooms the child*.
	Celebrities *set trends*.	*It *seems cat*.
	Corporations *share profits*.	*Heat *rises the cake*.
IV	Some people *go to church*.	The pitcher *threw* the ball to the *shortstop*.
	Bats *dwell in caves*.	*The doctor grafted* the skin skillfully.
	Jesse Norman *sings at the opera*.	
	Some people *live in apartments*.	

emerges. Compare *Sarah looks good* with **Sam wants grim*. (The asterisk (*) indicates that the sentence is ill formed (or ungrammatical).) *Good* and *grim* in these sentences are also the first words in their corresponding compounds in group I of table 2.3. *Grim-wanting* is not an acceptable compound, and interestingly, the sentence based on the verb *want* with *grim* adjacent to the verb is also unacceptable. However, the compound *good-looker* is a well-formed compound, and the sentence based on the verb *look* with *good* to its right is also well formed. Each example exhibits this pattern. That is, whenever the compound is well formed, the first word of that compound can appear in a sentence to the immediate right of the verb (ignoring *a*) that corresponds to the second word of the compound.

Many of the examples in group IV illustrate that the first word in the compound can correspond to a noun that occurs in a prepositional phrase immediately following the verb in the sentence (*go to church*, *dwell in caves*). The compounds in group IV that are ill formed (such as **shortstop-thrower*) do not conform to this pattern. In the example *The pitcher threw the ball to the shortstop*, the noun phrase *the ball* intervenes between the verb and the prepositional phrase containing *shortstop*. In the example *The doctor grafted the skin skillfully*, it is the noun phrase *the skin* that immediately follows *grafted*, not the noun phrase *the doctor*.

The pattern that has emerged can be captured by the following statement (an adaptation of Roeper and Siegel's (1978) *First Sister Principle*):

(25)

All deverbal compounds of the form W1 + W2 (= word 1 + word 2) are formed by taking W1—the first noun, adjective, or adverb that follows the verb (W2) in a sentence—and combining it with W2.

Exactly how to incorporate such a condition in a theory of compounds is the focus of much current research. Our interest here is to illustrate that compounding, like other morphological and grammatical processes, involves referring to such notions as category (here, "verb") and to properties of that category. Verbal compounding does not involve random combinations of words. Quite the contrary: just as the suffix *-able* cannot attach to just any verb, not just any word can serve as W1 with just any deverbal W2. Thus, compounding is governed by principles that are sensitive to numerous properties of the words involved.

Morphological Anaphora

One very important theme in current linguistic studies concerns *anaphora*. Anaphora involves a relation between, for example, a pronoun and an antecedent noun phrase where the two are understood as being used to refer to the same thing. The linguistic system uses various mechanisms to signal this phenomenon. Below we examine morphological data related to anaphora.

In English the morpheme *self* signals when two words or phrases are being used to pick out one individual:

(26)

Mary sees her*self*.

The person who is "seeing," Mary, is the same person who is being "seen." *Self* attaches not only to pronouns but also to other categories of words:

(27)

admirer	–	self-admirer
denial	–	self-denial
amusement	–	self-amusement
deceived	–	self-deceived
employed	–	self-employed
employable	–	self-employable
closing	–	self-closing
destructive	–	self-destructive
inhibitory	–	self-inhibitory

The data in (27) illustrate that *self* may attach to a noun (*admirer, denial, amusement*) or an adjective (*deceived, employed, destructive*). However, *self* does not attach to just any noun or adjective:

(28)
*self-red
*self-cat
*self-chalk

In fact, notice that the nouns and adjectives in the left-hand column of (27) are all morphologically complex and that they are all based on verbs (*employable–employ, inhibitory–inhibit, amusement–amuse*). However, *self* does not attach directly to verbs:

(29)
deceive   –   *self-deceive(s)
employ   –   *self-employ(s)
deny   –   *self-deny(s)
admire   –   *self-admire(s)

Clearly, there is some kind of dependency between *self* and the verb, yet *self* cannot directly attach to the verb. We can make the following descriptive observation: the deverbal nouns and adjectives in (27) are all based on transitive verbs (note in contrast that *self-fidgety*, based on the intransitive verb *fidget*, is odd):

(30)
admire the child
deny the truth
amuse the class
deceive the public
employ the elderly
close the door
destroy the argument
inhibit the boy

This is not too surprising since *self* functions to indicate that, for example, the subject and the object refer to the same entity. Therefore, a *self-admirer* is *someone* who admires *himself* or *herself*, *self-destruction* involves *someone* destroying *himself* or *herself*, and so on. This is another instance of word formation where the properties of the base word are crucial. In this case the relevant properties may have more to do with whether or not the word is "transitive" than with the category to which the word belongs (though

there must be an explanation for why verbs—even though they may be transitive—do not attach to *self*).

In the chapters that follow, we will look at other linguistic devices for signaling "coreference."

Exercises

1. In this chapter we noted that *radar* and *laser* are acronyms. List three other recent English words that are acronyms and state their origin.

2. Below is a list of acronyms. Provide original words for as many of these acronyms as you can.

UNICEF	REM
OPEC	SUNY
RIP	CUNY
BART	WIN
ROM	

3. List three additional recent words that, like *TV* and *ID*, are abbreviations of longer words, and state their origin.

4. For the purposes of this exercise, use only the words in the following list:

sidewalk
daughter
laugh
cactus
alligator

A. Using these words, invent five new compounds and provide a meaning for each one.
B. What would you guess is a possible meaning of the compound *sidewalk alligator cactus*?
C. What is the "head" of the compound listed in question B? State the reason(s) for your answer.

5. English has a suffix *-en* whose use is illustrated in the following lists:

List A	*List B*
red	redden
black	blacken
mad	madden
soft	soften
hard	harden
sweet	sweeten
short	shorten
wide	widen
sharp	sharpen

In regard to these data, answer the following questions:

A. What part of speech does the suffix *-en* attach to? That is, what is the part of speech of the words in list A? For evidence to support your answer, consider what other morphemes attach to the words in list A (consult the section "Categories (Parts of Speech)").

B. When the suffix *-en* is attached to a word, what part of speech is the resulting word? That is, what part of speech do the words in list B belong to? Give some specific morphological properties of one of the words in list B, in order to justify your answer.

C. In what way does the suffix *-en* change the meaning of the word it is attached to?

6. English also has a prefix *un-*, whose use is illustrated in the following lists:

List A	List B
true	untrue
likely	unlikely
acceptable	unacceptable
wise	unwise
real	unreal
common	uncommon
natural	unnatural
graceful	ungraceful
refined	unrefined
tamed	untamed

A. What part of speech are the words that the prefix *un-* attaches to? That is, what part of speech are the words in list A?

B. When *un-* is prefixed to a word, what part of speech is the resultant new word? That is, what part of speech are the words in list B?

C. In what way does the prefix *un-* change the meaning of the word it attaches to?

D. Very recently, new words such as *Uncola* (a type of soft drink) and *Uncar* (used in a bus company advertisement to refer to a bus) have been added to the English language. Given the pattern established above in lists A and B, why are words such as *Uncola* and *Uncar* "irregular"?

7. Exercise 6 involved examples of a prefix *un-* in English. Now consider a new set of data, involving another prefix *un-*:

List A	List B
tie	untie
wrap	unwrap
cover	uncover
wind	unwind
dress	undress
fold	unfold
buckle	unbuckle
lock	unlock
fasten	unfasten
stick	unstick

How does the prefix *un-* illustrated here differ from the prefix *un-* illustrated in exercise 6? To answer this, answer the following specific questions:

A. What is the part of speech of the words that this second prefix *un-* attaches to? That is, what part of speech are the words in list A? Where a given word could be classified as belonging to more than one part of speech, what is the part of speech that *un-* attaches to?

B. When this prefix *un-* is attached to a word, what part of speech does the resultant new word belong to? That is, what part of speech are the words in list B?

C. In what way does this prefix *un-* change the meaning of the word that it attaches to? Describe this meaning change as carefully as you can.

D. How is the meaning change associated with this prefix *un-* different from the meaning change associated with the prefix *un-* illustrated in exercise 6?

8. Based on the evidence in exercises 6 and 7, we note that English has two prefixes *un-*. Consider now the word *unlockable*. If you think about this word long enough, you will realize that it has two different meanings. Show how these two different meanings are in part determined by the fact that English has two different prefixes *un-*.

9. Use the following two lists for this exercise:

List A	*List B*
redo	*rego
rewrite	*recry
rework	*resleep
recook	*resit
reimport	*revanish
rebuild	*rechange
restate	*reelapse
reset	*redie
resharpen	
reshape	

State the word formation rule for the prefix *re-*. Follow the format given for the *-able* rule in this chapter. In particular, answer the following questions:

A. What phonological changes, if any, does the prefix *re-* cause in the word or stem to which it attaches?

B. What part(s) of speech does the prefix *re-* attach to? Note the contrast between list A and list B. What is the difference between these sets of words?

C. When *re-* is attached to a word or stem, what is the part of speech of the resulting word or stem?

D. In general, what meaning change(s) are caused by the addition of the prefix *re-*? In the ideal case, what meaning does the prefix *re-* add to the word or stem to which it is attached?

E. Can you find any words with *re-* that have erratic or unexpected meanings? (Are there any *re-* words that systematically mean more than you would expect from the simple meaning of *re-* and the simple meaning of the base?)

F. Why can you *reshoot* a movie but not *reshoot* a terrorist?

G. Why are the following *re-* words problematic? Discuss three of them: *reduce, reflect, refine, refuse, repeat, relax, release, renew, replicate, revive, remember.*

10. Analyze the following words, in the manner shown in table 2.2:

a. orderliness   e. fastest
b. capitalizers   f. digestion
c. lengthen   g. UNICEF's
d. employer   h. employee

11. For this exercise, consider the following data from Turkish:

el "the hand"	evimiz "our house"
eller "hands"	evde "in the house"
elim "my hand"	elimde "in my hand"
ev "the house"	evlerimiz "our houses"
eve "to the house"	evlerimden "from my houses"
ellerimiz "our hands"	evleriniz "your (pl.) houses"
ellerimde "in my hands"	evim "my house"
evlerde "in the houses"	ellerimden "from my hands"
evden "from the house"	evler "houses"
ellerim "my hands"	eline "to your (sing.) hand"
ellerinize "to your (pl.) hands"	ellerin "your (sing.) hand"
evlerim "my houses"	elimden "from my hand"
elin "your (sing.) hand"	evine "to your (sing.) house"

In the English translations, *your* is listed as singular (sing.) when it refers to one person, and plural (pl.) when it refers to more than one person.

Using the data given above, answer the following questions:

A. Fill in each blank with the appropriate Turkish morpheme:

(the) hand _____   your (sing.) _____
(the) house _____   your (pl.) _____
plural _____   to _____
my _____   in _____
our _____   from _____

B. Given the Turkish data, what is the order of the morphemes (indicating possession, person, and so forth) of the suffixes in a word?

C. Based on your answers to questions A and B, how would you translate the following English forms into Turkish?

from your (pl.) house _____
to our house _____
in my house _____

Bibliography and Further Reading

Adams, V. (1973). *An introduction to modern English word formation*. London: Longman.

Allen, M. (1978). Morphological investigations. Doctoral dissertation, University of Connecticut, Storrs.

Aronoff, M. (1976). *Word formation in generative grammar*. Cambridge, Mass.: MIT Press.

Bloomfield, L. (1933). *Language*. New York: Holt, Rinehart and Winston. (See chaps. 13 and 14.)

Bradley, D. C., M. F. Garrett, and E. B. Zurif (1980). Syntactic deficits in Broca's aphasia. In Caplan 1980.

Caplan, D., ed. (1980). *Biological studies of mental processes*. Cambridge, Mass.: MIT Press.

Jackendoff, R. S. (1975). Morphological and semantic regularities in the lexicon. *Language* 51, 639–671.

Jespersen, O. (1911). *A modern English grammar*. London: Allen and Unwin. (See vol. VI.)

Lieber, R. (1983). Argument linking and compounds in English. *Linguistic Inquiry* 14, 251–285.

Marchand, H. (1969). *The categories and types of present-day English word-formation*. 2nd ed. Munich: Beck.

Matthews, P. H. (1972). *Inflectional morphology*. Cambridge: Cambridge University Press.

Matthews, P. H. (1974). *Morphology: An introduction to the theory of word structure*. Cambridge: Cambridge University Press.

Miller, G., and P. Gildea (1987). How children learn words. *Scientific American* 257.3, 94–99.

Roeper, T., and M. Siegel (1978). A lexical transformation for verbal compounds. *Linguistic Inquiry* 9, 199–260.

Sapir, E. (1921). *Language*. New York: Harcourt, Brace & World. (See chap. 4.)

Selkirk, E. O. (1982). *The syntax of words*. Cambridge, Mass.: MIT Press.

Williams, J. M. (1975). *Origins of the English language*. New York: Free Press.

Zepeda, O. (1983). *Papago grammar*. Tucson, Ariz.: University of Arizona Press.

PHONETICS: THE STUDY OF SPEECH SOUNDS

We take it for granted that we can write a language with discrete symbols (an alphabet), even though speech itself is for the most part continuous. Neither the movements of the speech articulators nor the acoustic signal can be broken down into the kind of discrete units that alphabetic symbols represent. You can observe the overlap in articulation by pronouncing the syllables *bee, bah, boo*. You will find that when you pronounce the *b*, your tongue is already in position to pronounce the "following" vowel. Moreover, you will find that your lips are already pursed when you pronounce the *b* in *boo*, even though the pursing is part of the following vowel. With its set of linearly ordered discrete symbols, then, an alphabetic writing system is actually an idealization whose reality is not found in the *physical* instantiations of speech. So as we begin our study of the properties of the speech sounds of a language, we see that what appears to be their most concrete aspect—alphabetic representation—is ultimately highly abstract in nature.

3.1 SOME BACKGROUND CONCEPTS

Phonetics is concerned with how speech sounds are produced (articulated) in the vocal tract (a field of study known as *articulatory phonetics*), as well as with the physical properties of the speech sound waves generated by the vocal tract (a field known as *acoustic phonetics*). Whereas the term *phonetics* usually refers to the study of the articulatory and acoustic properties of sounds, the term *phonology*, the subject of chapter 4, is often used to refer to the abstract rules and principles that govern the distribution of sounds in a language. In this chapter we will examine the ways in which speech sounds are produced, discussing the articulation of English speech sounds in particular. We will focus on articulation rather than on the

Table 3.1
Different pronunciations of the plural morpheme

Example word	cat<u>s</u>	dog<u>s</u>	bush<u>es</u>
Pronunciation of plural morpheme for that word	<u>s</u>-sound	<u>z</u>-sound	vowel + <u>z</u>

acoustic properties of speech sounds; for further information on acoustic phonetics, see Ladefoged 1982 and Denes and Pinson 1973.

In chapter 2 we discussed the English plural morpheme -s. It turns out that plural nouns formed by attaching the plural morpheme, which is a suffix, do not all end with the same sound (see table 3.1). In chapter 4 we will explore a principled account of the difference, but first we must study the nature of these sounds in order to be equipped with the relevant notions and vocabulary.

Physiology of Speech Production

One commonsense view is that learning to speak a language requires only the control of a few muscles that move the lips, jaw, and tongue. These anatomical structures are the most easily observed in any case. In reality the situation is much more complex, for over 100 muscles exercise direct and continuous control during the production of the sound waves that carry speech (Lenneberg 1967). These sound waves are produced by a complex interaction of (1) an outward flow of air from the lungs; (2) modifications of the airflow at the larynx (the Adam's apple or "voice box" in the throat); and (3) additional modifications of the airflow by position and movement of the tongue and other anatomical structures of the vocal tract. We will consider each of these components in turn.

Airflow from the Lungs during Speech

The flow of air from the lungs during speech differs in several important respects from the airflow during quiet breathing. First, during speech, three to four times as much air is exhaled than during quiet breathing. Second, in speech, the normal breathing rhythm is changed radically: inhalation is more rapid and exhalation is much more drawn out. Third, the number of breaths per unit time decreases during speech. Fourth, the flow of air is unimpeded during quiet breathing, whereas in speech the airflow encounters resistance from the obstructions and closures that occur in the throat and mouth. While these alterations in the normal breathing pattern are occurring during speech, the function of breathing (exchange of oxygen and carbon dioxide) continues with no discomfort to the speaker.

One of the primary mechanisms for expanding the lungs during both quiet breathing and speech is the contraction of the *diaphragm* (see figure 3.1), a sheet of muscular tissue that separates the chest cavity from the abdominal region. This contraction causes the diaphragm to lower and flatten out, leading to an increase in the size of the chest cavity. The other primary mechanism for the expansion of the chest cavity is the set of muscles between the ribs in the rib cage (the *external intercostals*). Contraction of these muscles causes the ribs to lift up, and because of the way that the ribs are hinged, they swing out, increasing the volume of the chest cavity. Since the lungs are attached to the walls of the chest cavity, when the chest cavity expands, either from diaphragm contraction or rib movement, the lungs, being elastic, also expand. As the lungs expand, the air flows in, up to the point when inhalation is completed. In quiet breathing, the diaphragm relaxes at this point, and the stretched lungs begin to shrink, allowing air to flow out quite rapidly at the beginning, as with air escaping from a filled balloon. During speech, however, the muscles of the diaphragm and the rib cage continue to be active, restraining the lungs from emptying too rapidly. Without this checking force, speech would be loud at first and then become quieter as the lungs emptied. Thus, humans have developed special adaptations for breathing during speech: speech is not merely "added" to the breathing cycle; rather, the breathing cycle is adapted to the needs of speech.

The Role of the Larynx in Speech

The first point where the airflow from the lungs encounters a controlled resistance is at the *larynx*, a structure of muscle and cartilage located at the upper end of the *trachea* (or *windpipe*) (see figure 3.1). The resistance can be controlled by the different positions and tensions in the *vocal cords* (or *vocal folds*), two muscular bands of tissue that stretch from front to back within the larynx (see figure 3.2). During quiet breathing the cords are relaxed and spread apart to allow the free flow of air to and from the lungs. During swallowing, however, the cords are drawn tightly together to keep foreign material from entering the lungs. For speech the most important feature of the vocal cords is that they can be made to vibrate if the airflow between them is sufficiently rapid and if they have the proper tension and proximity to each other. This rapid vibration is called *voicing* (or *phonation*). The *frequency* of vibration determines the perceived *pitch*. Because the vocal cords of adult males are larger in size, their frequency

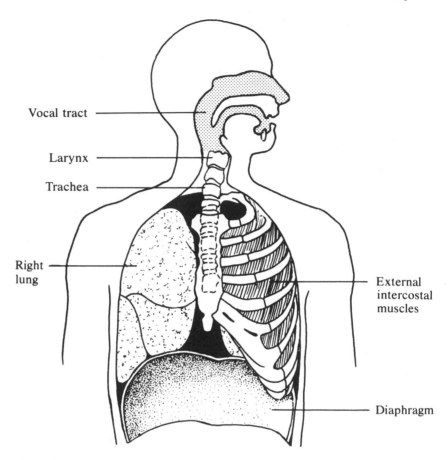

Figure 3.1
Major anatomical structures involved in the production of speech. Air driven from
the lungs through the trachea and the larynx into the vocal tract is the primary
source of the acoustic energy in speech. The lungs are attached to the chest wall
and diaphragm, and when the diaphragm lowers, the size of the chest cavity is
increased, the elastic lungs expand, and air flows inward. Similarly, air also flows
inward when the muscles between the ribs (the *external intercostals*) contract and
the rib cage expands outward, thus increasing the size of the chest cavity. The
muscles of the diaphragm and rib cage remain active during speech, acting as a
check on the outward flow of air.

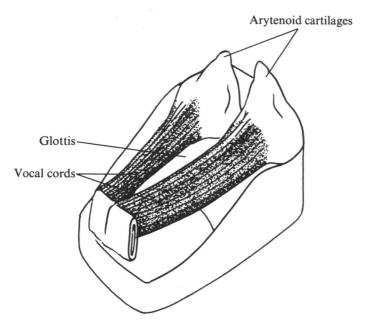

Arytenoid cartilages

Glottis

Vocal cords

Figure 3.2
View of the vocal cords. The mechanical vibration of these cords during speech is called *voicing* (or *phonation*). The space between the cords is called the *glottis*.

of vibration is relatively lower than the frequency of vibration in females and children. The pitch of adult males' voices is thus perceived as lower than that of females and children.

Voicing is the "extra noise," the "buzz" that accompanies the production of the *z*-sound version of the plural morpheme shown in table 3.1. We say that the *z*-sound is *voiced*, whereas the *s*-sound is *voiceless*. The lack of voicing in *s* is due to the fact that the vocal cords are more spread apart and tenser than during the production of *z*, thus creating conditions that inhibit vocal cord vibration.

Other speech sounds found in human language also require other types of vocal cord configurations and movements. We will examine some of these later in the chapter.

Speakers have a high degree of control over the sounds the vocal cords can produce. The ability to sing a melody, for example, depends on being able to change the vocal cord positions and tensions rapidly and accurately to hit the right notes. Although the ability to sing well is subject to much individual variation, the ability to control the vocal cord positions and

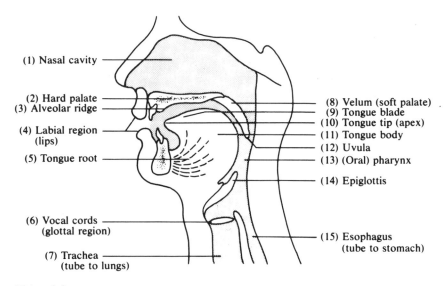

(1) Nasal cavity

(2) Hard palate
(3) Alveolar ridge

(4) Labial region
    (lips)

(5) Tongue root

(6) Vocal cords
    (glottal region)

(7) Trachea
    (tube to lungs)

(8) Velum (soft palate)
(9) Tongue blade
(10) Tongue tip (apex)
(11) Tongue body
(12) Uvula
(13) (Oral) pharynx

(14) Epiglottis

(15) Esophagus
     (tube to stomach)

Figure 3.3
Cross section of the human vocal tract

tensions necessary for speech is well within the ability of all normal speakers.

Finally, the space between the vocal cords is called the *glottis* (see figure 3.2), and linguists frequently refer to sounds that involve a constriction or closure of this space between the vocal cords as *glottal sounds*.

The Vocal Tract

The *vocal tract*, the region above the vocal cords that includes the (oral) pharynx, the oral cavity, and the nasal cavity, is the space within which the speech sounds of human language are produced (see figure 3.3). We will examine the anatomical features of the vocal tract in the course of discussing how the consonants and vowels of English are formed.

3.2 THE REPRESENTATION OF SPEECH SOUNDS

Phonemic Transcription versus English Orthography

In discussing the sounds of English, and the sounds of human language in general, we need a set of symbols to *represent* those sounds. What sort of representational system will be most useful? If we try using the conventional English *orthography* (spelling system) to represent speech sounds, we face problems of two major types: first, a single letter of the alphabet often represents more than one sound; and conversely, a single speech sound is represented by several different letters (see figure 3.4).

As for problems of the first type, we have already seen that the letter *s* represents a *z*-sound in the word *dogs* and an *s*-sound in the word *cats*. To take another case, the letter *t* can represent a *t*-sound, as in the word *tin*; but it can also represent a *sh*-like sound, as in *nation*.

Conversely, consider the *k*-sound in the word *kick*. This sound is orthographically represented in two different ways: the letter *k* at the beginning of the word and the letters *ck* at the end of the word. The word *cow* also begins with a *k*-sound, but here it is represented by the letter *c*. Similar problems arise with the initial *j*-sound in *jug*. This initial sound is represented by the letter *j*, but it is sometimes called "*soft g*" (and is spelled *g*) in words such as *giraffe*. Even the sequence of letters *dge* in words such as *ridge* and *edge* represents the *j*-sound.

In sum, English orthography is inadequate as a representation of the current speech sounds of American English. This lack of consistency in representing sounds is due in part to the fact that the English writing system became fixed several hundred years ago, although the pronunciation of the words has continuously changed since that period. But what system of symbols should we use to represent the speech sounds of English? More importantly, what should the symbols represent? The writing system introduced in this chapter uses symbols that represent for the most part the *sounds produced by particular configurations of the vocal tract*. A symbol such as *s* therefore represents the vocal tract configuration in which the tongue tip and/or blade are lightly pressed against the roof of the mouth near the teeth ridge so that when air from the lungs passes between the tongue and the teeth ridge a hissing sound is produced.

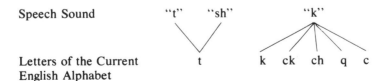

Figure 3.4
Types of inconsistencies in current English orthography. A single letter can stand for more than one sound, and vice versa—several letters or groups of letters can stand for the same sound. On the left, the letter *t* represents both the *t*-sound in *tin* and the *sh*-sound in *nation*. On the right, the *k*-sound is represented by the letters *k* and *ck* as in the word *kick*, *ch* as in *choir*, *q* as in *quick*, and *c* as in *cow*.

The first writing system that we will look at is called a *phonemic transcription system*. Later we will have occasion to discuss and distinguish a *phonetic transcription system*. The crucial property of a phonemic system is that each significant speech sound of a language is represented with a unique symbol (or unique combination of symbols). This transcription system therefore overcomes the deficiencies of the current English alphabet.

The Consonants of American English

Table 3.2 displays the phonemic consonant symbols of English. A *consonant* is a speech sound produced when the speaker either stops or severely constricts the airflow in the vocal tract. In addition to being classified as *voiceless* (like the *s*-sound in *cats*) or *voiced* (like the *z*-sound in *dogs*), consonants are described in terms of (1) the *place* and (2) the *manner* of their articulation. The *places* of articulation (see the top of table 3.2) are labeled in terms of anatomical structures, which include the lips and regions along the roof of the mouth. In the production of most consonants, the lower lip or some part of the tongue approaches or touches the designated places of articulation along the roof of the mouth. The *manners* of articulation (see the left-hand side of table 3.2) refer for the most part to how the articulators (lips or tongue) achieve contact or proximity with the places of articulation.

We will now describe the consonants of English in terms of the framework given in table 3.2, making use of the anatomical descriptions shown in figure 3.3.

The phonemic symbols we will use here are the ones generally used by American linguists. These symbols are easier to type than most other phonemic symbol systems and for this reason are preferred by many linguists. There are other symbol systems, however, among them the commonly used International Phonetic Alphabet (IPA). Where the IPA symbols differ from our symbols, we will include them in parentheses next to the symbols used in this text. We enclose our symbols in slant lines, a tradition common in linguistics when discussing *phonemic* symbols.

Stops

Stops are sounds produced when the airflow is completely obstructed during speech.

/p/   A voiceless bilabial stop. The speech sound symbolized by /p/ does not have accompanying vocal cord vibration and is therefore voiceless. The

Table 3.2
The consonants of English

MANNER OF ARTICULATION		PLACE OF ARTICULATION						
		Bilabial	Labiodental	Interdental	Alveolar	Alveopalatal	Velar	Glottal
Stops	voiceless	p			t		k	
	voiced	b			d		g	
Fricatives	voiceless		f	θ	s	š		h
	voiced		v	ð	z	ž		
Affricates	voiceless					č		
	voiced					ǰ		
Nasals		m			n		ŋ	
Liquids	lateral				l			
	nonlateral				r			
Glides						y	w (ʍ)	

airflow is stopped by the complete closure of the two lips, which gives rise to the term *bilabial* (see 4, figure 3.3). The symbol /p/ represents the first sound in the word *pin*.

/b/   A voiced bilabial stop. The sound represented by /b/ has the same articulation as /p/, but it is accompanied by voicing. The symbol /b/ represents the first and last sounds in the name *Bob*.

/t/   A voiceless alveolar stop. The *alveolar* consonants of English are produced when the tongue tip (or apex; see 10, figure 3.3) approaches or—in the case of /t/ and /d/—touches the roof of the mouth at or near the alveolar ridge *behind* the upper teeth (see 3, figure 3.3). The English sound represented by the symbol /t/ thus differs from the *t*'s of many European languages in which the tongue tip touches the upper teeth. A Spanish /t/, for example, is a voiceless *dental* stop. The symbol /t/ represents the initial sound in the English word *tin*.

/d/   A voiced alveolar stop. The sound represented by the symbol /d/ has the same articulation as /t/ but is accompanied by voicing. The symbol /d/ represents the first and last sounds in the word *Dad*.

/k/   A voiceless velar stop. *Velar* consonants are formed when the body of the tongue approaches or—in the case of /k/ and /g/—touches the roof of the mouth on the *palate* (the soft palate is called the *velum*; see 8, figure 3.3). The symbol /k/ represents the first sound in the word *kite*.

/g/   A voiced velar stop. The sound represented by the symbol /g/ has the same articulation as /k/ but is accompanied by voicing. The symbol /g/ represents the first and last sounds in the word *gag*.

Fricatives

Fricatives are sounds produced when the airflow is forced through a narrow opening in the vocal tract so that noise produced by *friction* is created.

/f/   A voiceless labiodental fricative. The term *labiodental* indicates that the point of contact involves the (lower) lip and the (upper) teeth. The symbol /f/ represents the first sound in the word *fish*.

/v/   A voiced labiodental fricative. The sounds represented by the symbols /f/ and /v/ differ only in voicing, /v/ being voiced. The symbol /v/ represents the initial sound of the word *vine*.

/θ/   A voiceless interdental fricative. The sound symbolized as /θ/, as well as its voiced counterpart /ð/, are spelled with *th* in the current English writing system. The *interdental* sounds are produced when the tongue tip is placed against the upper teeth, friction being created by air forced between the upper teeth and the tongue. For most English speakers, the tongue tip is projected slightly when it rests between the upper and lower teeth. The symbol /θ/ represents the first sound in its own name, the Greek letter *theta*, and in the word *thin*.

/ð/   A voiced interdental fricative. The symbol /ð/ is called *eth* (or *crossed d*). You can hear the difference between the sounds symbolized by /ð/ and /θ/ if you say *then* and *thin* very slowly. You will hear (and feel) the voicing that accompanies the /ð/ at the beginning of *then*, and you will note that the initial consonant of *thin* is not voiced. The symbol /ð/ also represents the initial sound of the words *this* and *that*.

/s/   A voiceless alveolar fricative. Note that the fricative sound represented by the symbol /s/ is much harsher than the fricative sound represented by the symbol /θ/. The turbulence for /s/ is created by air passing between either the tongue tip or blade (for some English speakers) and the alveolar ridge, which then strikes the teeth at a high velocity. The symbol /s/ represents the initial sound of the word *sit*.

/z/   A voiced alveolar fricative. The sounds represented by the symbols /s/ and /z/ differ only in voicing, /z/ being voiced. The symbol /z/ represents the first sound in the name *Zeke*.

/š/   (IPA ʃ)   A voiceless alveopalatal fricative. The symbol /š/, usually spelled *sh* in English orthography, represents a fricative similar to /s/, but the region of turbulent airflow lies just behind the alveolar ridge on the hard palate (hence *alveopalatal*; see 2 and 3, figure 3.3). During the articulation of /š/ the tongue tip can be positioned either near the alveolar ridge itself (with the tongue blade arched) or just behind the alveolar ridge (in which case the tongue blade does not need to be arched). The symbol /š/ represents the initial consonant in the word *ship*.

/ž/   (IPA ʒ)   A voiced alveopalatal fricative. Unlike /š/, the voiced counterpart /ž/ is rare (and for some speakers, nonexistent) in word-initial position in English. The symbol /ž/ represents the first sound in foreign names such as *Zsa-Zsa* and *Jacques*. More commonly, /ž/ occurs in the middle of English words. For example, the letter *s* in *decision* and *measure* is pronounced as the sound represented by /ž/.

/h/   A "glottal" fricative. The /h/ sound is often called a *glottal* fricative because the vocal cords are positioned so that a small amount of turbulent airflow is produced across the glottis. However, the primary noise source for this speech sound is turbulence created at different points along the vocal tract where the tongue body (or blade) approaches the roof of the mouth. The point where the friction is created is determined by the vowel that follows the /h/. In the articulation of the English word *heap*, for example, the tongue body is positioned high and forward, and the fricative noise is produced in the palatal region. The symbol *h* represents the first sound in the words *how* and *here*.

Affricates

An *affricate* is a single but complex sound, beginning as a stop but releasing secondarily into a fricative.

/č/   (IPA tʃ)   A voiceless alveopalatal affricate. The symbol /č/ represents the first sound in the word *chip* (/č/ is usually spelled as *ch*). In articulating this sound, the tongue makes contact at the same point on the roof of the mouth as in the articulation of the sound represented by /š/. Unlike /š/, though, /č/ begins with a complete blockage of the vocal tract (a stop), but then is immediately released into a fricative sound like /š/.

/ǰ/   (IPA dʒ)   A voiced alveopalatal affricate. The sounds represented by the symbols /č/ and /ǰ/ differ in voicing, /ǰ/ being voiced. The symbol /ǰ/ represents the first and last sounds of the word *judge* (/ǰ/ being spelled as both *j* and *dge*, in this case).

Nasals

In English, the *nasals* are oral stops similar to voiced stops in that they are voiced and are produced with a complete obstruction in the *oral* cavity. With nasals, however, the airflow and sound energy are channeled into the nasal passages (see 1, figure 3.3), due to the lowering of the velum (see 8, figure 3.3).

/m/   A bilabial nasal. The sounds represented by the symbols /m/ and /b/ are articulated in the same manner, except that for /m/ the velum is lowered to allow airflow and sound energy into the nasal passages. The symbol /m/ represents the first sound in the word *mice*.

/n/   An alveolar nasal. The sound represented by the symbol /n/ is articulated in the same position as /d/, with the velum lowered. The symbol /n/ represents the first sound in the word *nice*.

/ŋ/   A velar nasal. The symbol /ŋ/ is called *eng* (or even *engma* or *engwa*) and represents the final sound in the word *sing*. The normal English spelling for this single sound is *ng*. In order to hear the sound—and to hear that it *is* only one sound—compare the words *finger* and *singer*. For most speakers of American English the middle consonants of the word *finger* consist of a sequence of the velar nasal /ŋ/ followed by the velar stop /g/. In *singer*, however, only /ŋ/ occurs as the middle consonant, with no following /g/. Similarly, the word *long* ends only in a single consonant, the velar nasal. Note, however, the existence of a dialectal pronunciation of the word *long* in the expression *Long Island*. Certain speakers from the New York City area actually pronounce the final /g/ (*Long Island* = *LonGisland*).

The "*g*-like" quality of /ŋ/ is due to its being articulated in the same position as /g/, except that the velum is lowered. Thus, just as /m/ and /n/ are the nasal counterparts of /b/ and /d/, so /ŋ/ is the nasal counterpart of /g/. The sound represented by the symbol /ŋ/ does not occur in initial position in English words, being found only in medial and final positions, as our examples show. Finally, despite the fact that English orthography uses a *digraph* (a combination of two letters) to represent /ŋ/ (namely, the letters *ng*), it should be stressed once again that the velar nasal is a *single* speech sound. Recall that other consonant sounds of English are represented by two-letter sequences in the current spelling system: *th* for /θ/ and /ð/, *sh* for /š/, and *ch* for /č/. Yet each of these consonants—/ŋ/, /θ/, /ð/, /š/, and /č/—is a single speech sound.

Liquids

Liquid sounds are found in the overwhelming majority of the world's languages. English has two: /l/ and /r/. The term *liquid* is a nontechnical, impressionistic expression indicating that the sound is "smooth" and "flows easily." Liquids share properties of both consonants and vowels: as in the articulation of certain consonants, the tongue blade is raised toward the alveolar ridge; as in the articulation of vowels, air is allowed to pass through the oral cavity without great friction.

/l/   A lateral alveolar liquid. In the articulation of English /l/, the tongue blade is raised and the apex makes contact with the alveolar ridge. The sides of the tongue are lowered, permitting the air and sound energy to flow outward. The symbol /l/ represents the initial sound in the word *life*.

/r/   A nonlateral alveolar liquid. American English /r/ is produced with a tongue blade that is raised toward the alveolar ridge. Many speakers also curl the apex into a *retroflexed position* (curled upward and backward). This sound is also produced with lip rounding (a pursing of the lips) and a retraction of the tongue root (see 5, figure 3.3). The symbol /r/ represents the first sound in the word *red*.

Glides

Glides are vowellike articulations that precede and follow true vowels. The term *glide* is based on the observation that the sequence of a glide and a vowel is a smooth, continuous gesture. Because the tongue position in articulating the glides *y* and *w* is similar to the tongue position of the vowels in *beet* and *boot*, respectively, these glides are sometimes referred to as *semivowels*.

/y/   An alveopalatal glide. The sound represented by the symbol /y/ is formed with the body and the blade of the tongue arched in a high, front position, toward the hard palate. The symbol /y/ represents the first sound in the word *yes*.

/w/   A (labialized) velar glide. The sound represented by the symbol /w/ is formed with the body of the tongue arched in a high, back position, toward the soft palate (velum). Lip rounding also accompanies the production of this sound. The symbol /w/ represents the initial sound in *wood*.

(/ʍ/)   A (labialized) velar glide (with a voiceless beginning). Some speakers of English have different initial sounds in the words *which* and *witch*. For these speakers the initial sound in *which* begins as a voiceless sound, followed immediately by the glide *w*. Some linguists write this initial sound as the digraph *hw*.

The Vowels of American English

Whereas consonants are formed by obstructions—either partial or total—in the vocal tract, vowels are produced with a relatively open vocal tract, the latter functioning as a resonating chamber. The different vowels are formed by the different *shapes* of the open resonating vocal tract, and the variety of shapes is determined by the position of several anatomical structures: the position of the tongue body and blade, the relative opening of the lips, the relative opening of the oral pharynx (see 13, figure 3.3), and the position of the jaw (see figure 3.5). Although these articulators are, to some extent, anatomically connected, they can be independently controlled to produce the different vowels.

There are three major types of vowels in American English: *lax* (or *short*), *tense* (or *long*), and *reduced*. As the labels suggest, the lax vowels are produced with somewhat less muscular tension than the tense ones and are also somewhat shorter in duration. The reduced vowels could equally well be called the *unstressed* vowels, a point we return to below.

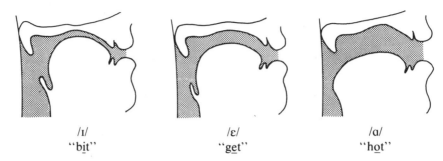

/ɪ/   /ɛ/   /ɑ/
"b<u>i</u>t"   "g<u>e</u>t"   "h<u>o</u>t"

Figure 3.5
Vocal tract shapes for given English vowels

Lax (Short) Vowels

The symbols for the English lax vowels are displayed in figure 3.6. If we imagine this figure superimposed on a cross section of the vocal tract (such as that depicted in figure 3.3), then the positions of the vowels in the chart represent the relative positions of the part of the tongue closest to the roof of the mouth (assume the mouth opening to be on the left, as in figure 3.3). We can simplify our description of the articulation of vowels by limiting our discussion to this relative position of the tongue during vowel production.

/ɪ/   A lax high front vowel. The terms *high* and *front* describe the position of the tongue in the mouth (see figure 3.5). The symbol /ɪ/ represents the vowel sound in the words *bit* /bɪt/ and *wish* /wɪš/.

/ɛ/   A lax mid front vowel. The tongue body is relatively forward, as in the production of /ɪ/, but it is slightly lower (see figure 3.6). The symbol /ɛ/ represents the vowel sound in words such as *get* /gɛt/ and *mess* /mɛs/.

/æ/   A lax low front vowel. This vowel (and the symbol for it) is called *ash* by many linguists, and the symbol /æ/ in fact represents the vowel sound in the word *ash* /æš/. It is produced with a front tongue body and with a lowered tongue body and jaw.

/ʊ/   A lax high back vowel. The vowel sound represented by the symbol /ʊ/ is found in words such as *put* /pʊt/ and *foot* /fʊt/. As you start to pronounce the vowel /ʊ/, you can feel your tongue move back and upward toward the velum. You can also feel your lips become rounded (pursed and brought closer together) during the production of this vowel; hence, it is called a *rounded* vowel.

/ʌ/   A lax mid back vowel. The vowel sound represented by the symbol /ʌ/, sometimes called *wedge*, occurs in words such as *putt* /pʌt/ and *luck*

	Front	Back
High	ɪ	(ɨ) ʊ
Mid	ɛ	(ə) ʌ ɔ
Low	æ	ɑ

Figure 3.6
Lax (short) vowels and reduced vowels of American English

/lʌk/. Note that the words *put* and *putt*, which differ in the number of final *t*'s in the English spelling system, actually differ in their vowels, /ʊ/ versus /ʌ/, respectively.

/ɑ/   A lax low back vowel. The position of the tongue is low and retracted in the articulation of the vowel /ɑ/ (see figure 3.6). There are several varieties of /ɑ/-like vowels in English; these vowels constitute one of the most difficult aspects of the study of English sounds. The difficulty is due in part to the fact that there is considerable dialectal variation in the pronunciation of these vowels. We leave it to your instructor to help you assign the appropriate symbols to represent vowels of your own speech or of the English spoken in your area. The vowel sound represented by the symbol /ɑ/ (*script-a*) is the low back vowel shared by most speakers of American English. It is typically found in words such as *hot* /hɑt/ and *pot* /pɑt/.

/ɔ/   A lax low back (rounded) vowel. If you pronounce the words *cot* and *caught* differently, you probably have the vowel /ɔ/ in your pronunciation of *caught*. There is minor lip rounding in the articulation of this vowel.

For many (if not most) speakers of American English the pronunciation of the low vowels in the words *father, froth,* and *fraught* will be the same. However, you may speak a dialect (for example, if you are a speaker of British English) in which the low vowels in the three words may all be different.

Reduced Vowels

There are two so-called *reduced* vowels in English, shown in parentheses in figure 3.6. The most common reduced vowel is called *schwa*, a *mid back vowel* whose symbol is an upside down and reversed *e* /ə/. It is the last vowel sound in the word *sofa* and sounds very much like the lax vowel represented by the symbol /ʌ/ (some linguists in fact use the same symbol for both of these sounds). Schwa /ə/ is called a *reduced* vowel because it is frequently an unstressed and shortened variant of a stressed (accented) vowel. Note how the accented vowel /ɛ/ in the base word *democrat*

/démkrét/ "reduces" or "corresponds to" the unaccented vowel /ə/ in the derived word *democracy* /dəmákrəsiy/.

The other reduced vowel of English is a *high back vowel* represented by the symbol /ɨ/; it is referred to as *barred-i*. It is typically the vowel sound in the second syllable of *chicken* /čɪkɨn/. The vowel /ɨ/ also occurs only in unstressed (unaccented) syllables in a word.

There is considerable variation in the pronunciation of these two vowels. Most likely, English has only one basic reduced vowel, and the appearance of one or the other is determined by the phonetic environment. In chapter 4 we will discuss the reduced vowel and some properties of English words that account for its distribution.

Tense (Long) Vowels and Diphthongs

In addition to its inventory of lax and reduced vowels, English has a set of tense vowels (see figure 3.7), which, in terms of their structure, appear to be quite different both from the lax vowels and from each other. Despite their apparent differences in structure, however, they pattern together in various ways. The tense vowels are all relatively longer than the lax vowels, and all tense vowels in Standard English end with the tongue body high in the mouth; this is because tense vowels end with /y/ or /w/. Comparing the vowel sounds of *raid* and *red*, note that the tense vowel in *raid* not only is longer than the lax /ɛ/ of *red* but also sounds higher (closer to /iy/). The tense vowels are made up of two parts: an initial vowel and a transition into a less loud vowellike sound (in other words, into one of the two glides /y/ or /w/). We will therefore transcribe the English tense vowels as a combination of two symbols: an initial vowel symbol indicating where the tongue position begins, followed by one of the symbols *y* or *w* representing the second half of the vowel sound. We should note that single vowel sounds that begin in one vowel position and end in another vowel or glide position are frequently referred to as *diphthongs*. The English tense vowels are thus diphthongs.

/iy/ (IPA /i/) A tense high front vowel (with an accompanying /y/-offglide). For this vowel, the /y/-offglide is difficult to hear since it is

	Front		Back
High	iy		uw
Mid	ey		ow, oy
Low	(æw)	(a)	aw, ay

Figure 3.7
Tense (long) diphthongs of American English

articulated in essentially the same position as the initial vowel. You never-theless can feel your tongue moving upward throughout the /iy/ articula-tion, demonstrating the two-part nature of this sound. The transcription /iy/ represents the vowel sound in words such as *bead* /biyd/ and *three* /θriy/.

/ey/   (IPA /e/)   A tense mid front vowel (with an accompanying /y/-offglide). When you pronounce this vowel, you can easily follow the change that occurs in pronunciation from a mid front vowel to a /y/-offglide. This vowel is found in words such as *clay* /kley/ and *weigh* /wey/.

/uw/   (IPA /u/)   A tense high back (rounded) vowel (with an accompany-ing /w/-offglide). For this vowel, the /w/-offglide is difficult to hear since it is articulated at the same position as the initial /u/ vowel. You will neverthe-less be able to perceive the continual and increasing rounding of your lips as you pronounce this diphthong. This transcription represents the vowel sound in words such as *crude* /kruwd/ and *shoe* /šuw/.

/ow/   (IPA /o/)   A tense mid back (rounded) vowel (with an accompany-ing /w/-offglide). This transcription represents the vowel sound in the words *boat* /bowt/ and *toe* /tow/.

/oy/   (IPA /ɔy/)   A tense mid back (rounded) vowel (with an accompany-ing /y/-offglide). The vowel sound represented by this transcription is found in words such as *boy* /boy/ and *Floyd* /floyd/.

/aw/   A tense low back vowel (with an accompanying /w/-offglide). This transcription represents the vowel sound in the words *cow* /kaw/ and *blouse* /blaws/. In some dialects of American English, for example in Maryland and Michigan, this diphthong begins with a low front vowel and should be transcribed as /æw/.

/ay/   A tense low back vowel (with an accompanying /y/-offglide). This transcription represents the vowel sound in words such as *my* /may/ and *thigh* /θay/.

East Coast Dialectal Variant

/a/   A tense low vowel. The vowel sound represented by the symbol /a/ (*printed-a*) is found—among other places—in the speech of New England, especially in Maine and eastern Massachusetts. One characteristic expres-sion of the Boston area, "Park the car," contains two instances of the vowel represented by the symbol /a/.

To conclude our discussion of vowels, we point out that one of the reasons that speakers of English have some difficulty in pronouncing the vowels of languages such as Spanish and Italian is that the tense (long) vowels of English are diphthongs, whereas the corresponding vowels in Spanish and Italian are not. For example, an American learning Italian is likely to pronounce the word *solo* /solo/ "alone" with two English *o*'s as in /sowlow/. For this reason, teachers of foreign languages such as Italian often tell American students to use "pure" vowels, rather than the long diphthongs of American English.

The Form of the English Plural Rule: Three Hypotheses

Now that we have a set of symbols that permit us to transcribe the consonant and vowel sounds of English in a precise way, we can reformulate table 3.1, more accurately, as table 3.3. Here the plural morpheme can appear as either /s/, /z/, or /ɨz/.

Even though we can now represent the different pronunciations of the plural morpheme, we are still left with accounting for the *distribution* (pattern of occurrence) of the different plural forms. What factors govern, or predict, this distribution? We will pursue this problem by formulating several hypotheses, which we will then test and revise in light of new data.

Nouns can take only one of the three different forms of the plural. Thus, for example, the plural /ɨz/ that occurs with *bush* to make *bushes* cannot be added to *cat* or *dog*. The result of doing so (/kætɨz/, /dɑgɨz/) sounds "foreign" to a native speaker of English. Thus, there must be some principle governing the occurrence of the different plural shapes. One account for the plural distribution would be to say that the form of the plural morpheme to be used with any given noun is unpredictable, and that we must simply list, for each individual noun of the language, which form it takes. This would amount to saying that speakers of English have simply memorized the phonological form of the plural for each individual noun. The distribution of the forms of the plural would then be given by sets of statements such as the following:

Table 3.3
Phonemic transcription of different forms of the plural morpheme

Example word	cat<u>s</u>	dog<u>s</u>	bush<u>es</u>
Phonemic transcription of plural morpheme for that word	/s/	/z/	/ɨz/
Phonemic transcription of that word	/kæts/	/dɑgz/	/bʊšɨz/

(1)

Hypothesis 1 (Listing of words)
Every lexical item is listed with its plural.
{kæt, kæts} "cat"
{mæp, mæps} "map"
{bæk, bæks} "back"
{dɑg, dɑgz} "dog"
{kæn, kænz} "cans"
{tæb, tæbz} "tabs"
{bʊš, bʊšɨz} "bush"
{dɪš, dɪšɨz} "dish"
{rɪǰ, rɪǰɨz} "ridge"
and so forth

Hypothesis 1 is consistent with the fact that there are nouns such as *child, ox, sheep*, and *man* for which the shape of the plural ending does seem to be a property of the word itself. However, hypothesis 1 implies that for any new word (not already found in our lists) we will not be able to predict which of the three forms it will take. But this is clearly false. Speakers of English spontaneously and with consensus form the plural for nouns they have never heard before and therefore could not have memorized. We may never have heard the noun *glark* before (since it is a nonsense word), yet we know that the form of the plural would be /s/ and not /z/ or /ɨz/; in fact, it seems that *every* noun that ends in /k/ takes the plural form /s/ whether it is a nonsense word or not. Similarly, every noun that ends in /g/, such as *dog*, takes the plural form /z/; and every noun that ends in /š/, such as *bush*, takes the plural form /iz/. It is, in fact, possible to *group* the nouns that take only /s/, or only /z/, or only /ɨz/ in terms of their *last sound*. This leads us to a second hypothesis about the /s/, /z/, and /ɨz/:

(2)

Hypothesis 2 (Listing of final sounds)
The forms of the plural are distributed according to the following *speech sound lists*:

a. The plural morpheme takes the form /s/ if the noun ends in /p, t, k, f, or θ/.

b. The plural morpheme takes the form /z/ if the noun ends in /b, m, d, n, g, ŋ, v, d, l, r, w, y/, or any vowel.

c. The plural morpheme takes the form /ɨz/ if the noun ends in /s, z, š, ž, č, or ǰ/.

Notice that hypothesis 2 now reflects a native English speaker's judgments concerning the form that the plural will take for any new word. Accordingly, the task faced by the language learner in learning the distribution of the plural forms is different under hypothesis 2 than under hypothesis 1. That is, language learners do not need to memorize the particular plural form for every noun; rather, they learn to associate a particular plural form with the last sound in a noun. Of course, there are still nouns whose plural form has to be memorized, as with the exceptional nouns *children, oxen, sheep, men*, and so forth. We can say, then, that there are nouns whose plural follows hypothesis 1 (the exceptional nouns), but the overwhelming majority are subject to hypothesis 2.

To see that hypothesis 2 is still not sufficient to handle all cases of plural formation, we turn to cases in which foreign words are made to undergo English plural formation—in particular, foreign words that contain speech sounds not found in English. Some people, especially announcers on radio stations that play classical music, pronounce the name of the German composer Bach as it is pronounced in German, with a final voiceless velar fricative. This sound, symbolized as /x/, is not part of the English phonemic system. If the name *Bach* (/bɑx/) is used in the plural, as when someone refers to two generations of *Bachs*, it takes /s/ and not /z/ or /ɪz/ (*Bachs* = /bɑxs/). The problem is that the sound /x/ does not appear in the list in hypothesis 2. We therefore need to develop a new hypothesis that reflects the English speaker's ability to assign plurals to words that end in sounds that are foreign to English.

If we compare words that end in, say, /f/ (which take the plural form /s/) and words that end in /v/ (which take the form /z/), we can observe that /f/ and /v/ represent similar sounds that differ only in a single feature —namely, /f/ is *voiceless*, whereas /v/ is *voiced*. Further, words that end in /k/ (which is voiceless) take the plural /s/, whereas words that end in /g/ (which is voiced) take the plural /z/. If we set aside for a moment the nouns that take /ɪz/, we can make the following observation: if a noun ends with a voiceless sound, then it will take the voiceless plural form /s/; but if it ends with a voiced sound, then it will take the voiced plural form /z/. Notice that we now have an account for why hypothesis 2 groups nouns ending in *vowels* with nouns ending in *voiced consonants* such as /b/, /d/, /m/ (see hypothesis 2, part (b)): those final sounds are all voiced, and so it follows automatically that all nouns ending in voiced sounds will take the plural form /z/.

Let us now return to the nouns that take the plural form /iz./ We note that the final consonants of these nouns (/s, z, š, ž, č, ǰ/) are either *alveolar fricatives, alveopalatal fricatives*, or *alveopalatal affricates*.

(3)

Hypothesis 3 (Use of phonetic features)
The forms of the plural morpheme are distributed according to the following conditions:
a. The plural morpheme takes the form /iz/ if the last sound in the noun to which it attaches is an *alveolar fricative*, an *alveopalatal fricative*, or an *alveopalatal affricate.*
Otherwise:
b. The plural morpheme takes the voiced form /z/ if the last sound in the noun is *voiced.*
c. The plural morpheme takes the voiceless form /s/ if the last sound in the noun is *voiceless.*

English plural formation demonstrates the interaction of two parts of English grammar, where the concept of grammar includes morphology and phonology as well as syntax. English grammar includes a morphological part specifying that plurals are formed by adding a suffix to nouns, and a phonological part containing rules that determine the actual phonetic shape (or shapes) of the suffix. Linguists hypothesize that grammars of all languages contain a morphological component, discussed in chapter 2, in which morphemes are combined to form complex or compound words. In this chapter we have seen that combinations of morphemes are often subject to phonological rules that alter the basic shape of the underlying morphemes, both stems and affixes.

Some affixes are invariant in their phonological form. Such a case is the prefix *re-*, which is pronounced /riy/ regardless of the phonological shape of the verb to which it is attached. Other affixes are subject to rules that specify their phonological shape depending on their phonological environment. The English plural morpheme is one of these. Other examples of shape-changing rules are given in the exercises at the end of this chapter and in Demers and Farmer 1986.

Phonetic Variations on a Phonemic Theme

So far we have assumed that the sounds represented by the phonemic transcription system of English are articulated exactly the same way each time they are produced. This assumption ignores an important aspect of the pronunciation of some phonemes. We discuss below several examples of variation in the pronunciation of certain American English consonants, variations that are common to most speakers of American English.

Types of /t/ in English

Aspirated t. When the sound /t/ occurs at the beginning of a syllable, its pronunciation is accompanied by a puff of air called *aspiration*. You can observe the presence of aspiration if you hold a thin, flexible piece of paper close to the front of your mouth when you say the word *tin* /tɪn/. The paper will flutter immediately after the *t* is pronounced. In contrast, the pronunciation of the /t/'s in the word *stint* /stɪnt/ are unaspirated; they will not cause the piece of paper to flutter. In order to represent more detailed aspects of pronunciation (such as aspiration), linguists use a system called (close) *phonetic transcription.* By convention, phonetic symbols are enclosed in square brackets [ ], as opposed to the more general transcription system we have been using that encloses symbols in slant lines / /. This more general transcription system, when it satisfies conditions to be discussed below, is called a *phonemic transcription.* We will discuss the difference between phonetic and phonemic transcriptions after we have discussed some of the finer phonetic details of American speech. A phonetic symbolization for the pronunciation of the /t/ in the words *tin* and *stint* would be [tʰɪn] and [stɪnt], respectively. A superscripted *h*, as in [tʰ], indicates that a sound is aspirated, whereas its absence in phonetic transcription indicates that the sound, in this case [t], is unaspirated.

Unreleased t. The pronunciation of final /t/ in words such as *kit* is frequently *unreleased* in the speech of many Americans: the tongue touches the alveolar ridge but does not immediately drop away to "release" the sound. (In contrast, in most American dialects the pronunciation of the final stop /t/ in words such as *fast* is in fact released.) For most speakers of American English, in the pronunciation of the word *kit*, the voicing ends and the airflow stops *before* the tongue reaches the alveolar ridge in articulating the final /t/. Where and how is the airflow stopped in this case? It turns out that before the /t/ in the word *kit* is articulated, the airflow is stopped by a closure at the vocal cords. Thus, the primary stop articulation in the pronunciation of final /t/ in words such as *kit* occurs in the larynx, rather than in the region of the alveolar ridge, even though the tongue tip does indeed make contact with the alveolar ridge immediately *after* the closure of the vocal cords. Recall that the *glottis* is the space between the vocal cords; and a stop created by closure at the glottis is called a *glottal stop*, represented as the symbol [ʔ]. A glottal stop appears between the two *oh's* of the expression *oh oh!*, which we can phonetically transcribe as [ʔʌʔow] or [ʔowʔow]. An unreleased /t/ that is produced with a glottal stop immediately preceding the alveolar articulation is symbolized as [ʔt]. Such sounds are sometimes referred to as *preglottalized*. Thus, the characteristic pronunciation of the word *kit* for most American dialects is represented phonetically as [kɪʔt].

Glottal stop replacement of t. In certain words the tendency to have a glottal closure with the articulation of /t/ in certain environments reaches such an extreme that the glottal stop actually replaces /t/. In many speakers' pronunciation of words such as *button* and *kitten*, the stop articulation is actually carried out at the glottis, and the tongue does not, in fact, move toward the alveolar ridge until the /n/ of the final syllable is articulated. The /t/ is generally replaced by the glottal stop if the following syllable contains a *syllabic* /n/. The term *syllabic* here refers to the fact that nasal consonants (such as /n/) can function as syllables by themselves, without any accompanying vowel. In the word *button*, for example, the only sound in the second syllable is the nasal [n̩]—there is no true vowel at all in that syllable. A syllabic /n/ is indicated by placing a straight apostrophe (or tick mark) under the symbol: [n̩]. The phonetic transcription of *kitten* would thus be [kʰɪʔn̩]. In section 3.3 we will discuss another syllabic consonant.

Flapped t. In words such as *pitted*, /t/ is regularly pronounced as a voiced "*d*-like" sound by most speakers of American (but not British) English. This sound is articulated by making a quick "tap" with the tongue tip on the alveolar ridge. Because of the rapidity of the articulation of this sound, it is referred to as a *flap* (or a *tap*), transcribed phonetically with the symbol [D] (or in the IPA with the symbol [ɾ]). Thus, a word such as *pitted* is phonetically transcribed as [pʰɪDɨd]. The flap [D] is always voiced, and occurs primarily intervocalically (between vowels).

Alveopalatal t. [ṭ] Children who are learning to write English sometimes spell the word *truck* as *chruk* or *chuk*. In doing so, they reveal that they are quite good phoneticians. What they are noticing is that the *t* in the word *truck* is pronounced much farther back along the roof of the mouth than is the regular *t*. For many speakers, in fact, the tongue tip touches *behind* the alveolar ridge at exactly the point where the /č/ phoneme is produced. Moreover, the /r/ phoneme is voiceless following *t* and sounds similar to /š/. Since the combination of the alveopalatal stop followed by the alveopalatal "fricative" (a voiceless *r*) sounds like the /č/ phoneme, it is understandable that children might spell initial *tr* sequences as *ch*.

Table 3.4
Phonetic variants of the phoneme /t/ in American English

Articulatory Description	Phonetic Symbol	Conditioning Environments	Example Words
Released, aspirated	[tʰ]	when syllable-initial	tin [tʰin]
Unreleased, preglottalized	[ʔt]	word-final, after a vowel	kit [kʰɪʔt]
Glottal stop	[ʔ]	before a syllabic *n*	kitten [kʰɪʔn̩]
Flap	[D]	between vowels, when the first vowel is stressed (approximate environment)	pitted [pʰíDɨd]
Alveopalatal stop	[ť]	syllable-initial before *r*	truck [ťrʌk]
Released, unaspirated	[t]	when the above conditions are not met first	stint [stɪnt]

To sum up, there are quite a few phonetic realizations of the phoneme /t/ in American English. These variations and their conditioning environments are shown in table 3.4. These variations are all heard as *t*'s by speakers of English in spite of the wide phonetic variation.

The Relationship between Phonetic and Phonemic Representation

We have seen that the phoneme /t/ has a number of phonetic variants depending on its *position* in a word. Keeping this in mind, we can see that the phonemic symbol /t/ is actually a *cover symbol* for a range of different sounds (or *phones*). We can refer to all of the *sounds/phones* for which /t/ is a cover symbol as its *allophones* (sometimes also called *positional variants*, since they occur in specific environments). The positional variants that we transcribe as [t], [tʰ], [ʔt], [ʔ], [ť], and [D] are all instances of the same /t/ phoneme. It is important to stress that every positional variant is represented by a phone. Indeed, every phone is an allophone of some phoneme. Thus, we can refer to the allophones [kʰ], [tʰ], or [t], but we must keep in mind that [kʰ] is an allophone of the phoneme /k/, whereas [t] and [tʰ] are allophones of the phoneme /t/. Criteria for determining whether two or more phones are members of the same phoneme or different phonemes are discussed below.

It is clear, then, that we are using two different systems of representation for the sounds of English (and of human language in general) and that different information is encoded in each system. For example, the phonetic representation system explicitly represents information concerning aspiration, preglottalization, and flapping, using notational devices such as superscripted *h* and other special symbols summarized in table 3.4. In contrast, the phonemic representation system is more abstract in nature; it ignores such features as aspiration, preglottalization, and flapping.

Since we are using two representation systems for sounds, the question immediately arises, Why should this be so? How can we justify two systems for encoding phonological information? Why should one representation system ignore (or leave unrepresented) articulatory information encoded by the other system? Why shouldn't we simplify our phonological theory and use only one representation system for sounds?

There are some fairly intuitive ways to answer these questions, and so we must stress that we will provide informal answers here rather than precise definitions. Furthermore, we must point out that part of our discussion will assume certain traditional (or "classical") views on the distinction between phonemic and phonetic representations, in which, for the sake of exposition, we will gloss over a number of problems that have arisen in recent work.

The basic idea behind the distinction between phonetic and phonemic representation systems can best be illustrated by considering pairs of words that linguists refer to as *minimal pairs:* pairs of words that (1) have the same number of phonemes, (2) differ in a single sound in a corresponding position in the two words, and (3) differ in meaning. An example is the pair of words *fine* and *vine*. They differ in meaning, but phonologically they differ only in the *contrast* between initial /f/ and initial /v/. Thus, *fine* and *vine* constitute a minimal pair.

Now let us consider two possible pronunciations of the word *kit*: [kʰɪt] and [kʰɪʔt]. As noted earlier, for some speakers of English, the final consonant of *kit* is sometimes released (= [t]) and sometimes unreleased (= [ʔt]). The important point is that no meaning difference is associated with the different pronunciations [kʰɪt] and [kʰɪʔt]: both versions are perceived by native speakers of American English as instances of the same word *kit*. Thus, the distinction between the allophones [t] and [ʔt] in word-final position is not contrastive, and we can say that, for some speakers, these allophones of /t/ are in *free variation* (or of optional occurrence) in that position.

The substitution of /v/ for /f/ can create a minimal pair, as we saw in the case of the words *fine* and *vine*. The sounds /f/ and /v/ are therefore members of different phonemes whereas [t] and [ʔt] are members of the same phoneme.

The allophones of a phoneme can also occur in what is called *comple-mentary distribution*: that is, one allophone can occur in a position where the other allophone(s) can never appear, and vice versa. The term comple-mentary distribution is used because the distribution of one allophone is the complement of the distribution of the other(s). For example, in the position following /s/, the phoneme /t/ has the obligatory positional variant [t], and the allophones [tʰ] and [ʔt] never occur in this position. Allophones of a single phoneme, then, are always either in free variation or in comple-mentary distribution, but in either case they are not contrastive with one another. To repeat, it is only when phones function contrastively that they are members of different phonemes.

The phoneme is actually more than just a cover symbol for a collection of sounds (its allophones)—it has a psychological aspect as well. The phoneme can be viewed as the speaker's internalized representation of a single speech sound, which, however, can have different phonetic shapes depending on the environment in which it appears. To speakers of American English, for example, the phones [tʰ], [t], [ʔt], and so forth, are all heard as a "single *t*-sound," the phoneme /t/.

Some linguists understand the phoneme somewhat more concretely and view it as a representation of an ideal articulatory target. Because of the effects of the environment in which the phoneme occurs, however, it may be produced in different allophonic versions. In any case, phonemic writing represents the *contrasting* sound units of a language, and many languages use the phonemic principle as the basis of their alphabet.

Linguists also have occasion to represent the finer phonetic details of a language. The aspiration of syllable-initial *t*'s is a regularly observable feature of English pronunciation, and we want to represent this phonetic feature in some way. To fail to do so would be to fail to give a true description of American English pronunciation. For these reasons, we require a phonetic representation system as well as a phonemic representa-tion system in order to characterize the sounds of English (and of human language in general).

So far we have taken care to specify that our phonemic and phonetic generalizations are based on American English. It is important to note that languages can differ with respect to what phonetic features function dis-tinctively. For example, in Hindi, a language spoken in India, the feature of aspiration does in fact function distinctively in voiceless stops. For speakers of Hindi, /kʰ/ (aspirated) and /k/ (unaspirated) are perceived as two completely different consonant sounds, and indeed we can find mini-mal pairs in Hindi showing the contrast between the two. For example,

/kʰiil/ means "parched grain," whereas /kiil/ means "nail." Speakers of English tend to hear Hindi /kʰ/ and /k/ as free variants of one another, or else they perceive Hindi unaspirated /k/ as English /g/, given that voiced stops in English are unaspirated. But Hindi /kʰ/ and /k/ also contrast with Hindi /g/. This example brings up an important point: whether or not a phonetic feature is contrastive (phonemic) is a language-particular phenomenon. That is, a phonetic distinction that functions phonemically in one language may or may not function phonemically in another language. Aspiration functions phonemically in Hindi, but it has no such function in English.

In contrast, no phonemic distinction exists between the consonants [r] and [l] in Japanese and Korean; they are allophones of a single phoneme. Japanese has both [r] and [l], but they are free variants of a single phoneme, which is usually written /r/. Speakers of American English are baffled by the fact that to a native Japanese speaker the English words *red* and *led* sound like the same word. How can sounds that seem so different sound the same? The answer is that differences that function phonemically in a language are easy for a native speaker to distinguish. In contrast, differences that do not function distinctively may be hard to distinguish. Speakers of Japanese have trouble distinguishing English /r/ and /l/ in the same way that English speakers have trouble distinguishing Hindi /k/ and /kʰ/ as two separate phonemes.

In most cases the distinction between phonemic and phonetic representations will not be crucial for our purposes. Generally speaking, we will use phonetic representations, using [ ], when discussing specific details of the pronunciation of a word or syllable, and phonemic representations, using / /, when discussing individual consonants and vowels at a more abstract level, as part of a phonological system. When we are discussing sounds and neither the phonemic nor the phonetic transcription is relevant, we will italicize the letter representing the sound under discussion.

3.3 SPECIAL TOPICS

In this section we present additional details concerning the pronunciation of American English. There are hundreds of conditions on the pronunciation of English, conditions that ultimately define both our individual accent and our overall American accent. As you read the descriptions of the following phonetic details, compare your own pronunciation with the one described.

Vowels before *r*

American English *r* is one of the most difficult features of pronunciation for foreigners to learn. It is even hard for Americans themselves, being one of the last sounds that children acquire when they learn English. It is also one of the sources of extreme dialectal variation—for instance, imagine the word *fire* being pronounced by Ted Kennedy (U.S. Senator from Massachusetts), Chuck Yeager (test pilot, now a TV advertising personality; raised in West Virginia), and Tom Brokaw (NBC Evening News anchor; native of the Midwest). In fact, differences in the pronunciation of /r/ are so complex that we leave it to your instructor to explore with you the features of /r/ in your region.

An interesting aspect of the pronunciation of /r/—one that also has a bearing on dialectal variation, as we will see—lies in the relationship between /r/ and the vowel that precedes it in a word. When beginning students of linguistics transcribe the word *fear*, they often use the tense vowel /iy/: */fiyr/. They notice that the vowel in *fear* sounds higher than the lax vowel /ɪ/ in *bid*, even though they admit that it doesn't seem quite as high as the tense vowel /iy/ in *bead*. In reality, the vowel in *fear* lies between /ɪ/ and /iy/. In fact, the vowel before /r/ is a positional variant—namely, a raised variant of the vowel phoneme /ɪ/, the raising of which is due to the anticipated articulation of the /r/. You can hear that /ɪ/ is the correct vowel by pronouncing both high vowels in the context *s—r*. When you use /ɪ/, the word will sound like *sear* /sɪr/. When you use /iy/, it will sound like *seer* /siyr/. Listening to these two words, you will hear that *sear* contains one syllable and *seer* two—the second syllable of *seer* being a syllabic /r/ (syllabic /r/ is analogous to the syllabic /n/ discussed earlier). This is because in current American English only a lax vowel can appear in the same syllable with a following /r/; if /r/ follows a tense vowel, the /r/ must always occur in a second, immediately following syllable. Figure 3.8 displays words that contain the sequence *vowel* + /r/.

The lax vowels that do not appear in figure 3.8 are /æ/ and /ʌ/. /æ/ does not occur before /r/ in the speech of most Americans. /ʌ/ has actually merged with /r/ to form an /r/-colored vowel written variously as /ɚ/, /ɝ/, or /ɹ̩/.

As an example of dialectal variation involving vowels before /r/, consider the words *marry, merry,* and *Mary*. Speakers in most parts of the United States, especially in the West, pronounce these words the same: /mɛriy/. However, many speakers on the East Coast, especially those in New York City, pronounce them all differently: *marry*/mæriy/, *merry* /mɛriy/, *Mary*

(a)

sear	/sɪr/			tour	/tʊr/
air	/ɛr/	fur	/fɹ̩/		
				for	/fɔr/
				are	/ɑr/

(b)

seer	/siyɹ̩/	sewer	/suwɹ̩/
Bayer	/beyɹ̩/	blower	/blowɹ̩/
		lawyer	/loyɹ̩/
tire	/tayɹ̩/	tower	/tawɹ̩/

Figure 3.8
Vowels that can appear before *r*: (a) lax, (b) tense

/mariy/, where the last vowel is the tense /a/ discussed earlier. Since the tense /a/ does not occur in most dialects, it is not available before *r*.

Contractions in Casual Spoken English

In discussing the phonetic properties of English, we have so far focused our attention on phonetic details within single words. Now we must note that in casual spoken forms of American English there are a number of phonological contraction processes in which a sequence of words is contracted, or reduced, to a shorter sequence. For example, consider the various phonological contractions of forms of the verb *to be*, illustrated in tables 3.5 and 3.6. Taking table 3.5 first, notice that a sequence of words from formal written language such as *she is* will be pronounced in careful, or formal, speech as a sequence of two separate words [šiy] [ɪz], whereas in more casual, rapid speech they are "merged" into a single bisyllabic (two-syllable) form [šíyɨz], with stress on the first syllable, indicated by an accent mark, ´, above the first vowel. Notice further that in the bisyllabic form [šíyɨz], the vowel [ɪ] of [ɪz] is reduced to [ɨ], a reduction phenomenon that also takes place when the two-word sequence *I am* becomes a single bisyllabic form [áyəm], where [æ] is reduced to [ə] in the unstressed syllable. Recall that the reduced vowels [ɨ] and [ə] occur only in unstressed syllables of a word, as in, for example, *sofa* [sówfə] and *chicken* [číkɨn]. In other words, the bisyllabic forms [šíyɨz] and [áyəm] reflect phonetic patterns characteristic of single words, and indeed we can consider such bisyllabic contractions as single phonological words.

Table 3.5
Phonetic form of contractions of the verb *to be* with personal pronouns in American
English: Bisyllabic forms

Formal Written	Formal Spoken	Casual Spoken Bisyllabic Forms
I am	[ay æm]	[áyəm]
you are	[yuw ɑr]	[yúwr̩]
she is	[šiy ɪz]	[šíyɨz]
he is	[hiy ɪz]	[híyɨz]
it is	[ɪt ɪz]	[íDɨz]
we are	[wiy ɑr]	[wíyr̩]
they are	[ðey ɑr]	[ðéyr̩]

Table 3.6
Phonetic form of contractions of the verb *to be* with personal pronouns in American
English: Monosyllabic forms

Casual Written	Casual Spoken Monosyllabic Forms
I'm	[aym] or [ɑm]
you're	[yʊr] or [yər]
	[yr̩]
she's	[šiyz]
he's	[hiyz]
it's	[ɪts]
we're	[wɪr]
they're	[ðɛr]

To take a final example from table 3.5, consider the sequences with the
verb *are: you are, we are, they are*. Notice that in the bisyllabic contracted
forms of casual speech, *are* [ɑr] is reduced to [r] alone (the vowel [ɑ] having
been lost), and in fact this [r] functions as the second (unstressed) syllable.
Syllabic [r], like the syllabic nasal [n̩], is represented by placing a straight
apostrophe beneath the symbol, [r̩], indicating that it can function as a
syllable by itself, without an accompanying vowel. In the forms [yúwr̩],
[wíyr̩], and [ðéyr̩], notice that the tense vowels [uw], [iy], and [ey] are in the
first (stressed) syllable, and [r̩] forms the second syllable. This sequence of
tense vowel + *r* reflects a syllabic pattern found quite generally in single
words of American English: two members of the sequence *tense vowel* + /r/
must be in different syllables. Therefore, this syllabic pattern is just what
we find in the bisyllabic contractions [yúwr̩], [wíyr̩], and [ðéyr̩]. As we have
seen, however, lax vowels and /r/ can appear in the same syllable.

Notice that in the very casual speech pronunciations of the contractions in table 3.5, the bisyllabic (two-syllable) forms can be realized as mono-syllabic (one-syllable) forms (table 3.6). In these examples we see that *am*, *are*, and *is* have lost their vowels entirely and have become reduced to [m], [r], and [z], respectively. Thus, *I'm* is pronounced as a monosyllabic [aym] or [ɑm], having lost the schwa [ə] of the bisyllabic [ayəm]. In the forms *you're* ([yʊr] or [yr̩]), *we're* ([wɪr]), and *they're* ([ðɛr]), notice that [r] is now in the same syllable as the preceding vowel; however, the vowel is now a *lax vowel* ([ʊr] ([r̩]), [ɪr], and [ɛr]) and thus [r] can occur with it as part of the same syllable. In fact, [r] can even be the only vowellike sound in a contraction such as *you're* [yr̩]. That the phoneme /r/ "acts like" a vowel is a rather striking property of American English, though for expository reasons we did not introduce this fact earlier. Consider words such as *bird* [br̩d] and *fur* [fr̩]. In these words there is no accompanying "pure" vowel preceding the [r] in the syllable containing the [r]. Thus, to the list of tense vowels in figure 3.7, we need to add syllabic [r̩].

Consonant Clusters

The sequence of English speech sounds in a word is not arbitrary. In fact, there are strict conditions on the order and type of speech sounds that can appear. At the beginning of a word all consonants except /ŋ/ can appear. If two consonants occur at the beginning, however, the possibilities become quite limited. Consider the sequences in (4).

(4)
*bt, *nk, *gb, *pb, *pt, *pk, . . .

None of these combinations can begin an English word, even though they can all be found word-internally (for instance, *napkin*). By contrast, all the combinations in (5) are permissible word-initial sequences of English.

(5)
br, dr, gr, bl, gl, pr, tr, kr, pl, kl

Native speakers of English can instantly tell whether a given combination of sounds is possible, suggesting that speakers have internalized a set of principles that determine well-formedness. To begin to form an idea of what these principles are, note that the difference between the disallowed sequences in (4) and the allowed sequences in (5) is that the former consist of two stops and the latter consist of a stop followed by a liquid. A start to understanding the conditions on the sequences of English consonants must include the observation that a word-initial sequence of two stops is not possible, but a sequence of a stop plus a liquid is possible (with a couple of exceptions). Conditions of this type are generally called the *phonotactics* of a language.

Stress in English Words

An important feature of the pronunciation of English words is that one syllable in every word is pronounced more prominently than the others. In the two words *TORment* and *torMENT*, the first syllable in the first word and the second syllable in the second word are the more prominent, so we say that the first syllable in the noun *torment* is stressed, and the second (or last) syllable of the verb *torment*. The position of main stress is not arbitrary but instead follows from certain other properties of the word. These properties are discussed in more detail in chapter 4.

English words also have *unstressed* syllables. It is easy to identify unstressed syllables in an English word: they are the only ones with the vowel /ə/ or /i/. In fact, the reduced vowels only occur in unstressed syllables. There are also levels of stress between main stress and unstressed, but a discussion of these additional levels goes beyond the scope of this introductory chapter.

In this section we have only sketched the outlines of a few of the phonetic properties of American English. In chapter 4 we will discuss many of these phonetic details in a more explanatory fashion and begin to look at the principles that shape human language sound systems.

Exercises

1. George Bernard Shaw, in ridiculing the English spelling system, claimed that a possible spelling for *fish* could be *ghoti*. Why did he claim this?
(Hint: The *o* in *women* /wɪmɪn/ is pronounced as an /ɪ/.)

2. Give the English speech sound symbol that corresponds to the following articulatory descriptions:

a. voiceless bilabial stop   f. voiced interdental fricative
b. voiced alveolar stop   g. voiceless alveopalatal affricate
c. lax high front vowel   h. tense high back vowel
d. voiceless alveolar fricative   i. lax low front vowel
e. lateral   j. voiceless velar stop

3. Describe each of the following speech sound symbols using articulatory features:

a. /n/   f. /ɑ/
b. /ʊ/   g. /ɛ/

c. /s/   h. /h/
d. /z/   i. /g/
e. /m/   j. /ʌ/

4. Write the speech sound symbol for the *first* sound in each of the following words. Examples: *fish* /f/, *chagrin* /š/.

a. psychology   f. though
b. use   g. pneumonia
c. thought   h. cybernetics
d. cow   i. physics
e. knowledge   j. memory

5. Write the speech sound symbol for the *last* sound in each of the following words. Examples: *bleach* /č/, *sigh* /ay/.

a. cats   f. judge
b. dogs   g. rough
c. bushes   h. tongue
d. sighed   i. garage
e. bleached   j. climb

6. Write the speech sound symbol for the *vowel* in each of the following words. Examples: *fish* /ɪ/, *table* /ey/.

a. mood   f. five
b. caught   g. bait
c. cot   h. toy
d. and   i. said
e. tree   j. soot

7. Note the following pairs of words:

a. /bæd/ *bad* and /bæg/ *bag*
b. /sɪn/ *sin* and /sɪŋ/ *sing*
c. /bɛd/ *bed* and /bɛg/ *beg*

You may speak a dialect of American English in which the vowels in the words on the right differ from those on the left. Describe the differences and determine why the vowels are so different. (Hint: Consider tongue movement.)

8. Write the following words in the transcription system given in this chapter:

a. 1. through   6. though
   2. rough   7. blink
   3. gouge   8. hinge
   4. Knox   9. hang
   5. draft   10. try

b. 1. miss   6. three
   2. his   7. paste
   3. shoe   8. trash
   4. edge   9. blunt
   5. foot   10. thigh

c. 1. bow (bend at waist)   6. lose
   2. bow (for shooting arrows)   7. which
   3. hand   8. witch
   4. hands   9. tasks
   5. loose   10. chat

d. 1. strengths   6. yeast
   2. halve   7. gym
   3. salve   8. mend
   4. cloths   9. sixths
   5. clothes   10. boil

9. Write the names of the letters of the alphabet using the *phonemic* symbols given in this chapter. For example, a = /ey/, b = /biy/, c = /siy/, and so forth. Can you find any "rhyme or reason" to the vowels that appear with the alphabetic consonants?

10. Write the following words using the *phonetic* symbols discussed in this chapter:

a. water   f. splat
b. lit   g. tin
c. eaten   h. beading
d. pull   i. beating
e. craft   j. beatin' (casual speech)

11. In some of the following words (for example, *play*) the *l*'s and the *r*'s are voiceless. Identify these words and try to establish the conditions under which *l* and *r* lose their voicing.

a. Alpo   f. try
b. archive   g. splat
c. black   h. spread
d. play   i. leap
e. dream   j. read

12. Transcribe the following words exhibiting vowels before *r*. (See section 3.3; be aware that dialect variations will abound in these words.)

a. boor   f. dear
b. bore   g. fir
c. poor   h. mire
d. care   i. sewer
e. car   j. mirror

13. Write the following combinations as contractions (monosyllables, if possible), using the phonetic symbols given in this chapter. Example: *she will* = /šɪl/.

a. I will   g. I would
b. you will   h. you would
c. he will   i. she would
d. it will   j. it would
e. we will   k. we would
f. they will   l. they would

14. Using phonetic symbols where possible, write a contracted form (there is more than one version for each of these expressions) for the following sequences, as though they were pronounced in the frame "_____want?" Example: in *What do I want?*, *what do I* = [wʌDəway].

a. what do I
b. what do you
c. what does she
d. what does it
e. what do we
f. what do they

15. Transcribe the following words that contain the reduced vowels (/ə/ or /i/). Example: *sofa* = /sowfə/.

a. attitude   f. torrent
b. predator   g. Arab
c. about   h. Arabian
d. demonstrate   i. police
e. compensate   j. potato (Is the sound symbolized by the first *o* voiced?)

Bibliography and Further Reading

Chomsky, N., and M. Halle (1968). *The sound pattern of English*. New York: Harper and Row.

Demers, R., and A. Farmer (1986). *A linguistics workbook*. Cambridge, Mass.: MIT Press. (2nd. ed., 1991.)

Denes, P., and E. Pinson (1973). *The speech chain*. Garden City, N.Y.: Anchor Books.

International Phonetic Association (1949). *Principles of the International Phonetic Association*. Rev. ed. London: IPA.

Ladefoged, P. (1982). *A course in phonetics*. 2nd ed. New York: Harcourt Brace Jovanovich.

Lenneberg, E. (1967). *Biological foundations of language*. New York: Wiley.

MacKay, I. R. A. (1987). *Phonetics: The science of speech production*. 2nd ed. Boston: Little Brown.

Smalley, W. (1963). *A manual of articulatory phonetics*. Rev. ed. South Pasadena, Calif.: William Carey Library.

Chapter 4

PHONOLOGY: THE STUDY OF SOUND STRUCTURE

In the introduction to chapter 3 we noted that the discrete, linear transcription system that we use to write languages is an idealization. There is nothing in the physical realization of speech (articulation and the acoustic signal) that corresponds to the discrete linear properties of our writing system. Speech is continuous and the phonetic segments overlap, yet speakers have little trouble accepting that speech can be represented by a writing system that uses discrete and linearly written symbols. Such writing systems have been in use for more than two thousand years, since the Greeks, inspired by the Phoenician writing system, developed an orthography that represented, for the first time, both vowels and consonants as separable and autonomous units. The idea that the fundamental sound units of a language were consonants and vowels has persisted since that time, and only in this century was it discovered that consonants and vowels are in turn composed of the more basic units that will be discussed in this chapter.

4.1 WHAT IS PHONOLOGY?

Phonology is the subfield of linguistics that studies the structure and systematic patterning of sounds in human language. The term *phonology* is used in two ways. On the one hand, it refers to a description of the sounds of a particular language and the rules governing the distribution of those sounds. On the other hand, it refers to that part of the general theory of human language that is concerned with the universal properties of natural language sound systems (that is, properties reflected in many, if not all, human languages). In this chapter we will describe a portion of the phonology of English, but we will also discuss some properties of the more general and universal theory of phonology that underlies the sound pattern of all languages. In addition, we will survey some of the phonological rules that are found in most dialects of American English.

As an initial strategy, we will take the alternation in pronunciation of the English plural morpheme as an organizing theme for several topics in this chapter. For example, in regard to the plural morpheme, we can ask the following questions:

What is the proper description of the three different *sounds* of the English plural morpheme shown in table 3.1?

What are the *conditions on the alternation* that account for where the different phonological forms of the English plural morpheme occur?

These two questions lead naturally into the more general topics of this chapter:

What is the proper description of the various sounds that are found generally in human language?

What is the proper general framework for describing the sound patterns of human language?

We provided tentative answers to the first two questions in chapter 3, but in order to develop all the answers in sufficient detail we must investigate some further properties of the phonology of English as well as of other languages.

4.2   THE INTERNAL STRUCTURE OF SPEECH SOUNDS: DISTINCTIVE FEATURE THEORY

We will see in this section that speech sounds (phones and phonemes) are not the smallest units of phonological systems; rather, the speech sounds themselves are composed of yet smaller features of articulation. We already noted in chapter 3 that generalizations (rules) regarding plural forms are best stated in terms of phonetic features such as voicing. In formulating the English Plural Rule, we made use of the feature of voicing to state an important generalization about the plural shapes: aside from cases where a noun ends in one of the consonants /s, z, š, ž, č, ǰ/, the phonological form of the plural morpheme is determined by a general assimilation process, whereby the plural form is voiceless if the final phoneme of the noun is voiceless but is voiced if the final phoneme of the noun is voiced. The feature of voicing, then, allows us to state a generalization that we miss by merely listing phonemes (compare, again, the discussion of hypotheses 2 and 3 of the Plural Rule).

The English Plural Rule exemplifies an important point about determining which phonetic features of a language are in fact the significant ones for a theory of phonology. In English, the feature of voicing plays two important roles: (1) it plays a crucial role in the statement of phonological regularities, such as the Plural Rule; and (2) it is minimally distinctive in that it serves to distinguish phonemes such as /z/ and /s/ in minimal pairs such as /zip/ and /sip/. In general, then, the significant phonetic features of human language are those that play a crucial role in the statement of phonological rules and/or distinguish phonemes from one another. Because of the latter function, these features are commonly called *distinctive features*.

Three questions immediately present themselves: What are the correct features? How many are there? Are the same ones found in all languages? We indirectly introduced a feature system in chapter 3. The point- and manner-of-articulation features represent a prima facie acknowledgment that speech sounds can be characterized by the phonetic features that make up these sounds. The features presented in table 3.2 appear to satisfy the criteria of insightfully characterizing phonological regularities and serve to minimally distinguish phonemes. Using these features, we can pick out *classes* of sounds; for example, the manner feature of voicing from table 3.2 was necessary for insightfully characterizing the plural forms.

But the system embodied in table 3.2 is not quite right for a general theory of phonology. This is because the table is stated entirely in terms of the way consonants are articulated in English. For example, the stops /t/ and /d/ are listed as *alveolar*, given that in English these stops are articulated with the tongue tip making contact with the alveolar ridge. But this is not how *t* and *d* are articulated in all languages. For example, in Japanese and in certain continental European languages (such as Spanish), *t* and *d* are *dental* stops: that is, the tongue tip makes contact on the teeth, rather than on the alveolar ridge. Thus, the feature system that forms the basis for table 3.2 would not be accurate for Spanish and Japanese, at least not with respect to the phonemes /t/ and /d/.

This leaves us in an unsatisfactory position: after all, there is an intuitively natural sense in which we want to say that Spanish, Japanese, and English all have the stop consonants *t* and *d*, and whether one type is basically dental and the other type is basically alveolar should not be significant. Furthermore, even in diverse languages the same rules are applicable to both kinds of *t*'s and *d*'s. For example, *t* and *d* become *palatalized* (articulated farther back on the hard palate), typically resulting in the creation of affricates such as /č/ and /ǰ/. Such palatalization processes usually happen in the environment of high, front sounds such as /i/ and /y/. For instance, in the English casual speech contraction of *don't* plus *you* as *dontcha* /downčə/, the final /t/ of *don't* becomes [č] when combined with the glide /y/ of *you*. In Japanese, the phoneme /t/ has the positional variant [č] when followed by the high vowel /i/ or /y/, a palatalization process also found in Brazilian Portuguese, which like Spanish has dental stops. These examples illustrate that despite minor differences in the articulation of *t* that exist across languages, these stops undergo very similar palatalization processes (and other rules as well). Therefore, we want to be able to talk about stops such as *t* and *d* across a number of languages, in a general way that will overlook irrelevant details in articulation.

To this end, a good deal of research in phonology has been aimed at defining a set of phonetic features that will, in fact, allow us to abstract away from English and other languages in such a way that we can refer to consonants and vowels in a general fashion and with cross-linguistic validity. For example, instead of using the phonetic feature *alveolar* to describe /t/ and /d/, phonologists have postulated a feature *coronal* to describe *all* articulations in which the tongue blade raises to approach or contact the teeth, the alveolar ridge, or the prepalatal region of the roof of the mouth. The feature *coronal* is clearly a more general feature than the feature *alveolar*, in that it includes a wider range of possible articulations. Thus, regardless of the fact that Spanish and Japanese have dental *t*, and that English has alveolar *t*, we can say that these languages all have (*voiceless*) *coronal stops*. Cross-linguistic considerations have compelled us to propose a feature (coronal) that is more general than the traditional feature(s) (alveolar, dental).

Sometimes, however, we are compelled to propose features that result from decomposition of a traditional feature. We saw in chapter 3 that the phoneme /k/ in English is a voiceless *velar* stop (that is, it is produced when the tongue touches the soft palate or velum). But in fact it is not always completely velar. Under certain circumstances /k/ is articulated with the body of the tongue making contact with the roof of the mouth at the point where the hard palate joins the velum, producing a prevelar (or postpalatal) *k*. For example, whenever /k/ is followed by the tense vowel diphthong /iy/ or the glide /y/, *k* has a prevelar articulation. In words such as *key* /kiy/ and *cute* /kyuwt/, /k/ is prevelar because of a coarticulation effect; in articulating /iy/ or /y/, the tongue body must be raised into a high position near the *hard palate*, and in articulating /k/ before these phonemes, the articulation of /iy/ or /y/ is anticipated so that the tongue shifts forward and makes contact in the prevelar region. In contrast, when /k/ is followed by a back vowel, as in *cool* /kuwl/, it is indeed a velar consonant. However, there is an important feature that all instances of /k/ share: all [k]'s of English are articulated with a *high* tongue body, and they differ only in how far *front* or *back* the high tongue body makes contact with the roof of the mouth. Thus, phonologists have proposed that the features *high* and *back*—the same features used in the description of certain vowels—should characterize /k/, rather than a feature *velar*. The /k/ that precedes front vowels, such as /iy/, will be characterized as *high* but *nonback*; the /k/ that precedes back vowels, such as /uw/, will be characterized as both *high* and *back*. In other words, /k/ is in both cases *high*, but its specification for *backness* is determined by the adjacent vowel. Recall that distinctive features serve to distinguish phonemes. Separating the single feature *velar* into two features *high* and *back* now makes a prediction: there could be a language that has two contrasting /k/-phonemes, one that is *high* and *back* and another that is *high* and *nonback*. Romanian is just such a language. By replacing the feature *velar* with the features *high* and *back*, we can now properly distinguish the /k/ in English from those in other languages, at the same time capturing what all the different types of [k] have in common. In addition, we will see when we discuss Mongolian that using the same tongue body features (such as *high* and *back*) to describe consonants as well as vowels yields insightful descriptions of phonological regularities.

As we examine a range of languages, the need to devise a feature system that has universal validity will become even clearer. This set of features must describe all phonemic contrasts in all languages and must also express all the phonological regularities (rules) in a perspicuous manner.

For the reasons discussed above, it is clear that the manner- and place-of-articulation features listed in table 3.2 are not the optimum set of phonetic features for describing the world's languages. Because of such problems a number of linguists have proposed alternative phonetic feature systems, and we will now examine one of the most influential of these in some detail.

An *SPE*-Based System

In tables 4.1 and 4.2 we have listed the consonants and vowels of English as they are classified in a distinctive feature system based on the one proposed by Morris Halle and Noam Chomsky in their 1968 work, *The Sound Pattern of English* (*SPE*). Their proposals in turn build on the pioneering work in distinctive feature theory done by Halle and by Roman Jakobson (Jakobson and Halle 1956). In the *SPE* system, the articulatory

Table 4.1
Distinctive feature composition of English consonants

	p	b	m	t	d	n	k	g	ŋ	f	v
Syllabic	−	−	−	−	−	−	−	−	−	−	−
			(+)			(+)					
Consonantal	+	+	+	+	+	+	+	+	+	+	+
Sonorant	−	−	+	−	−	+	−	−	+	−	−
Voiced	−	+	+	−	+	+	−	+	+	−	+
Continuant	−	−	−	−	−	−	−	−	−	+	+
Nasal	−	−	+	−	−	+	−	−	+	−	−
Strident	−	−	−	−	−	−	−	−	−	+	+
Lateral	−	−	−	−	−	−	−	−	−	−	−
Distributed	−	−	−	−	−	−	−	−	−	−	−
Affricate	−	−	−	−	−	−	−	−	−	−	−
Labial	+	+	+	−	−	−	−	−	−	+	+
Round	−	−	−	−	−	−	−	−	−	−	−
Coronal	−	−	−	+	+	+	−	−	−	−	−
Anterior	+	+	+	+	+	+	−	−	−	+	+
High	−	−	−	−	−	−	+	+	+	−	−
Back	−	−	−	−	−	−	+	+	+	−	−
Low	−	−	−	−	−	−	−	−	−	−	−

features are viewed as basically *binary*, that is, as having one of two values: either a *plus* value (+), which indicates the presence of the feature, or a *minus* value (−), which indicates the absence of the feature. Each phonetic feature represents an individually controllable aspect of articulation. For example, the feature *nasal* is related to the raising or lowering of the velum. The phoneme /m/ thus has the feature [+nasal], whereas the phoneme /b/ has the feature [−nasal]; this indicates that in the articulation of /m/ the velum is lowered, and in the articulation of /b/ the velum is raised. (Distinctive features, by convention, are enclosed in square brackets [ ], and we will use this convention in the rest of this chapter.) In a similar fashion, all phonemes in the *SPE* system are regarded as *bundles of features*, that is, as groups of binary features with pluses and minuses, as can be seen in tables 4.1 and 4.2. Notice that the features allow us to distinguish all the consonant phonemes from one another and at the same time to refer to classes of sounds (for instance, the class of *voiceless consonants*). The distinctive features of the *SPE* system, which we will now briefly consider

	s	z	θ	ð	š	ž	č	ǰ	l	r	w	y	h
Syllabic	−	−	−	−	−	−	−	−	− (+)	− (+)	−	−	−
Consonantal	+	+	+	+	+	+	+	+	+	−	−	−	−
Sonorant	−	−	−	−	−	−	−	−	+	+	+	+	+
Voiced	−	+	−	+	−	+	−	+	+	+	+	+	−
Continuant	+	+	+	+	+	+	−	−	+	+	+	+	+
Nasal	−	−	−	−	−	−	−	−	−	−	−	−	−
Strident	+	+	−	−	+	+	+	+	−	−	−	−	−
Lateral	−	−	−	−	−	−	−	−	+	−	−	−	−
Distributed	−	−	−	−	+	+	+	+	−	−	−	−	−
Affricate	−	−	−	−	−	−	+	+	−	−	−	−	−
Labial	−	−	−	−	−	−	−	−	−	−	+	−	−
Round	−	−	−	−	−	−	−	−	−	+	+	−	−
Coronal	+	+	+	+	+	+	+	+	+	+	−	−	−
Anterior	+	+	+	+	−	−	−	−	+	+	−	−	−
High	−	−	−	−	+	+	+	+	−	−	+	+	−
Back	−	−	−	−	−	−	−	−	−	−	+	−	−
Low	−	−	−	−	−	−	−	−	−	+	−	−	(+)

individually, are proposed as universal features, and not merely as features peculiar to English.

Syllabic. The feature [+syllabic] is assigned to phonemes that can be the head (or peak) of a syllable (we will define "syllable" more accurately in section 4.3). The vowels of English are, of course, syllabic.

Consonantal. Phonemes with the feature [+consonantal] are formed in the vocal tract with an obstruction that is at least as narrow as that of a fricative. Note that the glides are therefore not true consonants—nor, as we will see, are they true vowels.

Sonorant. "Sonorant sounds are produced with a vocal tract cavity in which spontaneous voicing is possible" (*SPE*, 302). In other words, the vocal tract is not constricted to the extent that airflow across the glottis is inhibited. Vowels, glides, liquids, and nasals are all [+sonorant]. [−sonorant] consonants are frequently referred to as *obstruents*.

Table 4.2
Distinctive feature composition of English vowels

	i	ɪ	e	ɛ	æ	u	ʊ	ʌ	o	ɔ	ɑ	ə*	ɨ
	(iy)		(ey)			(uw)			(ow)				
Syllabic	+	+	+	+	+	+	+	+	+	+	+	+	+
High	+	+	−	−	−	+	+	−	−	−	−	−	+
Back	−	−	−	−	−	+	+	+	+	+	+	+	+
Low	−	−	−	−	+	−	−	−	−	+	+	−	−
Round	−	−	−	−	−	+	+	−	+	+	−	−	−
Tense (long)	+	−	+	−	−	+	−	−	+	−	−	−	−

* ə is in fact different from ʌ, but a discussion of the difference would take us beyond the limits of an introductory text.

Voiced. Phonemes are [+ voiced] when their articulation is accompanied by a periodic vibration of the vocal cords. All of the phonemes in the word /bɪd/ are [+ voiced], whereas the phonemes /p/, /t/, and /k/ are [− voiced].

Continuant. [− continuant] sounds are made with a complete blockage of the oral tract. [+ continuant] sounds are made without such a blockage. By this definition nasals are oral [− continuant] stops, although air is shunted through the nasal cavity.

Nasal. Phonemes have the feature [+ nasal] when the velum is lowered during speech, thus permitting the airflow and sound energy to activate resonances in the nasal cavity.

Strident. [+ strident] sounds are characterized by the high-frequency turbulent noise that accompanies the production of some fricatives and affricates. The phoneme /s/ is [+ strident], whereas the phoneme /θ/ is [− strident].

Lateral. If the tip of the tongue is partially blocking the airstream, but the air is allowed to pass along one or both sides of the tongue, the resulting sound is [+ lateral]. The phoneme /l/ is the only [+ lateral] sound in English.

Distributed. The term *distributed* refers to the relative length of contact that the tongue makes along (not across) the roof of the mouth. The tongue has a relatively longer region of contact along the roof of the mouth in articulating /š/ as opposed to /s/; thus, /š/ is [+ distributed] but /s/ is [− distributed]. The terms *laminal* ([+ distributed]) and *apical* ([− distributed]) have been used in the past to characterize this articulatory difference.

Affricate (or *Delayed Release*). Recall that affricates are produced by articulatory gestures during which the airstream is temporarily stopped, but the stoppage is secondarily released into a fricative. This sequence of a stop plus a fricative functions in English as a single phoneme, as in /č/ and /ǰ/.

Labial. A labial articulation involves a bringing together or closing of the lips. The phonemes /f/, /b/, /m/ are all [+labial].

Round. A round articulation involves an extension and pursing of the lips. All sounds that are [+round] are redundantly [+labial], but [+labial] sounds are not necessarily [+round]. /b/ for example, though [+labial], is produced with no rounding.

Coronal. The blade of the tongue is raised toward or touches the teeth or the alveolar ridge. Dental, alveolar, and alveopalatal consonants are [+coronal] phonemes.

Anterior. [+anterior] sounds are made with the primary constriction in front of the alveopalatal position. Labials, dentals, interdentals, and alveolar articulations are [+anterior].

High. The body of the tongue is raised toward or touches the roof of the mouth. The phonemes /k/, /ŋ/, /č/ are all [+high].

Back. [+back] phonemes are made with the tongue body slightly retracted from the rest (quiet breathing) position. [−back] phonemes (also called *front*) are made with the tongue body in a relatively forward position. The phoneme /č/ in *chuck* is [−back], whereas the /k/ in that word is [+back].

Low. Phonemes with this feature are made with the tongue body lowered and retracted. American English /r/ is [+low] because of its associated pharyngeal constriction.

We now turn to the phonetic features of the vowels given in table 4.2. The features [high], [low], and [back] are the same tongue body features used for characterizing consonants. The gestures associated with these features in vowels are not as extreme, however, as they are for consonants. Two other features found in vowels, [syllabic] and [round], have also already been discussed in connection with vowels. The feature [+tense] (long) is associated with a more extreme articulatory gesture than its [−tense] (lax) counterpart. The [+tense] vowel /iy/ is higher and more front than the [−tense] vowel /ɪ/.

The feature [tense] is used to distinguish /ɛ/ and /ey/, although we have already noted that there is more than a difference in length and muscle tension between these vowels: /ey/ begins in a higher position in the mouth than /ɛ/, and /ey/ also has a high offglide. We have therefore listed the tense (long) vowels /iy/, /ey/, /uw/, /ow/ in terms of the features of their *first* segment. The remaining diphthongs /ay/, /aw/, /oy/ are not listed in table 4.2; they are to be analyzed as clusters of two phonemes: for example, /ay/ = /a/ + /y/.

Phonemes as Groups of Distinctive Features

As we have seen, the phonemes of all languages may be described in terms of differing subsets of the universally available set of distinctive features, some of which have already been discussed in the description of English phonemes. Although all languages draw from the same universal set of features, individual languages differ in the groups of features that make up their phonemes. For example, the features [coronal], [lateral], [affricate], and [distributed] are all found in English, but they never occur together in a single phoneme. In contrast, in Navajo, as well as in many other Native American languages of North America, these features do occur together in a single consonant called a *lateral affricate*; the Navajo word *tlah* "ointment" begins with this phoneme, which is represented by the two letters *tl* in the Navajo writing system. To take another example, English does not have the feature of rounding in front vowels, but many European languages do, among them French, German, Hungarian, and Finnish. Thus, the widely differing sounds that occur in the world's languages are actually based on different combinations of a relatively small, restricted set of features such as those given in tables 4.1 and 4.2.

In spite of the fact that languages draw upon different features to make up their phonemes, there is a surprising amount of convergence in the sound systems in human language. To gain a somewhat wider perspective, consider now the consonants listed in table 4.3, drawn from four unrelated, geographically separated languages. Notice that all four languages form their stops at the same general points along the vocal tract: the [labial], the [coronal] (dental/alveolar), the [+high, −back] (palatal), and the [+high, +back] (velar) regions.

It is striking that, despite minor differences in the details of pronunciation, the consonant systems of these diverse languages, and indeed in the majority of the world's languages, cluster around these same regions of articulation. There is intriguing evidence that these particular points of articulation are regions of *acoustic stability* (Stevens 1972). For example, the sound produced by tongue-tip contact throughout the dental and alveolar region is relatively stable acoustically, in that the sound is rela-

Table 4.3
Stop and affricate consonants in four unrelated and geographically separated languages

	[labial]	[coronal]	$\left[\begin{array}{c}+\text{high}\\-\text{back}\end{array}\right]$	$\left[\begin{array}{c}+\text{high}\\-\text{back}\end{array}\right]$
English (Europe, Australia, North America)	p	t	č	k
	b	d	ǰ	g
Navajo (North America)	(missing)	t	č	k
	b	d	ǰ	g
Ganda (Africa)	p	t	c (stop)	k
	b	d	j (stop)	g
Japanese (Asia)	p	t	č	k
	b	d	ǰ	g

tively constant regardless of minor shifts in the position of the tongue within this region. In contrast, the regions of articulation between the commonly occurring points of articulation—for example, the region on the border between the dental/alveolar region and the palatal region—are regions of acoustic instability, where even a small shift in the position of the tongue leads to radical changes in the acoustic properties of the sound. Thus, it is apparently only for articulations made in the vocal tract's regions of acoustic stability that there is considerable "leeway" for tongue position. It is probably not an accident, therefore, that the majority of the world's languages have consonantal systems with places of articulation similar to those shown in table 4.3, involving the features [labial], [coronal], [high], and [back].

We do not wish to underestimate the fact that there are important differences between languages. For example, in the African language Xhosa, certain "click" phonemes are an integral part of the consonant system that are not found in most other languages. (English speakers do, however, make click sounds that are not part of the language. For example, the sound that is made to get a horse to move is a click sound. The sound that is written *tsk! tsk! tsk!* is not to be pronounced "tisk, tisk, tisk." The *tsk!* is a single click sound made with air rushing in between the tip of the tongue and the alveolar ridge.) In the production of clicks, the tongue makes contact with the roof of the mouth not just at one point, but at two points (both at the velum and at one other point farther forward). A partial vacuum is created by lowering the tongue between the two points of articulation, and when the front stoppage is finally released and air rushes into the partial vacuum, a click sound results. Very few languages in fact make use of the "suction feature" (not described in our abbreviated list of

SPE distinctive features) that is necessary to characterize clicks; thus, we see that the set of universal phonetic features is a set that is *available* to languages and that not all features and combinations of features are found in all languages.

The Role of Distinctive Features in the Expression of Phonological Rules

We have been arguing that the fundamental contrasting units of a language are not the phonemes but the features that make up the phonemes. Additional support for analyzing phonemes into their constituent features comes from the explanatory way that phonological regularities can be stated in terms of the features that make up the phonemes.

Let us return one final time to the English Plural Rule and reformulate it in terms of the *SPE* distinctive features.

As part of the reformulation we need to address another point. We assumed in chapter 3 that the plural had "three shapes" (/s/, /z/, /ɪz/) and that these were assigned to a noun depending on the phonetic features of the last phoneme of the noun. Recall the final formulation of the Plural Rule:

(1)
Hypothesis 3 (Use of phonetic features)
The forms of the plural morpheme are distributed according to the following conditions:
a. The plural morpheme takes the form /ɪz/ if the last sound in the noun to which it attaches is an *alveolar fricative*, an *alveopalatal fricative*, or an *alveopalatal affricate*.
Otherwise:
b. The plural morpheme takes the voiced form /z/ if the last sound in the noun is *voiced*.
c. The plural morpheme takes the voiceless form /s/ if the last sound in the noun is *voiceless*.

There is no evidence for the assumption that there are three different plural forms, given as a list. In fact, there is an alternative: namely, that the plural morpheme has *one* shape and that there are conditions on pronunciation (or phonological rules) that determine the phonetic realization of the different shapes. We will incorporate this proposal directly below.

It has been argued (Pinker and Prince 1988) that the basic shape of the plural is /z/ and that all variations are due to phonological rules of English. If we assume that /z/ is added to form the plural of all nonexceptional

English nouns, then we must have some explanation for the fact that we actually say and hear three different shapes, /s/, /z/, and /ɨz/. Part (a) of hypothesis 3 states that the "plural ending" /ɨz/ follows *alveolar fricatives*, *alveopalatal fricatives*, and *alveopalatal affricates*. There is nothing in the place and manner features that suggests why the six consonants /s, z, š, ž, č, ǰ/ should pattern together. In contrast, the *SPE* distinctive features offer a ready explanation for this grouping: namely, they are uniquely described as the consonants containing the features [+strident, +coronal]. Referring to table 4.1, you will see that all and only the six final consonants /s, z, š, ž, č, ǰ/ contain the features [+strident, +coronal]. So the *SPE* features have the obvious advantage of making clear the basis for the patterning together of a *natural class* of English phonemes.

Second, the statement in part (a) of hypothesis 3 does not explain *why* the /ɨz/ form of the plural morpheme should appear in the environment of this particular natural class of phonemes. Using *SPE* distinctive features, however, the occurrence of this form can be understood, if not explained. Note that if the plural morpheme is /z/, then an /ɨ/ must be inserted between the plural morpheme and the final phoneme of the noun, if the latter is [+strident, +coronal]. Such vowel insertion is known as *epenthesis*, a common occurrence in the world's languages. The insertion of the /ɨ/ has the likely function of keeping the [+strident, +coronal] /z/ of the plural ending apart from the final [+strident, +coronal] consonants of the nouns. This separation increases the audibility of the plural ending. Try pronouncing the plural of *bush* with just a /z/ or /s/ instead of the normal /ɨz/. The other two plural endings tend to be lost.

Epenthetic vowels also occur elsewhere in English. Some dialects insert an epenthetic ə between consonants and *l*, as in the words *padlock* [pædəlɑk] and *athlete* /æθəliyt/. This common pronunciation of the latter word often leads to the misspelled form *athelete*.

When the /z/ ending is added to a noun that ends in a ([−strident]) voiceless consonant, the plural ending becomes voiceless (/s/) to match the ending of the noun. Finally, the /z/ plural form remains unchanged when it is attached to nouns ending in a [−strident] voiced segment.

With the above remarks we are now able to formulate the final version of the Plural Rule, which ironically is not really a plural rule at all, as we will soon see:

(2)

Conditions on plural formation
a. The plural morpheme is /z/ and is subject to the following conditions (rules).

b. If the noun ends in a [+strident, +coronal] consonant, an epenthetic /i/ is inserted between the plural ending and the noun.

c. Otherwise, if the noun ends in a voiceless consonant, this property of nonvoicing is spread to the plural morpheme.

Note that we no longer have a "unified" set of statements that specify all of the forms of the plural. The /z/ shape is not the result of a rule at all, but is rather the basic form that is unchanged by rule. It is only /s/ and /iz/ (or /i/, actually) that are the result of rules. But these rules are valid for more than plural formation. They are the same rules that apply in the following components of English morphology:

(3)
a. Third person possessive
   John's /z/, Dick's /s/, Butch's /iz/
b. Third person verb agreement
   runs /z/, hits /s/, pushes /iz/
c. Contraction of the verb *is*
   John's /z/ coming, Dick's /s/ coming, Butch's /iz/ coming

If we were to state rules separately for the plural, third person possessive, third person verb agreement, and contraction, we would miss the generalization that all four of these alternations are subject to *exactly the same principles*, namely, (1b,c).

The patterning of regularities seen in the English plural formation process offers substantial justification for the analysis of phonemes as distinctive feature clusters. The phoneme classes that participate in the formulation of rules can usually be defined by a relatively small number of distinctive features. As we have noted, each of these small lists of phonetic features is the basis for isolating a *natural class* of phonemes (see also Halle 1962), which we can roughly define as follows:

(4)
Natural class (informal definition)
A natural class is a set of phonemes uniquely defined by a small number of distinctive features such that the set plays a significant role in expressing the phonological regularities found in human language.

For example, in the conditions on plural formation (2) the groupings of phonemes used to state the rules are natural classes: the class of phonemes that take the /iz/ ending is the class of *strident coronal consonants*; the class of [−strident] phonemes that condition the devoicing of the plural ending is defined by their possessing the feature [−voiced].

Next we present an additional example of a phonological regularity from a distinct language that exhibits further evidence that (1) phonemes pattern in terms of natural classes, and (2) the nature of the phonological regularity is insightfully expressed by a rule written in distinctive features.

Mongolian

Mongolian has two sets of stops made in the velar region, a front set [g], [k], which are pronounced in a more forward position in the vocal tract, and a back set [G], [q], which are pronounced farther back in the vocal tract. [g] is the front variant and [G] is the back variant of a single voiced phoneme. Likewise, [k] is the front variant and [q] is the back variant of a single voiceless phoneme. (Additional phonetic qualities of these stops are not important for this example and will not be discussed here, although interested readers can find more details in Grønbech and Krueger 1955.) Some examples are listed in (5):

(5)

(Front) velar	*(Back) velar*
nigen "one"	qoyar "two"
degü "younger brother"	qudurGa "tail strap"
köbegün "son, boy"	Gajar "land, country, place"
ker "how"	Gobi "barren steppe, Gobi"

The more forward allophones [g], [k] occur before the vowels /e/, /ö/, /ü/, and the back allophones [G], [q] occur before /a/, /o/, /u/. The vowels /ö/ and /ü/ are the front vowels /e/ and /i/ pronounced with lip rounding (like the vowels found in French and German). The distribution of the front allophones [g], [k] versus the back allophones [G], [q] is predictable, in that the former set appears before front vowels and the latter before back vowels, as shown in (6):

(6)
a. The ([−back]) allophones [g], [k] occur before [−back] (front) vowels.
b. The ([+back]) allophones [G], [q] occur before [+back] vowels.

Once again, if we stated the facts in terms of two lists of phonemes, /e/, /ö/, /ü/ versus /a/, /o/, /u/, we would fail to express the relevant generalizations that are captured by the distinctive feature formulation in (6). This notation reveals that the groups of phonemes /e/, /ö/, /ü/ and /a/, /o/, /u/ pattern as the two natural classes of front ([−back]) and back vowels, respectively.

We leave as undecided whether the Mongolian consonants are basically [+back] and become [−back] by a phonological rule that fronts the consonants before [−back] vowels, or whether basically front consonants become back before back vowels. Our point about natural classes is made in either case. This example also reveals that the use of the same tongue-body features ([high], [low], and [back]) to describe vowels as well as consonants leads to a natural explanatory account of the distribution of the two different types of consonants. The [−back] variants of the "velar" consonants occur before the [−back] vowels, and the [+back] variants occur before the [+back] vowels. As was the case in the statement of the English Plural Rule, the exact nature of the assimilation process between two adjacent phonological segments is explicitly expressed.

Note, however, that the assimilation differs in a major way from the assimilation occurring in the English plural morpheme. The assimilation "goes in the other direction" in Mongolian. The feature [back] is transferred to a temporally earlier phoneme. When features of one phoneme are transferred backward to a (temporally) earlier phoneme, the assimilation is called *regressive assimilation*. When features are transferred forward to an adjacent segment, as in the case of English plural assimilation, the process is called *progressive assimilation*. Psychologists (and some linguists) use the terms *perseverative coarticulation* (progressive assimilation) and *anticipatory coarticulation* (regressive assimilation), respectively. These are terms that reflect more accurately the psychological nature of the assimilation phenomena. In any case, assimilation rules are very common in the world's languages, and they are clearly best stated with rules based on distinctive features.

One task currently being carried out by phonologists, then, is to establish the set of distinctive features and the properties of the phonological rules of the world's languages. For further discussion of the issues involved, see the readings given in the bibliography at the end of this chapter.

4.3 THE EXTERNAL ORGANIZATION OF SPEECH SOUNDS

In this section we survey the principles of organization that govern the combination of phonemes. We learned in chapter 2 that sounds make up morphemes, which may or may not be words, and that certain conditions govern the way these morphemes can be combined. The phonemes that make up morphemes and words are themselves subject to phonologically based conditions on their combination, and this is what we will be referring to when we talk about the *external organization* of sounds. The first level of organization that governs phonemes is made up of conditions defined by the *syllable*.

The Syllable

Although native speakers of English can determine, with a high degree of reliability, how many syllables a word has (*cat* has one syllable /kæt/, *catfish* has two syllables /kǽt-fiš/, *catalogue* has three syllables /kǽ-tə-lɑg/, and *catatonic* has four syllables /kæ-tə-tá-nɪk/, there has been little consensus about exactly what a syllable is. In this chapter we will look at the definition of syllable that guides current research. We will see that the syllable represents a *level of organization* of the speech sounds of a particular language. The expression "particular language" is important here, because languages vary in their syllable structure. Across the world's languages the most common type of syllable has the structure CV(C), that is, a single consonant C followed by a single vowel V, followed in turn (optionally) by a single consonant (C). As figures 4.1a and 4.1b together illustrate, vowels usually form the "center" or "core" of a syllable and hence are often called its *nucleus*; consonants usually form the beginning

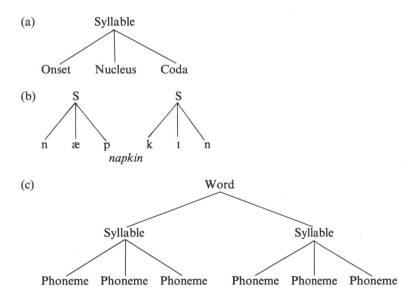

Figure 4.1
(a) Typical syllable structure, (b) syllable analysis of sample word, and (c) hierarchical organization of phonological units

(*onset*) and the end (*coda*) of the syllable. A word such as *napkin* has the syllable structure shown in figure 4.1b.

The properties of syllables are more complex than the above paragraph indicates, however. In the first place, it is not only vowels that can serve as the nucleus of a syllable. We have already seen that /r/ and /n/ can function as syllables in English. The consonants /m/ and /l/ also have syllabic variants, as seen in words such as *bottom* [bɑDm̩] and *apple* [æpl̩]. In each case the second syllable (/m/ and /l/, respectively) consists solely of a consonant. Second, we must allow for *ambisyllabic* consonants, that is, consonants that function simultaneously as the coda of one syllable and the onset of the immediately following syllable (*ambi-* is a prefix of Greek origin meaning "both"). For example, in slow, careful speech one might pronounce the name *Emma* as either *e-ma* or *em-a*. In normal conversational speech, the *m* is actually part of both syllables. We perceive it to close the first syllable as much as we perceive it to function as the onset of the second syllable.

There are nevertheless reasons for associating the *m* with the second syllable at a more abstract level of representation. It is true for all human languages that given a sequence VCV, the basic syllabification is V-CV, the medial C forming the onset of the second syllable. To see that this is the correct grouping, we can test it with an observation made in chapter 3.

Recall that the phoneme /t/ has an aspirated allophone [tʰ] in syllable-initial position and that it is not aspirated in syllable-final position. In the word *tot*, for example, only the initial /t/ is accompanied by aspiration. The aspiration rule is actually more general, applying not only to /t/ but also to /p/, /k/, and /č/. In other words, the sounds that undergo the aspiration rule form a natural class defined by the features [−continuant, −voiced]. We can write the Aspiration Rule as shown in (7):

(7)
Aspiration Rule (informally stated)
Phonemes with the features [−continuant, −voiced] are aspirated in syllable-initial position.

The Aspiration Rule now provides a test to determine which syllable an intervocalic consonant is associated with. With the sequence *ata*, for example, the intervocalic /t/ will only be aspirated if it is the onset of the second syllable and is not the coda of the first. As you pronounce the sequence *ata*, you will feel the puff of air that accompanies the release of the /t/. The aspiration demonstrates that *ata* is divided *a-ta*.

The principle that associates an intervocalic consonant with the second vowel is only a special case of the more general rule known as the *Maximal Onset Principle*:

(8)

Maximal Onset Principle
The consonants that combine to form an onset with the vowel on the right are those that correspond to the maximal sequence that is available at the beginning of a syllable anywhere in the language.

To see how this principle functions, consider the word *constructs*. Between the two vowels of this bisyllabic word lies the sequence of consonants *n-s-t-r*. Which, if any, of these consonants are associated with the syllable to the right? In pronouncing the word *constructs*, you may judge that the sequence *str* forms the onset of the second syllable. In other words, *con-structs* would be syllabified as *con-structs*. We can adduce evidence that supports this analysis. If the syllabification were *ns-tr*, then the *t* would appear in syllable-initial position, and as we have just seen, syllable-initial *t*'s must be aspirated. But the *t* in the sequence *nstr* is not aspirated, ruling out the putative syllabification *ns-tr*. Other considerations, which we will not discuss here (but think about the domain of the lip rounding caused by the *u*), rule out all but the division *n-str* (see Kahn 1976). This syllabification is the one that assigns the maximal number of "allowable consonants" to the second syllable.

A sufficient criterion test to define "maximal allowable" (in English) is to consider what consonant combinations can begin a *word*. Note that in this position all consonants must be in the onset of the first syllable.

This brings us back to a topic that we discussed in chapter 2: conditions on the type and number of allowable consonants at the beginning of a word (*phonotactics*). These conditions are actually conditions on syllable onsets, and so conditions that apply at the beginning of a word apply to any syllable within the word as well. Thus, the Maximal Onset Principle is related to the *sequential constraints* that apply to the series of consonants at the beginning of a word or syllable. The Maximal Onset Principle simply states that within a word, any intervocalic series of consonants is divided so that the syllable on the right ends up with the *maximal allowable number that satisfies the conditions of English syllable onsets*. Not surprisingly, these sequential conditions are best expressed in terms of natural classes of sounds (Clements and Keyser 1983). It is well known that English permits at most three consonants to form an onset; and once the second and third consonants are determined, only one consonant can appear in the first position. For example, if the second and third consonants in a word are *pr*, the only consonant that can precede them is *s*, forming *spr* as in *spring*. Whenever someone invents a new word—say, to use as a brand name—this word must conform to the syllable (and word) rules of English. The syllable-initial sequence in a word such as *ftik* is not possible in English, although it is possible in other languages. English speakers recognize immediately whether or not a word conforms to the English rules of syllable well-formedness, arguing strongly that they have access to principles of some sort that enable them to do so.

In addition to accounting for how speakers judge whether or not a newly encountered sequence of phonemes is a possible word in their language, syllable sequential constraints (along with phonological rules) cause borrowed words to conform to the principles of a language. Some languages —for example, Japanese—allow only a single consonant in onset position. When English words are borrowed into Japanese, Japanese speakers with little knowledge of English insert vowels between the English consonants. (What baseball term do you think *suturaiku* is?)

In our characterization of the phonology of a language as consisting of *sounds* and *rules*, then, we see that there are rules that specify the order of phonemes and that the unit in which these combinations are specified is the syllable.

To return to the Maximal Onset Principle, we note its role in dividing up the following internal sequences: $VnsV$, $VnstV$, $VnstrV$, $VftV$, and VtV. Through the application of the Maximal Onset Principle, the onset consonant(s) of the second syllable become(s) $Vn\text{-}sV$, $Vn\text{-}stV$, $Vn\text{-}strV$, $Vf\text{-}tV$, and $V\text{-}tV$. Other possible combinations—$V\text{-}nsV$ or $Vns\text{-}tV$— either represent an impermissible onset sequence (*ns*) or do not incorporate the maximal sequence possible (*t* instead of *st*). Thus, to return to our original example, it is the Maximal Onset Principle that ultimately associates the *m* in *Emma* (or indeed any consonant) with the vowel on its right.

Now that we have established some of the properties of the syllable in English, we can consider how these syllables play a role in patterns of prominence in English words.

Patterns of Prominence (Stress)

The syllables in English words are not all pronounced with the same degree of prominence. They vary in emphasis, length, and (as we will see later) pitch. In a word of four syllables, for example, one syllable is pronounced more prominently than the other three, and typically one of the remaining three is pronounced more prominently than the other two. It turns out that the position of the most prominent syllable in an English word is in large part predictable given certain information about the word. In the following abbreviated and therefore simplified proposal for stress assignment in English, we will see that the stress of a given word can be predicted given its syllabification and given the existence of yet another level of structure above the syllable: the foot.

The term *foot* is common in the study of poetry, where it plays an important role in scansion; you are probably familiar with (for example) iambic, trochaic, and dactylic feet. The foot also plays a fundamental role in English phonology. Feet serve to provide external organization for syllables.

Types of Feet

English has three foot types: one with one branch (*unary* foot), one with two branches (*binary* foot), and one with three branches (*ternary* foot). These are displayed in figure 4.2.

Assigning Feet to English Words

For purposes of exposition we will make some simplifying assumptions regarding the underlying form of English words, in particular with respect to their phonemes. It is sufficient for our purposes to assume that the lexical form of words consists of *full* vowels (tense and lax) and *reduced* vowels (ϑ or i).

It is a property of English feet that the leftmost branch is associated with (or dominates) a *full* vowel, whereas any other branch is associated with a *reduced* vowel. To assign feet to an English word, then, one need only begin at its right end and associate feet with its vowels from right to left. Because an English word consists of just a few different types of alternating patterns of full and reduced vowels, all vowels (syllables) will be associated with a foot.

It is possible, then, to follow a mechanical procedure that will associate every syllable in a word with a foot:

Figure 4.2
Types of feet (unary, binary, ternary) that are found in English words

(9)
a. Link every full vowel to the leftmost branch of a foot.
b. Link all reduced vowels to the right branch of a binary foot or to the
rightmost branches of a ternary foot.

Some examples will clarify the application of these principles. Consider
the word *anticipate* [æntɪsɨpeyt]. Scanning from the right side, the first
vowel that we encounter is the full vowel *ey* in the syllable *peyt*. Only a
unary foot can be assigned to this syllable, as shown in figure 4.3.

Continuing to scan from right to left, we encounter the reduced vowel
ɨ. Since it follows from (9a) and (9b) that the syllable containing this vowel
cannot by itself constitute a foot, we must defer assigning it to a foot until
we reach a full vowel to associate it with. Scanning leftward again, we come
upon such a vowel, *ɪ*. Together, the full vowel *ɪ* and the reduced vowel *ɨ*
satisfy the conditions for a binary foot. The assignment of this foot is
shown in figure 4.4.

Finally, one vowel remains, a full vowel, and the only foot that corresponds to it is the unary foot. The complete foot assignment for *anticipate*
is shown in figure 4.5. Note that the number of full vowels in a word

Figure 4.3
Association of the first foot to the rightmost syllable

Figure 4.4
Association of the second foot

Figure 4.5
Association of the third and last foot

determines the number of its feet. The number of reduced vowels, in turn, determines the type of foot that is associated with a full vowel. Since the number of syllables with reduced vowels between syllables with full vowels is either zero, one, or at most two, all English syllables can be associated with feet.

The word *anticipate* therefore consists of three feet, which in turn organize four syllables, which in turn organize nine speech sounds. The last unit of organization above the foot is the word, which we will discuss shortly.

Given the above principles, we can discuss certain properties of the foot. It is apparent from the pattern of full and reduced vowels that the leftmost branch of the foot is in some sense stronger than the other branches. In fact, the three foot types directly represent the important patterns of prominence in English pronunciation. In a sequence of a full vowel followed by one or two reduced vowels, the full vowel is louder, longer, and generally more prominent. Because words consist of a series of feet, English words have a characteristic pattern of pronunciation, consisting of *beats*, and each of these beats is determined by the strong member of each foot in the word. We are now ready to discuss how the idea of *relative* prominence is precisely represented by each of the feet. Following a convention used in linguistics, we will assign to the nodes (points where the branches join) labels representing the relative strength of pronunciation: *s* (for *strong*) and *w* (for *weak*).

In the feet shown in figure 4.6, for instance, the syllable labeled *s* is relatively stronger than the syllable labeled *w*. This labeling corresponds to the perceived level of stress: the syllable labeled *s* is pronounced with relatively heavier stress than the syllable labeled *w*. Words such as *butter*, *sofa*, and *apple* contain two syllables organized into a foot like the one shown in figure 4.6a. The foot shown in figure 4.6b is associated with words such as *camera* and *Pamela*.

We have seen, then, that the syllables in a word are organized into feet. How are the feet themselves organized? Returning to the word *anticipate*,

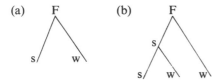

Figure 4.6
Feet labeled with relative prominence

as displayed in figure 4.7, we see that the feet are gathered up into a *word* (W). It is a property of English that this word-level structure must be *right branching*—in other words, that successive branching of a tree must occur to the right (see figure 4.8). (Right branching will come up again in chapter 5 when we study how words are organized into sentences. The ternary foot, by the way, is a left-branching structure; see figure 4.6b.)

The nodes in figure 4.7 must now be marked with the strong and weak labels. The following principles of English (based loosely on Liberman and Prince 1977) assign strong and weak marking to foot nodes in a word tree:

(10)

English Word-Level Prominence Assignment

For all nodes below the W node, assign *s/w* labels according to the following conventions:

a. If the rightmost node branches below, then assign that node an *s* and the left node a *w*.

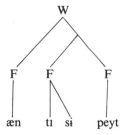

Figure 4.7
A word-level branching structure

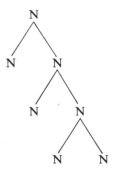

Figure 4.8
A right-branching structure

b. If the rightmost node does not branch, then assign that node a *w* and the leftmost node an *s*.

These assignments are shown in figure 4.9.

Note in figure 4.9 the nodes labeled 1 and 2. Node 2, which is the rightmost, is assigned an *s* because it branches into nodes 3 and 4. Node 1, opposite node 2, is then assigned a *w*. Of the two nodes 3 and 4, 4 does not branch, so it is marked with a *w*, causing node 3 to be marked, by default, with an *s*. The syllable that is dominated only by *s*'s is the most prominent in the word. The sequence of *s*'s in the branching structure in figure 4.9 indicates that *tɪ* is the strongest syllable in the word *anticipate*, the correct result.

The above principles, structures, and node labels lead to the correct assignment of stress in *anticipate*. For reasons of space, this general approach is simply presented here; the range of examples needed to justify it is not furnished. We will, however, look at one more example and see that no additional principles are needed to construct the word tree that yields the correct stress assignment.

Consider figure 4.10, which displays the word *anticipation* with all structures already in place. The sounds in this word are organized into five syllables and three feet. English Word-Level Prominence Assignment provides the following labelings: Node 2 branches; therefore, it is marked *s* and node 1 is marked *w*. Node 4 branches; therefore, it is marked *s* and node 3 is marked *w*. Nodes 6 and 8 do not branch (only branching structure at the foot level counts; branching within a syllable does not); therefore, nodes 6 and 8 are marked *w* and nodes 5 and 7 are marked *s*. The strongest

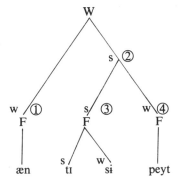

Figure 4.9
Word tree on which the strong and weak relationship is marked

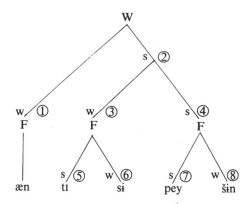

Figure 4.10
Word tree for *anticipation*

syllable is therefore *pey*, a result that corresponds with a native speaker's pronunciation.

It was noted earlier that the position of main stress is largely predictable. This is not to say that speakers can always correctly pronounce a word that they have never encountered before. Many place names have "correct" pronunciations that are known only to the locals. Newcomers' "incorrect" pronunciation indeed obeys the general principles of English phonology. Their problem lies in having to guess what to apply the principles to—in other words, in having to guess whether vowels in the name are tense, lax, or reduced, or how many feet are in the word. A particular guess about the vowels automatically leads to a foot assignment (by principle (9)) and a stress pattern (by English Word-Level Prominence Assignment). For example, *Sacaton* is a town in Arizona just south of Phoenix. If you assume that the second *a* is tense (/ey/), you will pronounce it /səkéytən/. But if you assume that the first *a* is /æ/ and that the *o* is /ɑ/, you will pronounce it—correctly—as /sǽkətɑn/.

Finally, notions such as *syllable*, *foot*, and *word* are not needed only to account for patterns of prominence in English words. They are needed independently in—and their existence is therefore independently supported by—other parts of the phonology of English as well. We have already seen one case of this: the Aspiration Rule, which requires reference to the notion of syllable for its most general statement:

(11)

English Aspiration Rule
Voiceless stops are aspirated in *syllable*-initial position.

Such rules provide additional evidence that notions such as the syllable must be a part of our representation of English words.

There is also independent evidence for the foot. When we discussed the Flap Rule in chapter 3, we gave the approximate environment as "between two vowels, if the first vowel is stressed." A more accurate formulation is that /t/ and /d/ become flapped when they occur between vowels, and both vowels are *members of the same foot*. In other words, flapping occurs foot-internally. We can write the rule roughly as follows:

(12)

English Flap Rule

The stops /t/ and /d/ become flapped between [+syllabic] segments, foot-internally.

In a word such as *attitude* the first /t/ is internal to a binary branching foot, whereas the second /t/ is the onset of a syllable that makes up the following unary foot. Since the second /t/ is syllable-initial, it is aspirated; since the first /t/ is foot-internal, it is flapped.

Rule (9) predicts that in a ternary foot, if /t/ or /d/ occurs both between the first and the second vowels in the foot and between the second and the third, then both are flapped. In this case the second vowel is very weakly stressed and in fact is weaker than the third. Consider now the pronunciation of *editor*, the foot pattern of which is shown in figure 4.11. Both /d/ and /t/ are flapped, and both appear within a single ternary foot. We see now the inadequacy of our earlier formulation in which the Flap Rule was stated as requiring that the /t/ or /d/ occur between two vowels and that the first vowel have some degree of stress. In the case of the ternary foot in *editor*, /t/ occurs between an *unstressed* vowel on the left and a vowel on the right. The point is that the general statement of the Flap Rule requires reference to the foot and therefore that this rule provides additional evidence for the existence of this category.

The presence of feet as a level of organization in the phonology of English readily accounts for many contractions. Contractions that consist in part of question words such as *what* and *how* and auxiliary words such

εditr = [εDɨDɾ]

Figure 4.11
Flapping within a ternary foot

Figure 4.12
Ternary foot organizing *what do you*

as *will*, *does*, and *do* actually involve the restructuring of these words into
(word) feet. For example, in the casual pronunciation of *What do you
want?*, the first three words are combined into a new word, in which the
original words have become syllables (see figure 4.12). That [wʌDəyə]
should indeed be analyzed as a word is shown by the facts that (1) it has
the prosodic structure of a single ternary foot (a left branch dominating a
stressed vowel and two right branches dominating reduced vowels) and (2)
the Flap Rule has applied.

In the next section we will look at an example of a rule that has the word
as its domain of application.

4.4 SPECIAL TOPIC

The Word-Level Tone Contour of English

In addition to differing in loudness, the syllables of an English word differ
in pitch (a perception based on the frequency of a sound). Consider the
pair *INsult* (noun) and *inSULT* (verb). If you pronounce the noun *insult*
several times, you will hear the pitch of your voice change between the two
syllables, the first syllable being higher pitched than the second. In fact,
you can hum the pitch pattern, high-low, extracting the pitch from the
sounds. Now compare the pattern in the verb *insult*. In this case the higher
pitch is associated with the second syllable. Again, humming the pitch
pattern reveals a low pitch followed by a higher pitch. The pattern on these
two words, then, is high-low (*INsult*) and low-high (*inSULT*).

Consider next the pitch patterns in the words in figure 4.13. There seem
to be quite a few of them, but in fact they are all instances of a single English
pattern (see Goldsmith 1981). Note first that each word has a single high
tone and that this high tone is associated with the most prominently
stressed syllable. Note also that all of the tones to the right of the high tone
are low. Rather than assume that there is a series of patterns in which high
tones are followed by one low tone, two low tones, three low tones, and

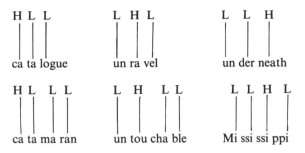

Figure 4.13
Different tone patterns on English words. H = high tone, L = low tone

so forth, we make the assumption that there is but a single low tone to the right of the high tone, but that this low tone spreads to link with all available syllables to the right. What happens to the left of the high tone? It appears that a low tone is also assigned to the left, followed by spreading if possible.

Thus, the tone pattern for English words is as follows:

(13)
English tone pattern
low-high-low

We need only specify that the high tone links with the most strongly stressed syllable in the word (namely, the syllable dominated by all *s*'s in its word tree) and that the low tones spread to any available syllables to the right and left.

There is only one additional detail to consider: namely, the variable behavior of the above tonal contour when the high tone is assigned to a syllable on the periphery of the word. When main stress falls on the first (leftmost) syllable, there is no evidence of a low tone to its left. In contrast, when main stress falls on the last (rightmost) syllable, there is evidence of a low tone to its right. If you utter the verb *insult* a few times, you will hear the pitch fall off on the last syllable. This fact can be accounted for if we assume that the English tonal contour has the following structure:

(14)
English tone pattern
(low)-high-low

The parentheses indicate that the first low tone is optional; and if there is no syllable to the left of the stressed syllable with the high tone, this tone will not be realized. In contrast, the low tone on the right must be realized on any syllables present to the right of the stressed syllable. If no such syllables are present, the low tone will be conjoined with the high tone, forming a high-low falling tonal contour. Words with tonal contours assigned by the principle in (14) are displayed in figure 4.14.

The principles of tone assignment and spreading described above are not just found in English. Similar principles are extremely common in the languages of Africa and are also found in Japanese. In Japanese a single high tone appears on a particular syllable in a word, and all tones to the right of the high tone are low. The fact that so many different languages from different language families have similar tone assignment principles suggests that tonal properties are part of the shared language facility in the human species.

At the beginning of this chapter we posed the following questions:

What is the proper description of the various sounds that are commonly found in human language?
What is the proper general framework for describing the sound patterns of human language?

We are now in a position to provide partial answers for these questions:

The speech sounds of human language at either the phonemic or the phonetic level of representation are best viewed as complexes of phonetic (distinctive) features, out of which the speech sounds are composed.

Phonological regularities are best expressed in terms of the phonetic (distinctive) features that make up phonemes. The statements (rules) typically refer to small classes of features that identify natural classes of phonemes.

In sum, a phonology consists of two major parts: sounds and rules (where the term *rule* covers the statement of all the regularities that char-

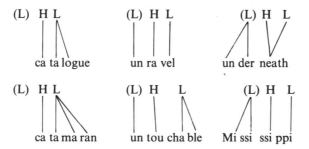

Figure 4.14
Words exhibiting the spreading of the English tone contour (L)-H-L

acterize English). As yet linguists have no idea how many rules are involved in the phonology of English, but the number may be in the hundreds. What is remarkable is that children acquire this system with little conscious effort. Moreover, phonology is but one part of the system of grammar that they must learn. In the following chapter we will explore the rules that children must learn to create (or understand) a phrase or sentence.

Exercises

The problems given here are drawn from various languages and serve to illustrate the role of natural classes of phonemes in the phonological regularities of these languages. In each of the problem sets a small number of distinctive features will serve to describe the class of segments that condition the change described in each problem. Assume that the data are representative of the phonological system of the language in question and that the phonemic symbols have the same phonetic feature specifications as the symbols in tables 4.1 and 4.2; refer to the tables in solving these problems. A sample problem and solution are given first, in order to acquaint you with some strategies to follow in solving these problems.

Sample Problem: In English, the vowel /ɪ/ becomes long (and is thus written [ɪ:], where the colon indicates length) under certain conditions. Consider the examples listed below, then (1) list the phonemes that condition the change of /ɪ/ to [ɪ:], and (2) state what feature(s) uniquely specify this class of phonemes.

a. [hɪs]   h. [hɪ:d]
b. [wɪš]   i. [mɪθ]
c. [pɪ:g]   j. [rɪ:b]
d. [pɪt]   k. [lɪ:z]
e. [lɪ:m]   l. [snɪp]
f. [trɪk]   m. [rɪ:ǰ]
g. [bɪ:l]   n. [kɪ:ŋ]

Start with the fact that [ɪ] is basic—that short [ɪ] becomes long [ɪ:]. The change from short [ɪ] to long [ɪ:] is phonologically determined; that is, the lengthening takes place in the presence of certain phonemes. A good strategy is first to list the phonemes to the right of long [ɪ:], then to list those to the left. Since [h] is on the left in both item (a) and item (h), it is not possible that the lengthening in question is caused by a phoneme to the left. As an answer to part (1), then, you would next propose that /ɪ/ becomes [ɪ:] whenever the phonemes to the right (/d, m, l, b, z, ǰ, ŋ/) occur immediately after that vowel. This hypothesis looks promising because, in fact, the short variant [ɪ] never occurs before these segments. The next question is, What is it about the phonemes on the right that unifies them as a class? If you look at their feature specifications in table 4.1, you will find that these phonemes are all voiced ([+voiced]), and, in fact, the short variant /ɪ/ never lengthens before voiceless segments. Thus, the answer to part (2) of the problem is that the vowel [ɪ] is lengthened before (the natural class of) voiced consonants.

1. A particular dialect of English exhibits a predictable variant /ʌy/ of the diphthong /ay/.

A. What phonetic segments condition this change?

B. What feature(s) uniquely describe the class of conditioning segments?

a. /bʌyt/ bite   i. /fʌyt/ fight
b. /tay/ tie   j. /bay/ buy
c. /rayd/ ride   k. /rʌys/ rice
d. /fayl/ file   l. /tʌyp/ type
e. /lʌyf/ life   m. /naynθ/ ninth
f. /taym/ time   n. /fayr/ fire
g. /rayz/ rise   o. /bʌyk/ bike
h. /rʌyt/ write

2. In Tohono O'odham (formerly Papago), a Native American language of the southwestern United States, the phone [č] is a variant of /t/.

A. Find and list the set of phonemes that condition this change.

B. What feature(s) characterize this class?

C. How would a Tohono O'odham speaker pronounce the word [tuksan] "Black Base (of a mountain)"? This pronunciation is found in southern Arizona, and the word is the source of the city name *Tucson*.

A colon after a vowel symbol indicates that the vowel is long; /ṣ/ is a voiceless fricative similar to English /š/; and /ɨ/ is a high, back, unrounded vowel. Other unfamiliar phonemic symbols are not important for the solution to this problem.

a. ta:t "touched"   g. tako "yesterday"
b. to:n "knee"   h. čɨkwo "ankle"
c. čiñ "mouth"   i. čuʔi "flour"
d. čɨm hekid "always"   j. to:bi "rabbit, cottontail"
e. čuk "black"   k. taṣ "sun"
f. čikpan "is/was working"   l. towa "turkey"

3. In the following words from Luganda, a Bantu language spoken in East Africa, the phone [ř] (a flapped "r" sound) is a predictable variant of [l].

A. What are the phonemes that condition the change of [l] to [ř]?

B. What feature(s) characterize the class of conditioning segments?

A rising accent mark indicates high pitch; the absence of an accent mark indicates low pitch. Double vowels represent long vowels. Data from Cole 1967.

a. mukířa "tail"   g. kutúulá "to sit down"
b. lumóóndé "sweet potato"   h. okútábáála "to attach"
c. kulímá "to cultivate"   i. eříñá "name"
d. éfířímbí "to whistle"   j. oolwééyó "a broom"
e. kuwóólá "to scoop or hollow out"   k. kwaanířízá "to welcome, invite"
f. kuwólá "to lend money"   l. kuujjúkířa "to remember"

4. For the following English words, state the conditions under which the different forms of the past tense appear. What determines whether /t/, /d/, or /ɨd/ is used? Hint: Write the past tense marker phonemically in order to discover whether the ending for a given verb is pronounced /t/, /d/, or /ɨd/. For example, *crushed* has

final /t/, but *pitted* has final /id/. What distinctive features define each conditioning environment?

a.	crushed	k.	turned
b.	heaped	l.	hissed
c.	kicked	m.	plowed
d.	pitted	n.	climbed
e.	deeded	o.	singed
f.	bagged	p.	hanged
g.	killed	q.	cinched
h.	nabbed	r.	played
i.	thrived	s.	hated
j.	breathed	t.	branded

5. Draw feet (unary, binary, or ternary) over the following words. First write the words phonemically to determine where the reduced vowels are.

a. phoneme

b. elephant

c. gymnast (two possibilities, but your dialect may only have one)

d. fundamental

e. phonological

Bibliography and Further Reading

Anderson, S. (1974). *The organization of phonology*. New York: Seminar Press.

Chomsky, N., and M. Halle (1968). *The sound pattern of English*. New York: Harper and Row.

Clements, G. N., and S. J. Keyser (1983). *CV phonology: A generative theory of the syllable*. Cambridge, Mass.: MIT Press.

Cole, D. (1967). *Some features of Ganda linguistic structure*. Johannesburg: Witwatersrand University Press.

Denes, P., and E. David, Jr. (1972). *Human communications: A unified view*. New York: McGraw-Hill.

Fodor, J., and J. Katz, eds. (1964). *The structure of language: Readings in the philosophy of language*. Englewood Cliffs, N. J.: Prentice-Hall.

Goldsmith, J. (1981). English as a tone language. In D. Goyvaerts, ed., *Phonology in the 1980's*. Ghent: E. Story-Scientia.

Grønbech, K., and J. Krueger (1955). *An introduction to classical (literary) Mongolian*. Wiesbaden: Harrassowitz.

Halle, M. (1962). Phonology in a generative grammar. *Word* 18, 54–72. Reprinted in Fodor and Katz 1964.

Halle, M., and G. N. Clements (1982). *Problem book in phonology: A workbook for introductory courses in linguistics and modern phonology*. Cambridge, Mass.: MIT Press.

Hyman, L. (1975). *Phonology: Theory and analysis.* New York: Holt, Rinehart and Winston.

Jakobson, R., and M. Halle (1956). *Fundamentals of language.* The Hague: Mouton.

Kahn, D. (1976). Syllable-based generalizations in English phonology. Doctoral dissertation, MIT, Cambridge, Mass.

Kenstowicz, M., and C. Kisseberth (1979). *Generative phonology: Description and theory.* New York: Academic Press.

Liberman, M., and A. Prince (1977). On stress and linguistic rhythm. *Linguistic Inquiry* 8, 249–336.

Pinker, S., and A. Prince (1988). On language and connectionism: Analysis of a parallel distributed processing model of language. In S. Pinker and J. Mehler, eds., *Symbols and connections.* Cambridge, Mass.: MIT Press.

Stevens, K. (1972). The quantal nature of speech: Evidence from articulatory-acoustic data. In Denes and David 1972.

Chapter 5

SYNTAX: THE STUDY
OF SENTENCE
STRUCTURE

5.1 SOME BACKGROUND CONCEPTS

So far in our study of language, we have focused on morphology, phonetics, and phonology, and thus we have been focusing on the level of the *word*. Now we turn our attention to the analysis of larger structural units of language: *phrases* and *sentences*. In focusing on these larger structural units, we will discover some rather striking properties of the syntax of human language.

Let us begin by considering a sentence that you have never heard before:

(1)
All the passengers on the plane would rather listen to Abbott and Costello than watch another crummy movie.

This sentence has probably never before been written or uttered. Yet, as a native speaker of English, you are able to comprehend the sentence (as long as you know the meaning of the individual words). That is, even if you have not encountered a particular sentence in your previous linguistic experience, you are nevertheless able to understand it because you recognize familiar units (words that you know) combined in a novel but appropriate way.

All of us, as native speakers of a language, are able to produce and comprehend an infinitely large number of phrases and sentences of that language, many of which we have never heard or produced before. How is it possible that speakers of a language can carry out such an impressive task? One thing is clear: we know that speakers cannot simply have memorized all the phrases and sentences of a language. This is suggested by example (1): if you had simply memorized all the sentences of English, how could you understand a sentence you had never had a chance to commit to memory (because you had never heard it before)? As it turns out, it is in principle impossible for speakers to memorize all the sentences of their native language.

Some simple examples will suffice to show this. Consider first a simple sentence of English: *Sara is a graduate student*. We can create a longer sentence of English using this first sentence, by *embedding* it within a larger sentence: *William believes that Sara is a graduate student*. In turn, this sentence can be embedded, yielding an even larger sentence: *Ruth said that William believes that Sara is a graduate student*. Indeed, there is in principle no limit on this embedding process: *Mary remarked that Tom read that everyone in Troy knew that Ruth said that William believes that Sara is a graduate student*. (In section 5.3 we will return to a more formal discussion of embedding.) Of course, such a long and unwieldy sentence might not ever be uttered in actual speech—it has become long enough to put a strain on our memory—but as native speakers of English we can make an *intuitive* judgment that all of the examples we have discussed so far are well formed: that is, they conform to regular patterns of English syntax that we encounter in many other well-formed sentences and phrases. We will return to a discussion of such intuitive judgments, which form a crucial part of each speaker's linguistic knowledge. But at this point, note that no matter how long we make a certain sentence, we can always embed that sentence, producing a still longer one. This means that the number of well-formed sentences in English (or any other language) is *infinite*. Since no matter how many sentences we had on the list there would always be other sentences that were longer that we had not put on the list, it is not possible to exhaustively list all the sentences of a language. Of course, any individual sentence itself is finite in length, but the number of sentences in any language is infinite; that is, the set of sentences is infinite. An infinite set is, in effect, a list that never ends, and for that reason such a list could not possibly be committed to memory.

Since native speakers of a language cannot have memorized each phrase or sentence of their language, given that the set of phrases and sentences is infinite, their linguistic knowledge cannot be characterized as a list of phrases or sentences. (This issue brings up some of the same problems and questions we encountered in chapter 2 in the course of arguing that simply making a list of words inadequately represents our knowledge of words.) If a list of phrases is insufficient, then how can we characterize the native speaker's linguistic knowledge? We will say that a speaker's linguistic knowledge can be characterized as a grammar consisting of a *finite set* of rules and principles that form the basis for the speaker's ability to produce and comprehend the infinite number of phrases and sentences of the language. The rules and principles of the grammar also serve to capture the regularities in the language.

In referring to the linguistic knowledge of the native speaker, we begin to touch upon a distinction between two concepts that have figured prominently in discussions of syntax in recent years: the distinction between *competence* and *performance*. In discussing these concepts, we will be following, in general outline, the work of the linguist Noam Chomsky (see the bibliography at the end of the chapter); indeed, our general approach to syntax in this entire chapter is based on his influential work.

Competence and Performance

Consider the fact that native speakers of a language are able to make numerous *intuitive judgments* about their language. For example, as native speakers of English we can make the intuitive judgment that examples (2a) and (3a–b) are well-formed sentences of English, whereas examples (2b) and (3c) are ill formed.

(2)
a.   The dog bit the horse.
b.   *Dog the horse the bit.

(3)
a.   Who(m) did Mary grow up with?
b.   With whom did Mary grow up?
c.   *Up with whom did Mary grow?

We do not have to consult grammar books or interview large groups of English speakers in order to determine that (2a) and (3a–b) are all well formed, whereas (2b) and (3c) are not. Rather, as native speakers we are able to make certain judgments, known as *grammaticality judgments*, about whether sentences are well formed or not. Our ability to make such judgments concerning examples like (2a) and (3a–b), on the one hand, and (2b) and (3c), on the other, reflects our linguistic knowledge; by virtue of knowing English, we know that the former examples are fine, whereas the latter are somehow "odd." This knowledge is part of our linguistic *competence* as native speakers of English.

The competence-performance distinction (see Chomsky 1965) is intended to reflect the difference between the linguistic knowledge of fluent speakers of a language (*competence*) and the actual production and comprehension of speech by those speakers (*performance*). To take a simple example, suppose that a fluent speaker of English has undergone extensive dental surgery on a certain day, which leaves him temporarily unable to talk. Would we want to say that he has lost his knowledge of English? Surely not. That is, in terms of *competence* we would say that the speaker still maintains a fluent grasp of the English language; however, because of *performance limitations* (aching jaw muscles and tooth pain) his vocal apparatus happens to be temporarily afflicted.

We can also observe the competence-performance distinction if we carefully examine the actual speech of native speakers in a conversation. Actual speech is characterized by false starts and stops, hesitations, lapses of memory, coughing, clearing of the throat, and so on. A detailed transcription of actual speech would reveal numerous *uhh*'s and *umm*'s and other extraneous sounds. Although such details reflect the actual performance of a given speaker on a given occasion, they do not necessarily reflect that speaker's competence. In other words, a speaker's competence is his or her *linguistic capacity*, and although that capacity is reflected in actual speech, it may also be obscured by performance factors such as memory limitations, coughing, inebriation, and so on. In a similar fashion, we can say that a Lamborghini sports car has the *capacity* to travel at 150 mph, even if it happens to be sitting in the shop right now with four flat tires. The point is that we must distinguish between what it *can do* (under ideal circumstances) and what it is *actually doing* (in the given circumstances of the moment).

Our study of syntax in this chapter will be based on our intuitive judgments as native speakers of English. In the pages that follow we will be examining numerous expressions, some of which we will judge to be ill formed. Hence, the primary data for our study of syntax will come from our own introspection about English sentences—that is, our own linguistic competence. Not only will the rules and principles that we discover from our study be part of the grammar of English, they will also be of a general type found in numerous other languages. We will proceed in our study of syntax first by examining the concept of *syntactic structure*. Having determined some of the central aspects of the concept of structure, we will then examine certain properties of syntactic *rules*. We will not attempt to discuss a wide range of structures or rules; rather, we will focus on a small number of structures and rules in English, in order to get a feel for how syntactic analysis is carried out. But for now, let us begin by examining what we mean by *structure*.

The Concept of Structure

In all languages, sentences are structured in certain specific ways. What is syntactic structure, and what does it mean to say that sentences are structured? Like many other questions that can be posed about human language, it is difficult to answer this one in any direct fashion. In fact, it is impossible to answer the question *What is structure?* without actually constructing a theory of syntax, and indeed one of the central concerns of current theories of syntax is to provide an answer to this question. Thus, it must be stressed that we cannot define the concept of structure before we study syntax; rather, our study of syntax will be an attempt to find a definition (however elaborate) of this concept.

To begin to find such a definition, we will adopt the following strategy: let's assume that sentences are merely unstructured strings of words. That is, given that we can recognize that sentences are made up of individual words (which we can isolate), it would seem that the minimal assumption we could make would be that sentences are nothing more than words strung out in linear order, one after the other. If we examine some of the formal properties of sentences in light of this strategy, we will quickly discover whether our unstructured string hypothesis is tenable or whether we will be forced to adopt a hypothesis that attributes greater complexity to sentences. That is, we do not want to simply *assume* that sentences are structured; rather, we want to find out whether this hypothesis is *supported* by evidence.

If we adopt the hypothesis that sentences are unstructured strings of words, then almost immediately we must add an important qualification. One of the first things we notice about the sentences of human languages is that the words in a sentence occur in a *certain* linear order. Although some languages display considerable freedom of word order (standard examples being Latin, Russian, and aboriginal Australian languages), in no human language may the words of a sentence occur in any random order whatsoever. No matter how free a language is with respect to word order, it will inevitably have some word order constraints (see exercise 10). Furthermore, in many languages the linear order of words plays a crucial role in determining the meaning of sentences: in English, *The horse bit the dog* means something quite different from *The dog bit the horse*, even though the very same words are used in both. Hence, we might say that sentences are unstructured strings of words, but we must ensure that we specify at least *linear order* for those words (see exercise 9).

Structural Ambiguity

Even with the important qualification just made about word order, our unstructured string hypothesis runs up against an interesting puzzle. Consider the following sentence:

(4)
a. The mother of the boy and the girl will arrive soon.

This sentence is ambiguous; that is, it has more than one meaning. It is either about one person (the mother) or about two people (the mother in addition to the girl). In sentences with the verbs *is* and *are*, these two possibilities clearly emerge:

(4)
b. The mother of the boy and the girl *is* arriving soon.
c. The mother of the boy and the girl *are* arriving soon.

The interesting feature of sentence (4a) is that the ambiguity cannot be attributed to an ambiguity in any of the words of the sentence. That is, we cannot attribute the ambiguity of the sentence to an ambiguity in *mother* or *boy* or *girl*. In contrast, consider the sentence *The sentence was a long one*. This too is ambiguous, but the ambiguity in this case is attributable to an ambiguity in the word *sentence*: it can mean either "prison sentence" or the linguistic unit "sentence." For (4a), however, we cannot appeal to such an explanation.

At this point, then, we are faced with a puzzle: how is it that a sentence consisting entirely of unambiguous words can nonetheless be ambiguous? Our unstructured string hypothesis does not lead us to expect this sort of ambiguity, nor does it provide any mechanism for accounting for the phenomenon. Abandoning the unstructured string hypothesis, let us instead assume that the words in (4a) can be grouped together and furthermore that they can be grouped together in more than one way. If we make this assumption, which is motivated by our example, we can provide an account of the kind of ambiguity exhibited in sentences such as (4a) by saying that although the sentence consists of a single set of unambiguous words, those words can in fact be grouped in two different ways:

(5)
a. The mother (of the boy and the girl) will arrive soon.
b. (The mother of the boy) and the girl will arrive soon.

When the phrases *of the boy* and *and the girl* are grouped together, as in (5a), the sentence is interpreted to mean that only the mother will arrive.

When *of the boy* is instead grouped with *the mother*, as in (5b), then the sentence is interpreted to mean that both the mother and the girl will arrive. Thus, depending on how the words are grouped (how they are *structured*), one interpretation rather than the other is possible. One string of words may have more than one well-formed set of groupings, creating a source of ambiguity that is totally separate from lexical (word) ambiguity.

By saying that words in a sentence can be grouped together, we have started to define the concept of sentence structure. Notice that by appealing to a notion of grouping, we have, even with this simple example, already gone beyond superficial observations concerning properties of sentences to postulating abstract, or theoretical, properties. Although the linear order of words is something we can check by direct observation of a sentence, the grouping of words in that sentence is generally not directly observable. Rather, word grouping is a theoretical property that we appeal to in order to account for abstract characteristics of sentences—such as structural ambiguity.

Given what we have said so far, it would appear that in specifying the structure of a sentence we specify (1) the linear order of words and (2) the possible groupings of the words. Indeed, these are two important properties of the structure of sentences, but by no means are they the only important properties. Given that we have initial evidence that requires us to attribute some kind of structure to sentences, let us examine in more detail what is involved in specifying the structure of English sentences (and, more generally, the sentences of many other languages).

5.2   AN INFORMAL THEORY OF SYNTAX

So far we have drawn our evidence for structure from ambiguous sentences that do not contain ambiguous words. We are not limited by such examples. One of the most important ways of discovering why and how sentences must be structured is to try to state explicitly grammatical rules for a given language. For example, consider the following English declarative sentences and their corresponding question (interrogative) forms:

(6)
a. John can lift 500 pounds.
    Can John lift 500 pounds?
b. Mathematicians are generally thought to be odd.
    Are mathematicians generally thought to be odd?
c. They will want to reserve two rooms.
    Will they want to reserve two rooms?

d. Mary has proved several theorems.
   Has Mary proved several theorems?

Any native speaker of English knows how to form interrogative and declarative sentences of the sort illustrated in (6). We will now engage in an apparently simple exercise: that is, to state as precisely as we can how such English questions are structured.

The English Question Rule

For the purposes of this discussion, we will assume that interrogative sentences are formed from declarative sentences. There is independent evidence that the two sentence types should be related; however, we will not go into those arguments here.

How can we describe the way the questions in (6) are formed from the declarative sentences? One approach would be to number each word of the declarative sentence, as in (7), and state a set of instructions for forming a question based on this sentence, as in (8). Note that the rule in (8) does not refer to structure but refers only to linear order and to the notion "word."

(7)
John can lift 500 pounds.
  1   2   3   4   5

(8)
Question Rule I (QR-I)
To form a question from a declarative sentence, place word 2 at the beginning of the sentence.

Given (7) as input, QR-I produces (9) as output:

(9)
Can John lift 500 pounds?
  2   1   3   4   5

Thus, QR-I properly produces the interrogative in (6a). A simple check will reveal that QR-I also works for the other examples in (6).

However, QR-I is inadequate. Though it does account for the sentences in (6), it cannot be extended to other declarative/interrogative pairs. Consider the following declarative sentences:

(10)
a. Yesterday John could lift 500 pounds.
b. Many mathematicians are thought to be odd.
c. Those people will want to reserve two rooms.

QR-I predicts that the corresponding questions should be as follows:

(11)
a.   John yesterday could lift 500 pounds?
b.   *Mathematicians many are thought to be odd?
c.   *People those will want to reserve two rooms?

Though (11a) might be a possible (albeit awkward) sentence, it is certainly not the question that corresponds to (10a)—which should be *Yesterday, could John lift 500 pounds?* As for (11b) and (11c), they are not the questions corresponding to (10b) and (10c), respectively. Moreover, they are ungrammatical—no native speaker would accept them as being well formed.

It is clear, then, that we must reformulate QR-I so as to account for the counterexamples in (11). We see that English questions are not formed by simply moving the second word of the sentence to the beginning. After all, the second word of an English sentence can be any type of word: a noun, a verb, an adjective, an article, and so on. However, the examples in (6) show that in forming a question in English, it is always a *verb* that is moved, that is, a word such as *can, are, will,* and *has.*

In order to state the Question Rule more accurately, we are now forced to suppose that the words of a sentence are not only strung out in some linear order but also classified into different morphological categories—what have traditionally been called *parts of speech.* We have already seen evidence in chapter 2 that words must be classed into parts of speech in order to state word formation rules properly. If we make this assumption for syntax as well as for morphology, then we can restate the Question Rule so that it is sensitive to this morphological information:

(12)
Question Rule II (QR-II)
To form a question from a declarative sentence, place the first verb at the beginning of the sentence.

In *John can lift 500 pounds*, the first verb is *can*; by placing it at the beginning of the sentence, we derive the question *Can John lift 500 pounds?* Similarly, in *Many mathematicians are thought to be odd*, the first verb is *are*; by placing it at the beginning, we derive *Are many mathematicians thought to be odd?* Indeed, the reformulated rule gives the right results for the examples in both (6) and (10), with one exception. For sentence (10a), *Yesterday John could lift 500 pounds*, the first verb is *could*; by placing it at the beginning of the sentence, we derive *Could yesterday John lift 500 pounds?*—which seems to be unnatural. Instead, we want to arrive at the form *Yesterday, could John lift 500 pounds?* We will return to this problem shortly.

We have now been forced to assume that the words in a sentence must be classified into parts of speech. It should be stressed that this classification is not a matter of convenience or conjecture; rather, it turns out to be impossible to state the Question Rule properly if we cannot appeal to such a classification.

Just as we found counterexamples to QR-I, however, we can easily find counterexamples to QR-II. Consider the following examples:

(13)
a. You know those women.
b. Mary left early.
c. They went to Phoenix.

Here, the first verbs are *know, left,* and *went,* respectively. Applying QR-II yields the following questions:

(14)
a. *Know you those women?
b. *Left Mary early?
c. *Went they to Phoenix?

If QR-II were the correct rule, then the questions in (14) would be well formed. Although English once formed questions of this general sort (similar forms occur in Shakespeare's writing, for example), they are ill formed in present-day English. Why are these sentences different from the ones we considered earlier? Let us review some of the sentences we have examined so far (15a–c, e–f) and add a new one (15d):

(15)
a. John can lift 500 pounds.
   Can John lift 500 pounds?
b. They will want to reserve two rooms.
   Will they want to reserve two rooms?
c. Mary has proved several theorems.
   Has Mary proved several theorems?
d. Bill is doing the dishes.
   Is Bill doing the dishes?
e. You know those women.
   Do you know those women?
f. They went to Phoenix.
   Did they go to Phoenix?

In the pairs of sentences in (15a–d) a verb has changed position in deriving the question from the statement. Note that each of these four sentences has two verbs: an auxiliary verb and a main verb, of which the former is involved in the question formation process. In fact, we may interpret the form of *do* that appears in the questions in (15e–f) as a "placeholder" auxiliary verb.

We will see in the next section that the distinction between main and auxiliary verbs plays a role elsewhere in the grammar. This is important since it further supports the need to draw such a distinction in accounting for the formation of interrogatives.

Auxiliary Verbs versus Main Verbs in English

The auxiliary verbs of English include the following forms:

(16)
a. Forms of the verb *be* (*is, am, are, was, were*)
b. Forms of the verb *have* (*have, has, had*)
c. Forms of the verb *do* (*do, does, did*)
d. The verbs *can, could, will, would, shall, should, may, might, must*, and a few others. Members of this group are usually called *modal auxiliaries*.

The distinction between auxiliary verbs and main verbs shows up very clearly in several grammatical process in English, among which are the following.

1. Auxiliary verbs, but not main verbs, are fronted in forming questions:

(17)
a. John *is* running.
    Is John running?
b. They *have* left.
    Have they left?
c. I *can* sing.
    Can I sing?
d. Mary *speaks* French.
    *Speaks Mary French?

When a sentence contains no auxiliary verb but has only a main verb, then the auxiliary verb *do* is used in forming questions:

(18)
a. You *know* these women.
   Do you know these women?

b. Mary *left* early.
   Did Mary leave early?
c. They *went* to Phoenix.
   Did they go to Phoenix?

 2. The contracted negative *n't* can attach to auxiliary verbs:

(19)

a. John *is* running.
   John *isn't* running.
b. They *have* left.
   They *haven't* left.
c. I *can* sing.
   I *can't* sing.

However, main verbs cannot be negated in this way:

(20)

a. You *know* those women.
    *You *known't* those women.
b. Mary *left* early.
    *Mary *leftn't* early.

When a sentence contains only a main verb and no auxiliary verb, the auxiliary verb *do* is used in forming the negative version:

(21)

a. You *know* those women.
   You *don't* know those women.
b. Mary *left* early.
   Mary *didn't* leave early.
c. They *went* to Phoenix.
   They *didn't* go to Phoenix.

In addition, auxiliary verbs can be followed by the uncontracted negative *not* (as in *John is not running, They have not left, I cannot sing*). Main verbs cannot be followed by uncontracted *not* in current spoken American English: expressions such as *We know not what we do* are possible only in highly stylized forms of English in which an archaic flavor is preserved (as in religious preaching styles and highly formal oratory).

 3. Auxiliary verbs, but not main verbs, can appear in *tags*. A tag occurs at the end of a sentence and contains a repetition of the auxiliary verb found in that sentence:

(22)

John *has* not been here, *has* he?

$\underbrace{\qquad\qquad}_{\text{main sentence}}$ $\underbrace{\qquad}_{\text{tag}}$

When the auxiliary verb of the main sentence is positive in form, the repeated auxiliary verb in the tag may be positive or negative in form:

(23)

a. Herman is threatening to leave, is he!

b. Herman is threatening to leave, isn't he?

The positive and negative tags are used under different circumstances (the positive tag often having the force of a challenge; the negative tag being used to request confirmation of the main sentence). But in both cases the auxiliary verb of the tag is a repetition of the auxiliary verb of the main sentence. In addition, when the auxiliary verb of the main sentence is negative in form, the auxiliary in the tag is always positive:

(24)

Herman isn't threatening to leave, is he?

In other words, we do not find cases like (25):

(25)

*Herman isn't threatening to leave, isn't he?

Unlike auxiliary verbs, main verbs cannot appear in tags. For a sentence such as *You know those women*, there is no corresponding tagged form, *_You know those women, know you?_ Instead, when a sentence contains only a main verb, the auxiliary verb *do* is used in forming the tag:

(26)

a. You know those women, *don't* you?

b. Mary left early, *did* she!

c. They went to Phoenix, *didn't* they?

Thus, auxiliary verbs and main verbs differ not only with respect to question formation but also with respect to negation and tag formation. These differences are summarized in table 5.1.

Given this distinction in English verbs, and given the impossibility of question forms such as those in (14), we must now amend the Question Rule to take account of the new data:

Table 5.1
Comparison of auxiliary verbs and main verbs

	Auxiliary Verbs	Main Verbs
Fronted in forming questions?	Yes: *Is* John running? *Have* they left? *Can* I sing?	No: *Know you those women? *Left Mary early? *Went they to Phoenix? Use *do*: *Do* you know those women? *Did* Mary leave early? *Did* they go to Phoenix?
Negative form can have *n't* attached?	Yes: John *isn't* running. They *haven't* left. I *can't* sing.	No: *You known't those women. *Mary leftn't early. *They wentn't to Phoenix. Use *do*: You *don't* know those women. Mary *didn't* leave early. They *didn't* go to Phoenix.
Can occur in tag sentence?	Yes: John isn't running, *is* he? They haven't left, *have* they? I can't sing, *can* I?	No: *You know those women, know you? *Mary left early, left she? *They went to Phoenix, went they? Use *do*: You know those women, *do* you! Mary left early, *did* she! They went to Phoenix, *did* they!

(27)

Question Rule III (QR-III)

a. To form a question from a declarative sentence, place the auxiliary verb at the beginning of the sentence.

b. If there is no auxiliary verb, but only a main verb, place an appropriate form of the verb *do* at the beginning of the sentence and make appropriate changes in the main verb.

As we can verify, this amended rule covers the cases we have cited so far. For a sentence such as *Mary has left*, the auxiliary verb is *has*; by fronting this, we derive the question form *Has Mary left?* A sentence such as *You knew those women* has no auxiliary verb; thus, we must insert an appropriate form of the auxiliary verb *do*. In this case, the appropriate form is *did* (past tense), and we must make appropriate changes in the main verb (changing past tense *knew* to tenseless *know*), thus deriving the question form *Did you know those women?* And so on for the rest of the examples given. We will not be concerned with the details of the use of auxiliary *do*, and thus we leave part (b) of the Question Rule stated in a rather vague way. Since our interest from this point on will be in part (a), we will omit further mention of part (b)—keeping in mind, however, that part (b) is to be understood as being included in further revisions of the rule.

We now have a revised version of the Question Rule, amended to take account of the distinction in English between auxiliary and main verbs. In other words, the Question Rule must be sensitive not only to the distinction among major parts of speech (such as *noun* versus *verb*) but also to the distinction(s) among *subcategories* of a major category. The Question Rule does not involve just *any* verb; it involves only a specific subcategory of verbs, namely, the auxiliaries. With this additional refinement, our Question Rule has become more adequate.

Structural Grouping: The Subject Constituent

Question Rule III makes reference to *auxiliary verb*. However, what happens if more than one auxiliary verb occurs in the sentence? Consider the examples in (28):

(28)

a. John *will have* left.

b. Sharon *should be* going to Chicago.

c. Tim *has been* studying very hard.

The corresponding interrogative sentences for these examples are
(29a–c)—*not* (30a–c):

(29)

a. *Will* John have left?
b. *Should* Sharon be going to Chicago?
c. *Has* Tim been studying very hard?

(30)

a. **Have* John will left?
b. **Be* Sharon should going to Chicago?
c. **Been* Tim has studying very hard?

Have and *be* are auxiliary verbs in (30). They share all the relevant properties of other auxiliary verbs. To see this, consider the examples in (31):

(31)

a. John has left.
   Has John left?   (interrogative)
   John hasn't left.   (negation)
   John has left, hasn't he?   (tag)
b. Sharon is going to Chicago.
   Is Sharon going to Chicago?   (interrogative)
   Sharon isn't going to Chicago.   (negation)
   Sharon is going to Chicago, is she!   (tag)
c. Tim is studying very hard.
   Is Tim studying very hard?   (interrogative)
   Tim isn't studying very hard.   (negation)
   Tim is studying very hard, is he!   (tag)

As we can see, *have* and *be* (realized here as *has* and *is*) front to form an
interrogative, can appear with the negative *n't*, and can appear in tags.
Why, then, can these auxiliaries not front when they cooccur with *will*,
should, and *has*? What distinguishes "good" fronting of an auxiliary verb
from illicit fronting is linear order. The *first* auxiliary verb in a sequence
of auxiliary verbs is the one targeted for fronting. In other words, the rule
needs to refer to linear order as well as to categorial information.

(32)

Question Rule IV (QR-IV)
To form a question from a declarative sentence, place the first auxiliary
verb at the beginning of the sentence.

Let us look at other sentences containing more than one auxiliary verb.
Examples in (33) constitute a class of sentences we have yet to examine:

(33)

a. The people who *are* standing in the room *will* leave soon.

b. Many mathematicians who you *will* meet *are* thought to be odd.

c. Anyone that *can* lift 500 pounds *is* eligible for our club.

Notice that in (33a) the first auxiliary verb is *are*. If we place this first auxiliary verb at the beginning of the sentence, we will derive the following ungrammatical question:

(34)

*Are the people who ——— standing in the room will leave soon?

Clearly, in this example it is not the first auxiliary verb that should be moved; instead, it is the second auxiliary verb, *will*:

(35)

Will the people who are standing in the room ——— leave soon?

Is this a counterexample to our previous conclusion? Is this a case where it is really the *second* auxiliary verb that fronts? To answer this question, we need more data. In the following examples, the auxiliary verb that fronts (which is boxed) does not correspond to any particular number; it can be the third, fourth, or any other number:

(36)

a. The people who <u>were</u> saying that John <u>is</u> sick <u>|will|</u> leave soon.
$$\qquad\qquad\qquad\quad\ \ 1\qquad\qquad\qquad\quad 2\qquad\quad 3$$

b. The people who <u>were</u> saying that Pat <u>has</u> told Mary to make Terry
$$\qquad\qquad\qquad\quad\ \ 1\qquad\qquad\qquad\qquad\ \ 2$$

quit trying to persuade David that many mathematicians <u>are</u> thought
$$\qquad\qquad\qquad\qquad\qquad\qquad\qquad\qquad\qquad\qquad\qquad 3$$

to be odd <u>|will|</u> leave soon.
$$\qquad\ \ 4$$

An important point to notice here is that such examples can be extended indefinitely—as noted earlier in this chapter, there is simply no limit on the length of the sentences we can construct or on the number of auxiliary verbs we can place before the auxiliary verb that fronts. Naturally, when sentences become this long, they become difficult to understand and remember; consequently, they would normally not occur in everyday conversation as single uninterrupted sentences. However, this is a practical problem, a problem of performance limitations on memory, and we will consider sentences such as (36b) as data that our grammar must be able to account for.

In (36a–b) we see that in each instance the auxiliary verb *will* is the correct verb to move to the beginning of the sentence. However, that auxiliary verb does not occupy any particular fixed slot in the linear order of words. Further, it is in principle impossible to specify exactly what can come between that auxiliary and the beginning of the sentence (because there is no limitation on the length of the sentence between the beginning point and the point where the appropriate auxiliary is located). It should be clear that for (36a–b), QR-IV will give the wrong results if we apply it strictly. A more general rule is needed.

If we look more carefully at examples (33a–c), we see that the auxiliary verb that must be moved to the front of the sentence is the auxiliary that immediately follows an intuitively natural *grouping* of words traditionally referred to as the *subject* of the sentence:

(37)
a. <u>The people who are standing in the room</u>   will   ...
                   Subject   Auxiliary
b. <u>Many mathematicians that you will meet</u>   are   ...
                   Subject   Auxiliary
c. <u>Anyone that can lift 500 pounds</u>   is   ...
             Subject   Auxiliary

The underlined words listed in (37a–c) form a unit; that is, they form a single *constituent*. The subject constituent of the sentence (discussed further in the next section) plays an important role in the statement of the Question Rule, since it allows us to locate the appropriate auxiliary verb in the formation of questions. Given the notion of subject constituent, we can now amend QR-IV as follows, to take into account examples such as (33a–c):

(38)
Question Rule V (QR-V)
To form a question from a declarative sentence, locate the first auxiliary verb that *follows the subject of the sentence* and place it at the beginning of the sentence.

Given this reformulation of the Question Rule, we can pick out the proper auxiliary verb to front in forming questions (you might want to verify that QR-V covers all the cases discussed so far), and we will successfully avoid the problem illustrated by example (34), which plagued QR-IV.

However, it turns out that even QR-V must be further modified. As we have already seen, the appropriate auxiliary verb is not always moved to the *front* of the sentence. Recall the following examples:

(39)

a.   Yesterday John could lift 500 pounds.

b.   *Could yesterday John lift 500 pounds?

c.   Yesterday, could John lift 500 pounds?

These examples suggest that the appropriate auxiliary verb of the sentence must be placed *immediately to the left of the subject*—not actually at the beginning of the sentence. This leads to the following modification:

(40)

Question Rule VI (QR-VI)

To form a question from a declarative sentence, locate the first auxiliary verb that follows the subject of the sentence and place it *immediately to the left of the subject*.

This reformulation will cover all the cases we have examined so far.

We began with the minimal assumption that sentences are unstructured strings of words, and we attempted to state an adequate rule for characterizing well-formed questions in English. Successive counterexamples forced us to revise our assumptions about how sentences are structured. For example, notice that the latest statement of the Question Rule forces us to refer to *linear order* (by referring to the *first* auxiliary verb after the subject), to categorize words into *parts of speech* (by referring to *auxiliary verbs*), and to refer to *constituent structure* (by referring to a structural grouping called *subject*). It is important to note that at each stage the added assumptions were not merely a matter of convenience. For example, we sought independent evidence for the distinction between main verb and auxiliary verb, noting various properties that auxiliary verbs, but not main verbs, share. We have yet to demonstrate the importance of the constituent we referred to as *subject*. We now turn to providing independent evidence for such a grouping.

The Notion "Subject"

In our latest reformulations of the Question Rule we have referred to the subject of a sentence, and it would be useful here to note that subjects play an important role in other grammatical processes in English (and indeed, in many other languages). To begin with, what exactly is a *subject*? This notion has never been precisely defined, despite its significant role in linguistic analysis. Like many linguistic notions, it has an intuitive basis. The classic example of a subject comes from simple sentences with action verbs, such as *The farmer fed the duckling*, in which the subject, in this case *the farmer*, is understood as the *agent* ("the doer") of the action, and the *object*, in this case *the duckling*, is understood as that which undergoes the action. Not every subject is an agent; in the sentence *Mary resembles her Aunt Bettina, Mary* is the subject, but no action is involved. In general, trying to characterize subjects in terms of meaning is an extremely complex undertaking, if indeed it is possible at all.

In any given language we can find grammatical processes that crucially (and uniquely) involve subjects of sentences, however, and we can use these processes as tests for identifying the subject of a sentence in that language. For example, in English, tag questions provide a good test for identifying the subject of a sentence, because the pronoun in the tag *agrees with* the subject:

(41)

a. You will persuade Aunt Bettina, won't you?

b. John can't sing, can he?

c. The woman in the photo is your mother, isn't she?

d. The man who hated everybody didn't leave early, did he?

e. The students in the class voted for me, didn't they?

f. The girl and the boy are playing, aren't they?

The pronouns in the tags illustrated in (41) agree with the subjects of the main sentences in terms of *person* (1st, which is the speaker; 2nd, which is the hearer; or 3rd, which is neither the speaker nor the hearer), *number* (singular or plural), and *gender* (masculine, feminine, or neuter). For example, in (41c) the subject, *the woman in the photo*, is third person singular feminine, and these features are reflected in the pronoun *she* in the tag. The features of person, number, and gender serve to classify the personal pronouns of English, as shown in table 5.2.

In English, then, subjects of sentences have a number of properties:

(42)

a. The subject of a declarative sentence generally precedes the auxiliary and main verb in linear order.

b. It forms the constituent around which an auxiliary is fronted in forming a question (see (40)).

c. It is the constituent with which a pronoun in a tag agrees in terms of person, number, and gender. (See exercise 7 for another grammatical process that makes reference to subjects.)

Table 5.2
Classification of English personal pronouns in terms of person, number, and gender

	Singular	Plural
1st person	I	we
2nd person	you	you
3rd person		
Masculine	he	
Feminine	she	they
Neuter	it	

Table 5.3
Subject and nonsubject pronouns in English

	SUBJECT PRONOUNS	NONSUBJECT PRONOUNS	
	As subject of sentence	As object of verb	As object of preposition
1st person			
Singular	*I* love movies.	They like *me*.	She spoke to *me*.
Plural	*We* enjoy cars.	You follow *us*.	It ran from *us*.
2nd person			
Singular or Plural	*You* left early.	I found *you*.	I work for *you*.
3rd person			
Singular	*He* collapsed.	Watch *him*!	I'll sit by *him*.
	She won.	I copy *her*.	Go after *her*!
	It blew up.	Why buy *it*?	Look under *it*!
Plural	*They* are nice.	I hired *them*.	It flew over *them*.

In languages other than English, subjects can have other grammatical properties. For example, recall the Japanese sentence discussed in section 2.1, *John-ga hon-o yonda* "John read the book." We noted that the subject of the sentence, *John*, has the particle *-ga* attached to it, which serves to indicate the subject function in this particular sentence. (The particle *-o* in turn indicates the object function of *hon* "book.") The subject, then, is overtly marked and is recognized by its marker. It is not recognized by its linear order in the sentence, as in English. In fact, it can occur either before or after the object; the sentence means the same, in either case.

Most English pronouns are marked according to their function as subjects or objects (see table 5.3). The pronoun *you* has the same form in all uses (singular and plural, subject and nonsubject), and the pronoun *it* has the same form in subject and nonsubject uses. Otherwise, English pronouns assume two different forms to reflect their subject or nonsubject function:

I–me, we–us, he–him, she–her, and *they–them*. The subject pronouns *I, we, she, he*, and *they* are sometimes called *nominative* (or *subjective*) *case* pronouns; the nonsubject pronouns *me, us, him, her*, and *them* are sometimes called *accusative* (or *objective*) *case* pronouns. Nonsubject (that is, nonnominative) pronouns cannot be used in subject position (except in pidgin expressions such as *Me Tarzan, you Jane* or in expressions such as *What, me worry?*), and subject pronouns cannot be used in nonsubject positions (note the ungrammatical *You saw I). Therefore, the form of the pronoun may serve as a clue to the role, subject or object, that the pronoun plays in the sentence.

Aside from the pronouns listed in table 5.3, no other words (noun(s)) in English change morphological form to reflect subject versus nonsubject function. Thus, in sentences such as *Mary saw the dog* or *The dog saw Mary*, the nouns *dog* and *Mary* have the same shape whether they function as subject or object.

These examples illustrate some of the ways in which subjects can be marked, or function in grammatical processes (also see exercise 8). We have not yet defined the notion "subject." In the section on constituent structure tests we will work out a definition that is structural in nature. In order to understand this definition, we must learn something about constituent structure, a matter to which we now turn.

Constituent Structure and Tree Diagrams

We have now seen two kinds of evidence in favor of the hypothesis that sentences are structured. First, if we do not assume that sentences are structured—that words are grouped into *constituents*—then we cannot account for the fact that a sentence consisting of a set of unambiguous words can nevertheless be ambiguous. Second, it is impossible to state certain grammatical rules (such as the Question Rule for English) without appealing to constituent structure. Not only can we say that sentences are indeed structured, but we can also indicate (at least partially) how they must be structured. That is, we have found at least three important aspects of sentence structure:

(43)
a. The *linear order* of words in a sentence
b. The categorization of words into *parts of speech*
c. The grouping of words into *structural constituents* of the sentence

These three types of structural information can be encoded into what is called a *tree diagram* (or *phrase marker*) of the sort illustrated in tree 5.1.

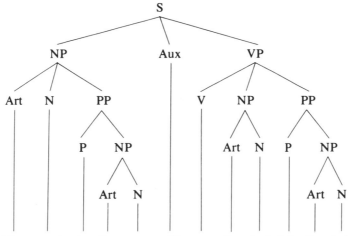

Symbols used: S—sentence; NP—noun phrase; Aux—auxiliary verb; VP—verb phrase; PP—prepositional phrase; Art—article; N—noun; V—verb; P—preposition.

Tree 5.1

Consider the structure in tree 5.1. Such tree diagrams can at first seem quite complicated. But in fact they represent in a simple and straightforward way the kinds of structural information summarized in (43). The trick is learning how to read them (and reading them is an important part of doing syntax). Let's begin by reading tree 5.1, in a step-by-step fashion, to see how it represents the structural information that we have been talking about. Learning how to decode this particular tree will give us an idea about how to read tree diagrams in general.

Tree 5.1 represents the structure of the sentence *The people in the room will move the desk into the hall*. Beginning at the bottom of the tree, note that each word of the sentence is connected by a line—called a *branch* of the tree—to a certain symbol of the tree:

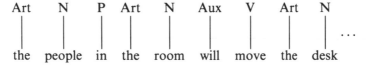

In this way, each word of the sentence is assigned to a certain *lexical category* (part of speech). Thus, the word *the* is connected by a branch to the symbol *Art*, standing for *Article*, indicating that *the* is an article. The word *people* is connected by a branch to the symbol *N*, standing for *Noun*, indicating that *people* is a noun. The word *in* is connected by a branch to the symbol *P*, standing for *Preposition*, indicating that *in* is a preposition. Shifting over to the right, the word *move* is connected by a branch to the symbol *V*, standing for *Verb*, indicating that *move* is a verb. In a similar fashion, all the words of the sentence are connected by branches to appropriate symbols indicating their lexical category. Notice that the words, as well as the lexical category symbols *Art*, *N*, *P*, and so on, are all shown in a specific *linear order* (reading the tree from left to right). Thus, tree 5.1 represents the information cited in (43a) and (43b): the *linear order* of words, and the *categorization* of words into parts of speech.

Now, how do tree diagrams represent *structural constituents* of a sentence? To see this, we will move up the tree a bit, focusing on the subject phrase, *the people in the room*. Notice that this string of words is shown as having a certain constituent structure. For example, the sequence of words *the room* is shown as a *noun phrase* (NP); that is, the symbols *Art* and *N* are connected by branches to the symbol *NP*:

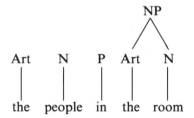

Both *Art* and *N* are connected by branches to the *same* symbol, *NP*; hence, *Art* and *N* form a *single constituent*. The noun phrase *the room* and the preposition *in* are shown as forming a prepositional phrase (*PP*); that is, the symbols *P* (*in*) and *NP* (*the room*) are both connected by branches to the symbol *PP*:

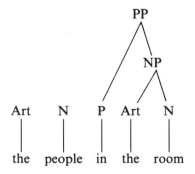

Both *P* and *NP* are connected by branches to the *same* symbol *PP*; hence, *P* and *NP* form a single constituent. Thus far, then, in tree 5.1 the sequence of words *the room* is a single constituent—a noun phrase (*NP*)—and the sequence of words *in the room* is a single constituent—a prepositional phrase (*PP*).

Finally, let us consider the sequence of words *the people*. This phrase is structurally similar to the phrase *the room*: it consists of an article followed by a noun, thus forming a noun phrase:

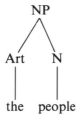

But noun phrases do not only consist of articles followed by nouns. Sometimes the noun in a noun phrase can be followed by a "modifying phrase." For example, in the phrase *the people in the room*, the prepositional phrase *in the room* is a modifying phrase: that is, it provides *additional information* about the noun *people*. To put it simply, when we use the phrase *the people in the room*, we are not talking about any random group of people; rather, we are talking about the people who are *in the room*, and in this sense the modifying phrase *in the room* provides "additional" information about the people. In tree 5.1 this modifying prepositional phrase is shown as part of the subject noun phrase:

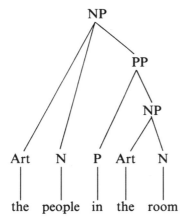

The article *the*, the noun *people*, and the prepositional phrase *in the room* are all connected by branches to the *same* symbol *NP*; hence, *Art*, *N*, and

PP all form a *single constituent*, which functions as the subject of the sentence, *The people in the room will move the desk into the hall.*

Let us now turn to the verb phrase (*VP*) of tree 5.1. The symbols *V* (*move*), *NP* (*the desk*), and *PP* (*into the hall*) are all connected by branches to the *same* symbol, *VP*; this means that the sequence *V-NP-PP* forms a single constituent—namely, the verb phrase *move the desk into the hall.* Finally, moving up to the highest level of the tree, the subject *NP* (*the people in the room*), the auxiliary verb *will* (symbolized as *Aux*), and the *VP* are all connected by branches to the same symbol, *S* (standing for *Sentence*); hence, the sequence *NP-Aux-VP* forms a single constituent, namely, a *Sentence*. A tree diagram represents syntactic constituent structure in terms of the particular way that its lines branch. The particular points in a tree that are connected by branches to other points are called *nodes* of the tree, and these nodes are labeled with specific symbols such as *S*, *NP*, *Aux*, *VP*, *V*, *N*, *Art*, and *P*. Particular labeled nodes represent single constituents, made up of the items connected to them by branching lines.

In section 5.3 we will discuss how tree diagrams can be *generated* by a type of rule. For the time being, however, it is sufficient merely to know how to read a tree diagram, without worrying yet where the tree "comes from." In decoding tree diagrams, notice that you can start from the top and work your way "down," to see how larger constituents are *broken down* into their constituent parts. For example, in tree 5.1 you can start at the top, *S*, and trace the branches down from *S* to see what constituents *S* is broken down into (and so on, for other phrases). Or you can start from the bottom of a tree and work your way "up," to see how individual words make up smaller constituents, and how smaller constituents make up larger ones, as we did in our earlier discussion. In any event, with practice you will find that reading tree diagrams becomes quite easy.

Tree 5.1 in effect encodes the important structural properties of a sentence. As we have seen, the various parts of the sentence are shown in a fixed linear order. Each word is assigned a part of speech: Art, N, P, and so on. And different elements in the sentence are shown as being grouped into successively larger constituents of the sentence: NP, Aux, and VP make up a sentence (S); V, NP, and PP make up a verb phrase (VP); and so on. What is important about this diagram is the information that it encodes, and we must note that the same information could be encoded in other (equivalent) ways. For example, the syntactic constituent structure of phrases and sentences can also be represented in terms of "box diagrams" of the sort illustrated in figure 5.1. This particular box diagram provides a structural analysis of the phrase *the people in the room*: (1) the words are

NOUN PHRASE				
Article	Noun	Prepositional Phrase		
		Preposition	Noun Phrase	
			Article	Noun
the	people	in	the	room

Figure 5.1
Constituent structure represented by box diagram

represented in a linear order; (2) each word is assigned to a part-of-speech category; and (3) a hierarchical grouping is defined (the diagram indicates that a Noun Phrase can consist of an Article followed by a Noun followed by a Prepositional Phrase, which in turn consists of a Preposition followed by a Noun Phrase, and so on). In effect, then, the box diagram of figure 5.1 encodes the same information as the tree structure in tree 5.1 with respect to the subject noun phrase *the people in the room*. In the tree, structural grouping is indicated by branching of the lines, rather than by levels in a box. Even though box diagrams might adequately represent constituent structure information for our purposes at this point, we will continue to represent syntactic structure by means of tree diagrams, since in the theory of syntax we are adopting in this chapter—the theory known as *transformational grammar*, developed by the linguist Noam Chomsky (see references)—transformational rules are traditionally defined as operating on tree structures. For present purposes, the point is that the same structural information can be encoded in a number of equivalent ways.

The same type of arbitrariness holds for the symbols we have chosen; although we have used the traditional names for the parts of speech, any system of labeling that made the same distinctions would be just as good for our purposes. Hence, we could call articles *Class 1 words*, nouns *Class 2 words*, and so on. As long as the right distinctions were made and similar words were assigned to similar categories, this system of naming parts of speech would be perfectly adequate.

Constituent Structure Tests: Using Rules, Clefts, and Conjunction

At this point, a natural question arises: namely, what evidence do we use to arrive at particular tree diagrams such as tree 5.1? How do we know that the sentence represented by that tree is structured as we have shown it? The answer is that tree diagrams represent hypotheses in our theory of syntax and are motivated by empirical evidence.

One of the ways in which we arrive at a particular formulation of a phrase marker (tree diagram) is to use certain *constituent structure tests*. Such tests usually involve stating a grammatical rule of the language, and then formulating the phrase marker (tree) in such a way as to allow the grammatical rule to be stated as simply as possible. For illustration, let us return to tree 5.1. We have good reasons for supposing that the phrase *the people in the room* forms a single NP constituent and is not merely an unstructured string of words. One important reason (but by no means the only one) is that if we represent this set of words as a single NP constituent, we can state the Question Rule in the simplest possible way: we can say simply that the auxiliary verb is to be moved to the left of the subject NP constituent of the sentence, and not, for instance, that the auxiliary verb should be moved to the left of the string of words *the people in the room*. More to the point, however, recall that since there is no limit on the length of the subject of a sentence (see example (36)), it is impossible to state the Question Rule in terms of the linear string of words that make up a subject: we would never be able to exhaustively list all the strings of words that could make up the subject of a sentence. Hence, we are forced to postulate an NP constituent as the subject of a sentence.

In the foregoing discussion, we have used the Question Rule in a constituent structure test. Since grammatical rules (such as the Question Rule) are stated in terms of tree structures, we formulate these structures in such a way as to allow the simplest statement of the rules. In a certain sense, then, grammatical rules of a language tell us what the tree structures ought to look like, and for this reason we can use such rules as constituent structure tests.

Cleft Sentences

In addition to using relationships between sentence types (such as declaratives and interrogatives) as constituent structure tests, we can also use certain *sentence frames*. For example, English has a construction referred to as the *cleft sentence*, with the following general form:

(44)
Cleft sentence

It $\left\{ \begin{matrix} \text{is} \\ \text{was} \end{matrix} \right\}$ X that Y

That is, cleft sentences consist of *it* followed by some form of the verb *to be*, followed by some constituent *X*, followed by a clause introduced by *that* from which *X* has been "extracted":

(45)

a. It was *the burglar* that broke the lamp.
b. It is *Mary* that I want to meet.
c. It was *under the mattress* that we found the money.
d. It is *at three o'clock in the afternoon* that they change guards.

In these examples, *X* is respectively *the burglar, Mary, under the mattress,* and *at three o'clock in the afternoon,* and *Y* is *broke the lamp, I want to meet, we found the money,* and *they change guards.*

An important fact about cleft sentences in English is that the phrase that fits into position *X* of the frame [*It is/was X that ...*] is always (1) a single constituent and (2) either a noun phrase (NP) or a prepositional phrase (PP). Sentences (45a–b) have NPs in position *X* of the cleft frame; (45c–d) have PPs in that position.

Returning to tree 5.1, we can use the cleft test to determine certain aspects of its constituent structure. Consider the sequences of words *the desk* and *into the hall.* In tree 5.1 *the desk* is shown as a single NP constituent, and *into the hall* is shown as a single PP constituent. Is there any corroborating evidence for this? We can test the validity of the tree by inserting those two phrases into position *X* of appropriate cleft sentences:

(46)

a. It is *the desk* that the people will move into the hall.
b. It is *into the hall* that the people will move the desk.

Given what we have seen about cleft sentences, (46a) confirms that the phrase *the desk* is a single constituent (an NP) and (46b) confirms that the phrase *into the hall* is a single constituent (a PP). Tree 5.1 accurately reflects this constituent structure by representing *the desk* as an NP and *into the hall* as a PP.

Continuing with tree 5.1, can we determine whether or not the sequence *the desk into the hall* is a single NP (or PP) constituent? The cleft test can help us here:

(47)

*It is *the desk into the hall* that the people will move.

Sentence (47) is ungrammatical. If the sequence *the desk into the hall* were a single NP constituent, then it would be able to occur in position *X* of the cleft frame [*It is X that* ...]. But it cannot, suggesting that this sequence is not a single constituent. Tree 5.1 reflects this property accurately, by representing *the desk* and *into the hall* as two distinct constituents. Those two constituents do not, in themselves, make up another constituent (however, note that those two constituents *along with* the verb *move* make up a verb phrase constituent). Hence, tree 5.1 assigns a constituent structure in which *move the desk into the hall* is a single constituent (VP) and the three phrases *move* (V), *the desk* (NP), and *into the hall* (PP) are each single constituents, but the sequence *the desk into the hall* is not a single NP constituent. Thus, the constituent structure represented by the tree seems consistent with what we know about the sentence so far.

Conjunction

Another test frame that has been used in linguistic analysis is the *conjunction* test. The assumption underlying this test is that only single constituents of the same type can occur in the frame [____ and ____] (that is, only single constituents of the same type can be conjoined with *and*):

(48)
a. *The teacher* and *the student* argued. (NP and NP)
b. Mary *played the harmonica* and *danced a jig*. (VP and VP)
c. We moved the desk *through the door* and *into the hall*. (PP and PP)

These examples include conjoined noun phases (*the teacher* and *the student*), conjoined verb phrases (*played the harmonica* and *danced a jig*), and conjoined prepositional phrases (*through the door* and *into the hall*). Such examples have been used to show that the conjunction *and* is used to conjoin two constituents of the same type. Indeed, when we attempt to conjoin two constituents not of the same type, a decidedly odd sentence results:

(49)
a. Sandy expects *to leave town*. (*to leave town* = VP)
b. Sandy expects *a good time*. (*a good time* = NP)
c. *Sandy expects *to leave town* and *a good time*.

In (49c) we have conjoined a verb phrase with a noun phrase, and the sentence is clearly much less acceptable than any of those in (48). On the basis of the conjunction test, we can establish in English such constituents as NP, PP, and VP: these are all types of expressions that can be conjoined with *and*. Given such a test for constituency, we can assume that structures such as tree 5.1 represent typical constituent structures of English.

Tree 5.2

There are other aspects of the structure shown in tree 5.1 for which we have presented little or no evidence. For example, we represent the auxiliary verb *will* as a constituent outside the verb phrase. But another logical possibility is to consider the constituent Aux to be part of the verb phrase, as in tree 5.2. This structure may or may not be more adequate than the structure shown in tree 5.1. We have not considered evidence here to support one version over another. It is important to be aware that although the gross outline of the structure shown in tree 5.1 is probably correct, many fine details of the structure are, for the moment, left undetermined.

We could devote a great deal of space to attempting to justify the various features of the structure shown in tree 5.1; indeed, much work in syntax has been concerned with this sort of issue. Nonetheless, this structure provides a rough illustration of the general sort of structural diagrams used in current syntactic work, and that will suffice for our purposes at the moment. Let us turn now to certain important ideas about phrase markers in general.

Grammatical Relations

We have already alluded to the distinction between *structural concepts* such as noun phrase (NP) and *grammatical relations* such as subject and object. This distinction reflects the fact that we can ask two questions about any given phrase: (1) What is its *internal structure*? (2) How does it *function* grammatically within a sentence? Diagrams such as tree 5.1 can also be used to give a structural definition of the grammatical relations *subject* and *object*. In English, the *subject* of a sentence can be structurally defined as the particular NP in the structural configuration that is immediately dominated by S and precedes Aux VP, as illustrated in tree 5.3. The *object* of a main verb can be structurally defined as the NP in the structural configuration that is immediately dominated by VP, as shown in tree 5.4.

Trees 5.3 and 5.4 illustrate that the same structural constituent in a sentence can have distinct relational functions. For example, take the phrase *the people in the room*. Structurally, this phrase is an NP, but this NP can function in different ways in different sentences. In tree 5.1 the NP

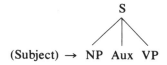

Tree 5.3

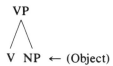

Tree 5.4

the people in the room functions as the subject of the sentence. However, in sentence (50) this same NP functions as the object of the main verb:

(50)
The police arrested *the people in the room*.

Hence, the phrase *the people in the room* is structurally an NP and only an NP; but relationally this phrase can be either a subject or an object, depending on its position in the structure of a particular sentence.

The distinction between structural and relational concepts is crucial in determining the meaning of a sentence, as illustrated by the fact that the sentences represented by trees 5.5 and 5.6 have exactly the same structural NP constituents, but those structural constituents have quite different grammatical relations in the two sentences. (Following a common practice, we have used triangles in trees 5.5 and 5.6 to simplify the representation of the internal structure of the NPs.) These two sentences mean different things, and these different meanings result from the fact that the subject in one tree diagram is the object in the other tree diagram.

So far, then, we have isolated the following structural properties and grammatical relations, and we have shown how these can be represented in, or defined on, tree diagrams:

(51)
Structural properties
a. The linear order of elements
b. The labeling of elements according to lexical categories (parts of speech)
c. The grouping of elements into structural constituents (phrases)

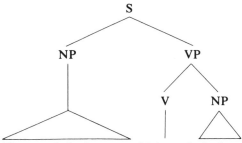

The people in the room frightened the boy

Tree 5.5

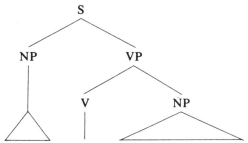

The boy frightened the people in the room

Tree 5.6

(52)
Grammatical relations
a. Subject (structural configuration given in tree 5.3)
b. Object (structural configuration given in tree 5.4)

Tree Diagrams and Structural Ambiguity

So far we have seen that tree diagrams (phrase markers) can represent a certain variety of structural and relational concepts. Now we must turn to the question of whether tree diagrams can be used to explain other important linguistic phenomena. To address this issue, let us recall the ambiguous sentence (4a), repeated here as (53):

(53)
The mother of the boy and the girl will arrive soon.

In a theory of syntax using phrase markers to represent syntactic structure, the explanation of the phenomenon of structural ambiguity is straightforward: whereas an unambiguous sentence is associated with just one

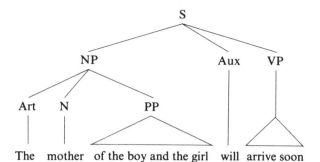

Tree 5.7

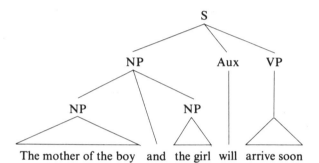

Tree 5.8

basic phrase marker, a structurally ambiguous sentence is associated with more than one basic phrase marker. For example, sentence (53) would be assigned two phrase markers, which we could formulate as trees 5.7 and 5.8.

As before, we have simplified the structure in the diagrams by using triangles for certain phrases rather than indicating the internal structure of those phrases. But these trees suffice to show the difference in structure that we postulate for the two phrase markers associated with sentence (53). In tree 5.7 the "head" noun of the subject, *mother*, is modified by a prepositional phrase that has a conjoined noun phrase in it: *of the boy and the girl*. In tree 5.8, on the other hand, the subject noun phrase is itself a conjoined noun phrase: *the mother of the boy* followed by *the girl*. We see, then, that a system of representation using phrase markers allows us to account for structurally ambiguous sentences by assigning more than one phrase marker to each ambiguous sentence. In this way the system of tree diagrams can be used to describe instances of ambiguity that are not lexical.

Discontinuous Dependencies

A natural assumption to make about phrase markers is that each sentence of a language is assigned exactly one phrase marker, except for those sentences that are structurally ambiguous. In the latter case, as we have seen, we assign more than one phrase marker—one for each particular meaning of the sentence, roughly speaking. But now let us examine some sentences that are not structurally ambiguous in the sense in which we have been using that term, but that nevertheless display interesting structural properties. Consider the following pair of sentences:

(54)
a. Mary stood up her date.
b. Mary stood her date up.

These sentences illustrate what is known as the *verb + particle construction* in English—in this particular case, the verb + particle construction *stand up* (where *stand* is the verb and *up* is the particle. *Stand up* is also referred to as a *phrasal verb* (see Radford 1988)). The interesting feature of this construction is that the particle can occur separated from its verb, as in (54b). Indeed, in many cases English speakers prefer the version in which the particle is separated from the verb:

(55)
a. ?John threw *down* it. (OK in British English)
b. John threw it *down*.

(56)
a. ?Mary called *up* him. (OK in British English)
b. Mary called him *up*.

It is natural to suppose that *stood up* is a single constituent in sentence (54a). For one thing, we have used the phrase *stood up* in its idiomatic sense, synonymous with *broke a social engagement without warning*, and we have ignored the other meaning synonymous with *propped up*. In its idiomatic sense the combination *stood up* has a single meaning that is not associated with the literal meaning of *stood* and *up* in isolation. A good guess at the structure of (54a) would be that shown in tree 5.9.

Now, what phrase marker would we assign to (54b)? The most obvious candidate, in terms of what we have done so far, would be tree 5.10. Because the particle *up* comes last in the linear order of words in (54b), we place it at the end of the VP in tree 5.10. (Keep in mind that we could just as easily place the particle at the end directly attached by a branch to S

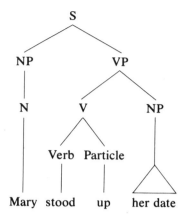

Tree 5.9

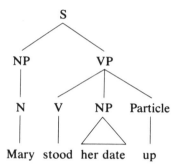

Tree 5.10

rather than to VP—again, we have not looked at any evidence for choosing between these two structures.)

Tree 5.10, though accurate in representing the linear order of words, is nonetheless inadequate in other ways. Given the idiomatic use of *stood up* in *Mary stood her date up*, we know that the particle *up* goes with the verb *stand*: even though the particle is separated from the verb, it is nevertheless the case in this sentence, as in (54a), that neither the verb nor the particle has the literal meaning it would have in isolation; it is still the combination of the two items that determines the single meaning. English speakers feel that *stand up* is a verb (albeit a complex one) analogous to *run*, *avoid*, and so forth. Yet tree 5.10 does not represent this affinity between verb and particle in any way; it gives no indication whatever that *up* is associated with *stood*. Whenever a single constituent of a sentence is broken up in this

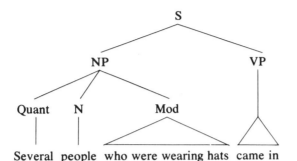

Tree 5.11

way, we say that we have a *discontinuous constituent* or, more generally, a *discontinuous dependency*. It turns out that phrase markers, though very useful for representing certain kinds of information about sentences, do not adequately represent discontinuous dependencies.

For another illustration of the same kind of phenomenon, consider a sentence whose subject contains a modifier:

(57)
Several people *who were wearing hats* came in.

In this case a phrase, *who were wearing hats*, known as a modifying *clause*, serves to supply additional information about the head noun, *several people*. We would assign this sentence a phrase marker such as tree 5.11. (Here the symbol *Mod* indicates a modifying clause; the symbol *Quant* stands for *Quantifier*, the grammatical category that includes words such as *several*, *many*, *few*, and *all*.)

In English there is a rather general grammatical process known as *extraposition*, whereby modifying clauses (and other types of clauses that need not concern us) can be shifted to the end of the sentence. Therefore, sentence (57) also has the following version:

(58)
Several people came in *who were wearing hats*.

This sentence is likely structured as shown in tree 5.12. This diagram correctly indicates that the linear position of the modifying clause is at the end of the sentence. However, it completely fails to show that the modifying clause goes with the subject NP, *several people*. It does not indicate in any way that *who were wearing hats* in fact modifies *several people*. In contrast, in tree 5.11 the head noun (*several people*) and modifying clause (*who were*

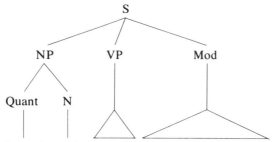

Tree 5.12

wearing hats) are shown as part of a single syntactic constituent, indicating that the head noun and the modifier are related. It is not possible to show the relation between the two in tree 5.12, however, because the head noun and the modifier are separated by the verb phrase (*came in*). Consequently, this is another case of a discontinuous dependency, and this dependency is not represented in any way by tree 5.12.

It turns out that discontinuous dependencies are quite common in human language; in fact, such dependencies can be much more complex than we have seen so far. To take just one example, note that the two processes just examined—separation of the verb particle and extraposition of the modifying clause—can interact in the same sentence. Consider (59):

(59)
She stood up all those men who had offered her diamonds.

Recall that the particle *up* can be shifted to the end of the verb phrase:

(60)
She stood ＿＿ all those men who had offered her diamonds up.

This produces an awkward sentence that is difficult to understand: the particle and verb are separated by a constituent that is quite long. But, since modifying clauses can be extraposed in English, we can extrapose the clause here to produce the following perfectly natural sentence:

(61)
She stood all those men ＿＿ up who had offered her diamonds.

In this example the dependencies actually "cross" each other, as illustrated in the final line of figure 5.2. As we see, *up* goes with *stood*, and *who had offered her diamonds* goes with *all those men*; both constituents are broken

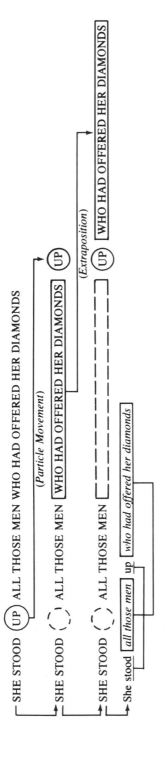

Figure 5.2
Crossing dependencies in Particle Movement and Extraposition

up in such a way that parts of one constituent intervene between parts of the other (in particular, *up* occurs between *all those men* and its modifying clause). This is a striking example of how sentences of natural language exhibit discontinuous dependencies that may even be "interwoven."

Transformational Rules as an Account of Discontinuous Dependencies

The examples we have been discussing show that some properties of sentences in natural language cannot be accounted for in terms of single phrase markers alone, that is, in terms of relations between contiguous words. It turns out that we need to account for relations between items in a sentence that are connected (in some sense), dependent, or related, but that are nonetheless not contiguous in the linear order of words. One way to account for discontinuous dependencies of this sort is to devise a means by which two or more phrase markers can themselves be related to each other in a special way. In this case two (or more) sentences (that is, two (or more) different phrase markers) need to be related to one another (an interesting contrast to the case of structural ambiguity, in which a single sentence has two (or more) different phrase markers, each corresponding to a different meaning). Relating phrase markers to one another is in fact a fundamental insight of the theory of transformational grammar.

As an illustration, consider again the pair of sentences in (54), repeated here as (62):

(62)
a. Mary stood up her date.
b. Mary stood her date up.

We will assume as before that sentence (62a) is assigned a single phrase marker, shown as tree 5.9. But what about sentence (62b)? This is the sentence with the discontinuous constituent, *stood ... up*. In order to express the dependency between *stood* and *up* in (62b), let us suppose that this sentence derives from the same phrase marker as (62a), shown as the *input tree* in figure 5.3. Call this the *input structure* or *base structure* for sentence (62b), *Mary stood her date up*.

Now we postulate a structural operation known as a *transformational rule* (or *transformation*), which we can state informally as follows:

(63)
Particle Movement
Given a verb + particle construction, the particle may be shifted away from the verb, moved immediately to the right of the object noun

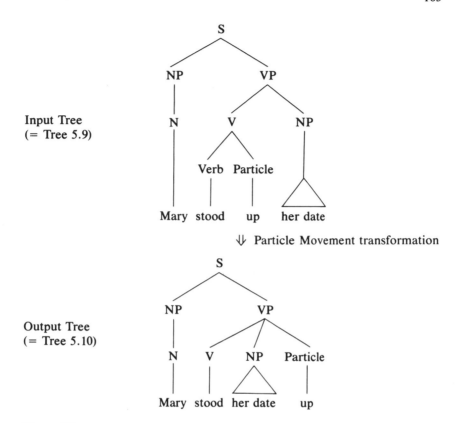

Figure 5.3
Input and output of the Particle Movement transformation

phrase, and made a sister to that noun phrase. (This movement is obligatory when the object noun phrase is a pronoun.)

Transformational rules are operations on tree structures that convert an *input* tree structure (or *base* structure) into an *output* tree structure (or *derived* structure). The operation of the Particle Movement transformation is illustrated in figure 5.3. The output structure in figure 5.3 corresponds to what is called the *surface structure* of sentence (62b); that is, this output phrase marker correctly represents the actually occurring word order and structure for the elements of sentence (62b).

We now have a way of accounting for discontinuous dependencies. The output tree in figure 5.3 is the correct surface phrase marker for the sentence *Mary stood her date up*: the particle is correctly represented as following the object NP. Nevertheless, we can account for the dependency between

the particle and the verb because we are claiming that the output tree
derives from the input tree in figure 5.3, and in that base phrase marker
the verb and its particle are in fact contiguous and form a single constituent.
Thus, the base (or "underlying") structure of the sentence shows the basic
constituency of the verb and its particle, but the surface structure of the
sentence correctly shows the particle as separated from its verb.

Now let us consider another case, involving the other discontinuous
dependency discussed earlier: extraposition of a modifying clause. Once
again, consider pairs of sentences such as (64a–b):

(64)
a. Several people who were wearing hats came in.
b. Several people came in who were wearing hats.

As before, we would assign to sentence (64a) the phrase marker 5.11
(shown as the input tree in figure 5.4). This phrase marker accurately
represents the word order and structure of the elements of sentence (64a).

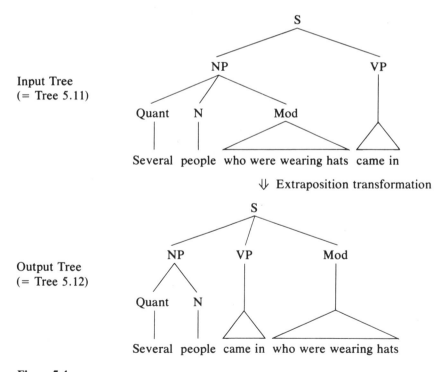

Figure 5.4
Input and output of the Extraposition transformation

But what about sentence (64b)? This is the sentence containing the discontinuous constituent *several people . . . who were wearing hats*. We will account for this sentence in a manner parallel to the case of particle movement, namely, by postulating that sentence (64b) derives from the base structure given as the input tree in figure 5.4. In that input structure, then, the head noun and the modifying clause form a single constituent. We will now postulate the following transformational rule:

(65)

Extraposition
Given a noun phrase containing a head noun directly followed by a modifying clause, the modifying clause may be shifted out of the noun phrase to the end of the sentence.

As shown in figure 5.4, by applying this transformation to the input tree, we derive the output tree, which is the correct surface structure for the sentence *Several people came in who were wearing hats*.

We have been able to account for the discontinuous dependency between the modifying clause and the head noun in sentence (64b) by deriving that sentence from the input tree in figure 5.4, in which the discontinuous elements are actually represented as a single constituent. This is another example of a transformational account of a discontinuous dependency. The effect of the transformational rule of Extraposition, like that of Particle Movement, is to set up a relationship between phrase markers: it states, in effect, that for every phrase marker containing a noun phrase with a modifying clause directly following the head noun, there is a corresponding phrase marker in which that same modifying clause has been shifted to the end of the sentence. (Although this is not strictly true—in certain cases extraposition of the modifying clause is prohibited—it is nonetheless quite adequate for present purposes, and we need not add any refinements.)

The kind of analysis we have just looked at is illustrative of the transformational model of syntax. This general sort of model (including numerous variations) has dominated the field of syntax ever since the publication of Noam Chomsky's 1957 book *Syntactic Structures*, the first major work to propose the transformational approach (see Newmeyer 1980 for discussion). Even though the transformational analysis we have considered is one means of accounting for discontinuous dependencies, the question remains whether there is any reason to suppose it is the best means, or the most insightful means. It is difficult to answer this question in any definitive way, but it is possible to give additional evidence for the model that will illustrate its descriptive and explanatory power.

Interaction between Transformations

We have examined two cases in which a transformational analysis can account for discontinuities, but that in itself is not enough to indicate whether the transformational model is a particularly revealing account. It is time to look at some rather striking evidence for this model. It turns out that individual transformational rules, established for independent reasons, can in fact interact with each other to account for a complex array of surface data in a straightforward and simple fashion.

Consider tree 5.13. One function of this phrase marker is to accurately represent the surface structure of sentence (66):

(66)
She stood up all those men who had offered her diamonds.

However, tree 5.13 also functions in another way, that is, as an input structure from which we can derive another (surface) structure. Notice that this structure contains both a verb + particle construction and a complex noun phrase composed of a head noun and a modifying clause. Hence, this is a tree to which the Particle Movement transformation (63) may apply (see figure 5.5). If we apply Particle Movement to the top input tree in figure 5.5, we derive the output structure shown as the middle tree in that figure. The particle has been placed after the object noun phrase, as dictated by the rule. This derived structure is not yet a well-formed surface structure (recall the awkwardness and difficulty of the sentence *She stood all those men who had offered her diamonds up*). However, this output tree can, in turn, become a new input tree: we can now apply the Extraposition

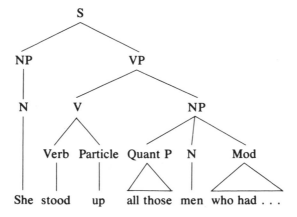

Tree 5.13

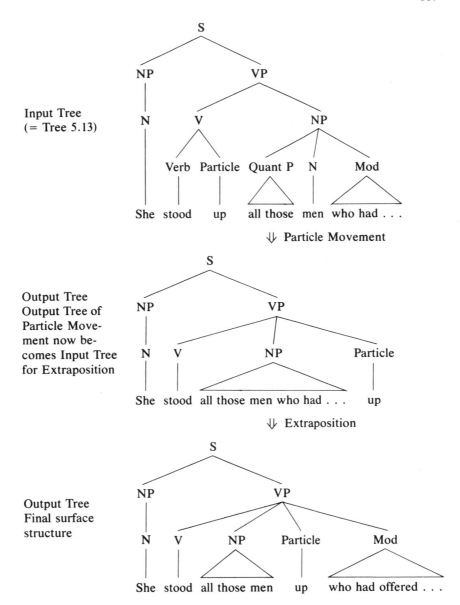

Figure 5.5
Interaction of Particle Movement and Extraposition transformations

transformation to yield yet another derived structure, namely, the bottom output tree shown in figure 5.5. We have now arrived at the final (surface) structure for the sentence *She stood all those men up who had offered her diamonds.* Recall that this sentence has two discontinuous dependencies, which actually "cross" each other, as shown in figure 5.2. Yet we can account for this complicated pattern of dependencies in a simple way: we have already postulated the Particle Movement and Extraposition transformations for independent reasons. If we simply allow both rules to apply in sequence, they will automatically interact as shown in figure 5.5. We can now specify precisely what elements of the bottom output tree are dependent upon each other, because we have claimed that it derives from the base structure shown at the top of figure 5.5, and that structure represents the surface discontinuities as underlying constituents.

The important point here, then, is this: individual transformations are postulated to account for certain dependencies; but even stronger evidence for the transformational model comes from the interaction of the independently established transformations. We have seen that the interaction of two transformations applying in sequence automatically leads to a simple account of a complex set of surface structure dependencies.

We began our investigation of syntactic structure by posing the questions, What is structure? and How do we know that sentences are structured? As we have seen, there is no simple answer to these questions nor any way to answer them without actually constructing a theory of syntax. We have provided a partial answer, though, by arriving at the conclusion that sentence structure involves both structural and relational aspects: specification of the linear order of words, classification of words into lexical categories (parts of speech), grouping of words into structural constituents, and assignment of grammatical relations to certain NPs in a sentence (such as the subject of the sentence). We did not arrive at this view for the sake of convenience, or because it was handed down to us by ancient grammatical authorities. Rather, we found it impossible to state some of the most fundamental syntactic processes of a language—such as how to form questions—without appealing to these properties. On further investigation we found that in order to account for discontinuous dependencies, we needed to postulate not just structural properties of sentences but structural relations between phrase markers as well. These relationships are stated in terms of formal rules (that is, transformational rules). In this way our view of what constitutes syntactic structure is very much determined by what phenomena we are trying to explain, and there is no doubt that theories of syntactic structure will become increasingly subtle and complex as syntactic theorists are faced with an ever-expanding range of new and heretofore unexplained data on the formal properties of sentences.

Finally, we should note that the constituent structure of sentences is not merely an artifact of syntactic theory; as we will see in chapter 10, there is reason to think that aspects of constituent structure have some reality in the minds of speakers.

5.3 A MORE FORMAL ACCOUNT OF SYNTACTIC THEORY

The type of transformational analysis sketched informally in section 5.2 has, in fact, been given a more precise and formal description by theorists working within the transformational framework. The references at the end of this chapter give a number of alternative accounts of the more formal theory (see Kimball 1973 and Wall 1972 for formalizations of "classical" transformational grammar). In this section we will provide only a brief description to give some idea of how transformational theory has been developed. It should be stressed that we will present here a description of some of the more basic features of standard, or classical, transformational theory, keeping in mind that at present many linguists are working on significant modifications and variations of these basic concepts (for discussion, see Newmeyer 1980, Radford 1988, Van Riemsdijk and Williams 1986, Horrocks 1987, Lasnik and Uriagereka 1988).

The Formal Statement of Transformations

Recall that a single phrase marker alone cannot account for a discontinuous dependency and that transformational rules are introduced into the theory in order to express syntactic relations between pairs of phrase markers. Transformational rules have been formalized in standard transformational theory; to illustrate the formalism used, we restate the Particle Movement transformation:

(67)
Particle Movement
Structural Description (SD): X – Verb – Particle – NP – Y
$$1 \quad 2 \quad 3 \quad 4 \quad 5$$
Structural Change (SC): $\quad 1 \quad 2 \quad \emptyset \quad 4+3 \quad 5$

A transformational rule consists, first, of an input: a *structural description* (SD), which is an instruction to analyze a phrase marker into a sequence of constituents (in this case Verb followed by Particle followed by NP).

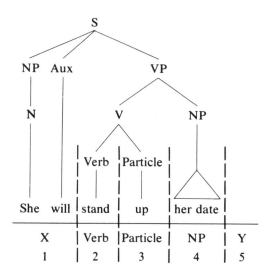

Tree 5.14

The variables X and Y indicate that the constituents to the left of the verb and to the right of the NP (should there be any) are irrelevant to this transformation—they can represent anything at all. In order for a transformation to be applied, the analysis of a phrase marker must *satisfy* the structural description of the particular transformation. As we can see, tree 5.14 can be analyzed—that is, can be cut up into chunks—in a way that matches exactly the sequence of constituents listed in the structural description of the Particle Movement transformation. Hence, this phrase marker satisfies the SD of the rule.

The second part of the transformational rule is the output: a *structural change* (SC), which in the case of Particle Movement is an instruction to modify the structural description by shifting term 3 (the particle) immediately to the right of term 4 (NP), as illustrated in tree 5.15. The particle (term 3) has correctly been placed immediately after the NP (term 4), and the plus sign (+) between them in the SC indicates that these two constituents are to be *sisters*; that is, they are to be daughters of the same node (in this case, VP). The symbol $\emptyset$ ("zero") indicates that nothing remains in the slot where the particle had been and marks the spot from which the particle was moved.

We can provide independent evidence that the particle is a daughter of the VP and not, say, of the S. Consider example (68):

(68)
Mary stood up her date yesterday.

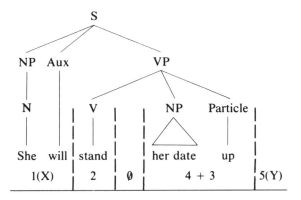

Tree 5.15

Yesterday is an adverbial of time that is a daughter of the VP. Now consider the examples in (69):

(69)
a.   Mary stood her date up yesterday.
b. *Mary stood her date yesterday up.

If the particle were a daughter of the S-node, then (69b) would be acceptable. This is so because the adverb *yesterday* would be a constituent of the VP, and any daughter of the S-node following the VP would naturally follow all the daughters of the VP. However, (69b) is definitely unacceptable, supporting the claim reflected in the Particle Movement transformation (67) that the particle becomes a sister to the NP-object (that is, a daughter of the VP).

There are many other details of transformational formalism that we cannot go into here; for these, see the works listed at the end of the chapter.

Phrase Structure Grammars

Within the standard transformational model it is assumed that basic phrase markers are generated by *phrase structure rules* (PS rules) of the following sort:

(70)
a. S   →   NP Aux VP
b. NP →   Art N
c. VP   →   V NP

Each rule is essentially a formula, or specification, for how the constituent

Tree 5.16

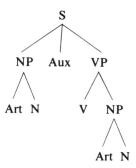

Tree 5.17

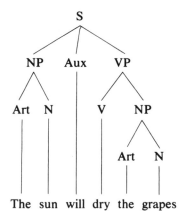

Tree 5.18

represented by a certain symbol—the symbol on the left of the arrow—can be constituted in a tree diagram. For example, PS rule (70a) tells us that S (sentence) can *consist of*, or can be *expanded as*, the sequence NP Aux VP. This is shown in tree form as tree 5.16. The rules also tell us that NP (noun phrase) can be expanded as Art N and that VP (verb phrase) can be expanded as V NP. These expansions are illustrated in tree 5.17. By inserting appropriate words, we derive a structure like tree 5.18.

As noted earlier, each labeled point in a tree is referred to as a *node*; thus, tree 5.18 includes an S-node, an NP-node, an Aux-node, a VP-node, and so on. We say that the node S *dominates* the nodes NP, Aux, and VP; the node NP *dominates* the nodes Art and N; the node VP *dominates* the nodes V and NP; and so on. We also use a certain type of genealogical terminology when discussing the relationships between nodes in a tree. For example, the nodes NP, Aux, and VP in tree 5.18 are referred to as the *daughter nodes* of the node S, which is the *mother node*. Hence, NP, Aux, and VP are *sister nodes* with respect to each other. Notice that the NP-node *the sun* and the V-node *dry* are not sisters, because the NP is a daughter node of S, whereas the V is a daughter node of VP. In other words, sister nodes must be daughters of the same mother node. (We should note, in passing, that linguistic convention has settled on the mother/daughter/sister terminology, and thus we do not speak of father nodes, brother nodes, and so on.)

Returning to tree 5.17, how do we know what words to insert into that structure? We will assume that part of our grammar consists of a *lexicon*, that is, a list of words of a language. In the lexicon, words are listed with their parts of speech: for example, *the* is listed as an *article*, *sun* is listed as a *noun*, *will* is listed as an *auxiliary verb*, *dry* is listed as a *verb*, and so on. Given a tree such as tree 5.17, we can insert the word *the* under the node Art, the word *sun* under the node N, the word *will* under the node Aux, the word *dry* under the node V, and so on, as shown in tree 5.18. We could not, for example, insert the word *the* under the node V, because *the* is an article, and not a verb.

It is not the case that every noun phrase of English must contain an article, nor is it the case that every verb phrase must contain an object NP. We say that these are *optional constituents*, and we indicate this by placing them within parentheses:

(71)
a. S → NP Aux VP
b. NP → (Art) N
c. VP → V (NP)

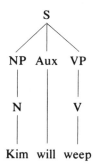

Tree 5.19

Items in parentheses *may* be chosen in generating a tree structure; the other items *must* be chosen if a structure is to be well formed. Actually, (71b–c) collapse two rules each. The uncollapsed versions are as in (72) and (73):

(72)
NP → (Art) N
a. NP → N
b. NP → Art N

(73)
VP → V (NP)
a. VP → V
b. VP → V NP

The rules in (71a–c) therefore allow us to form both structures like the one in tree 5.18 and structures like the one in tree 5.19.

As we have seen, noun phrases in English may contain various sorts of modifiers after the head noun (for instance, clauses, as in *the men who offered her diamonds*). We have seen that nouns can also be followed by prepositional phrases (PP) as modifiers:

(74)
a. the house *in the woods*
b. the weather *in England*
c. a portrait *of Mary*
d. the prospects *for peace*

In order to form such phrases—or *generate* them, to use the technical term—we can modify our PS rule for NPs as follows:

(75)
NP → (Art) N (PP)

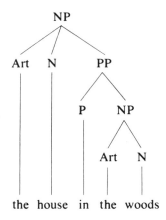

Tree 5.20

Rule (75) collapses the following rules:

(76)

	Rule			*Example*
a.	NP	→	N	*Mary* in *Mary is nice.*
b.	NP	→	Art N	*the boy* in *The boy is nice.*
c.	NP	→	N PP	*water in the basement* in *Water in the basement is a bad sign.*
d.	NP	→	Art N PP	*the boy on the swing* in *The boy on the swing fell.*

We now need to add a PS rule to expand prepositional phrases:

(77)

PP → P NP

This set of PS rules, called a *phrase structure grammar*, now generates NPs such as the one in tree 5.20.

Consider again the phrase structure rules in (71), in particular the rules for NP and VP. Notice that an NP must consist at least of an N, which forms the *head* of the NP; and a VP must consist at least of a V, which forms the *head* of the VP. A noun phrase is called a noun phrase because it has a noun as its head; and a verb phrase is called a verb phrase because it has a verb as its head. This has led to the suggestion that for each of the *lexical categories* N (noun), V (verb), A (adjective), and P (preposition), there is a corresponding *phrasal category* NP (noun phrase), VP (verb phrase), AP (adjective phrase), and PP (prepositional phrase). We have already seen how this works for NPs and VPs. What about PPs? Notice that in rule (77) PP is expanded as P NP; in fact, a prepositional phrase *must* contain a preposition, and we say that the preposition is the *head* of the prepositional phrase. (In our discussion, we have not touched on PS rules for adjective phrases (AP).) Generally speaking, then, if we let the symbol X stand for the lexical categories N, A, V, and P, and if we let the symbol XP stand for "phrase of the type X," then it seems that we can state a general formula for certain PS rules: $XP \to \ldots X \ldots$. This says that a phrase of the type X has a lexical category X as its head, and in this sense it seems that there is a regular relation between lexical categories and phrasal categories (see Radford 1988, chap. 3, and Van Riemsdijk and Williams 1986 for further discussion).

Embedding

An interesting consequence of rules (75) and (77) is that we can generate a potentially infinite number of noun phrases. This is because the PS rule for NP may be expanded to contain a PP, which in turn contains an NP, which itself may be expanded to contain a PP; and so on, indefinitely, as in tree 5.21. This is one of the ways in which a finite set of rules—in this case, the two rules (75) and (77)—can generate an infinite set of structures. PS grammars containing such pairs of rules that "feed" one another are said to be *recursive*.

Suppose that we now allow the rule for VP to include an optional symbol S following V:

(78)
VP   →   V (S)

If we allow such a rule, then the PS rule for S will contain a VP, and the PS rule for VP can contain an S:

(79)
a. S   →   NP Aux VP
b. VP   →   V (S)

This is another instance of recursion, as we can see by examining tree 5.22. Beginning on the very lowest level (on the far right) in this tree, notice the sentence, S, *Kim didn't leave*. This sentence is *embedded* in a VP of a larger sentence, *Bill will say Kim didn't leave*. That S in turn is embedded within the VP of an even larger sentence, *Pat may think Bill will say Kim didn't leave*. A sentence embedded within a larger sentence is referred to as an *embedded clause*, a *subordinate clause*, or just an *embedded sentence*. A

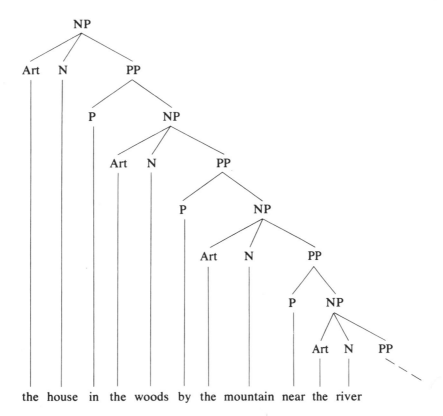

the house in the woods by the mountain near the river

Tree 5.21

sentence that contains an embedded clause is called a *matrix sentence*; in tree 5.22 the sentence *Kim didn't leave* is embedded within the matrix sentence that begins *Bill will...*, and the sentence *Bill will say Kim didn't leave* is embedded within the matrix sentence that begins *Pat may think....* The "highest" matrix sentence in tree 5.22 (*Pat may think...*) is referred to as the *main clause*. A sentence such as *Kim didn't leave* is referred to as a *simple sentence* because it contains no embedded sentences; a sentence such as *Bill will say Kim didn't leave* is referred to as a *complex sentence* because it contains a matrix sentence and an embedded sentence.

The pair of PS rules in (79) thus constitutes another example of recursion: sentences contain verb phrases, which in turn may contain sentences, which in turn contain verb phrases, and so on. Again, we see how a finite set of rules can generate an infinite number of sentences, and we now have an account for the kinds of examples discussed at the very beginning of this chapter.

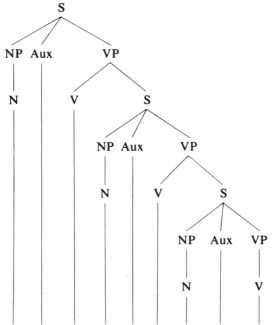

Tree 5.22

We now have the following two PS rules for VP, each of which collapses two rules:

(80)
VP → V (NP)
a. VP → V
b. VP → V NP

(81)
VP → V (S)
a. VP → V
b. VP → V S

Both rules allow for the possibility that the VP contains just a verb (V) (since the NP and S are optional); or the VP may contain a V followed by an NP; or it may contain a V followed by S. We can collapse rules (80) and (81) into a single rule using notation involving *braces*, {   }:

(82)

$$\text{VP} \quad \rightarrow \quad \text{V}\left(\left\{\begin{matrix} \text{NP} \\ \text{S} \end{matrix}\right\}\right)$$

This rule states that VP must contain at least a V, and that V may optionally be followed by *either* an NP *or* an S *or* nothing:

(83)

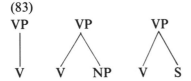

Thus, the parentheses notation, ( ), indicates optionality; the braces notation, { }, indicates an either-or choice.

Center Embedding

In tree 5.21, beginning at the lowest level (rightmost end), every prepositional phrase (PP) is on the extreme right branch of a noun phrase (NP), which is itself on the extreme right branch of some PP. Structures of this general sort are called *right branching*.

Now consider tree 5.23 (where the symbol *Poss* stands for *Possessive Phrase*). We could generate such a tree with the following PS rules:

(84)
a. NP   →   (Poss) N
b. Poss   →   NP Poss-Affix

These rules state that an NP may have an optional possessive phrase preceding the head noun. A possessive phrase consists of an NP followed by an Affix (in this case, '*s*). Tree 5.23 once again illustrates the property of recursion, in that an NP may contain a Poss, which in turn contains an NP, which in turn may contain a Poss, and so on. In tree 5.23, beginning at the lowest level (leftmost end), every possessive phrase (Poss) is on the extreme left branch of an NP that is itself on the extreme left branch of a Poss. Structures of this general sort are called *left branching*.

Phrases with right- or left-branching structures are relatively easy to comprehend, provided they are within memory limitations. In other words, the degree of right or left branching itself does not seem to lead to excessive difficulty in comprehension. Of course, if any given phrase becomes very long, we may well forget what was at the beginning of the phrase by the time we come to the end.

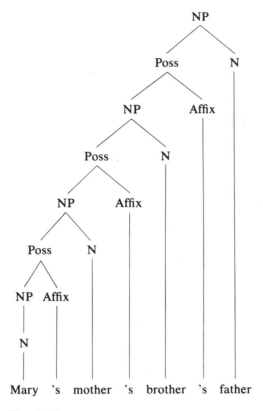

Tree 5.23

Linguists have also noted another class of phrases with a property known as *center embedding*, which can pose serious problems for sentence comprehension. Let's begin with the simple sentence *The rat ate the cheese*. Noun phrases such as *the rat* can be modified by clauses (as we have seen in examples of extraposition). In this case, we can modify the NP *the rat* with a clause such as *that the cat chased*, producing the sentence *The rat that the cat chased ate the cheese*. Given that noun phrases can be modified by clauses, there is nothing in principle to prevent us from modifying the noun phrase *the cat* with a clause such as *that the dog bit*:

(85)
The rat that the cat that the dog bit chased ate the cheese.

Notice that the sentence has become extremely difficult to comprehend. If we examine these sentences schematically, a pattern emerges:

(86)

a. The rat ate the cheese

b. The rat [that the the cat chased] ate the cheese

c. The rat [that the cat [that the dog bit] chased] ate the cheese

(86a) is a simple sentence, *The rat ate the cheese*. (86b) is an example of center embedding: that is, the modifying sentence *the cat chased* is embedded *within* the larger sentence *The rat ate the cheese*. With one level of center embedding, as in (86b), the sentence remains comprehensible. However, (86c) involves two center embeddings: the modifying sentence *the dog bit* is embedded within the matrix sentence *the cat chased*, which is in turn embedded within the main sentence *The rat ate the cheese*. We see that two (or more) levels of center embedding render the sentence extremely difficult to comprehend. It is not fully understood why center embedding causes such perceptual complexity (that is, not enough is known about the psychological mechanisms underlying our perceptual abilities); nevertheless, the perceptual difficulties posed by center embedding form an interesting feature of human language processing and comprehension.

5.4 SPECIAL TOPIC

Sentence Structure and Anaphora

In chapter 2 we investigated the morpheme *self*. Recall that *self* indicates when, say, the subject and the direct object are "linked" to the same entity (*John's self-abuse* means, roughly, "John's abuse of himself" or "John abuses himself"). This is an example of *morphological* anaphora, where the morpheme *self* signals when, for example, the subject and the object are associated with the same individual. We now turn to evidence that syntactic *structure* also makes a contribution to anaphora phenomena. Consider the following examples, where italicized expressions can refer to the same individual:

(87)

a. *Nicholas* left after *he* found the tricycle.
b. He left after Nicholas found the tricycle.
c. After *he* found the tricycle, *Nicholas* left.

In (87a) *Nicholas* and *he* can easily be understood as referring to the same person. This contrasts with (87b), where *he* and *Nicholas* are presumed to

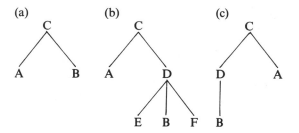

Figure 5.6
C-command configurations

be different people. One difference between (87a) and (87b) is the order of
the two noun phrases. In (87a) *Nicholas* precedes *he* and in (87b) *he*
precedes *Nicholas*. But does linear order account for the difference? (87c)
provides evidence that order cannot be the answer. In (87c) *he* precedes
Nicholas and yet they can be interpreted as referring to the same individual.

Even though the pronoun *he* precedes the noun phrase *Nicholas* in both
cases, only in (87b) does *he* appear "higher" in the tree than *Nicholas*.
Specifically, in (87b) the pronoun *c(onstituent)-commands* the noun, but
in (87c) it does not. C-command is defined as follows:

(88)
Node A c-commands node B if and only if the first branching node that
dominates A also dominates B (condition: A does not dominate B and
vice versa).

Consider the trees in figure 5.6. In figure 5.6a node A c-commands node
B (and vice versa) since the first branching node dominating A, which is
node C, also dominates B. In figure 5.6b A c-commands B because the first
branching node that dominates A (again C) also dominates B. But in this
case B does not c-command A. Why? Because the first branching node that
dominates B is D, and D does not dominate A. In figure 5.6c A and B bear
the same c-command relation to each other as they do in figure 5.6a. The
linear order is different but that is not what is important for c-command.
C-command is a relationship between nodes that is *structural* in nature. It
appears, then, that when a pronoun c-commands a nonpronoun noun
phrase, as is the case with *he* and *Nicholas* in (87c), the speaker is understood as intending to refer to different individuals. (In chapters 6 and 9 we
will consider whether this constraint is semantic or pragmatic in nature.)

More data confirm the importance of c-command in constraining the
interpretation of pronouns. (Examples (89) and (90) are from Postal 1971,
20, 24; again, italics indicate coreference.)

(89)

a. If *he* can, *John* will run.

b. *John* will run if *he* can.

(90)

a. The man who [investigated *him*] hates *Charley*.

b. The man who investigated *Charley* [hates *him*].

(91)

a. Mary told *John* about the woman who [admired *him*].

b. Mary told him about the woman who admired John.

In (89a–b) and (90a–b) the pronouns *he* and *him* do not c-command the nouns *John* and *Charley*. The first branching node in (89a–b) is an S that does not dominate *John*, and in (90a–b) the VP (indicated with brackets), which is the first branching node dominating *him*, does not dominate *Charley*. In (91a) the first branching node dominating *him* (the VP) does not dominate *John*; therefore, *him* does not c-command *John* and they can be understood as the same individual. However, in (91b) the pronoun *him* does c-command *John* because the first branching node dominating *him* is a VP that also dominates *John*—hence the interpretation that *him* and *John* are two different individuals.

The exact nature of the association of pronouns with expressions such as *Nicholas*, *John*, *Mary*, *Charley* is a topic of much current debate. Structure does indeed seem to play an important role here and we have, following one tradition (see Chomsky 1981, Reinhart 1983, and references cited there) captured this by stating the structural contribution in terms of the c-command relations between pairs of nodes.

Exercises

1. The following tree structures have been left incomplete, in the sense that no words have been filled in. For each structure, list an appropriate sentence that would fit the structure (that is, supply an appropriate word for each blank):

a.

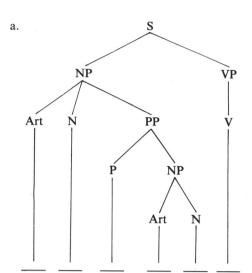

b.

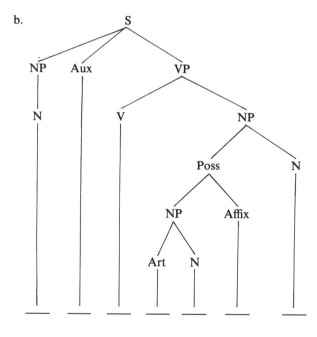

c.

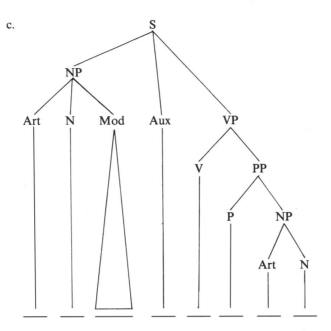

(For more practice with trees, see the exercises in *A Linguistics Workbook* entitled "Simple Phrase Structure Rules," "Simple NPs, VPs, and PPs," "Ill-formed Trees," and "Possessive NP with a PP.")

2. Using tree 5.1 as your reference, answer the following questions:
A. What are the daughter nodes of the node VP?
B. The subject NP, *the people in the room*, contains a PP-node. What are the *sister* nodes of that PP?
C. The phrase structure rule for VP given in example (71c) of the text will not generate the VP shown in tree 5.1. Why not (that is, what constituent is missing from rule (71c))? How would you reformulate rule (71c) so that it will generate the VP in tree 5.1?
D. Is the sequence of words *the room will move* represented as a *single* constituent in tree 5.1?

3. Draw tree diagrams for the following noun phrases:

a. the weather in England
b. John's uncle in England
c. John's uncle in England's company

4. The sequence of words *light*, *house*, *keeper* is structurally ambiguous.
A. How many meanings can you detect for this sequence?
B. What structural groupings would you assign to the phrase, to represent each meaning you have found? (Use parentheses, in the manner of example (5) of the text.)

(See the exercise entitled "Tree and Sentence Matching" in *A Linguistics Workbook* for another example of syntactic ambiguity.)

5. In American English, the word *so* can be used as an intensifier, or emphasizer, as in the following example:

(i)
a. I can lift this weight.
b. I can *so* lift this weight.

In (ib) *so* functions to indicate emphasis. The following examples show that there is a restriction on the placement of *so* in a sentence (recall that * indicates an ill-formed expression):

(ii)
a. I will pass the test.
b. I will *so* pass the test.

(iii)
a.   I know the answer.
b.   *I know *so* the answer!
c.   I do *so* know the answer.

(iv)
a. Mary is running in tomorrow's race.
b. Mary is *so* running in tomorrow's race!

(v)
a.   They took our money.
b.   *They took *so* our money!
c.   They did *so* take our money!

(vi)
a. He is nice.
b. He is *so* nice.

What is the restriction on the placement of *so*? That is, where can *so* be inserted within a sentence, and when is it impossible to insert *so*? Use yes/no questions, tag formation, and negative placement to support your answer.

6. Example (42) of the text describes a number of properties of the *subject* constituent of English sentences. For example, the pronoun in a tag agrees with the subject of a sentence in person, number, and gender (see example (41)). Now consider the following sentences:

a. That John arrived late annoyed Bill.
b. There were three men in the park.
c. It was Mary who solved the problem.
d. The car, truck, and train collided with each other.
e. Thirty or forty bees have built a hive.
f. That movie, the boys really like a lot.

A. For each sentence, construct an appropriate tag.
B. For each case, indicate what constituent (group of words) of the main sentence the pronoun in the tag *agrees* with. Do this by underlining the relevant words (that

is, the constituent) and connecting it to the tag pronoun (as in example (41)).

C. Based on your results in questions A and B, what is the subject of each sentence?

7. In the text we noted a number of grammatical properties of subjects in English. Now consider the following sentences, focusing in particular on the form of the italicized *verb*:

(i)

a. The boy *likes* that cake.
b. The boys *like* that cake.
c. The boy and girl *like* that cake.
d. *The boy and the girl *likes* that cake.

(ii)

a. That cake, the boy *likes*.
b. That cake, the boys *like*.
c. *That cake, the boys *likes*.

Many verbs in English *agree in number* with some preceding constituent. That is, the verbs take on a singular form (*likes*) or a plural form (*like*) in the present tense (in the manner illustrated above), depending on whether certain preceding constituents are singular or plural. This process, illustrated in (i) and (ii), is known as *verb agreement*. Now consider the hypothetical verb agreement rules in (iii) and (iv) and answer the questions associated with each:

(iii)
The verb agrees in number with the noun immediately to its left.

A. Why is this rule inaccurate? Use the data in (i) to show that the rule makes a false prediction.

(iv)
The verb agrees in number with the noun phrase that comes at the very beginning of the sentence.

B. Why is this rule inaccurate? Use the data in (ii) to show that the rule makes a false prediction.
Now answer the following question:
C. What constituent of a sentence does the verb agree with in number? That is, what is the proper way to state the verb agreement rule?

8. As we saw in examining the notion "subject," in English the subject of a sentence can be identified by its structural position (see tree 5.3), among other things, and in Japanese by a special marking on the subject noun phrase (*-ga*). There are also languages in which the subject of a sentence can be identified by means of a special marking on the main verb. For example, in Navajo there are two verbal prefixes, *yi-* and *bi-*, illustrated in the following examples:

a. Łį́į́' dzaanééz yiztał   "The horse kicked the mule."
b. Łį́į́' dzaanééz biztał   "The mule kicked the horse."

(The translations of the words *łį́į́* and *dzaanééz* can be derived from exercise 9.)

A. In Navajo, for sentences of the form *NP1 NP2 yi + Verb*, which NP is interpreted as the subject and which as the object?

B. For sentences of the form *NP1 NP2 bi + Verb*, which NP is interpreted as the subject and which as the object?

(For more on the *yi/bi* alternation, see the exercise entitled "Pragmatics: Navajo" in *A Linguistics Workbook*.)

9. Basic word order for English is *Subject-Verb-Object*, as in *Gorillas eat bananas*. For the following two languages, isolate and identify the different words and determine what the basic word order is.

Language #1: Navajo (Native American language of the Southwest)

a. Łį́į́' dzaanééz yiztał	"The horse kicked the mule."
b. Dzaanééz łį́į́' yiztał	"The mule kicked the horse."
c. Ashkii at'ééd yiztsǫs	"The boy kissed the girl."
d. At'ééd ashkii yiztsǫs	"The girl kissed the boy."
e. Ashkii łį́į́' yo'į́	"The boy saw the horse."

horse _____ *łį́į́* _____
mule _____ *dzaanééz* _____
boy _____ *ashkii* _____
girl _____ *at'ééd* _____
kicked _____ *yiztal* _____
kissed _____ *yiztsǫs* _____
saw _____ *yo'į́* _____
Basic word order: _____ *subject – object – verb* _____

Language #2: Lummi (Native American language of the Pacific Northwest)

a. xčits cǝ-swǝy'qǝ' sǝ-słeni'	"The man knows the woman."
b. xčits sǝ-słeni' cǝ-swǝy'qǝ'	"The woman knows the man."
c. leŋnǝs cǝ-sčǝtxʷǝn cǝ-swǝy'qǝ'	"The bear saw the man."
d. leŋnǝs sǝ-słeni' cǝ-swi'qo'ǝł	"The woman saw the boy."

man _____ *cǝ-swǝy'qǝ* _____
woman _____ *sǝ-słeni* _____
bear _____ *cǝ-sčǝtxʷǝn* _____
boy _____ *cǝ-swi'qo'ǝl* _____
knows _____ *xčits* _____
saw _____ *leŋnǝs* _____
Basic word order: _____ *verb – subject – object* _____

10. As noted in the text, in some languages word order is quite free, as, for example, in Tohono O'odham, a Native American language of southern Arizona and northern Mexico. To see the possibilities for word order, consider the following sentence (data from Zepeda 1983):

(i)

Huan	'o	wakon	g-ma:gina.
Subject	Aux	Verb	Object
"John"	"3rd person"	"washing"	"the car"

"John is/was washing the car."

Sentence (i) can have the word order shown, or any of the following word orders:

(ii)

a. Huan 'o g-ma:gina wakon.
b. Wakon 'o g-ma:gina g-Huan.
c. Wakon 'o g-Huan g-ma:gina.
d. Ma:gina 'o wakon g-Huan.
e. Ma:gina 'o g-Huan wakon.

The auxiliary *'o* (which we label Aux) indicates a third person subject (in this case, *Huan* "John") and is used in sentences that describe ongoing or incompleted actions. (In the Tohono O'odham sentences, the symbol *:* is used to indicate a long vowel, and a "prefix" *g-* sometimes appears with nouns and sometimes does not. Both of these features can be ignored in this exercise.) Now answer the following questions:

A. For each sentence in (ii), indicate what the word order is. Use the labels Subject (= *Huan*), Aux (= *'o*), Verb (= *wakon*), and Object (= *ma:gina*), in the manner shown in the first example below:

Sentence	*Word order*
a. Huan 'o g-ma:gina wakon.	Subject-Aux-Object-Verb
b. Wakon 'o g-ma:gina g-Huan.	_____
c. Wakon 'o g-Huan g-ma:gina.	_____
d. Ma:gina 'o wakon g-Huan.	_____
e. Ma:gina 'o g-Huan wakon.	_____

B. As your answer to question A will have shown, word order in Tohono O'odham appears to be free (that is, any order of constituents seems possible), except for one particular constituent of the above sentences, which occurs in the same relative position in every sentence. What is this constituent, and in what position of a sentence must it appear?

C. Given your answer to question B, consider the following ungrammatical sentences of Tohono O'odham:

(iii)

a. *Huan g-ma:gina 'o wakon.
b. *Huan g-ma:gina wakon 'o.

Why are these sentences bad?

(See the exercise entitled "Simple Sentences: Tohono O'odham" in *A Linguistics Workbook* for more relevant data from Tohono O'odham (formerly Papago).)

11. Consider the sentence *I kicked the ball into the basket*. Is *the ball into the basket* a single constituent? Show how the cleft construction can be used to answer this question. (Review the discussion of examples (45)–(47); see also the exercise in *A Linguistics Workbook* entitled "Verb-Particle versus Verb-PP Structure.")

12. Under certain circumstances, the Particle Movement transformation seems to be obligatory; that is, the particle *must* be separated from the verb:

(i)

a. *She stood up them.
b. She stood them up.

(ii)

a. *I wrote down it.

b.   I wrote it down.

(iii)

a. *The bartender kicked out him.

b.   The bartender kicked him out.

Under what circumstances must the particle be separated from its verb?

13. The following sentences illustrate cases of extraposition similar to ones discussed in the text:

(i)

a. A review *of the new book by Chomsky* will soon appear.

b. A review will soon appear *of the new book by Chomsky*.

(ii)

a. Several theories *about the structure of language* were presented last night.

b. Several theories were presented last night *about the structure of language*.

The phrases *of the new book by Chomsky* and *about the structure of language* are single constituents that can be shifted to the end of a sentence by the Extraposition transformation.

A. Draw a tree structure for each of the following phrases:

a. a review of the new book by Chomsky

b. several theories about the structure of language

B. Now draw a tree structure for sentence (ia) and a tree structure for sentence (iia) (you will naturally incorporate the structures you have drawn in answering question A). If you are unsure about details of the verb phrase, simply use triangles to abbreviate the structure, as in trees 5.7, 5.8, 5.11, and 5.12.

C. Finally, draw tree structures for sentences (ib) and (iib). These will be the output trees of Extraposition. (Hint: A careful study of trees 5.11, 5.12, 5.20, and 5.21 should clear up any problems you might have in drawing your trees for this exercise.)

Bibliography and Further Reading

Akmajian, A., and F. W. Heny (1975). *An introduction to the principles of transformational syntax.* Cambridge, Mass.: MIT Press.

Bach, E. (1974). *Syntactic theory.* New York: Holt, Rinehart and Winston.

Baker, C. L. (1989). *English syntax.* Cambridge, Mass.: MIT Press.

Chomsky, N. (1957). *Syntactic structures.* The Hague: Mouton.

Chomsky, N. (1965). *Aspects of the theory of syntax.* Cambridge, Mass.: MIT Press.

Chomsky, N. (1976). *Reflections on language.* New York: Pantheon Books.

Chomsky, N. (1980). *Rules and representations.* New York: Columbia University Press.

Chomsky, N. (1981). *Lectures on government and binding*. Dordrecht, Holland: Foris.

Chomsky, N. (1986). *Knowledge of language: Its nature, origin, and use*. New York: Praeger.

Demers, R. A., and A. K. Farmer (1986). *A linguistics workbook*. Cambridge, Mass.: MIT Press. (2nd ed., 1991.)

Greenberg, J. H., ed. (1966). *Universals of language*. Cambridge, Mass.: MIT Press.

Horrocks, G. (1987). *Generative grammar*. London and New York: Longman.

Kimball, J. P. (1973). *The formal theory of grammar*. Englewood Cliffs, N.J.: Prentice-Hall.

Lasnik, H., and J. Uriagereka (1988). *A course in GB syntax*. Cambridge, Mass.: MIT Press.

Newmeyer, F. J. (1980). *Linguistic theory in America: The first quarter-century of transformational generative grammar*. New York: Academic Press.

Postal, P. (1971). *Crossover phenomena*. New York: Holt, Rinehart and Winston.

Radford, A. (1980). *Transformational syntax: A student's guide to Chomsky's Extended Standard Theory*. Cambridge: Cambridge University Press.

Radford, A. (1988). *Transformational grammar*. Cambridge: Cambridge University Press.

Reinhart, T. (1983). *Semantic interpretation and anaphora*. London: Croom Helm.

Riemsdijk, H. van, and E. Williams (1986). *Introduction to the theory of grammar*. Cambridge, Mass.: MIT Press.

Stockwell, R. P., P. Schachter, and B. H. Partee (1973). *The major syntactic structures of English*. New York: Holt, Rinehart and Winston.

Wall, R. (1972). *Introduction to mathematical linguistics*. Englewood Cliffs, N.J.: Prentice-Hall.

Zepeda, O. (1983). *A Papago grammar*. Tucson, Ariz.: University of Arizona Press.

SEMANTICS: THE STUDY OF MEANING AND DENOTATION

6.1 SEMANTICS AS A PART OF GRAMMAR

The study of linguistic units and their principles of combination would not be complete without an account of what these units mean, what they are used to talk about, and what they are used to communicate. The study of communication is a part of pragmatics, to which we will return in chapter 9. In this chapter we will take up the first two topics, which constitute a major portion of *semantics*.

In the field of linguistics, semantics is generally considered to be the study of *meaning* (and related notions) in languages, whereas in the field of logic, semantics is generally considered to be the study of linguistic reference or *denotation* and *truth conditions* in languages. Other disciplines, such as philosophy, psychology, and computer science, sample freely from both traditions. Although there is sometimes tension between these conceptions of semantics, the dispute is really one of emphasis: in the end, an adequate semantic description of natural languages must record facts of meaning and denotation. In chapter 2 we discussed some semantic notions at the word level. But semantic analysis also applies to those expressions that are made up of words: phrases and sentences. Indeed, traditionally, phrases and sentences have received more attention than the words that make them up.

Semantics has not always enjoyed a prominent role in modern linguistics. From World War II to the early 1960s semantics was viewed, especially in the United States, as not quite respectable: its inclusion in a grammar (as linguists sometimes call a scientific description of a language—see Chomsky 1965) was considered by many as either a sort of methodological impurity or an objective to be reached only in the distant future. But as Katz and Fodor (1963) pointed out in their influential article

"The Structure of a Semantic Theory" (see also Higginbotham 1985), there is as much reason to consider semantics a part of grammar as syntax or phonology. It is often said that a grammar describes what fluent speakers know of their language—their *linguistic competence*. If that is so, we can argue that whatever fluent speakers know of their language is a proper part of a description of that language. Given this, then the description of meaning is a necessary part of the description of a speaker's linguistic knowledge (that is, the grammar of a language must contain a component that describes what speakers know about the semantics of the language). In other words, if appealing to what fluent speakers know about their language counts as motivation for including a phonological fact or a syntactic fact in the grammar of that language, then the same sort of consideration motivates the inclusion of semantic facts.

A more general consideration also motivates us to include semantics in the grammar of a language. A language is often defined as a conventional system for communication, a system for conveying messages. Moreover, communication can be accomplished (in the system) only because words have certain meanings; therefore, to characterize this system—the language—it is necessary to describe these meanings. Hence, if a grammar describes a language, part of it must describe meaning, and thus the grammar must contain a semantics. Taking these two considerations together, it seems reasonable to conclude that semantic information is an integral part of a grammar.

In reading this chapter, though, bear in mind that the subfield of semantics is in a greater state of diversification than phonology or syntax; much that we will discuss is a cautious selection from among possible alternatives. There is no shortage of semantic theories, and it is widely acknowledged that serious open questions still lie at the very foundations of semantics. We suggest consulting the works listed at the end of this chapter, in order to get a general idea of the range and scope of semantics.

6.2   WHAT ARE MEANING AND DENOTATION?

It would take a whole semantic theory to answer the questions raised below, but in the history of semantics a few "leading ideas" have emerged concerning the nature of meaning and denotation, and a brief look at some of these conceptions is instructive.

Meaning

In everyday English, the word *mean* has a number of different uses, many of which are not relevant to the study of language:

(1)
a. That was no mean (insignificant) accomplishment.
b. This will mean (result in) the end of our regime.
c. I mean (intend) to help if I can.
d. Keep Off the Grass! This means (refers to) you.
e. His losing his job means (implies) that he will have to look again.
f. Lucky Strike means (indicates) fine tobacco.
g. Those clouds mean (are a sign of) rain.
h. She doesn't mean (believe) what she said.

These uses of the word *mean* can all be paraphrased by other expressions (indicated in parentheses above). None of them is appropriate for our discussion of word meaning. Rather, we will use the terms *mean* and *meaning* as they are used in the following examples:

(2)
a. *Procrastinate* means "to put things off."
b. In saying that, she meant that we should leave.

These two uses of the word *mean* exemplify two important types of meaning: *linguistic meaning* (2a) and *speaker meaning* (2b).

This distinction can be illustrated with an example. Suppose that you've been arguing with another person, who exclaims, "The door is right behind you!" You would assume, quite rightly in this context, that the speaker, in uttering this sentence, means that you are to leave—although the speaker's actual words indicate nothing more than the location of the door. This illustrates how speakers can mean something quite different from what their words mean. In general, the *linguistic meaning* of an expression is simply the meaning or meanings of that expression in the language. In contrast, the *speaker meaning* can differ from the linguistic meaning, depending on whether the speaker is speaking *literally* or *nonliterally*. When we speak literally, we mean what our words mean, and in this case there is no important difference between speaker meaning and linguistic meaning. But when we speak nonliterally, we mean something different from what our words mean.

Two nonliteral uses of language are irony and sarcasm, as when someone says of a film, "That movie was a real winner!", uttered in such a way that we understand the speaker to mean that the movie was a flop. Metaphorical uses of language (some of which we discussed in chapter 2) are also examples of nonliteral language use, as, for example, when someone is described as having raven hair, ruby lips, emerald eyes, and teeth of pearl. Taken literally, this description would indicate that the person in question is an inorganic monstrosity; however, taken metaphorically, it is quite a compliment. As we will see in part II of this text, a crucial feature in human communication is the ability on the part of the hearer to determine whether a speaker is speaking literally or nonliterally.

Returning now to the question of linguistic meaning, whenever we talk about the meaning of an expression, it is useful to keep in mind the distinction between the linguistic meaning of an expression and a given speaker's literal or nonliteral use of the expression. Furthermore, in talking about the linguistic meaning of an expression, we must note that meanings can vary across dialects and across individual speakers. To recall an example from chapter 2, in American English the word *bonnet* refers only to a type of hat, whereas in British English it can refer to the hood of a car. Hence, for a word such as *bonnet* we cannot isolate a single meaning valid for all forms of English; rather, our discussion of the meaning of the word will be relative to a specific dialect of English.

The matter is further complicated when we note that meanings of words can vary across individual speakers within the same dialect. For example, the word *infer* seems to have different meanings for different speakers. For some speakers, it has roughly the same meaning as *surmise* or *conclude*, as in *I infer from what you say that you are sick*. For other speakers, it has roughly the same meaning as *imply*, as in *He inferred that he was fed up with us*. The language of a particular individual is referred to as that person's *idiolect*, and it is clear that the idiolectal meaning of a word can differ from one person to another (even among people who can be said to speak the same dialect). The varieties of meaning we have specified so far are summarized in figure 6.1.

At this point we might ask, How can so many varieties of meaning exist? Isn't it the case, after all, that "official" dictionaries of a language tell us what the meaning of a word is? And isn't it the case that the only "valid" meanings for a word are those listed in the dictionary? In answering these questions, it is important to recall the distinction made earlier between prescriptive and descriptive grammar. Current dictionaries of English (and many other languages as well) derive from a tradition of prescriptive grammar and almost invariably have focused on the written language. You can probably think of numerous words and uses of words in current spoken,

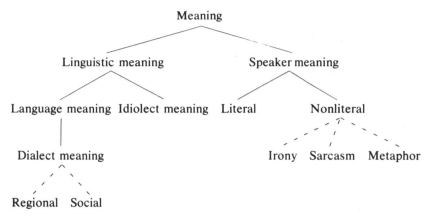

Figure 6.1
Some varieties of meaning

informal English that do not appear in dictionaries. From a prescriptive point of view these unlisted words and uses might be termed "incorrect" or "improper." From a descriptive point of view, however, the spoken language forms a central source of data for linguistic theory, and linguists are very much concerned with discovering meaning properties and relations in forms of spoken language actually used by speakers (rather than forms of language that prescriptive grammar dictates speakers "should" use). Hence, although dictionaries might be useful in providing certain basic definitions of common words, they do not, by and large, reflect accurately enough the meaning and variations in meaning of words in current use in everyday spoken language. And even where they are useful, they presuppose that the reader is already familiar with all the words used in the definition. But these words too eventually appear in other definitions, making the lexicon of a language look more like a densely connected network than a reductive pyramid with certain basic undefined words at the bottom, and all others defined in terms of them on top.

The descriptive point of view is sometimes misinterpreted as advocating "linguistic freedom"—that is, a situation in which speakers are free to use words any way they like and are allowed to "get away with" breaking the rules of proper English. This is, of course, an absurd parody of the descriptive point of view. It turns out that, quite aside from dictionaries and prescriptive grammar books, speakers are indeed not free to use words any way they like. There is tremendous social pressure for speakers of a language to use words in similar ways—successful communication depends on this, in fact—and the need to communicate effectively provides constraints on how "creative" an individual speaker can be in the use of words. What, then, is recorded in language as "meaning"?

What Is Meaning?

Historically, the most compelling idea concerning meaning has been that meaning is some sort of entity or thing. After all, we do speak of words as "having" a meaning, as meaning "something," as having the "same" meaning, as meaning the same "thing," as "sharing" a meaning, as having "many meanings," and so forth.

What sort of entity or thing is meaning? Different answers to this question give us a selection of different conceptions of meaning, and a selection of different types of semantic theory.

The Denotational Theory of Meaning

If one focuses on just some of the expressions in a language—for instance, proper names such as *de Gaulle, Chris Evert, Italy*, or definite descriptive noun phrases such as *the present president of the United States, the first person to walk on our moon*, and so forth—one is likely to conclude that their meaning is the thing they denote. For convenience we will formulate this conception of meaning in terms of the following slogan:

(D)
The meaning of each expression is the (actual) object it denotes, its *denotation*.

Although (D) does reflect the fact that we use language to talk about the world, there are serious problems with the identification of meaning as denotation.

For instance, if we believe that the meaning of an expression is its denotation, we are committed to at least the following additional claims:

(3)
a. If an expression has a meaning, then it follows that it must have a denotation.
b. If two expressions have the same denotation, then they have the same meaning.
c. Anything that is true of the denotation of an expression is true of its meaning.

Each of these consequences of (D) turns out to be false. For instance, (3a) requires that for any expression having a meaning there is an actual object that it denotes. But this is surely wrong. What, for instance, is the (actual) object denoted by such expressions as *Pegasus* (the flying horse), *the, empty, and, hello, very,* and *Leave the room*? Next, consider (3b). This says that if two expressions denote the same object, then they mean the same thing; that is, they are synonymous. But many expressions that can be correctly used to denote a single object do not mean the same thing. For instance, *the morning star, the evening star,* and *Venus* all denote the same planet, but they are not synonymous, as can be seen by the fact that the morning star is the last star seen in the morning and the evening star is the first star seen at night. Nor are the expressions *the first person to walk on our moon* and *Neil Armstrong* synonymous, but they denote the same person. Finally, consider (3c). As far as we know, Sir Edmund Hilary was the first European to climb Mt. Everest, and as a consequence he was knighted by the Queen. But by (3c) we must conclude that it is the meaning of the words *the first European to climb Mt. Everest* (*Edmund Hilary*) that climbed Mt. Everest and was knighted by the Queen. Since this is absurd, we conclude instead that the Denotational Theory will have to be either rejected or modified in some significant way.

Mentalist Theories of Meaning

Well, we might say, if meanings are not actual objects, perhaps they are mental objects; even if there is no real flying horse for *Pegasus* to denote, there is surely such an *idea*, and maybe this idea is the meaning of *Pegasus*. A typical example of this view can be seen in the following quotation from Glucksberg and Danks (1975, 50): "The set of possible meanings of any given word is the set of possible feelings, images, ideas, concepts, thoughts, and inferences that a person might produce when that word is heard and processed." As with the Denotational Theory, this conception of meaning can be formulated in terms of a slogan:

(M)
The meaning of each expression is an idea (or ideas) associated with that expression in the minds of speakers.

This sort of theory has a number of problems, but the most serious one can be put in the form of a dilemma: either the notion of an idea is too vague to allow the theory to predict anything specific and thus the theory is not testable; or if the notion of an idea is made precise enough to test, the theory turns out to make false predictions. The quotation from Glucksberg and Danks illustrates the first problem. How, with such a view of meaning, could one ever determine what an expression means? With such a view, could two expressions be synonymous, or would there always be feelings and thoughts associated with one expression that are not associated with the other?

Meaning as images. Turning to the second problem, suppose we sharpen the notion of an idea by saying that ideas are *mental images*. Though this might work for words like *Pegasus* and perhaps *the Eiffel Tower*, it is not obvious how it would work for nouns like *dog* and *triangle*, or a verb like *kick*. For instance, if one really does form an image of dog or a triangle, more than likely the dog will be of some particular species and will not comprise both a Chihuahua and a Saint Bernard; the triangle will be isosceles or equilateral but will not comprise all triangles. Similar problems arise with *kick*. If one really forms an image of *X* kicking *Y*, then that image probably will have properties not essential to kicking, such as the sex of the kicker, which leg was used, the kind of thing being kicked, and so forth. In general, mental images are just not abstract enough to be the meanings of even common nouns and verbs. But suppose for the moment that appropriate images could be found for these nouns and verbs. What about other kinds of words? What images are the meanings of words such as *only*, *and*, *hello*, and *not*? Worse still, can the theory apply to units larger than words, such as the sentence *She speaks French and Navajo*? How, for instance, does an Image Theory of meaning differentiate this sentence from *She speaks French or Navajo*?

Meaning as concepts. One way around this problem of the excessive specificity of images is to view ideas as *concepts*, that is, as mentally represented categories of things. As we will see in chapter 10, this version of the idea theory is also problematic. First, concepts also might be too specific in that various speakers' concepts of *X* might include information that is specific to the way they developed the concept but is not a part of the related word. There is psychological evidence that our system of cognitive classification is structured in terms of *prototypes*, in that some instances of a concept are more typical (closer to the prototype) than others: robins are more typical birds than penguins, chairs are more typical examples of furniture than ashtrays, and so on. Yet these are not features of the meaning of *bird* and *furniture*. And even if concepts work as meanings for some words, such as common nouns, adjectives, and maybe verbs, there are still many other kinds of words that do not have clear conceptual content, such as *elm tree*, *only*, *not*, and *hello*. Furthermore, it is not clear what concept would be assigned to a sentence, though sentences are clearly meaningful. The concept analysis of meaning is at best a theory of a restricted portion of the language. So although this way of understanding the notion "idea" makes the theory as testable as theories in general in cognitive psychology, there is as yet no such theory of meaning in cognitive psychology that is detailed enough to test. To succeed, such a theory must be capable of identifying and distinguishing concepts independently of meaning, which all current versions fail to do.

In short, theories of meaning as entities, whether they be objects denoted, images in the mind, or concepts, all face various difficulties. Perhaps the trouble lies with the initial assumption that meaning is an entity.

The Use Theory of Meaning

One of the last theories of meaning to emerge has been the (nonentitative) Use Theory of meaning. Advanced by Ludwig Wittgenstein in the 1930s, it has more or less dominated Anglo-American theorizing about meaning for the past fifty years. Properly construed, it is, we think, a promising theory. Like the previous theories of meaning, this one can be formulated as a slogan:

(U)
The meaning of an expression is determined by its use in the language community.

This theory does not suffer all the weaknesses of the previous "entity" theories of meaning. We can just as easily speak of the use of *hello* and various sentences as of the use of *table* or *Pegasus*. The main problem with the Use Theory of meaning is that the relevant conception of *use* must be made precise, and the theory must say how, exactly, meaning is connected to use. Such a theory is currently being developed by various authors (see the works of Grice and Schiffer, cited in the bibliography), and we will say more about language use in chapter 9.

In conclusion, it is fair to say that researchers do not have a very clear idea what meaning is. All of the theories we have surveyed are in various states of disarray. However, the situation is not hopeless, as there are still promising avenues of approach to this topic. As a student, you should not be deterred by present limitations on understanding but should consider theories of meaning a promising area for future research.

6.3   THE SCOPE OF A SEMANTIC THEORY

The foregoing discussion indicates that there are facts for a semantic theory to describe, and it leads us to consider what kinds of information are central to the description of the semantics of a language.

Words and Phrases

Meaning Properties

We now turn our attention to certain *meaning properties* of words that play an important role in the description of human languages. Perhaps the most central semantic property of words (and morphemes in general) is the property of being *meaningful* or being *meaningless*. Any adequate account of the lexicon of a language must specify the meaningful words of the language and must represent the meaning of those words (both simple and complex) in some fashion. For example, at the very least an adequate account of the English lexicon must tell us that *procrastinate* means "put things off," *bachelor* means "unmarried adult male," *mother* means "female parent," and so on for numerous other words of the language. In learning our native language, we obviously learn a large set of words that we know to be meaningful in the language, and at the same time we come to distinguish between meaningful words and meaningless expressions.

Another important semantic property of words is *ambiguity*, in particular what is referred to as *lexical ambiguity*, as illustrated in the following examples:

(4)
a. He found a *bat*.
    (*bat*: baseball bat; flying rodent)
b. She couldn't *bear* children.
    (*bear*: give birth to; put up with)

In each case, the italicized word is ambiguous in that it has more than one meaning. The ability to detect ambiguity is crucial in the communicative process, and successful communication can depend on both speaker and hearer recognizing the same meaning for a potentially ambiguous word.

Another important semantic property of words, in particular words put together into phrases, is *anomaly*. An expression is anomalous when the meanings of its individual words are incompatible:

(5)
a. gradually plummet
b. colorless green idea
c. dream diagonally

Of course, it is almost always possible to impose a meaning on such expressions—indeed, certain forms of poetry demand that the reader impose a meaning on anomalous expressions. For example, *to dream diagonally* might be taken to mean "to lie diagonally in a bed while dreaming," but this is the result of a special (and forced) interpretation, which speakers could argue about at length. The point is that expressions like those in (5) have no conventional interpretation in English. It is important to notice that a semantically anomalous expression can nevertheless be syntactically well formed (for example, *colorless green idea* is formed on a regular syntactic pattern of English exemplified by phrases such as *colorful red flower*), and this may be a major factor that makes it feasible for speakers to invent meanings for such anomalous expressions.

Meaning Relations

Not only do words have *meaning properties* (such as ambiguity, or having a meaning), they also bear various *meaning relations* to one another. Just as words can be related morphologically (for example, by word formation rules such as the *-able* rule), so they can also be related semantically, and words related by virtue of meaning form subgroups within the lexicon of a language. For example, one central meaning relation is *synonymy*, or "sameness" of meaning. Thus, we say that *automobile* is synonymous with *car*, *plane* (in one of its senses) is synonymous with *aircraft*, *kid* (in one of its senses) is synonymous with *child*, and so on. Synonymy is a relation that structures the lexicon of a language into sets of words sharing a meaning.

Words may also be *homophonous*; that is, they may have identical pronunciations but be different words with different meanings. An often-cited example of homophony is the word *bank* referring to the side of a river, versus the word *bank* referring to a financial institution. (Homophonous words often have distinct spellings in the written language, such as *Mary*, *marry*, and *merry*.) Of course, certain questions immediately arise. Is there a single word *bank* with two distinct meanings? Or are there two distinct, but homophonous, words, each with a single meaning? It is by no means easy to resolve such issues, and we can provide no firm solutions here.

Similarly for *polysemy*, which is often defined as the property of having more than one related meaning. Thus, *table* can mean a certain kind of furniture, or it can be the act of putting an item at a meeting on hold (*She tabled the motion*). One might argue that the same word cannot be both a noun and a verb, hence that these are two different words, hence that this is not a case in which one can speak of relations between the meanings of a single word. Still, there are examples of relations between the meanings of words from a single syntactic category. For instance, *Time magazine* can be bought for one dollar or 35 million dollars; the first is something you can read, the second is a particular company that produces the thing you just read. Sometimes dictionaries use history to decide whether a particular entry is a case of one word with two related meanings or two separate words, but this can be tricky. Even though *pupil* (eye) and *pupil* (student) are historically linked, in the current language they intuitively raise the same questions as *bank*.

Another important meaning relation is *meaning inclusion*, illustrated in (6a–c):

(6)

a. The meaning of *sister* includes the meaning of *female*.
b. The meaning of *murder* includes the meaning of *illegal*.
c. The meaning of *kill* includes the meaning of *dead*.

When we put words together that are related by meaning inclusion, we derive expressions that are *redundant* (such as *female sister*, *illegal murder*) and *idiomatic* (such as *She killed him dead*).

Even if two expressions are not synonymous and the meaning of one does not include the meaning of the other, they still may be semantically related in that they *overlap*, or *share* some aspect of meaning:

(7)

a. *Father*, *uncle*, *bull*, and *stallion* all express the property "male."
b. *Say*, *speak*, *whisper*, *yell*, *shout*, and *scream* all express the property "vocalization."
c. *Fortunately*, *luckily*, *happily*, and *fortuitously* all express the property "good for" something or someone.

Groups of words in the lexicon can be semantically related by being members of a set known as a *semantic field* (see Lehrer 1974). On a very general and intuitive level, we can say that the words in a semantic field, though not synonymous, are all used to talk about the same general phenomenon, and there is a meaning inclusion relation between the items in the field and the field category itself. Classical examples of semantic fields include color terms (*red, green, blue, yellow*), kinship terms (*mother, father, sister, brother*), and cooking terms (*boil, fry, bake, broil, steam*). The notion of a semantic field can be extended intuitively to any set of terms with a close relation in meaning, all of which can be subsumed under the same general label. Thus, in addition to the specific semantic fields just cited, we could also refer to labels such as "nautical terms," "plant names," "animal names," "automobile terms," and so on, as specifying semantic fields. It is difficult to be very precise about what counts as a semantic field. Do all time words form a semantic field? How about wearing apparel for the feet, or the things Napoleon thought about the day he died? Although there have been interesting attempts to make the notion of a field more precise (see Katz 1972, sec. 7.5, Miller and Johnson-Laird 1976, chaps. 4 and 5, Grandy 1987), so far they have not created much consensus for research.

Sometimes words can share one aspect of meaning but be "opposite" in some other aspect of meaning. We say that such sets of words are *antonymous*. Typical examples of word antonymy include the following:

(8)
a. *Small* and *large* share the notion "size" but differ in degree.
b. *Cold* and *hot* share the notion "temperature" but differ in degree.

The sense in which words such as *hot* and *cold* are "opposites" is not just that they are incompatible in meaning. Many words are semantically incompatible in the sense that they cannot both be true of something at the same time. For example, the words *cat* and *dog* are semantically incompatible (they cannot both be true descriptions of the same thing at the same time); nevertheless, they are not "opposites" in the sense of being antonyms. The examples in (8) are antonyms essentially because there is a scale containing the "opposites" at either end, with a midpoint (or mid-interval) between them:

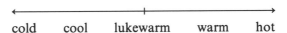

cold   cool   lukewarm   warm   hot

Thus, the words *hot* and *cold* can be said to be antonyms ("opposites") since they define the *extremities* of a scale (in this case, of temperature) that has a midinterval between them (in this case, represented by the word *lukewarm*, a word that can be used to refer to things that are neither hot nor cold). The comparative (*-er*) form of antonyms points in the direction of the scale, and so the midpoint will not take comparison (see Lehrer and Lehrer 1982):

(9)
a. smaller, *mediumsizeder, larger
b. colder, cooler, *lukewarmer, warmer, hotter

This completes our initial survey of semantic properties and relations in the area of word meaning. We note, once again, that the study of word meaning reveals that the lexicon of a language is not simply an unorganized list of words. Semantic relations such as synonymy, antonymy, and the relation defined by semantic fields all serve to link certain words with other words, indicating that the overall lexicon of a language has a complex internal structure consisting of subgroups, or "networks," of words sharing significant properties.

Sentences

Since sentences are composed of words and phrases, we can expect that certain semantic properties and relations of words and phrases will carry over to sentences as well. However, as traditional grammarians put it, a sentence (as opposed to a single word or phrase) expresses a "complete thought." This is not a very useful definition of a sentence, but it does suggest that sentences have a unique function, and thus we might expect to find semantic properties and relations that are unique to sentences.

Meaning Properties and Relations

Among the meaning properties and relations of words and phrases that carry over to sentences are ambiguity and synonymy:

(10)
a. *Ambiguity*
   She visited a little girl's school.
b. *Synonymy*
   His pants were too small.
   His pants were not big enough.

However, sentences also exhibit meaning properties and relations that words and phrases lack.

Communicative Potential

One important property of a sentence is its *communicative potential*. Sentences with different structures often have different communicative functions. Thus, a speaker who wants to assert or state that something is true will normally utter a declarative sentence such as *Snow is white*. On the other hand, if the speaker wants to issue an order, request, or command, then an imperative sentence such as *Leave the room!* is appropriate. Finally, if the speaker wants to ask a question, then the obvious choice is an interrogative sentence such as *What time is it?* As a first approximation we could diagram these facts as follows:

(11)

a. Declarative sentence → Used to assert, state, etc.

b. Imperative sentence → Used to order, request, command, etc.

c. Interrogative sentence → Used to ask questions

It seems to be a part of the semantics of these structural types (declarative, imperative, interrogative) that they have the distinct communicative functions cited above. In any event, no one could be said to understand sentences of these types if they did not understand the differences in communicative function.

That some types of sentences are used literally to assert that something is *true* is an important semantic fact. That an imperative sentence is normally used to request a hearer to do something (to *comply with* the request) and that an interrogative sentence is used literally to *ask a question* are also important semantic facts. However, the field of semantics has traditionally concentrated on the assertive function of language, concerning itself mainly with the properties and relations of declarative sentences with respect to truth.

Truth Properties

Not only do expressions in a language have meaning and denotation, they are also used to say things that are true or false. Of course, no semantic theory can predict which sentences are used to say something true and which are used to say something false, in part because truth and falsity depend upon what is being referred to, and because the same words can be used in identical sentences to refer to different things. Does this mean that the semantics of natural language cannot deal with truth and falsity? The answer is no, because some truth properties and truth relations hold regardless of reference, provided meaning is held constant.

Consider first the property of being *linguistically true* (also called *analytically true*) or *linguistically false* (also called *contradictory*). A sentence is linguistically true (or linguistically false) if its truth (or falsehood) is determined solely by the semantics of the language and it is not necessary to check any facts about the nonlinguistic world in order to determine its truth or falsehood. A sentence is *empirically true* (or *empirically false*) if it is not linguistically true or false—that is, if it is necessary to check the world in order to verify or falsify it; knowledge of the language alone does not settle the matter. Semantics is not concerned to explain empirical truths and falsehoods, but it is concerned to explain those sentences that are linguistically true or false. In each of the groups (12), (13), and (14) it is possible to determine truth values (true = T, false = F) without regard to the actual state of the world.

(12)

a. Either it is raining here or it is not raining here. (T)
b. If John is sick and Mary is sick, then John is sick. (T)
c. It is raining here and it is not raining here. (F)
d. If John is sick and Mary is sick, then John is not sick. (F)

(13)

a. All people that are sick are people. (T)
b. If every person is sick, then it is not true that no person is sick. (T)
c. Some people that are sick are not people. (F)
d. Every person is sick, but some person is not (sick). (F)

(14)

a. If John is a bachelor, then John is unmarried. (T)
b. If John killed the bear, then the bear died. (T)
c. If the car is red, then it has a color. (T)
d. John is a bachelor, but he is married. (F)
e. John killed the bear and it's (still) alive. (F)
f. The car is red, but it has no color. (F)

Again, knowing the language seems to be sufficient for knowing the truth or falsity of these sentences, and this being so, the semantics of these sorts of sentences will be relevant to a semantic theory that attempts to characterize the knowledge that speakers have about their language.

Truth Relations

We have noted that there are truth relations as well as truth properties that fall within the scope of semantics. The most central truth relation for semantics is *entailment*. One sentence S is said to entail another sentence S' when the truth of the first guarantees the truth of the second and the falsity of the second guarantees the falsity of the first, as in (15):

(15)

a. *The car is red* entails *The car has a color.*
b. *The needle is too short* entails *The needle is not long enough.*

We can see that the first sentence in each example, if true, guarantees the truth of the second; and the falsity of the second sentence in each example guarantees the falsity of the first.

Closely related to entailment is another truth relation, *semantic presupposition*. The basic idea behind semantic presupposition is that the falsity of the presupposed sentence causes the presupposing sentence not to have a truth value (T or F). Furthermore, both a sentence and its denial have the same semantic presupposition. Although this truth relation is somewhat controversial, (16) and (17) show typical examples of semantic presupposition in which both the positive (a) and the negative (b) sentences have the same presupposition (c):

(16)

a. The present king of France is bald.

b. The present king of France is not bald.

c. There is a present king of France.

(17)

a. John realizes that his car has been stolen.

b. John does not realize that his car has been stolen.

c. John's car has been stolen.

In sum, in addition to truth properties, there are at least two truth relations between pairs of declarative sentences that an adequate semantic theory must explain (or explain away), namely, entailment and semantic presupposition. Furthermore, since there are analogues of these properties and relations for nondeclarative sentences, an adequate semantics must ultimately account for how the world can *satisfy* a sentence of any type. In particular, semantics must explain how declaratives can be true, interrogatives can be answered, and imperatives can be complied with.

Goals of a Semantic Theory

We now come to the question of the goals of a semantic theory. What should a semantic theory do, and how?

The short answer to the first question is that a semantic theory should attribute to each expression in the language the semantic properties and relations that it has; moreover, it should define those properties and relations. Thus, if an expression is meaningful, the semantic theory should say so. If it has a specific set of meanings, the semantic theory should specify them. If it is ambiguous, the semantic theory should record that fact. And so on. Moreover, if two expressions are synonymous, or if one entails the other, the semantic theory should mark these semantic relations. We can organize these demands on a semantic theory by saying that an adequate theory of a language must generate every true instance of the following schemes for arbitrary expression E:

(18)

a. *Meaning properties and relations*

E is literally used to ____.

E means ____.

E is meaningful.

E is ambiguous.

E is anomalous (nonsense).

E is redundant.

E and E′ are synonymous.

E includes the meaning of E′.

E and E′ overlap in meaning.

E and E′ are antonymous.

b. *Truth properties and relations*

E is logically true (or false).

E is analytic.

E is contradictory.

E entails E′.

E semantically presupposes E′.

We can say in sum that the domain of a semantic theory is at least the set of properties and relations listed in (18); we should not be satisfied with a semantic theory of English that fails to explain them (or to explain them away).

The second question concerning the goals of a semantic theory is, How should the theory handle these semantic properties and relations? What kinds of constraints on a semantic theory are reasonable to impose? We will mention just two. First, it is generally conceded that even though a natural language contains an infinite number of phrases and sentences, a semantic theory of a natural language should be *finite*: people are capable of storing only a finite amount of information, but they nevertheless learn the semantics of natural languages. The second constraint on a semantic theory of a natural language is that it should reflect the fact that, except for idioms, expressions are *compositional*—in other words, that the meaning of a syntactically complex expression is determined by the meaning of its constituents and their grammatical relations. Compositionality rests on the fact that a finite number of familiar words and expressions can be combined in novel ways to form an infinite number of new phrases and sentences; hence, a finite semantic theory that reflects compositionality can describe meanings for an infinite number of complex expressions.

The existence of compositionality is most dramatic when compositional expressions are contrasted with expressions that lack compositionality.

The expression *kick the bucket* in (19a) has the two meanings shown in
(19b) and (19c):

(19)
a. John kicked the bucket.
b. John kicked the pail.
c. John died.

One of the meanings of (19a) is compositional: it is determined on the basis
of the meaning of the words and is synonymous with (19b). The other
meaning of (19a) is idiomatic and can be paraphrased as (19c). Idiomatic
meanings are not compositional in the sense of being determined from the
meaning of the constituent words and their grammatical relations. That
is, one could not determine the idiomatic meaning of (19a) by knowing just
the meaning of the words and recognizing familiar grammatical structure—
an idiomatic meaning must be learned separately as a unit. Idioms behave
as though they were syntactically complex words whose meaning cannot
be predicted, since their syntactic structure is doing no semantic work.

It would be a mistake to think of the compositionality of a complex
expression as simply adding up the meanings and references of its parts.
For adjective + noun constructions like that in (20a), adding up sometimes
works:

(20)
a. He was a *bearded Russian soldier.* =
b. He was a Russian and bearded and a soldier.

But even in such constructions the contributions of syntax can be obscure.
In (21), for example, we cannot simply add up the meanings of *occasional*
and *sailor*:

(21)
a. An occasional sailor walked by. ≠
b. *Someone who is a sailor and occasional walked by.

Modifiers can create other complications for compositionality, which
must also be reflected in a semantic theory of the language. Contrast the
arguments in (22) and (23):

(22)
a. That is a *gray* elephant. (T)
b. All elephants are animals. (T)
c. So, that is a *gray* animal. (T)

(23)
a. That is a *small* elephant. (T)
b. All elephants are animals. (T)
c. So, that is a *small* animal. (F)

In (22) the premises (a) and (b) jointly entail the truth of (c), but in (23) the premises (a) and (b) do not jointly entail the truth of (c). The only difference between (22) and (23) is the occurrence of *gray* in (22) and *small* in (23), so clearly there is some difference in the semantics of these two words.

More complicated and interesting examples of the interaction of semantics and syntax come from the functional relations of subject and object in a sentence. In sentences like (24a) and (24c) the words are the same, but the entailments (24b) and (24d) are importantly different:

(24)
a. John killed the snake.
b. The snake died.
c. The snake killed John.
d. John died.

This further illustrates the degree to which a semantic theory must be integrated with a syntactic theory in an adequate description of a natural language.

6.4   SPECIAL TOPICS

The issues we have just surveyed represent common ground for most semantic theories. However, many topics are the special concern of particular theories, and the problems they pose for semantics form part of its research agenda for the future.

Denotation and Reference

We have reserved the word *refer* for what speakers do, and the term *denote* for what words or phrases do. Under this terminology, the object (or objects) referred to by a person is called the *referent*, and the object (or objects) semantically referred to by a word or phrase is called the *denotation* of that word or phrase.

Speaker reference, which we will consider again in chapter 9, involves what the speaker is referring to in uttering an expression. The speaker's reference may coincide with what the speaker's words denote—for instance, when one refers to George Washington by using the phrase *the first president of the United States*. However, it can happen that what the speaker is referring to is not the same as the semantic reference or denotation of the words used. For instance, suppose that Jones believes himself to be the world's most famous linguist—much to the amusement of his friends. We might well *refer* (nonliterally of course—see chapter 9) to Jones in saying, "Well, here comes *the world's most famous linguist*," even though our words *denote*, say, Noam Chomsky. But even if we restrict ourselves to literal reference, we must still distinguish speaker reference from denotation. We have said that knowing the semantics of a language involves knowing its meaning. If actual reference were a part of semantics, then no one would understand words like *I*, *the book*, or *John Smith* unless they knew every referent of these words, and so in the case of *I*, every potential speaker of the language. Since no one could know all this, it follows that no one could understand the meaning of these words. So we must keep speaker reference (pragmatics) and denotation (semantics) separate.

Finally, there are nonreferential occurrences of forms that, in other contexts, would be used to refer. Consider, for example, the following sentences:

(25)
a. God exists; there is a God.
b. God does not exist; there is no God.

If *God* denotes something in (25a), then why doesn't (25a) seem redundant, since it can't denote something if there isn't something for it to denote? But worse, how could (25b) be true if *God* did denote something? If *God* denotes, there would have to be something that *God* denotes, and so (25b) would have to be false, since it says there is no such thing. Yet we do not have the pretheoretic intuition that (25b) is necessarily false. The unwanted redundancy of (25a) and necessary falsity of (25b) can be removed if we simply deny that *God* occurs as a referring expression in these contexts. Not all occurrences of a referring expression are referring occurrences, and in what follows we will restrict our remarks to referring occurrences.

Singular and General

It is important to emphasize that denotations are things and events in the world (or groups of them); what words or phrases denote are the things and events that the words correctly describe. For example:

(26)

a. *desks* denotes each and every desk

b. *is a desk* denotes each and every desk

c. *the first man to walk on our moon* denotes Neil Armstrong

d. *Richard Nixon* denotes those named Richard Nixon (including the former president of the United States)

These examples reveal a distinction that is important for more advanced work in semantics, and for pragmatics: the distinction between "general" expressions such as (26a) and (26b) and "singular" expressions such as (26c) and (26d). General expressions—such as common nouns, verbs, adjectives, and phrases that contain them—correctly describe potentially many different things or events. Thus, *red* applies to any red thing (and so denotes them all) and *table* applies to any table (and so denotes them all). Singular expressions include proper names, such as *Julius Caesar* and *Paris*; definite descriptive phrases such as *the first man to walk on our moon* and *the dents on the fender*; and pronouns such as *she*, *he*, and *they*. Singular denoting expressions have the property that they are used, on particular occasions, to refer to one single thing or collection of things. Even though there are many persons we can speak of as "she," and many collections of dents that can be referred to as "the dents on the fender," and even several different people named "Richard Nixon," when we use these singular denoting expressions in normal discourse we are still taken to have just one person or collection of dents in mind. The language makes available different types of expressions to do different types of jobs in connecting words to the world. Let us briefly look at these.

Indexicals, Definite Descriptions, and Proper Names

Indexical expressions (also called *deictic* expressions, from the Greek word for pointing) include personal pronouns (27), demonstratives (28), present and past tense, and such adverbs as those in (29):

(27)

a. I, we

b. you

c. he, she, it, they

(28)

a. this, these

b. that, those

(29)

a. now, yesterday, tomorrow

b. here, there

An indexical expression is one that has an indexical use, and an indexical use is a literal use to refer to something in virtue of its relation to the actual circumstances of the utterance. A good example is the word *I*, which is used to refer to Sam when Sam utters it but is used to refer to Jane when Jane utters it. And every moment the reference of *now* changes. Yet none of these words changes its *meaning* when it changes its reference. If it did, how would we know what it meant, and how could we understand what the speaker was trying to communicate?

The semantics of indexicals, on their indexical use, seems to involve rules such as the following:

(30)

a. *I*: used to refer to the speaker of this utterance of *I*.

b. *Now*: used to refer to the time of this utterance of *now*.

Like other singular terms, indexicals need not always be used indexically:

(31)

a. *Here* we go again, another bumpy landing.

b. *You* never know. *You* can't tell a book from its cover.

c. Come on *now*, you don't believe that!

d. I felt *this* crawly thing on my leg.

e. Everyone thinks *he* can do something well.

These uses are not indexical because they are not uses of the expression to refer to something via the actual production of the utterance.

Definite descriptions have the form *the F*, where *F* can be anything appropriate to a noun phrase:

(32)

a. the book on the table

b. the first man to walk on our moon

c. the dent on the fender

By far the most influential theory of the semantics of definite descriptions is Russell's (1905) "Theory of Descriptions." Russell proposed that sentences containing definite descriptions are to be semantically analyzed as *general* sentences. For instance, (33a) is schematized as (33b), and anything of this form, such as (33c), is analyzed as (33d):

(33)

a. *The first man to walk on the moon* is *right-handed*.

b. *The F* is *G*.

c. There is just one thing that is *the first man on the moon* and he is right-handed.

d. There is just one thing that is *F* and it is *G*.

Some theorists have objected that Russell's account fails to reflect an important "ambiguity" in descriptions. Consider normal uses of the following sentences:

(34)

a. *The fattest man in the world* must be lonely.

b. *The woman drinking a martini* is a famous linguist.

The first description is naturally used to refer to whatever man is the fattest man, no matter who he may be, and to say of that man that he must be lonely. If there is no single such man, then the statement is false, just as Russell's theory predicts. But in the second case the description is being used to refer to a particular woman, and even if she has ginger ale in her martini glass, the speaker will be saying something true—if the woman is in fact a famous linguist. On the first, "attributive" use of the definite description (as Donnellan (1966) has called it), the role of the description is to set down conditions that determine the referent. On the second, "referential" use, the description is not essential to picking out the referent, and the important thing is the object or person itself, not how it happens to be described. The description is picked mainly to help the hearer recognize what or who the speaker has in mind and is referring to.

Proper names, as Kaplan (1978) comments, "may be a practical convenience in our mundane transactions, but they are a theoretician's nightmare. They are like bicycles. Everyone easily learns to ride, but no one can correctly explain how he does it." J. S. Mill (1843) first proposed the *Direct Reference Theory* of proper names:

(35)

Direct Reference Theory

Proper names are like labels that stand directly for what they name.

Frege (1892) noted that if this were true, then sentences with two names for the same thing should be no more informative than sentences with the same name repeated. But clearly they are:

(36)
a. Bob Dylan is Bob Dylan.
b. Bob Dylan is Robert Zimmerman.

We learn something from the second sentence that we do not learn from the first. But how could that be if names merely introduce their bearer into the proposition expressed? Furthermore, almost all names have many bearers, even historically prominent ones such as *Moses*, *Aristotle*, and *Napoleon*. To which Moses, Aristotle, or Napoleon is the speaker referring? Or consider the issue of *vacuous* names, names that do not name anything. For instance, *Vulcan* was once taken to name a planet just opposite the Sun from Earth (that's why we could never see it). People asked, "Is there life on Vulcan?" But such questions should be as meaningless on the Direct Reference Theory as "Is there life on Csillam?" Neither word (*Vulcan*, *Csillam*) names anything; thus, neither makes any semantic contribution to the sentence it is a constituent of.

These problems led Frege to propose a *Description Theory* of proper names:

(37)
Description Theory
Semantically, proper names are abbreviated definite descriptions of what they name.

This theory explains our ability to refer using names in terms of our ability to refer using definite descriptions. It solves some of the puzzles mentioned for proper names. For instance, sentence (36b) can be informative because the different names abbreviate different descriptions.

Recently description theory has come under intense criticism (see Kripke 1980). One problem is how to choose the description we associate with a name; does each person associate his or her own description? Then how is communication possible? Is there just one description for the whole language? Which one? What is "the" description for *Aristotle*? In fact, it seems that no description is necessary because Aristotle might not have been the most famous student of Plato, teacher of Alexander the Great, author of *Metaphysics*, and so on.

What are we to think? According to the Direct Reference Theory, names mean their bearers, but that seems insufficient. According to the Description Theory, names mean some definite description, but none seems motivated or necessary. A compromise has recently been defended. According to Bach (1988), names have only nominal descriptive content, yielding the *Nominal Description Theory* of names:

(38)
Nominal Description Theory
Proper names have the meaning "the bearer of *N*."

Thus, *Aristotle* means just "the bearer of *Aristotle*." Unlike the Description Theory, this theory does not bring up the problem of choosing one description to associate with a name. It explains how sentences with different names for the same thing can be informative. It also explains how we can use a name to refer literally to things that bear that name. Still, it does not yet explain how we can use a name to refer to just one bearer of that name.

But settling questions of language use is the job of *pragmatics*—the study of the use of language in context. We have seen that semantics and pragmatics are intimately related in the theory of singular terms, and this will also be reflected in our discussion of later topics, such as anaphora.

Natural Kind Terms, Concepts, and the Linguistic Division of Labor

Putnam (1975, 1988) notes that elm trees are not maple trees and that most speakers know that elm trees are not maple trees—in other words, they know that *elm* does not mean the same as *maple*. Yet many of these same speakers cannot tell an elm tree from a maple tree; the knowledge they have in their heads is not sufficient to differentiate these kinds of trees. The same is true for many other *natural kind terms*—common nouns that denote kinds of things in nature, such as aluminum versus molybdenum, gold versus pyrite ("fool's gold"), diamonds versus zircons. We are all confident that these pairs of words are not synonymous, yet many people's concepts contain no information sufficient to distinguish one member of each pair from the other. Thus, it is clear that normal speakers do not have a determinate concept of the things these words denote. What then fixes their denotation?

Putnam suggests that there is a "division of linguistic labor" in language, in that normal speakers depend on and defer to "experts" in these matters. To determine whether a tree really is a beech or a maple, one consults a tree specialist. To determine whether a metal is gold or pyrite, one consults a metallurgist. And so on. These experts have procedures, based on scientific understanding, for determining the category of these samples. With respect to these terms, then, reference is in part a social phenomenon.

Anaphora, Denotation, and Reference

One phenomenon that has interested linguists and logicians for some time is the relation between pronouns (or noun phrases) and a set of "antecedent" noun phrases (see Chomsky 1981 and references cited there). Such relations, known as *anaphoric relations*, can be illustrated as follows:

(39)
Colinked

a. Reflexives: John shaves himself.

b. Reciprocals: The men liked each other.

c. Idioms: I lost my way.

d. *Wh*-antecedent: Who thinks that he has been cheated?

e. Quantified antecedent: Everyone said that he was tired.

f. Epithets: He stepped on my foot, the creep!

(40)
Disjointly linked

a. Robert saw Michael.

b. He likes Sam.

c. John believes him to be rash.

d. John believes that she is rash.

e. Sam believes that Sam is rash.

In each case the second item is linked to the first item in some way that is relevant to how a speaker and hearer communicate (there would be a misunderstanding if the speaker intended one linking, but the hearer understood another).

What sorts of linking are we dealing with here? This is a difficult question, and at present any answer would have to be considered tentative; but it seems likely that some of these links are syntactic or semantic, whereas others are pragmatic (see chapter 9 for further discussion). One way of getting a feel for this is to ask whether the sentence would be used nonliterally if the link were actually broken. For instance, in (40a) *Robert* and *Michael* are disjointly linked and thus are considered to be distinct in reference. But is this denotation or speaker reference? Well, imagine a person named both *Robert* and *Michael*, who sees himself in a mirror at an arcade. If a speaker were to say *No one saw Michael*, it would be possible to answer literally *That's not so, Robert saw Michael*. Although it can be true that Robert *is* Michael, it is still an odd way of *saying* what we want to say. Why is this so? Probably there is a pragmatic presumption to the effect that unless otherwise indicated, subject and object positions of verbs are to be taken as disjoint in speaker reference. This same principle would account for (40b). A case where the linkage is semantic—and therefore cannot be overridden pragmatically without being nonliteral—is given in (39a). Here the reflexive pronoun *himself* marks the fact that *him* has the same denotation as the subject of the verb, *John*. If *himself* is changed to *herself*, either one must assume that the speaker is speaking nonliterally in virtue of using the pronoun *her*, or one must assume that *John* is being used to refer to some female. These remarks extend to complex cases such as (40d). Notice that if the name *John* in these examples is changed to one without gender associations, as in (41), one has to know whether *Lee* is being used to refer to a male or a female in order to determine whether *she* is linked with *Lee* or not, preserving literality:

(41)
Lee believes that *she* is rash.

In some of the above cases, the linking is optional, in that there is another way of construing the sentence literally that does not involve the indicated links. For instance, (39d) and (39e) seem to admit the following interpretation:

(42)
a. Who thinks that he has been cheated? (That man over there)

b. Everyone said that he was tired. (That man over there)

Finally, notice that we can put more than one anaphoric device into a sentence and thereby affect its linking. For instance, (43) allows *he* either to be linked to *John* or to refer demonstratively to someone else:

(43)
John said that he was tired. (That man over there)

However, if we add *as for himself* to the sentence, we block the latter possibility:

(44)
John said that, as for himself, he was tired. (That man over there)

How can the phrase *as for himself* contribute to establishing the link between *John* and *he*? These are still matters of current research, but the above examples should serve to illustrate that anaphora is a topic rich in connections among morphology, syntax, semantics, and pragmatics.

How might we represent these kinds of facts in a semantic theory? Clearly, we will not want our semantics to represent information that is nonsemantical, but since the distinction is difficult to determine at times, we will illustrate how both a semantic case and a pragmatic case might work.

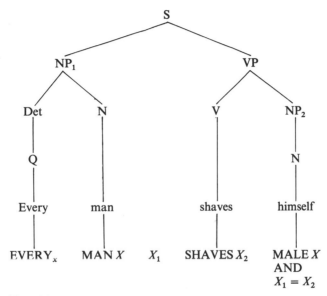

Tree 6.1

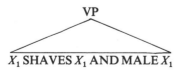

Tree 6.2

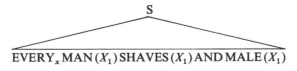

Tree 6.3

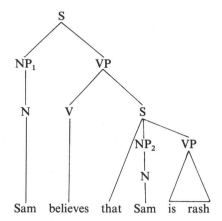

Tree 6.4

For a semantic case, consider *Every man shaves himself*. This sentence would receive roughly the syntactic and semantic analysis shown in tree 6.1. Combining NP_2 with the verb yields the result shown in tree 6.2, and combining this result with NP_1 in turn yields tree 6.3. The semantic rendition of our original sentence is imperfect, but the effect of the semantics is clear, and the result entails that all the people shave themselves and they are all males—which is what the original entails.

For a pragmatic case, consider (40e), *Sam believes that Sam is rash*. This sentence has roughly the syntactic structure shown in tree 6.4. When a noun phrase (such as NP_1) precedes another noun phrase that is a proper name (such as NP_2), and also c-commands the second NP, as in tree 6.4, then the two NPs are subject to the following presumption:

(45)

Presumption of Disjoint Reference

If a speaker utters a sentence with a structure such as that shown in tree 6.4, then the hearer may assume that the speaker intends to refer to two distinct persons (or things), unless there is some reason to think the same person or thing is being referred to.

Given this presumption, sentence (40e) is understood by a hearer to involve references to two different people, unless the context of utterance provides evidence that overrides it. This can happen in cases such as the following:

(46)
Speaker A: Everybody believes Sam is rash.
Speaker B: But does Sam believe *himself* to be rash?
Speaker A: Sure, since *everybody* believes Sam is rash, Sam (pointing to
                Sam) must believe that Sam is rash.

This example illustrates again the important difference between semantic constraints and these sorts of pragmatic constraints. By choosing to override semantic constraints, the speaker will be speaking nonliterally. By choosing to override the pragmatic constraint, the speaker can still be speaking literally; however, the hearer will now have to figure out what the speaker is referring to, given that the most obvious presumption is not in effect. In this way we can see that all levels of a grammar can be called upon to explain related aspects of language structure and communication.

Study Questions

1. Give two reasons for including a representation of semantic information in a grammar.

2. What is the Denotational Theory of meaning? Discuss at least one objection to it.

3. On the Denotational Theory of meaning, if an expression has a denotation, it has a meaning. Give at least one example of an expression for which this is false.

4. What is the Mentalist Theory of meaning? What two versions of it are discussed in the text? Discuss the problems with each version.

5. What is the Use Theory of meaning? Discuss its major weakness.

6. Consider the following dialogue:

Speaker A: What chances do I have for a raise?
Speaker B: Two. Slim and fat.

Does *fat* mean the same thing as *slim* in the language, or is one of these words being used nonliterally? Defend your answer.

7. Why should a semantic theory be finite?

8. What is it for a semantic theory to be compositional?

9. Anaphora involves two kinds of linking; what are they?

10. What is the difference between semantic and pragmatic linking?

11. What problems do natural kind terms pose for the conceptualist theory of meaning? Discuss.

12. Are descriptions semantically ambiguous between attributive and referential readings, or are these simply two different uses of descriptions? Discuss.

13. What problems do the following sentences pose for the Direct Reference Theory? Discuss.

a. Vulcan exists.
b. Budapest exists.
c. Vulcan does not exist.
d. Budapest does not exist.

14. How does the syntax of proper names differ from that of descriptions?

15. What are some further problems for the Nominal Description Theory? Discuss.

Exercises

1. Think of a reason, not given in the text, why semantics might be considered a part of a grammar.

2. Can you think of a reason why semantics should not be included in a grammar? Discuss.

3. What is *ambiguity* on the Denotational Theory of meaning? How might this semantic property be a problem for the theory? (Hint: Think of the number of possible denotations.)

4. What is *ambiguity* on the imagist version of the Mentalist Theory of meaning? How might this be a problem for the theory? Discuss.

5. Interpret the following sentences. What principles do you think you used to interpret them?

a. Ralph may not be a communist, but he's at least a *pinko*.
b. He traded his hot car for a *cold* one.
c. John is studying sociology and other *soft* sciences.
d. Who *killed* Lake Erie?

6. Think of five words, write down what you think they mean, then look them up in a good dictionary. Is your idiolect at variance with the dialect called Standard English?

7. Suppose someone said that a grammar must describe what a *speaker* means in uttering an expression from the language, and that it must do this for every meaningful expression. What problems are there for this proposal?

8. Entailment relations are transitive: if *cat* → *mammal*, and *mammal* → *animal*, then *cat* → *animal*. Now consider the "part of" relation. Is it transitive? Defend your answer.

a. A second is part of a minute.
   A minute is part of an hour.
   An hour is part of a day.
   Is a second a part of an hour? part of a day?

b. The toenail is part of the toe.
The toe is part of the foot.
The foot is part of the leg.
Is the toenail part of the leg?
c. Henry's toe is part of Henry.
Henry is part of the 23rd Battalion.
Is Henry's toe part of the 23rd Battalion?

9. Consider the following sentences and state what the denoting expression denotes:

a. *The chair you are sitting on* sells all over France for $200.
b. *Time Magazine* was bought out by Hearst, so now *it* is good for wrapping your garbage.

10. The words *mother*, *father*, *sister*, and *brother* all have religious as well as biological meanings. How would one represent the religious senses of each word?

11. How many different meanings can you see in the following sentences? (Hint: If you think of the possible meanings of the words in isolation, you may come up with more meanings.)

a. My dogs are very tired today.
b. The green giant is over the hill.
c. Time flies.

12. At the lexical level, how might the ten meaning properties and relations schematized in (18a) be defined? (Hint: Some of these were defined in the text.)

13. Suppose someone were to claim the following: "Given some combination of phonemes, we can *never* predict the meaning of the combination; given some combination of morphemes, we can *sometimes* predict the meaning of the combination; given some combination of words into a sentence, if we know the words and their grammatical relations, we can *always* predict the meaning of the sentence." Criticize or defend this claim in terms of evidence based on the information presented in chapters 3 through 6.

14. What other indexical expressions are there besides the ones discussed in the text? (Hint: Think of pronouns in the accusative and possessive.)

15. Find nonindexical uses for all the indexical expressions in the text (except the ones given).

16. Formulate plausible semantic rules for more indexicals on the model of *I* and *now*. For example, try *you*, *this*, *yesterday*, and *here*.

17. How would you state each of the nonindexical uses given in the text as a rule? Is this semantic? Discuss.

18. Consider the following grammatical and ungrammatical sentences containing proper names. Try to formulate a rule (or rules) describing their syntactic distribution. (Words set in capitals are pronounced with heavy stress.)

a.   Paris is beautiful.
b.   *The Paris is beautiful.
c.   THE Paris is beautiful.
d.   The Paris which is in France is beautiful.
e.   The French Paris is beautiful.
f.   Paris the capital is beautiful.
g.   * The Paris the capital is beautiful.
h.   *The Paris, which is in France, is beautiful.
i.   Paris, which is in France, is beautiful.
j.   I saw SOME Sam.
k.   *I saw some Sam.
l.   Sams are all quite similar, you know.
m.   A Sam is usually a funny guy.

Bibliography and Further Reading

Allan, K. (1986). *Linguistic meaning*. 2 vols. London: Routledge and Kegan Paul.

Alston, W. (1967). Meaning. In P. Edwards, ed., *The encyclopedia of philosophy*, vol. 5. New York: Macmillan.

Bach, K. (1988). *Thought and reference*. Oxford: Oxford University Press.

Chomsky, N. (1965). *Aspects of the theory of syntax*. Cambridge, Mass.: MIT Press.

Chomsky, N. (1981). *Lectures on government and binding*. Dordrecht, Holland: Foris.

Cruse, D. (1986). *Lexical semantics*. Cambridge: Cambridge University Press.

Devitt, M., and K. Sterelny (1987). *Language and reality*. Cambridge, Mass.: MIT Press.

Dillon, G. (1977). *Introduction to contemporary linguistic semantics*. Englewood Cliffs, N.J.: Prentice-Hall.

Donnellan, K. (1966). Reference and definite descriptions. *Philosophical Review* 67, 237–242.

Dowty, D., et al. (1981). *Introduction to Montague semantics*. Dordrecht, Holland: Reidel.

Evans, G. (1983). *Varieties of reference*. Oxford: Oxford University Press.

Farmer, A. (1984). *Modularity in syntax*. Cambridge, Mass.: MIT Press.

Fodor, J. D. (1977). *Semantics: Theories of meaning in generative grammar*. New York: Crowell.

Frege, G. (1892). On sense and reference. In P. Geach and M. Black, eds. (1960). *Translations from the philosophical writings of Gottlob Frege*. Oxford: Blackwell.

Glucksberg, S., and J. Danks (1975). *Experimental psycholinguistics*. Hillsdale, N.J.: L. Erlbaum Associates.

Grandy, R. (1987). In defense of semantic fields. In Lepore 1987.

Grice, H. P. (1957). Meaning. *Philosophical Review* 66, 377–388.

Grice, H. P. (1968). Utterer's meaning, sentence-meaning, and word-meaning. *Foundations of Language* 4, 225–242.

Grice, H. P. (1969). Utterer's meaning and intentions. *Philosophical Review* 78, 147–177.

Higginbotham, J. (1985). On semantics. *Linguistic Inquiry* 16, 547–593.

Jackendoff, R. (1972). *Semantic interpretation in generative grammar*. Cambridge, Mass.: MIT Press.

Jackendoff, R. (1983). *Semantics and cognition*. Cambridge, Mass.: MIT Press.

Kaplan, D. (1978). Dthat. In P. Cole, ed., *Syntax and semantics 9*. New York: Academic Press.

Katz, J. (1972). *Semantic theory*. New York: Harper and Row.

Katz, J. (1980). *Propositional structure and illocutionary force*. Cambridge, Mass.: Harvard University Press.

Katz, J., and J. Fodor (1963). The structure of a semantic theory. *Language* 39, 170–210.

Kempson, R. (1977). *Semantic theory*. Cambridge: Cambridge University Press.

Kripke, S. (1977). Speaker's reference and semantic reference. Reprinted in P. French et al., eds. (1979). *Contemporary perspectives in the philosophy of language*. Minneapolis, Minn.: University of Minnesota Press.

Kripke, S. (1980). *Naming and necessity*. Cambridge, Mass.: Harvard University Press.

Ladusaw, W. (1988). Semantic theory. In Newmeyer 1988.

Lehrer, A. (1974). *Semantic fields and lexical structure*. Amsterdam: North-Holland.

Lehrer, K., and A. Lehrer, eds. (1970). *Theory of meaning*. Englewood Cliffs, N.J.: Prentice-Hall.

Lehrer, K., and A. Lehrer (1982). Antonymy. *Linguistics and Philosophy* 5, 483–501.

Lepore, E., ed. (1987). *New directions in semantics*. New York: Academic Press.

Lyons, J. (1977). *Semantics*. 2 vols. Cambridge: Cambridge University Press.

McCawley, J. (1981). *Everything that linguists have always wanted to know about logic*. Chicago: University of Chicago Press.

Mill, J. S. (1843). *A system of logic*. London.

Miller, G., and P. Johnson-Laird (1976). *Language and perception*. Cambridge, Mass.: Harvard University Press.

Newmeyer, F., ed. (1988). *Linguistics: The Cambridge survey*, vol 1. Cambridge: Cambridge University Press.

Platts, M. (1979). *Ways of meaning*. London: Routledge and Kegan Paul.

Putnam, H. (1975). The meaning of "meaning." In K. Gunderson, ed., *Language, mind and knowledge*. Minneapolis, Minn.: University of Minnesota Press.

Putnam, H. (1988). *Representation and reality*. Cambridge, Mass.: MIT Press.

Russell, B. (1905). On denoting. *Mind* 14, 479–493.

Schiffer, S. (1987). *Remnants of meaning*. Cambridge, Mass.: MIT Press.

Schiffer, S. (1988). *Meaning*. 2nd ed. Oxford: Oxford University Press.

Schwartz, S., ed. (1977). *Naming, necessity and natural kinds*. Ithaca, N.Y.: Cornell University Press.

Sloat, C. (1969). Proper nouns in English. *Language* 45, 26–30.

Wittgenstein, L. (1953). *Philosophical investigations*. Oxford: Blackwell.

Chapter 7

LANGUAGE VARIATION

7.1 LANGUAGE STYLES AND DIALECTS

Consider the following sentence (from Dillard 1972):

(1)
You makin' sense, but you don't be makin' sense!

Speakers of the standard dialect of English are likely to conclude that this sentence is ungrammatical. The first clause lacks a (finite) verb (such as *are*) that the standard dialect requires, and the sequence *do* + *be* in the second clause is a combination that the standard dialect prohibits. Speakers of the standard dialect might also question the logic of the sentence (and hence, as has unfortunately happened, the logical abilities of its utterer). After all, the two clauses appear to contradict each other. However, we will see in this chapter that the sentence is grammatical in its dialect (a Washington, D.C., dialect of Black English) and is both logical and sophisticated. It represents one of the many variations in form that English can take.

No human language is fixed, uniform, or unvarying: all languages show internal variation. Actual usage varies from group to group, and speaker to speaker, in terms of the pronunciation of a language, the choice of words and the meaning of those words, and even the use of syntactic constructions. To take a well-known example, the speech of Americans is noticeably different from the speech of the British, and the speech of these two groups in turn is distinct from the speech of Australians. When groups of speakers differ noticeably in their language, they are often said to speak different *dialects* of the language.

Dialectal Variation

It is notoriously difficult, however, to define precisely what a dialect is, and in fact the term has come to be used in various ways. The classic example of a dialect is the _regional_ dialect: the distinct form of a language spoken in a certain geographical area. For example, we might speak of Ozark dialects or Appalachian dialects, on the grounds that inhabitants of these regions have certain distinct linguistic features that differentiate them from speakers of other forms of English. We can also speak of a _social_ dialect: the distinct form of a language spoken by members of a specific socio-economic class, such as the working class dialects in England or the ghetto languages in the United States (to which we will return). In addition, certain _ethnic_ dialects can be distinguished, such as the form of English sometimes referred to as Yiddish English, historically associated with speakers of Eastern European Jewish ancestry.

It is important to note that dialects are never purely regional, or purely social, or purely ethnic. For example, the distinctive Ozark and Appalachian dialects are not merely dialects spoken by any of the inhabitants. As we will see, regional, social, and ethnic factors combine and intersect in various ways in the identification of dialects.

In popular usage the term _dialect_ refers to a form of a language that is regarded as "substandard," "incorrect," or "corrupt," as opposed to the "standard," "correct," or "pure" form. In sharp contrast, the term _dialect_, as a technical term in linguistics, carries no such value judgment and simply refers to a distinct form of a language. Thus, for example, linguists refer to so-called Standard English as a dialect of English, which, from a linguistic point of view, is no more "correct" than any other form of English. From this point of view, the monarchs of England and teenagers in Los Angeles and New York all speak dialects of English.

Although dialects are often said to be regional, social, or ethnic, linguists also use the term _dialect_ to refer to language variations that cannot be tied to any geographical area, social class, or ethnic group. Rather, this use of _dialect_ simply indicates that speakers show some variation in the way they use elements of the language. For example, some speakers of English are perfectly comfortable using the word _anymore_ in sentences such as the following:

(2)
Tools are expensive _anymore_.

Here, _anymore_ means roughly the same as _nowadays_ or _lately_. Other speakers of English can use *anymore* only if there is a negative element, such as *not* , in the sentence:

(3)
Tools are *not* cheap *anymore*.

As far as we can tell, this difference between speakers cannot be linked to a particular region of the country or to a particular social class or ethnic group.

Language variation does not end with dialects. Each recognizable dialect of a language is itself subject to considerable internal variation: no two speakers of a language, even if they are speakers of the same dialect, produce and use their language in exactly the same way. We are able to recognize different individuals by their distinct speech and language patterns; indeed, a person's language is one of the most fundamental features of self-identity. The form of a language spoken by a single individual is referred to as an *idiolect*, and every speaker of a language has a distinct idiolect.

Once we realize that variation in language is pervasive, it becomes apparent that there is no such thing as a single language used at all times by all speakers. There is no such thing as a single English language; rather, there are many English languages (dialects and idiolects) depending on who is using the language and what the context of use is. Consider the well-known phenomenon of variation in vocabulary words that exists among speakers of English:

(4)
a. *Dope* means "cola" in some parts of the South.
b. *Pocketbook* means "purse" in Boston and in parts of the South.
c. *Fetch up* means "raise" (children) in the South.
d. *Pavement* means "sidewalk" in eastern Pennsylvania and in England.
e. *Happygrass* means "grasshopper" in eastern Virginia.
f. *Bubbler* means "water fountain" in Wisconsin.
g. *Knock up* means "to wake someone up by knocking" in England.
h. *Bonnet* means "hood" (of a car) in England.
i. *Fag* means "cigarette" in England.

As the last three examples indicate, vocabulary differences between American and British English are common and often amusing. Indeed, the Bell Telephone System has published a pamphlet entitled "Getting around the USA: Travel Tips for the British Visitor," which contains a section entitled "How to Say It." This section notes the following correspondences:

(5)

British	*American*
car park	parking lot
coach	bus
garage	service station
lay by	rest area
lift	elevator
lorry	truck
petrol	gasoline
underground (or tube)	subway
call box	telephone booth
telephonist	switchboard operator
gin and French	dry martini
minerals	soft drinks
suspenders	garters
vest	undershirt

These examples are typical of the sort of dialectal variation found in the vocabulary of British and American English.

Mutual Intelligibility

Given the existence of dialectal and idiolectal variation, what allows us to refer to something called English, as if it were a single, monolithic language? A standard answer to this question rests on the notion of *mutual intelligibility*. That is, even though native speakers of English vary in their use of the language, their various languages are similar enough in pronunciation, vocabulary, and grammar to permit mutual intelligibility. A New Yorker, a Texan, and a Californian may recognize differences in each other's language, but they can understand each other (despite all the jokes to the contrary) and they recognize each other as speaking the "same language." Hence, speaking the "same language" does not depend on two speakers speaking identical languages, but only very similar languages.

By way of contrast, it is interesting to note cases that might be called *one-way intelligibility*, involving speakers of different, but historically related, languages. For example, speakers of Brazilian Portuguese who do not know Spanish can often understand the forms of Spanish spoken in neighboring countries. The analogous Spanish speakers, however, find Portuguese largely unintelligible. A similar situation holds between Danish and Swedish: speakers of Danish can (more or less) comprehend Swedish, but the reverse situation is much less common. Even if one group of speakers can understand another group, they cannot be said to speak the same language unless the second group also understands the first, and thus the notion of *mutual* intelligibility is crucial in specifying when two languages are the "same" language.

Although the notion of mutual intelligibility seems like a reasonable criterion in defining dialects, the situation can be considerably complicated by social and political factors. In China, for example, a northern Chinese speaker of the Beijing dialect (also known as Mandarin) cannot understand the speech of a southern Chinese speaker of Cantonese, and vice versa. For this reason, a linguist might well label Mandarin and Cantonese as two distinct "languages." Nevertheless, in traditional studies of the Chinese language, both Mandarin and Cantonese are regarded as "dialects" of Chinese, given that they are historically related (that is, they may have been offshoots of several closely related dialects that existed earlier in the history of the Chinese language). Moreover, both Mandarin and Cantonese are spoken in the same nation (they are not languages of two different countries with different governments), and speakers of both "dialects" can use the written language (in the form of Chinese characters) as a common language of communication. For such reasons, the tendency has persisted to use the term "dialect" to refer to various mutually unintelligible forms of the Chinese language.

Historical and political factors can also give rise to the opposite situation, where two mutually intelligible forms are considered not dialects of the same language but rather two distinct languages. For example, Tohono O'odham (formerly Papago) and Akimel O'odham (formerly Pima) are two Native American languages spoken by members of tribal groups living in Arizona and in northern Mexico. In fact, Tohono O'odham and Akimel O'odham are mutually intelligible and are extremely close phonologically and grammatically, with only minor linguistic differences in pronunciation and syntax (the differences between them being less radical than the differences between American and British English). For this reason, a linguist could well consider Tohono O'odham and Akimel O'odham to be two dialects of the same language. Nevertheless, for historical and political reasons the two tribal groups consider themselves distinct political entities, and they consider their languages to be distinct languages rather than dialectal variations of a single language. Another example is provided by "Dutch" and "Flemish." Speakers of "Dutch" understand speakers of

"Flemish" and vice versa. However, there is an important political distinction between the two: "Dutch" is spoken in The Netherlands and "Flemish" is spoken in Belgium.

Having examined some of the complications involved in the term *dialect*, how can we define it? No satisfactory definition of *dialect* has yet been proposed, but for our purposes we will ignore complications and settle on a very general one. A dialect is simply a distinct form of a language, possibly associated with a recognizable regional, social, or ethnic group, differentiated from other forms of the language by specific linguistic features (for example, pronunciation, or vocabulary, or grammar, or any combination of these). This rough definition is intended to do no more than capture a certain intuitive idea of the term *dialect*, but one that seems useful. In any event, it must be kept in mind that from a linguistic point of view *dialect* is a theoretical concept. In reality, variation in language is so pervasive that each language is actually a continuum of languages from speaker to speaker, and from group to group, and no absolute lines can be drawn between different forms of a language.

Dialects and the Interplay of Regional and Social Factors: New York City /r/

As noted, the classic example of a dialect is the regional dialect, the assumption being that speakers of the dialect form a coherent speech community living in relative isolation from speakers outside the community. Such relative isolation between geographical areas is becoming increasingly rare, and in the United States the population as a whole is so geographically and socially mobile that it is becoming increasingly more difficult to speak of regional dialects in any pure sense. Especially in large urban areas, a particular linguistic feature of a regional dialect might well be influenced by social factors.

An interesting example of the effect of "social prestige" on a regional dialect is found in the pronunciation of /r/ in New York City speech. The so-called *r-less* dialect of New York City is so well known that it is often the subject of humor, especially on the part of the New Yorkers who themselves speak it. It is commonly thought that speakers of the dialect completely lack /r/ in words such as *car*, *card*, *four*, *fourth*, and so on, but this is a misconception, as an intriguing study by the sociolinguist William Labov (1972) reveals.

Labov began with the hypothesis that New York City speakers vary in their pronunciation of /r/ according to their social status. Labov interviewed salespeople at several New York City department stores that differed in price range and social prestige. Assuming that salespeople tend to "borrow prestige" from their customers, Labov predicted that the social stratification of customers at different department stores would be mirrored in a similar stratification of salespeople. These assumptions led him to hypothesize that "salespeople in the highest-ranked store will have the highest values of (r); those in the middle-ranked store will have intermediate values of (r); and those in the lowest-ranked store will show the lowest value" (1972, 45).

Labov chose three stores: Saks Fifth Avenue (high prestige), Macy's (middle level), and S. Klein (low prestige). He interviewed salespeople by asking them a question that would elicit the answer *fourth floor*:

The interviewer approached the informant in the role of a customer asking for directions to a particular department. The department was one which was located on the fourth floor. When the interviewer asked, "Excuse me, where are the women's shoes?" the answer would normally be, "Fourth floor."

The interviewer then leaned forward and said, "Excuse me?" He would usually then obtain another utterance, "*Fourth floor,*" spoken in careful style under emphatic stress. (1972, 49)

The phrase *fourth floor* has two instances of /r/, both of which are subject to variation in the pronunciation of New York City speakers, and Labov was able to study both casual and careful pronunciations of this phrase.

The result turned out to correlate in an interesting way with the hypothesis. For example, Labov found that at Saks, 30 percent of the salespeople interviewed always pronounced both /r/'s in the test phrase; at Macy's 20 percent did so; and at Klein's only 4 percent did. In addition, Labov found that 32 percent of the interviewed salespeople at Saks had variable pronunciation of /r/ (sometimes /r/ was pronounced and sometimes not, depending on context); at Macy's 31 percent of the interviewees had variable pronunciation; and at Klein's only 17 percent did. These overall results do suggest that pronunciation of /r/ in New York City is correlated, at least loosely, with social stratification of the speakers.

What about the differences in pronunciation between the casual and the emphatic styles? It turns out that in the casual response the /r/ of *floor* was pronounced by 63 percent of the salespeople at Saks, 44 percent at Macy's, and only 8 percent at Klein's. In contrast, in the careful, emphatic response the /r/ of *floor* was pronounced by 64 percent at Saks, 61 percent at Macy's, (note the jump from 44 percent), and 18 percent at Klein's. In other words, at Saks there was very little difference between casual and careful pronunciations, whereas at Macy's and Klein's the difference between these styles was significantly larger. This suggests that speakers at the middle and lower levels of the New York City social scale are perfectly aware that a final /r/ occurs in words such as *floor*. Even though they omit this /r/ in casual pronunciation, it reappears in careful speech:

In emphatic pronunciation of the final (r), Macy's employees come very close to the mark set by Saks. It would seem that r-pronunciation is the norm at which a majority of Macy employees aim, yet not the one they use most often. In Saks, we see a shift between casual and emphatic pronunciation, but it is much less marked. (1972, 51–52)

As we will see again in section 7.2, the difference between casual and careful language styles is important in syntactic variation as well.

Hypercorrection

In connection with the pronunciation of New York City /r/, it is interesting to note that some New York City speakers insert /r/ in words where it does not actually occur in spelling. One can hear *Cuba* pronounced [kyuwbɹ], *saw* pronounced [sɔr], *idea* pronounced [aydiyɹ], and so on. It seems that the very speakers who drop /r/ in some words and positions will insert an /r/ in other words and positions. The cause of this phenomenon is sometimes thought to be *hypercorrection* (that is, overcorrection): speakers who have been persuaded that it is "incorrect" to drop /r/ will overcompensate or overcorrect for this by inserting the sound where it does not actually occur in spelling. (Syntactic hypercorrection occurs when speakers say *between you and I* instead of *between you and me* on the grounds that *I* is more "correct" and "cultured" than *me*.)

However, we might question whether, for given speakers, inserting /r/ involves only hypercorrection. For one thing, even those speakers who insert /r/ do not always pronounce words such as *idea* with a final /r/: the insertion of /r/ in such words happens only when the next word begins with a vowel (hence, we might hear phrases such as *the idear I heard about* but not **the idear John told me about*). The insertion of /r/ is thus at least partially governed by a phonological principle. In the second place, hypercorrection often involves imitating what is thought to be prestige language. For example, a hypercorrect phrase such as *It is I* is thought to sound more prestigious than *It's me*, even though there is nothing grammatically incorrect about the latter phrase. Returning to words such as *idear*, speakers who insert /r/ in *idear* may not think that such a pronunciation is presti-

gious. Since insertion of /r/ is governed partially by a phonological principle, and since it may not involve imitation of prestige language, for some
speakers this insertion of /r/ is not strictly a case of hypercorrection.

The Labov study illustrates once again that there is often no absolute
or simple distinction between one dialect and another: we cannot simply
say that the New York City dialect is *r*-less. Rather, the pronunciation of
/r/ in that dialect is variable, and this variation seems to be correlated both
with social factors and with the casual or careful context. Thus, just as no
language can be said to be unvarying or fixed, so no dialect of a language
can be said to be unvarying or fixed either. Finally, not even the language
of an individual speaker is unvarying: an individual New Yorker may well
show variation in pronouncing /r/.

"Standard" versus "Nonstandard" Language

A pervasive phenomenon of societies in the contemporary world is the
designation of one dialect of a language as the "standard," "correct," or
"pure" form of the language. In the contemporary United States, Standard
American English (or SAE, for short) is a form of the language used in
news programs in the national media (often referred to as "Network
English"); it is the language of legal and governmental functions; and it is
the language used in the schools as a vehicle for education.

As noted earlier, in linguistic terms no one dialect of a language is any
more correct, any better, or any more logical than any other dialect of the
language: all dialects are equally effective forms of language, in that any
idea or desire that can be expressed in one dialect can be expressed just as
easily in any other dialect. The idea that SAE is the correct form of the
language is a social attitude—more precisely, a language prejudice—that
is just as irrational as social prejudices involving race or sex. In the United
States the so-called standard language is perhaps most widely identified
with the educated white middle class; hence, a good case can be made that
the reverence for the standard language in our schools and official functions is a reflection of the far more general bias in the country toward
considering the white middle-class value system the correct or best value
system. It is important to realize at the outset that labeling one particular
dialect as standard and others as inferior reflects a sociopolitical judgment,
not a linguistic judgment. Indeed, in countries throughout the world, the
standard national language is the dialect of the subculture with the most
prestige and power.

Black English and the Verb *Be*

A well-known example of a social dialect that has been labeled as non-standard is Black English. In a certain sense the term Black English (or BE, for short) is misleading in that it suggests that all Black Americans speak the same dialect and use it all the time. Both impressions are incorrect. Black Americans show as much linguistic variation as any other social group in the nation; language is not determined by race. Further, even those who can be said to use BE do not necessarily use this dialect at all times. Essentially, BE refers to an informal style of language typically (though not exclusively) used by Black residents of low-income ghettos in large urban areas of the United States. Although BE is also used by certain Latinos and Whites who live in the same ghetto areas, BE is stereotypically associated with Black residents of the ghetto.

In recent years, BE has attracted a good deal of attention from linguists (see references), whose investigations have shown quite clearly that BE is every bit as rule-governed and as logical as SAE. In a series of important studies Labov (see references) has demonstrated that there are several important and highly systematic relationships between BE and SAE. To take what is perhaps the best-known example, consider the frequently noted fact that in BE present tense forms of the verb *to be* are often dropped in casual speech (examples taken from Labov 1969a):

(6)
a. She the first one started us off.
b. He fast in everything he do.
c. I know, but he wild, though.
d. You out the game.
e. We on tape.
f. But everybody not black.
g. They not caught.
h. Boot always comin' over my house to eat.
i. He gon' try get up.

The omission of the verb *to be* in BE can easily be misinterpreted by those untrained in linguistics as evidence that BE is a kind of defective dialect that violates rules of grammar or, worse yet, has no rules of grammar. As Labov (1969b) notes, this has even led to the mistaken view on the part of certain educators and psychologists that Black children entering school have a language deficit and are culturally deprived. Even though the omission of forms of the verb *to be* may at first appear to make

BE quite distinct from SAE, Labov (1969b, 203) points out that

The deletion of the *is* or *are* in [BE] is not the result of erratic or illogical behavior: it follows the same regular rules as standard English contraction. Wherever standard English can contract, [BE can] use either the contracted form or (more commonly) the deleted zero form. Thus, *They mine* corresponds to standard *They're mine*, not to the full form *They are mine*. On the other hand, no such deletion is possible in positions where standard English cannot contract: just as one cannot say *That's what they're* in standard English, *That's what they* is equally impossible in the vernacular we are considering.

In the examples already cited, the correspondence between SAE and BE is as follows:

(7)

SAE: Contraction	*BE: Deletion*
She's the first one . . .	She the first one . . .
He's fast . . .	He fast . . .
You're out . . .	You out . . .
They're not caught . . .	They not caught . . .

Both dialects have contraction, but only BE has the further option of deleting a contractible form of *to be*.

What appears at first to be a significant difference between SAE and BE actually turns out to be rather minor. Indeed, in both dialects the same general phenomenon is taking place: the verb *to be* (as well as other auxiliary verbs) becomes *reduced* in casual speech when it is unstressed. One dialect reflects the reduction process by contraction alone, the other dialect by contraction or deletion. As we will see, in fact, the deletion of the verb *to be* (and other auxiliary verbs) is by no means limited to BE but happens quite generally in the informal style in all dialects of American English.

Another grammatical feature of BE that has been noted in linguistic studies is a certain use of the verb *to be* illustrated by examples such as the following (taken from Fasold 1972, chap. 4):

(8)

a. I get a ball and then some children *be* on one team and some *be* on another team.

b. Christmas Day, well, everybody *be* so choked up over gifts and everything, they don't *be* too hungry anyway.

c. My father *be* the last one to open his presents.

d. Yes, there always *be* fights.

e. On Saturdays, I like to watch cartoons, but I *be* out working.

This use of *be* has been termed *invariant be* (since it does not vary either to reflect past or present tense, or to agree with the subject), and it indicates a habitual and repeatable action, state, or event. Thus, invariant *be* is typically used in general descriptions (as in (8a), a description of a game) and to indicate customary or typical states of affairs. Given this, note that it is unacceptable in BE to say **He be workin' right now*, since the time expression *right now* does not have a habitual interpretation but instead refers to the specific present. In addition, whereas one can say *He my brother* (SAE *He's my brother*), it is unacceptable to say **He be my brother*, since the sibling relation is permanent; that is, it is not repeatable in the way that the use of invariant *be* requires. The sentence *You makin' sense, but you don't be makin' sense* would seem very odd if one did not understand the use of invariant *be*. Dillard (1972, 46) suggests that one could, in uttering such a sentence, mean "You've blundered into making an intelligent statement for once" or "That's a bright remark—but it's not the usual thing for you." The use of invariant *be* has been cited as a grammatical feature unique to BE, representing what seems to be a genuine difference between BE and other American dialects.

In discussions of BE, there has been an all too unfortunate tendency to compare BE to SAE without paying sufficient attention to the level of formality of the languages being compared. That is, BE refers to an *informal*-style language used in the ghetto by ghetto residents (within the culture of the Black ghetto there are more formal styles of language as well: for example, Afro-American religious preaching styles—see Smitherman 1977). BE has been compared with an "official" language of news broadcasts, governmental functions, and school settings. It is no surprise that significant differences have been found. However, when we examine *informal* styles of American English, we find similar features across all dialects, and it turns out that certain features of BE are simply part of the general linguistic features of informal English. It is crucial to distinguish between formal and informal styles of language before one can compare dialects in an accurate way.

Formal and Informal Language Styles

Without being aware of it, each speaker of any language has mastered a number of language styles. To illustrate, in a formal setting someone might offer coffee to a guest by saying *May I offer you some coffee?* or perhaps *Would you care for some coffee?* In an informal setting the same speaker might well say *Want some coffee?* or even *Coffee?* This shift in styles is completely unconscious and automatic; indeed, it takes some concentration and hard introspection to realize that we each use a formal and an informal style on different occasions.

The clearest cases of formal speech occur in social contexts that are formal, serious, often official in some sense, in which speakers feel they must watch their language and in which *manner* of saying something is regarded as socially important. These contexts would include a formal job interview, meeting an important person, and standing before a court of law. Informal speech in our use of that term occurs in casual, relaxed social settings in which speech is spontaneous, rapid, and uncensored by the speaker. Social settings for this style of speech would include chatting with close friends and interacting in an intimate or family environment or in similar relaxed settings.

Some speakers of English, notably self-styled educated speakers, often equate the formal language style with the so-called standard language; the informal style, if discussed at all, is dubbed a form of sloppy speech or even slang, especially in language classes in public schools. But on closer investigation of the actual details of informal language, it turns out that the informal style, far from being merely a sloppy form of language, is governed by rules every bit as precise, logical, and rigorous as the rules governing formal language. (Of course, the informal style also has idiosyncrasies and irregularities—but, then, the formal style does too.) In section 7.2 we will concentrate on some of the rules of the informal style because a detailed study of the syntactic differences between formal and informal language styles reveals a number of important ideas about language variation in general, and about the question of standard versus nonstandard language in particular.

7.2 SOME RULES OF THE GRAMMAR OF INFORMAL STYLE IN ENGLISH

A well-known difference between formal and informal language styles in English (and indeed in many other languages) is that the informal style can be characterized as having a greater amount of abbreviation, shortening, contraction, and deletion. Compare the formal *Would you care for some coffee?* with the informal *Want some coffee?* The formal style is often redundant and verbose, whereas the informal style is brief, to the point, and grammatically streamlined. In this section we will concentrate on two important grammatical features of the informal style, (1) the dropping of the subject of the sentence and (2) the dropping of the auxiliary verb, these being two central features of the *abbreviated* style.

The abbreviated style we will describe here is based on the language of the authors of this book, and all grammatical judgments will be based on our own speech. We have tested and confirmed our judgments with those of numerous other speakers, however. Furthermore, it seems clear that the abbreviation processes we describe are quite general within American English. You may find that your own judgment differs from ours at certain points, and this will be entirely natural; indeed, there could be no better illustration of the topic of this chapter. The important point is that every speaker of English has an abbreviated style in casual speech. Consequently, you will be able to judge for yourself how accurate we are in describing the abbreviated style in general.

Tag-Controlled Deletion

To begin, let us consider sentences that end in tag questions:

(9)
a. You have been sneaking to the movies again, *haven't you*!
b. He wants me to pay the bill, *does he*!
c. She likes her new house, *doesn't she*?
d. He is failing his courses, *isn't he*?
e. They will steal my money, *will they*!
f. You are getting pretty excited, *aren't you*?
g. You are not ready to swim fifty laps, *are you*?

As we saw in chapter 5, tag questions—*haven't you*, *does he*, and so on—reflect at least two important properties of a sentence: (1) the tag contains the auxiliary verb found in the main sentence, or (in the case of *do*) the auxiliary appropriate to the main sentence, and (2) the pronoun in the tag agrees with the subject of the sentence. The tag question thus contains, in part, a repetition of some of the information found in the main sentence.

In the informal, abbreviated style, the subject and the auxiliary of the main sentence can in fact be dropped.

(10)
a. Been sneaking to the movies again, haven't you!
b. Wants me to pay the bill, does he!
c. Likes her new house, doesn't she?
d. Failing his courses, isn't he?

e. Steal my money, will you!

f. Not ready to swim fifty laps, are you?

Let us refer to the process illustrated here as *Tag-Controlled Deletion*, described as follows: given a sentence with a tag question, the subject and the auxiliary (if any) of the main sentence may be deleted. Tag-Controlled Deletion is a rule of the abbreviated style in informal language.

Notice that there is nothing incomplete about the sentences in (10). That is, even though the subjects and auxiliaries are missing from the main clauses, this information can easily be *recovered* from the tag. Now consider the sentences in (11) and (12), which, as far as we know, are not possible for any speaker:

(11)

a. *Have been sneaking to the movies again, haven't you?

b. *Is failing his courses, isn't he?

c. *Will steal my money, will you?

d. *Are getting pretty excited, aren't you?

e. *Are not ready to swim fifty laps, are you?

(12)

a. *You been sneaking to the movies again, haven't you?

b. *He failing his courses, isn't he?

c. *You steal my money, will you?

d. *You getting pretty excited, aren't you?

e. *You not ready to swim fifty laps, are you?

These examples show another regularity: if the subject is deleted, then the auxiliary must be deleted (11a–e) and vice versa (12a–e). We can make a firm judgment that these sentences are bad, indicating that the abbreviation process is hardly sloppy; that is, not just anything can be deleted or left behind.

How can we account for the fact that the auxiliary verb may not remain behind if the subject of the sentence has been deleted or that the subject cannot be left if the auxiliary is deleted? Labov's observations on contraction suggest that we consider the fact that subjects and auxiliaries are often contracted (compare (13a–e) with (9a, d–g)):

(13)

a. You've been sneaking to the movies again.

b. He's failing his courses.

c. They'll steal my money.

d. You*'re* getting pretty excited.

e. You*'re* not ready to swim fifty laps.

If the rule is that the subject of the sentence can be deleted only if the auxiliary verb is contracted onto it, sentences such as those in (11) will never occur: the auxiliary will always be deleted along with the subject. The examples in (12) will never occur since, in Tag-Controlled Deletion, it is the subject that is deleted, not the free-standing auxiliary. To form a sentence such as *Been sneaking to the movies again, haven't you?*, we do not delete the two separate elements *you* and *have*, but the single contracted element *you've*.

This suggests the following descriptive generalization for Tag-Controlled Deletion:

(14)

Tag-Controlled Deletion
The subject of the main sentence may be deleted, under the following conditions:

a. There is a tag.

b. If the main sentence contains an auxiliary, it *must* be contracted onto the subject if it *can* be contracted onto the subject.

We have not addressed examples where the auxiliary is not contractible. As it stands, (14) makes the following prediction: if the auxiliary is not contractible, then it stays behind in Tag-Controlled Deletion. This prediction appears to be correct. For example, consider what happens when the auxiliary is *could*:

(15)
It could get on your nerves, couldn't it.

Since *could* cannot contract onto the subject, the sequence **it'd* would be ill formed. This predicts that (16a) should be odd, whereas (16b) should be fine. This turns out to be correct:

(16)

a.   *Get on your nerves, couldn't it.

b.   Could get on your nerves, couldn't it.

We have now set up a system wherein deletion of the subject depends on contraction of the subject with the auxiliary, wherever this is possible. As we saw, in Black English the link between contraction and deletion is crucial, and it turns out that this link is just as crucial in the general abbreviated style of American English.

We have by no means exhausted the topic of Tag-Controlled Deletion. However, the tag cases are only one part of the general deletion processes that affect subject and auxiliary in abbreviated style. We now turn to the deletion of *be* in abbreviated questions.

Deletion of *Be*

Another informal style of English involves abbreviated questions. *Want some coffee?* is an example of one type of abbreviated question; another type, the one we will be examining here, involves the deletion of the verb *be*. The following sentences illustrate cases where deletion is possible:

(17)
a. (You) running a fever?
   (= Are you running a fever?)
b. (You) finally rich now?
   (= Are you finally rich now?)
c. Your car in the garage?
   (= Is your car in the garage?)
d. Satisfied?
   (= Are you satisfied?)
e. John a professor or something?
   (= Is John a professor or something?)
f. (You) gonna leave soon?
   (= Are you going to leave soon?)
g. (You) sposta do that?
   (= Are you supposed to do that?)

Our data show that deletion of the verb *be* and the subject *you* is possible. Note also that the subject *you* cannot be deleted unless the auxiliary verb is deleted as well:

(18)
a. *Are running a fever?
b. *Are finally rich how?
c. *Are satisfied?
d. *Are gonna leave soon?
e. *Are sposta do that?

The verb in question is a contractible verb, just as in the case of Tag-Controlled Deletion. For example, the various forms of *be* can contract with various subjects:

(19)

am I	=	'my	[may]
are you	=	'ryou	[ryuw]
is he	=	's he	[ziy]
is she	=	's she	[zšiy]
is it	=	's it	[zɪt]
is John	=	's John	[zǰɑn]
are we	=	'r we	[ɻwiy]
are they	=	'r they	[ɻðey]

As noted in chapter 3, *am* shortens and contracts as /m/, *are* as /r/, and *is* as /z/, showing that *be* is a contractible verb and hence can delete. Since the subject *you* is deleted only if *be* is contracted onto it, such ungrammatical cases as *Are running a fever?* can never arise. Thus, in forming an abbreviated question, the second person subject *you* can be deleted as long as *be* is contracted onto it. It turns out that abbreviated questions can be formed with other auxiliary verbs as well, but we will not venture into those cases here.

Rule-Governed Deletion

We have seen that abbreviated questions are formed by deleting certain elements (contractable forms of *be* and *you*), and we have posited certain rules to characterize these processes. It is important to realize that other apparent abbreviations also occur in the informal style in English. For example, in a situation where we might use the abbreviated question *Want some coffee?*, we might also be able to ask, simply, *Coffee?* To take another example, suppose you run into a friend wearing shoes you haven't seen before. You might point to them and ask, "New?" These single-word utterances are quite common in casual styles and are perfectly appropriate and comprehensible. The point is that there is no reason whatsoever to suppose that such single-word utterances are derived from whole sentences from which all the other words have been deleted. It is simply that we can use many kinds of short expressions (including single words), as long as the context (linguistic or nonlinguistic) makes it clear what we are talking about.

In sharp contrast, the deletion of subjects and contractable verbs in, for example, abbreviated questions is governed by a *systematic rule*, with strict conditions. Not just any kind of deletion of subject and verb is possible, even if the context would make the abbreviation perfectly clear. For example, recall that *Are running a fever?* is impossible. There is nothing incomprehensible about this question: its meaning is clear and nothing in the context of conversation would rule it out. However, the expression has violated a systematic grammatical rule: if the subject has been deleted, the contractible verb must also be deleted. An important point about grammatical rules is that expressions that violate those rules are ill formed and generally cannot be rescued, or made good, by appealing to meaning or to pragmatic context. In other words, such rules do not have to have logical or commonsensical reasons for existing: it is a plain and simple fact that when grammatical rules are violated, an ill-formed expression results. For these reasons, then, we say that an abbreviated question such as *Running a fever?* is in fact the result of a systematic deletion rule, whereas expressions such as *Coffee?* are not.

It turns out that the formation of abbreviated questions involves reference to a small, highly specific set of elements: the subject *you* and the contractible forms of *be* (and *do* and *have* as well, it turns out). It would appear that native speakers of English, as they learn how to form abbreviated questions, come to learn the specific elements that can be missing from these questions. Given that the set of elements is small, we already know what information to "look for" in interpreting abbreviated questions, and in cases of potential ambiguity the conversational (or linguistic) context can resolve the matter.

Black English in Relation to Other American Dialects

Returning now to the features of Black English that we discussed earlier, it is important to reemphasize that certain features of BE are in fact part of the general set of features for American dialects in the informal style. In particular, it appears that deletion of the verb *to be* is a property of all dialects in informal style. The difference is that BE allows deletion of *to be* in declarative sentences as well as abbreviated questions, whereas other dialects limit the deletion of the verb *to be* to abbreviated questions. Hence, BE has generalized a pattern that other dialects leave incomplete. These results are summarized in table 7.1.

Other features of BE seem distinctive, however (for instance, recall the use of invariant *be* in examples such as those given in (8)). Hence, not all the features of BE can be shown to be part of the general features of informal style, and we can speak of BE as a dialect with certain unique features. Regardless of whether features of BE turn out to be distinct or part of more general features of American dialects, the point to be stressed

Table 7.1
Comparison of formal and informal styles with regard to contraction and deletion of the verb *be*. The informal style sentences in the chart are variations of the formal style sentences at the top. Examples such as *You sick?*, spoken with the rising intonation pattern characteristic of questions, shows that deletion of the verb *be* (and other auxiliary verbs) is a feature of all American dialects, not just Black English. However, in Black English deletion of *be* is allowed in declarative sentences, a possibility not found in other dialects. Thus, Black English actually completes a pattern left incomplete in the informal style of other dialects.

	Questions	Declarative Sentences
Formal Style	Are you sick?	You are sick.
Informal Style:		
All Dialects	'Ryou sick?	You're sick.
Informal Style:		
Black English	You sick?	You sick.
(Deletion)		
Other Dialects	You sick?	(not possible)

is that this dialect, and other dialects of American English, are in no way defective or illogical.

Where Phonology, Morphology, Syntax, and Pragmatic Context Meet

The rules for the abbreviated informal style that we have discussed here not only provide insight into the nature of language variation; they also provide a concrete example of how different subfields of linguistics are integrated and unified at a broader level. The rules for the abbreviated style must refer to *phonological* information: the deletion process is dependent on the phonological process of contraction. *Morphological* information also plays a crucial role, since only certain kinds of morphemes can be (phonologically) contracted and then deleted. For example, only contractible verbs may delete, whereas other types of verbs may not; and both the information about the part of speech and the information about specific words are types of morphological information. The deletion process itself is a *syntactic* process, broadly speaking, since it concerns the way sentences are formed in the abbreviated style. Finally, in order to understand sentences that have undergone deletion, we must be able to infer, or recover, the missing information. The pragmatic context in which the abbreviated sentences are actually used plays a crucial role in this inference process, and hence *pragmatic* information is necessary in our overall account of the abbreviated style.

In other words, linguistic explanations are rarely purely syntactic, or purely morphological, or based on any single component of the grammar. More often than not, to account for linguistic phenomena we require diverse kinds of information from different components of a grammar. Even though various subfields of linguistics are presented in separate chapters of this book—reflecting the need to break down the broad questions about language into more manageable ones—we must not forget that these areas are ultimately integrated when we seek to give complete explanations for linguistic phenomena.

7.3 OTHER LANGUAGE VARIETIES

We have so far examined the phenomenon of language variation in terms of dialects and styles of American English. In this section we will examine certain additional examples of language variation (from other languages, as well as from English) that are of interest to linguists. In our brief survey, we will not attempt to be comprehensive; rather, we will focus on a small number of selected examples in order to give a basic idea of some of the significant ways in which forms of language can vary.

Lingua Francas, Pidgins, and Creoles

For various reasons, groups of people speaking diverse languages are often thrown into social contact. When this occurs, a common language must be found to serve as a medium of communication. Sometimes, by common agreement, a given language (not necessarily a native language of anyone present) known to all the participants is used, and a language used in this fashion is known as a *lingua franca*. The term *lingua franca* derives from a trade language of this name used in Mediterranean ports in medieval times, consisting of Italian with elements from French, Spanish, Greek, and Arabic. Until about the eighteenth century, European scholars used Latin as a lingua franca—a common language for treatises on science and other scholarly subjects. In the contemporary world, English serves as a lingua franca in numerous social and political situations where people require a common language. For example, English has become a lingua franca for international scientific journals and international scientific meetings—it is, by common agreement, the language in which scientific results are presented.

Historically, another kind of situation has often arisen in which people come into contact, sharing no common language: namely, when one group becomes politically and economically dominant over another. This has been typical of colonial situations, in which the dominant group desires trade with, or colonization of, the subordinate group. In such situations, *pidgin languages* (or *pidgins*) have developed, having the following important properties:

1. The pidgin has no native speakers but is used as a medium of communication between people who are native speakers of other languages.
2. The pidgin is based on linguistic features of one or more other languages and is a *simplified* language with *reduced* vocabulary and grammatical structure.

There have been pidgins based on English, French, Dutch, Spanish, Portuguese, Arabic, and Swahili, among others. Pidgin languages are sometimes called *contact languages* (reflecting the fact that such languages often arise when social groups come into contact) or *marginal languages* (reflecting the reduced grammar and vocabulary of the pidgin).

The word *pidgin* itself is said to derive from the English word *business* as pronounced in Chinese Pidgin English. Pidgin languages have limited vocabulary (most often drawn from the "dominant" language), and in terms of grammatical features they typically lack inflectional morphemes (nouns have no endings to indicate plurality, and verbs have no endings to indicate tense or subject agreement). In addition, forms of the verb *to be* are often entirely lacking in pidgins, and prepositions are often limited to a reduced set that serves multiple functions.

In an interesting discussion of Hawaiian Pidgin English, Bickerton (1981) notes that although the vocabulary of the pidgin comes primarily from English, its syntax may vary depending on the original native language of the individual user. For example, Bickerton cites cases such as the following (1981, 11):

(20)
a. da pua pipl   awl poteito it   (pidgin form)
   the poor people only potatoes eat (English gloss)
   "The poor people ate only potatoes." (translation)
b. wok had dis   pipl   (pidgin form)
   work hard these people (English gloss)
   "These people work hard." (translation)

Example (20a) is from a Japanese speaker using Hawaiian Pidgin; note that the verb (*it* "eat") comes last in the sentence, just as it does in Japanese. Example (20b) is from a Filipino user of the pidgin; note that the verb (*wok* "work") comes first, just as it does in Philippine languages of the sort this speaker used natively. Although word order in Hawaiian Pidgin is by no means fixed for any given group of speakers, Bickerton notes that the original language of the user of the pidgin has a significant influence on grammatical features of the pidgin. Thus, a pidgin language is not based exclusively on a single language, such as English. It may well have significant features of more than one language.

Although pidgin languages are said to have limited uses, as well as reduced vocabularies and grammars, they can be used in highly expressive ways. Bickerton (1981, 13) cites a striking example from Hawaiian Pidgin English, uttered by a retired bus driver:

(21)
samtaim gud rod get, samtaim, olsem ben get, enguru ["angle"] get, no? enikain seim. olsem hyuman laif, olsem. gud rodu get, enguru get, mauntin get—no? awl, enikain, stawmu get, nais dei get—olsem. enibadi, mi olsem, smawl taim.
"Sometimes there's a good road, sometimes there's, like, bends, corners, right? Everything's like that. Human life's just like that. There's good roads, there's sharp corners, there's mountains—right? All sorts of things, there's storms, nice days—it's like that for everybody, it was for me, too, when I was young."

Although we have not given a word-by-word English gloss of the pidgin, we suggest using the English translation as a basis for isolating words of the pidgin. (Pronouncing the pidgin words makes them easier to understand than seeing them in print.)

It is striking to see how a pidgin—a language with reduced vocabulary and structure—can be used as a vehicle for serious thought. *Chinook Jargon*, a pidgin used by Native Americans and Europeans in the northwestern United States, had a vocabulary of between 500 and 800 words, and users became so skilled that complex communication could take place—even church sermons were delivered in Chinook Jargon.

Certain pidgins have become well established, the most notable case being *Tok Pisin*, a pidgin widely used in Papua New Guinea. Tok Pisin has a writing system, a literature, and even radio programs.

As we have already noted, pidgins are generally used by native speakers of other languages as a medium of communication. Under certain circumstances, however, children may learn a pidgin as their first language. When a pidgin begins to acquire native speakers who use it as their primary language, it is referred to as a *creole language*. Creole languages are said to develop in situations where the adults in a community speak mutually unintelligible native languages and must rely on a pidgin to communicate with each other. As children acquire the pidgin, they use it with playmates and other children in their peer group. Such situations often arose on slave plantations in the Americas, where Africans from linguistically diverse backgrounds could only communicate in a pidgin. Their descendents began to use the pidgin as a first language, and from this sort of development came such creoles as Haitian Creole (based on French), certain forms of Jamaican English, and Gullah (or Sea Island Creole, spoken by descendents of African slaves living on the Sea Islands off the coast of Georgia and South Carolina). Some scholars believe that some of the current forms of Black English may have had their origins as a creole language (see Dillard 1972 for discussion), but this is by no means a firmly established conclusion.

When a pidgin becomes creolized—that is, when it comes to be used as a primary language of a group of speakers—it undergoes considerable *expansion* of its vocabulary and grammar and begins to acquire rules comparable in nature and complexity with the rules of any other human language. To take one example, Crowley and Rigsby (1979) have described an interesting English-based creole spoken in the northern part of the Cape York Peninsula in Australia. Some typical vocabulary words of this creole are listed in table 7.2. Among the grammatical features of this creole, common to many other creoles as well, Crowley and Rigsby note a system of marking verb tenses:

(22)

a. Im bin ran.
   "He ran." (*bin* used to mark past)
b. Im ran.
   "He is running."
c. Im go ran.
   "He will run." (*go* used to mark future)

(23)

a. Wan dog i bin singaut.
   "*A* dog was barking."
b. Plenti dog i bin singaut.
   "*Some* dogs were barking."

Wan (originally from the English word *one*) is generally equivalent to the indefinite article *a* in English; and *plenti* (originally from the English word

Table 7.2
Some vocabulary words of Cape York Creole. In the Cape York Creole orthography, the vowel *i* is pronounced [ɪ]; *e* is pronounced [ɛ]; *a* is pronounced [ə]; *aa* is pronounced [ɑ]; *o* is pronounced [ɔ], with *oo* having greater length; and *u* is pronounced [ʊ]. (See chapter 3 for explanation of phonetic symbols.) (From Crowley and Rigsby 1979, 206–207.)

English	Cape York Creole
bad	nogud (from "no good")
diarrhea	beliran (from "belly run")
cold (the illness)	koolsik (from "cold sick")
on your back	beliap (from "belly up")
live, stay	stap
a lot	tumach (from "too much")
beach	sanbich (from "sand beach")
return	kambek (from "come back")
other	nadha(wan) (from "another one")
the best	nambawan (from "number one")
the same	seimwei (from "same way")
shout	singaut (from "sing out")
stand	staanap (from "stand up")
sit	sidaun (from "sit down")
run away in anger	stoomwei (from "storm away")
grab, take, get	kech-im (from "catch him")
stingray	tingari
stop a vehicle for a lift	beil-im ap (from "bail it up")
throw	chak-im (from "chuck him")
deaf	talinga nogud (from "telling no good")
blind	ai nogud (from "eye no good")
smoke	faiasmouk (from "fire smoke")
be drunk	spaak (from "spark")
urine, urinate	pipi (from "pee-pee")
lie (tell a lie), pretend	geman (from "gammon")
cheat	blaf (from "bluff")
hide	stoowei (from "stow away")
father's elder brother	big ankl
father's younger brother	litl ankl
maternal grandmother	greni blo madha
Thursday Island	tiai (from "T.I.")
bow of canoe	foored (from "forehead")
Red Island Point	araipi (from "R.I.P.")

plenty) is generally equivalent to the English word *some*. Possession is marked with the preposition *blong* (from the English word *belong*):

(24)

a. stik blong olmaan

   "the old man's stick"

b. dog blong maan

   "the man's dog"

Certain morphemes that may function as *concord particles* (among other uses) precede the verb of the sentence and agree with the subject. For example, when the subject is a third person noun, the concord particle is *i*:

(25)

a. Dog i singaut.

   "The dog is barking."

b. Olmaan i kam ia.

   "The old man is coming here."

Concord particles such as *i* perform the function of "agreement" with the subject, and in this way are very similar to the English third person singular morpheme *-s*, which is suffixed to verbs in the present tense (as in *She/He runs* versus *I, you, we, they run*). The difference is that concord particles precede the verb, whereas *-s* is an inflectional suffix on the verb.

To sum up, then, grammatical features such as those illustrated in (22)–(25) often come into existence as a creole evolves from a pidgin.

This evolutionary process has sometimes been described in terms of a broader "creole continuum" (Bickerton 1975). In his study of Guyanese Creole, Bickerton noted that between the pure creole (the *basilect*) and the local variety of Standard English (the *acrolect*), there are a series of *mesolects*: language varieties that form a continuum beginning at the creole and gradually shifting toward Standard English, each successive mesolect approximating Standard English more closely. Individual speakers can often use a range of mesolects from the continuum and are not necessarily limited to a single mesolect. The evolutionary process of pidginization and creolization is concisely summed up by Naro (1979, 888):

In the broadest possible terms, many specialists accept a cyclic concept of pidgin/creole evolution. The start is some sort of reduction process in both inner and outer form (PIDGINIZATION); this leads to a non-standard linguistic system (a PIDGIN) different from any of the ingredients (SOURCE or SUBSTRATA) existing previously. The middle stage is achieved by re-expansion (CREOLIZATION) to a less-limited linguistic system (a CREOLE). The end of the cycle is a stage in which a standard language exerts influence on the creole (DECREOLIZATION), producing a result that can range up to a regional variety of the standard.

What "guides" the process of creolization? How can children acquiring a pidgin "expand" the pidgin so that it comes to have grammatical structures on a par with those of other human languages? Some scholars have suggested that the increased complexity of the creole reflects an innate "faculty of language"—that is, a biologically innate linguistic capacity (see Bickerton 1981 for discussion of a "bioprogram" along these general lines). Thus, speakers expanding a pidgin language into a creole are in some intuitive sense constrained by their innate linguistic capacity, and for this reason, perhaps, all creoles are predicted to have very similar structures regardless of where they have developed and what languages are involved.

Jargon and Slang

In virtually every recognized profession, a special vocabulary evolves to meet the special needs of the profession. This special, or technical, vocabulary is known as *jargon*. To take well-known examples, physicians and health professionals use medical jargon; lawyers use legal jargon; and linguists use a technical linguistic jargon with vocabulary items such as *phoneme*, *morpheme*, *transformation*, and so on. Jargon is not limited to professional groups, but also exists in what we might term "special-interest" groups. For example, sports enthusiasts, amateur rock-climbers, jazz and rock-and-roll fans, custom car hobbyists, art lovers, and many other groups all make use of technical jargons that are specially suited to the particular interests of the group. The jargon of the criminal underworld is often referred to as *argot*.

Despite its mysterious nature to an "outsider," jargon is not intended to be secret, but, for purely practical reasons, particular jargons are largely incomprehensible to those outside the particular profession or group that uses the jargon. The shared use of jargon is often the basis for a feeling of group solidarity, with the accompanying feeling that those who do not use the jargon are not part of the "elite."

Slang and Taboo Language

It has been said that slang is something that everyone can recognize but no one can define. Speakers show enormous creativity in their use of slang (it is, indeed, one of the most creative areas of language use), and it is often the source of a good deal of humor. Although a precise definition of slang seems extremely difficult (if not impossible), there are, nevertheless, some salient features of this form of language:

1. Slang is part of casual, informal styles of language use. Further, the term *slang* has traditionally carried a negative connotation: it is often perceived as a "low" or "vulgar" form of language and is deemed to be out of place in formal styles of language.

2. Slang, like fashions in clothing and popular music, changes quite rapidly. Slang terms can enter a language rapidly, then fall out of fashion in a matter of a few years or even months. This rate of turnover is much greater than for other areas of the vocabulary of a language.

3. Specific areas of slang are often associated with a particular social group, and hence one can speak of teenage slang, underworld (criminal) slang, the slang of the drug culture, and so on. In this respect slang is a kind of jargon, and its use serves as a mark of membership and solidarity within a given social group. To use outdated slang, or to use current slang inappropriately, is to be hopelessly "out of date" and to be excluded from an "in-group." Consider the slang in table 7.3 and compare it with slang you are exposed to.

Slang is sometimes referred to as *vernacular* (especially when it is associated with a particular social group), and some forms of slang fall under the term *colloquialism*, referring to informal conversational styles of language. These terms do not carry negative connotations; however, for convenience we will continue to use the popular term *slang*.

Slang vocabulary often consists of regular vocabulary used in specific ways. For example, the words *turkey* and *banana* are regular vocabulary

Table 7.3
Slang expressions used in a high school in Tucson, Arizona. Note the creativity in these expressions.

Word	Meaning
to hork	to beg someone to share (food, etc.) with you
fondo	a very, very bad joke
Gandhi	a red spot on your forehead that comes about from laying your head down on your hand when you fall asleep in class
pita	pain in the ass
to yom	to withhold, not share
Ronald	a male geek
to snake	to steal

items in English (and can be used in formal styles with their literal meaning), but in slang they can be used as insults (referring to stupid or foolish people). In addition to the use of regular vocabulary words, however, slang also makes use of regular word formation devices (of the sort discussed in chapter 2) to create new words. For example, new slang words can be coined, as was the case for forms such as *diddleysquat* (*He doesn't know diddleysquat* meaning "He doesn't know anything"). More recently *slam dunk* has become airline pilot slang for plunging an airliner down through congested air traffic, and auto sales slang for getting buyers to pay more than they had to (*Newsweek*, July 3 and August 7, 1989). Blends are common in slang—for example, *absotively* and *posilutely*, both of which are blends based on the words *absolutely* and *positively*. Affixes can be used also, as with the slang suffix *-ski* (or *-sky*), found on such words as *brewski* "beer," *tootski* "a puff on a marijuana cigarette," and *buttinski* "one who butts in." It is interesting to note that *brew* and *toot* (with the same meanings as *brewski* and *tootski*) are recent slang words that are becoming stale or outmoded; the addition of the slang suffix *-ski* "rejuvenates" the words. The origin of this slang use of *-ski* is unknown, but it may be a linguistic parody on Polish or Russian words that end in a similar phonetic sequence.

An interesting, and quite amusing, phenomenon in American slang is the use of the forms *city* and *ville* to create various compound expressions. For example:

(26)
a. We're in *fat city*.
b. What a bummer! It is, like, *bug city*.
c. You shouda seen all the cars—I mean, *lowrider city*!
d. She cried all night ... you know, *heartbreak city*.

(27)
a. This place was out in the boonies; I mean, *hicksville*, you know?
b. What a boring place—talk about *nowheresville*.
c. You shouda seen it: those people were so stoned, it was like *drugsville* all the way.
d. That guy's really strange—totally *weirdsville*.

The interpretation of expressions with *city* and *ville* is clear enough in specific contexts, but not so easy to explicate in general. Such expressions all seem to refer to situations where some maximum concentration or extreme degree is reached: *bug city* means "infested with bugs"; *lowrider city* means something like "lowriders [modified automobiles] everywhere";

heartbreak city means something like "maximum heartbreak"; *nowheres-ville* means something like "really nowhere"; *weirdsville* means something like "very weird." These are only rough paraphrases, and we leave the finer details to the brave reader. Both *city* and *ville* refer to locations, and it is interesting to note that other words denoting locations can be used in similar ways:

(28)
a. We're on easy *street*.
b. He's in fantasy-*land*.
c. I'm in chocolate *heaven*.

In addition to individual vocabulary items, and expressions on the pattern of *fat city*, there are also longer expressions (with idiomatic meanings) that are characteristic of slang usage, such as the following examples (all used in describing someone who appears unintelligent, foolish, or crazy):

(29)
a. He's got a few screws loose.
b. She doesn't have all her marbles.
c. He's not playing with a full deck.
d. Her elevator doesn't go all the way to the top.
e. He's running a quart low/not firing on all cylinders.

These examples contain no grammatical or morphological features that are uniquely slang-related (such as *-ski* or *-ville*). We nevertheless classify them as slang because of their insulting/humorous nature.

Discussion of verbal insults invariably raises the question of obscenity, profanity, "cuss words," and other forms of *taboo language*. Taboo words are those that are to be avoided entirely, or at least avoided in "mixed company" or "polite company." Typical examples involve common swear words such as *Damn!* or *Shit!* The former is heard more and more in "polite company," and both men and women use both words openly. Many, however, feel that the latter word is absolutely inappropriate in "polite" or formal contexts. In place of these words, certain *euphemisms*—that is, polite substitutes for taboo words—can be used, including words such as *darn* (a euphemism for *damn*), *heck* (a euphemism for *hell*), *gee* or *jeez* (euphemisms for the exclamation *Jesus!*), and so on. An amusing example is the current expression, *the "F" word*, which is a euphemism for that notorious English word that many newspapers spell as *f---*.

Taboo language is not limited to obscenity—sacred language can also be taboo, that is, language to be avoided outside the context of sacred ritual. In many societies the language of religious or magical rites can only be used by certain members of the society (priests or shamans).

What counts as taboo language is something defined by culture, and not by anything inherent in the language itself. There is nothing inherent in the sounds of the expression *Shit!* that makes it "obscene"—it is simply that in our cultural history the word has come to be known and used as a "swear word." Foreigners learning English as a second language will at first find nothing unusual about the word, and will not experience the "emotional charge" that often accompanies the use of a taboo word. For Americans learning French, there is nothing intrinsic in the expression *Merde!* (meaning "Shit!") that seems obscene.

It is interesting to note, however, that bilingual (or multilingual) speakers sometimes avoid words in one language that accidentally resemble taboo words in another language. This phenomenon of *interlingual word taboos* (Haas 1957) can be illustrated in various ways. For example, American students learning Brazilian Portuguese are often embarrassed to learn the word *faca* meaning "knife," since its pronunciation in Portuguese comes uncomfortably close to sounding like the tabooed English word *fuck*. Haas (1957) cites a case in which a Creek Indian informant avoided using certain words of the Creek language when whites were around. One of the words was *fakki*, meaning "soil, earth, clay." A particularly interesting case cited by Haas involved a group of Thai students in the United States, who noticed that the Thai word *phrig* (the sequence *ph* pronounced as an aspirated /p/, not as /f/), meaning "pepper," resembled the American English slang word *prick*. It was necessary to use this word frequently when dining in public, and not wanting Americans to overhear a word that sounded like a tabooed word of English, the students sought another term in Thai that could replace the word *phrig*. The substitute that they hit upon was the Thai word *lyn*, which in fact means "phallus" but secondarily came to mean "pepper" in the context of dining out. Ironically, then, the students found a term in Thai that did not sound like a tabooed American slang word (thus, they could freely talk about pepper with Americans in hearing distance); yet their substitute term had the same meaning as the tabooed English word they were trying to avoid!

Code Switching and Borrowing

The term *code switching* refers to a situation in which a speaker uses a *mixture* of distinct language varieties as discourse proceeds. This occurs quite commonly in everyday speech with regard to levels of style, as, for example, when speakers mix formal and informal styles:

(30)
We must not permit the State of California to deplete the water supply of the State of Arizona. Ain't no way we're gonna give 'em that water.

The speaker (in this case an Arizona politician) is mixing styles for a certain rhetorical effect: the juxtaposition of formal speech-making style with informal colloquial style adds emphasis to the speaker's position on the water issue; and the use of the informal style in this context is intended by the speaker to increase a feeling of solidarity with the audience.

Code switching can often happen within a single sentence (and at numerous points within a sentence). Among the most interesting cases of this sort of code switching are those in which a speaker mixes distinct (mutually unintelligible) languages, a situation that often arises in bilingual or multilingual areas such as the American Southwest. In the following example, Spanish is mixed with English (the Spanish forms are italicized, with the English glosses in parentheses):

(31)
It's now *ocho y media* ("eight-thirty") on a Saturday night, and we're gonna hear a new artist *con* ("with") his new group. You're in tune with *la máquina rítmica* ("the rhythm machine").

This example (taken from a radio broadcast on station KXEW, "Radio Fiesta," Tucson, Arizona) is predominantly based on English, with a mixture of Spanish words. The reverse situation is also common, where a few English words are mixed in with a predominantly Spanish utterance, as in the following example (where the English word *training* is italicized):

(32) Estaba *training* para pelear.
        "They were training to fight."

In cases of code switching, the speaker is in effect using two distinct language varieties at the same time. We can contrast this situation with that of *borrowing*. When speakers of one language borrow words from another language, the foreign words come to be used as regular vocabulary items. For example, when a speaker of English says, "They have a great deal of *savoir-faire*," we might well recognize that the term *savoir-faire* was originally a borrowed word (or *loanword*) from French, but it has come to be used as a vocabulary item in English (in fact, it is listed in Webster's). In contrast, the Spanish phrase *ocho y media* in (31) is not a borrowed vocabulary item that English speakers now use, but rather is a result of code switching between English and Spanish.

Conclusion

In this chapter we have covered several aspects of variation in language. We would like to conclude with the observation that variation, far from being a "defect" of language, actually reveals its true nature: human language is a rule-governed system within which an enormous amount of flexibility or creativity is possible. Variation is linguistically neutral, and there is no evidence that "nonstandard" dialects *themselves* are weaker in any way than the so-called standard dialect or that the standard dialect is stronger. In other words, variation in language does not entail any superiority or inferiority in language. One should not assume that "different is smarter" or that "different is dumber." Instead, the problem lies in the *attitudes* of the language community toward the *speakers* of these forms. The community as a whole ranks the various forms of language socially, thereby elevating some speakers and stigmatizing others to the point where listeners frequently perform on-the-spot assessments of a speaker's background and abilities based on the selection and pronunciation of a few words! To repeat, then, the fact that dialects occur readily is a natural consequence of humans using language in a creative manner. The force of variation and change in language is such that differentiation within a language will eventually lead to the formation of different languages, a topic to which we turn in the next chapter.

Exercises

1. If you are acquainted with a regional, social, or ethnic dialect, list as many features as you can that distinguish this dialect from the so-called standard language. What are some significant differences in pronunciation, vocabulary words, and syntax?

2. The following types of sentences (originally made famous by *Mad Magazine*) are frequently used in the informal style of English:

a. What, me worry?
b. What, John get a job? (Fat chance!)
c. My boss give me a raise? (Are you joking?)
d. Him wear a tuxedo? (He doesn't even own a clean shirt!)

How would you express each of these sentences in formal English? Do these informal sentences express any feeling or idea that is not expressed in the formal style?

3. Several acquaintances who were raised in Brooklyn inform us that the following sentences are good:

a. Let's you and him fight—how about it?
b. Let's you guys shut up, all right?

How does this informal use of *let's* differ from its use in formal English?

4. In the informal style it is quite common to hear sentences such as the following:

a. There's three cars in the garage.
b. There's a lot of problems with this car.
c. There's many ways to do this.

How would these sentences be expressed in formal English, and how do the formal and informal styles differ in the use of *there's*?

5. Sports announcers on TV and radio use a style of English that is both colorful and unique. Listen to a variety of sports broadcasts, paying careful attention to the language, and try to characterize as precisely as you can how this language differs from the formal style or standard language. To get started, you might consider the following sample of sportscaster language: "Smith on third. Jones at bat. Mursky winding up for the pitch." (This language should be reminiscent of the informal style discussed in this chapter.) Remember to include differences (if any) in pronunciation and vocabulary words, as well as syntax.

6. In this chapter we considered abbreviated questions of one type, namely, questions without question words (or *wh-words*) such as *who*, *what*, and *where*. The following sets of sentences illustrate the differences between *wh*-questions and the abbreviated questions we examined:

(i)
a.   Where have you been lately?
b.   Where've you been lately?
c.   *Where've been lately?
d.   Where ya been lately?
e.   *Where been lately?

(ii)
a.   Who are you taking to the prom?
b.   Who're you taking to the prom?
c.   *Who're taking to the prom?
d.   Who ya takin' to the prom?
e.   *Who takin' to the prom?

(iii)
a.   What do you want to do?
b.   Whattaya wanna do?
c.   *Whatta wanna do?
d.   Watcha wanna do?
e.   *What want to do?

How do these abbreviated *wh*-questions differ from the abbreviated questions studied in the chapter? That is, what are the differences in the rules for forming the

two types of abbreviated questions? In answering, pay careful attention to (1) the fact that some of the examples in (i)–(iii) are ungrammatical and (2) the way contraction works in these cases.

7. It is not quite true to say that *be* can never be deleted in declarative statements in the informal speech style of the authors, for the following sentences are good:

a. Odd that Mary never showed up.
b. Good thing you fixed your engine.
c. Too bad (that) she had to leave town so soon.
d. Amazing that he didn't spot that error.

What has been deleted from these sentences? Is this deletion general?

8. Questions typically come from a first person speaker and are addressed to a second person hearer. Can you relate this *use* of questions to the fact that *you* is deleted from abbreviated questions? Can *any* subject be deleted from abbreviated questions as long as use and context make the deletion recoverable?

Bibliography and Further Reading

Bailey, R. W., and J. L. Robinson, eds. (1973). *Varieties of present-day English.* New York: Macmillan.

Bickerton, D. (1975). *The dynamics of a creole system.* Cambridge: Cambridge University Press.

Bickerton, D. (1981). *Roots of language.* Ann Arbor, Mich.: Karoma Publishers.

Bodine, A. (1975). Androcentrism in prescriptive grammar: Singular 'they', sex-indefinite 'he', and 'he' or 'she'. *Language in Society* 4, 129–146.

Burling, R. (1973). *English in black and white.* New York: Holt, Rinehart and Winston.

Crowley, T., and B. Rigsby (1979). Cape York Creole. In Shopen 1979.

Dillard, J. L. (1972). *Black English: Its history and usage in the United States.* New York: Random House.

Dixon, R. M. W. (1971). A method of semantic description. In Steinberg and Jakobovits 1971.

Fasold, R. W. (1972). *Tense marking in Black English.* Urban Language Series. Arlington, Va.: Center for Applied Linguistics.

Folb, E. A. (1980). *Runnin' down some lines: The language and culture of Black teenagers.* Cambridge, Mass.: Harvard University Press.

Frank, F., and F. Anshen (1983). *Language and the sexes.* Albany, N.Y.: SUNY Press.

Giglioli, P. O., ed. (1972). *Language and social context.* Baltimore, Md.: Penguin Books.

Glissmeyer, G. (1973). Some characteristics of English in Hawaii. In Bailey and Robinson 1973.

Haas, M. R. (1957). Interlingual word taboos. *American Anthropologist* 53, 338–341. Reprinted in Hymes 1964.

Haviland, J. B. (1979). How to talk to your brother-in-law in Guugu Yimidhirr. In Shopen 1979.

Hudson, R. A. (1980). *Sociolinguistics.* Cambridge: Cambridge University Press.

Hymes, D. H., ed. (1964). *Language in culture and society.* New York: Harper and Row.

Hymes, D. H., ed. (1971). *Pidginization and creolization of language.* Cambridge: Cambridge University Press.

Labov, W. (1969a). Contraction, deletion, and inherent variability of the English copula. *Language* 45, 715–762.

Labov, W. (1969b). The logic of nonstandard English. In *Report of the Twentieth Annual Round Table Meeting on Linguistics and Language.* Washington, D.C.: Georgetown University Press. Reprinted in Bailey and Robinson 1973 and Giglioli 1972.

Labov, W. (1972). The social stratification of (r) in New York City department stores. In *Sociolinguistic patterns.* Philadelphia: University of Pennsylvania Press.

Labov, W. (1973). Some features of the English of Black Americans. In Bailey and Robinson 1973.

Lakoff, R. (1973). Language and woman's place. *Language in Society* 2, 45–79.

Naro, A. (1979). Review of Valdman 1977. *Language* 55, 886–893.

Pride, J. B., and J. Holmes, eds. (1972). *Sociolinguistics.* Middlesex, England: Penguin Books.

Shopen, T., ed. (1979). *Languages and their status.* Cambridge, Mass: Winthrop Publishers.

Smitherman, G. (1977). *Talkin and testifyin: The language of Black America.* Boston: Houghton Mifflin.

Steinberg, D. D., and L. A. Jakobovits, eds. (1971). *Semantics: An interdisciplinary reader in philosophy, linguistics, and psychology.* Cambridge: Cambridge University Press.

Thorne, B., and N. Henley, eds. (1975). *Language and sex: Difference and dominance.* Rowley, Mass.: Newbury House.

Valdman, A., ed. (1977). *Pidgin and creole linguistics.* Bloomington, Ind.: Indiana University Press.

Williams, F., ed. (1970). *Language and poverty.* Chicago: Markham.

Chapter 8

LANGUAGE CHANGE

8.1 SOME BACKGROUND CONCEPTS

The inherent flexibility of human language, along with its complexity and the creativity with which it is used, causes it to be extremely variable and to change over time. So changeable is human language, in fact, that were they to meet, speakers from one generation would not be able to understand speakers of another generation sufficiently far apart in time. Contemporary speakers of English find the language of Shakespeare's plays in large part intelligible (we can, for instance, extrapolate from the current word *chicken-livered* to guess what the now obsolete word *pigeon-livered* might have meant); nonetheless, small changes are made from time to time in Shakespeare's texts to keep some passages from becoming totally obscure. And our contemporary language will continue this process of change, as well, until eventually there will come a generation that will need subtitles in order to understand the English of twentieth-century movies. In section 3 of this chapter we will discuss in detail some of the changes that English has undergone in the last fourteen centuries.

Language change is one of the subjects of *historical linguistics*, the subfield of linguistics that studies language in its historical aspects. Sometimes the term *diachronic linguistics* is used instead of historical linguistics, as a way of referring to the study of a language (or languages) at various points in time and at various historical stages. *Diachronic* is often used in contrast to *synchronic*, a term referring to the study of a language (or languages) at a single point in time, without reference to earlier (or later) stages. For example, chapter 5 is a synchronic study of current American English syntax, but part of section 8.3 contains a brief diachronic study of syntax, that is, a study of the historical development of certain sentence constructions in English.

In considering the history and development of particular languages, one of the most fascinating questions—and indeed, a question that has intrigued scholars throughout the ages—concerns the origin and evolution of language in the human species in general. When in the history of our species did language originate? What was the nature of the first language(s)? As with many questions in linguistics, the most fascinating ones are often the very ones we cannot answer in any definitive way. Let us see why questions concerning the origin of language have so long resisted efforts to find clear answers.

The Origin and Evolution of Human Language

Considerable evidence suggests that the capacity for language is a species-specific, biologically innate trait of human beings. The question then naturally arises how this capacity may have originated and evolved in the species. Unfortunately, we have little, if any, solid evidence to indicate when language may have originated, why it might have developed in our particular species, and how it evolved from its earlier stages.

One idea concerning the origin of human language is that humans began to mimic the sounds of nature and used these sounds as referents for the sources of the sound. This theory is sometimes disparagingly referred to as the *"bow-wow"* theory. The existence of onomatopoeic words such as *bow-wow, meow, crash, boom*, and so forth, might be taken as evidence of such mimicking. But onomatopoeic words invariably form a very small portion of the words of any given language; and even if "imitation of nature" accounts for some words, we still have no explanation of how the rest of human language evolved.

According to another speculation, vocal language gradually evolved from spontaneous cries of pain, pleasure, or other emotions. Once again, absolutely no evidence has been advanced to show how a full-blown language—complete with phonology, morphology, syntax, and so on— could evolve from simple emotional cries. To this day all humans, and other animals as well, use response cries; and what is left unexplained is why humans developed language as well.

It has also been suggested that a *gestural language*—that is, a system of hand gestures and signals—may have preceded vocal language (see Hewes 1976). This might well be true, but again we are faced with the problem of understanding how gestural language came to be supplanted by vocal language as well as when and why this might have happened.

In addition, it is sometimes speculated that human language gradually evolved from the need for humans to communicate with each other in coordinating certain group tasks. The idea here is that people working in groups can cooperate more efficiently if they can use a vocal language to communicate. But such "functional" theories of the origin of language seem quite dubious. For one thing, it has never been shown that the carrying out of group tasks requires a *vocal* language. Why couldn't a sign language or gestural language suffice as a communication system in the context of groups at work? Further, it has never been shown that group tasks require a communication system anywhere near as complicated as human language. For example, wolf packs are extremely efficient hunting groups and yet have no complex language; further, many farming tasks carried out today by humans require no language and are learned by imitation. Generally speaking, "functional" theories of the origin of language all suffer from a similar defect: human language is vastly more expressive and more powerful than would be dictated by any given functional task involving groups at work. Of course, once human language did evolve, it came to be exploited fully for all kinds of social functions; but the needs involved in such functions cannot be identified as the first cause of language evolution.

At present the most reasonable suggestion about the origin and evolution of human language is that it was intimately linked with the evolution of the human brain. We know, for example, that over roughly the last 5 million years there has been a striking increase in brain size, ranging from about 400 cubic centimeters in our distant hominid ancestors to about 1,400 cubic centimeters in modern *Homo sapiens* (see Miller 1981 for a useful summary). The mere increase in brain size would not necessarily have led to superior intelligence and the evolution of language, since dolphins, for example, have brains of a size comparable to that of humans, yet they have only a rudimentary communication system. Furthermore, even a mere increase in general intelligence might not necessarily have led to the evolution of language. Dolphins and primates, for instance, are considered to be more intelligent than birds, yet their communication systems seem to be no more sophisticated or complex than that of birds. Indeed, as Lenneberg (1964) has pointed out, mentally retarded humans with IQ levels significantly below normal can nevertheless grasp the rudiments of language. Obviously, brain size is only one factor that may have played a role in the evolution of language; changes in the organization and complexity of the brain must also be supposed to have played a crucial role.

At what point in time language may have originated is far from clear: guesses range from 50,000 to 100,000 years ago and even earlier, but such figures are speculative at best. In any event it seems likely that language is a relatively recent development in the human species. There is an abrupt change in the quality and nature of tool development between 50,000 and 100,000 years ago, signaling to some anthropologists the emergence of modern man. It is plausible that this increased ability may have been associated with a qualitative change in language ability, but we have no evidence at all that this was the case.

The problem in determining the answer to questions concerning the origin and evolution of human language is that we have so little solid evidence on which to base any claims. Attempts have been made to reconstruct the vocal tract of Neanderthal man (see Lieberman 1975 for discussion), and although early reports claimed that Neanderthals had only a limited capacity for speech because their vocal tract was shaped differently from that of modern humans, recent evidence from Neanderthal remains suggests that they had a vocal tract shaped like ours (*National Geographic*, 1989).

We not only have no idea when language began, we do not even have an idea of what the earlier stages of language might have been like—even in the most recent stage before the modern era. We have stated that language is a biological phenomenon, and in the biological world it is frequently possible to find earlier forms of life existing simultaneously with more evolved forms. For example, the coelacanth was a biologically primitive fish known only in fossil form until a living specimen was discovered and identified in 1938. Might it be possible to encounter a group of people who speak a form of language that can be identified as an earlier form of modern language?

Small, previously unknown groups of people are indeed discovered from time to time in jungle areas in New Guinea and the Philippines (Molony 1988). These groups have apparently been isolated from other humans for long periods of time and have no knowledge of the modern world. Their existence, then, often gives rise to speculation that they may speak a more primitive language that could be an earlier form of modern human language. But despite the fact that the technology of such people is at a Stone Age level, their languages appear to be as developed and as complex as any other human language. So far, then, no natural language (with the possible exception of the pidgin languages discussed in chapter 7) has been shown to be more primitive than any other language in terms of grammatical organization, expressiveness, and so forth.

Hence, it may seem that we are limited to studying the history of languages on the basis of written records, dating back only 6,000 years. It is nevertheless possible to make deductions about stages of language before historical records. This is the subject of the next section.

8.2 THE RECONSTRUCTION OF INDO-EUROPEAN, THE NATURE OF LANGUAGE CHANGE, AND LANGUAGE FAMILIES OF THE WORLD

Similarities among Languages

The discovery in the early nineteenth century that the European languages, such as English, German, and French, were historically related to the languages of antiquity, such as Latin, Greek, and Sanskrit (an ancient language of India), led to a revolution in our understanding of the nature and history of language. Linguistic similarities among the different languages of Europe had not gone unnoticed before the nineteenth century. Already in the sixteenth century Filippo Sassetti pointed out similarities between Italian and Sanskrit. Even the philosopher Leibnitz observed that Persian and German were grammatically similar. A true understanding of the nature of the relationship among these languages did not come, however, until the early part of the eighteenth century. The person who is credited with the first and clearest statement concerning the relationships among the classical and other ancient languages was Sir William Jones, who in 1786 wrote:

The Sanskrit language, whatever be its antiquity, is of a wonderful structure; more perfect than the Greek, more copious than the Latin . . . yet bearing to both of them a stronger affinity, both in the roots of verbs and in the forms of grammar, than could possibly have been produced by accident; so strong indeed, that no philosopher could examine them all three, without believing them to have sprung from some common source, which, perhaps, no longer exists. There is a similar reason, though not quite so forcible, for supposing that both the Gothic and the Celtic . . . had the same origin with the Sanskrit; and the Old Persian might be added to the same family . . . . (quoted in Lehmann 1967, 15)

This language, "which no longer exists," is called (*Proto*)-*Indo-European* in the English-speaking world, a term reflecting the (earlier) geographical distribution of the speakers of this language family from India to Europe. Note that if it is possible to learn about an earlier form of a language for which no written records exist, then we may also be able to learn about the history of the world's languages and perhaps even something about the geographical origin of language itself. How can we learn about this language that no longer exists and for which no written records are available? In order to see how linguists establish historical relationships among languages, consider the words in (1):

(1) *Spanish*   *Navajo*   *Sanskrit*

Language A	Language B	Language C
uno *← vowel*	łáá'ii	eka *← vowel*
dos	naaki	dva
tres	táá'	tri
cuatro	dį́į'	catur
cinco	ashdla'	pañca
seis	hastą́ą́	ṣaṣ
siete	tsosts'id	sapta
ocho	tseebíí	aṣta
nueve	náhást'éí	nava
diez	neeznáá	daśa

vowel → (uno)

You may know (or be able to guess) that these are the words for the numerals one through ten in each of the three languages. You will also notice that languages A and C have some phonological similarities: six out of ten words begin with the same (or a similar) consonant; the words for *one* and *eight* are the only ones that begin with vowels; nine of the words have the same number of syllables; and so forth. Thus, we have some initial evidence that languages A and C (Spanish and Sanskrit, respectively) might be related; but neither of these two seems to be related to language B (Navajo). This brief exercise raises the central questions to be dealt with in this section: (1) How do we establish with a reasonable degree of certainty that two or more languages are related? (2) If languages are related but no longer the same in vocabulary and grammar, how and why did they change? and (3) Does language change involve an improvement or a decay in expressive ability? In attempting to answer these questions, we will be examining some of the most important aspects of *historical* or *comparative linguistics.*

Based on the similarities between Spanish and Sanskrit in the words for *one* through *ten*, we could hypothesize that Spanish and Sanskrit are related languages, meaning that they both are descended from a common ancestor language. However, in order to establish a *genetic relationship* between or among languages, more is needed than the presence of similar-sounding words. We need to rule out *chance overlap* in sound and meaning and the presence of *borrowed vocabulary*. Consider the words (2) and (3):

(2) *algonquian*   *Scots Gaelic*

Language A	Language B	Meaning
bhanem	ban	"woman"
alnoba	allaban	"person, immigrant," respectively
lhab	lion-obhair	"netting"
odana	dun	"town"
haʔlwiwi	na h-uile	"everywhere"
kladen	claden	"frost, snowflake"
pados	bata	"boat"
monaden	monadh	"mountain"
aden	ard	"height"
cuiche	cuithe	"gorge"

(3) *Latin*

Language A	Language B
cuprum	copper
planta	plant
cuppa	cup
discus	dish
coquīna	kitchen
cāseus	cheese

The languages in (2) are Scots Gaelic (language B) and Northeastern Algonquian (language A). Scots Gaelic is a Celtic language of Western Europe, whereas Algonquian is a Native American language of the northeastern United States.

The languages in (3) are Latin (language A) and, of course, Modern English (language B). The meanings of the Latin words are the same as those of their English counterparts, although the pairs of words differ somewhat in pronunciation.

Examples (1), (2), and (3) illustrate three situations in which languages can share a set of words that are individually similar in both sound and meaning. These similarities can be the result of a true historical relationship, of a chance overlap in sound and meaning, or of borrowing from one language to another. We discuss in reverse order these three ways that languages can have words that share sound and meaning.

Borrowing

Many terms relating to Western technology and culture have become part of the vocabulary of the world's languages, and English speakers in turn have borrowed many words from other languages. The vocabularies of

Modern Japanese and English, for example, share a significant number of common words, among them *karate, sushi, hibachi, bluejeans*, and *computer*. This common and shared vocabulary might lead a naive linguist at some future date to hypothesize that English and Japanese are somehow related—perhaps they are descended from a common language? (It may be that Japanese and English are in fact descended from a remote common language, but this is unprovable given our present state of knowledge.) In establishing *genetic relationships* among languages, then, one must exclude words that may have been borrowed and are therefore not part of a common inheritance. The Latin words in (3) were borrowed by English speakers, and although this vocabulary seems to refer to rather common objects, it does reflect the cultural influence of the Roman occupation of England. Even without records that establish evidence of borrowing, we will see that borrowed words can be distinguished from common inherited words by the principles discussed in the section on establishing genetic relationships among languages.

Chance Overlap in Sound and Meaning

The fact that languages often have similarities in sound structure and have words for common objects yields a significant probability that there will be accidental overlaps in sound-meaning correspondences between them. For example, all languages have a low vowel (such as *a*), and most have *i* and/or *u* vowels; most languages have *t, k,* and *p* and the nasal consonants *n* and *m*. Moreover, most languages have words referring to water, the numbers, male and female parents, and other items common to human existence. In Lummi, a Native American language spoken in northwestern Washington State, the word for "father" is /mæn/. In Chinese and Navajo the word for "mother" is /-má/, as in Chinese /mā/ and Navajo /shi-má/ "my mother." Thus, there are a few words in Chinese, Navajo, and Lummi that are phonetically and semantically similar to words in English, but this is insufficient evidence to demonstrate that any of these languages is genetically related to English.

Likewise, there is insufficient linguistic evidence that the languages in (2), Scots Gaelic and Algonquian, are genetically related. The meanings of the phonologically similar words shared by Scots Gaelic and Algonquian are typical of the type of vocabulary that would suggest a genetic relationship, in that the words generally refer to common objects, words that are unlikely candidates for borrowing. The number of shared words, however, is very small; more importantly, there are no *systematic* sound correspondences between the words of the sort that we will discuss in the next section. We conclude, therefore, that the similarities between Scots Gaelic and Algonquian are due to an accidental overlap in the sound-meaning associations of some of their words.

Establishing Genetic Relationships among Languages

The study of language history and the relationships among languages is one of the tasks of *comparative linguistics*. The traditional procedure that linguists use in determining a true historical (genetic) relationship is called the *comparative method*. The comparative method is not really a term referring to a fixed procedure that is to be followed rigidly. Rather, it refers to the analytical techniques linguists employ in reconstructing the history of languages that are hypothesized to be members of the same language family. We will demonstrate some of the aspects of the comparative method by considering the words in (4), whose phonetic and semantic similarities suggest a historical relationship:

(4)

English	Latin	Greek	Sanskrit
ten	decem	deka	daśa
two	duo	duo	dva
heart	cordia	kardía	hŕd-

t/d.
English + corresponds

Limiting ourselves to the word-initial and -final *t* of English, we note that this sound corresponds to the *d*'s of the other languages. The term *correspond* used here means that a particular sound occurring in some position in words of one language appears in the same relative position in semantically similar words of the other languages.

In the case of the forms in (4), we can establish the phonological correspondence set given in (5):

(5)

English	Latin	Greek	Sanskrit
t	d	d	d

Whenever extensive correspondence sets of sounds such as the one in (5)—which could be greatly expanded, if space permitted—can be established among groups of words in different languages, a historical phonological relationship among these languages can be inferred because of the combination of two principles:

(6)

a. Phonological changes are generally regular; that is, within the limits of certain conditions, the changes are exceptionless.

b. The relationship between sound and meaning in a word is arbitrary.

Principle (6a) expresses the fact that speakers of a language can modify their pronunciation in a systematic way. Linguists describe this type of change as the result of the *addition of a phonological rule to a speaker's grammar*. In the examples in (4), the *t*'s in English that correspond to the *d*'s in other languages are the result of some speakers' adding a rule that caused all the original *d*'s to change into *t*'s in their grammars. That the regular correspondence occurs in words among different languages that are the same or similar in meaning is crucial also. Since the meaning that a word has is not in any way determined by the sounds making up that word, then it is likely that such arbitrary sound-meaning relationships (principle (6b)) were inherited by each of them from a historically earlier language, because such far-reaching similarities could hardly be due to chance.

Linguists surmise, then, that Latin, Greek, and Sanskrit have preserved an original *d* articulation, whereas at some point in the history of English, certain speakers changed the pronunciation of their *d*'s into *t*'s. English is not the only language that appears to have undergone the change from *d* to *t*, however. German, Dutch, and the Scandinavian languages also participated in this change. These languages, including English, are all members of the *Germanic language family*, and the change of *d* to *t* most likely occurred within a single Germanic linguistic community before the community separated into the different groups just mentioned. The Germanic languages, then, share several innovations, such as the change of *d* to *t*, that differentiate this group from the other Indo-European languages.

Grimm's Law

The set of correspondences given in (4) is in fact only a part of a larger set of correspondences that can be established between English on the one hand and Latin, Greek, and Sanskrit on the other hand. The underlined portions of the words in (7) indicate the critical consonants involved in the correspondences.

(7)

Germanic (English)   *Other languages*

a. sli<u>pp</u>ery   lū<u>b</u>ricus (Latin) "slippery"

ten	decem (Latin) "ten"
yoke	iugum (Latin) "yoke"
b. father	pater (Latin) "father"
three	trēs (Latin) "three"
horn	cornū (Latin) "horn"
c. brother	bhråtar (Sanskrit) "brother"
bind	bandh (Sanskrit) "bind"
guest	hostis (Latin) "enemy" (note meaning change)

As noted earlier, the consonants of Latin and Sanskrit are for the most part closer to what is reconstructed as the original Indo-European pronunciation. It is hypothesized that Sanskrit and Latin preserve the original *d, b,* and *g* pronunciation of Indo-European, and that these sounds all became voiceless in Germanic. But not all consonants are preserved in their original form in Sanskrit and Latin either, or in any member of the Indo-European language family for that matter. For example, the *g* in English *guest* corresponds to the *h* in Latin *hostis.* Many linguists have hypothesized that the original Indo-European sound was close to a voiced aspirated velar stop, symbolized **gh.* (An asterisk used with transcriptions indicates here that they are hypothetical forms for which no written records are available.) Thus, the original Indo-European **gh* became *g* in Germanic and *h* in the language that was ultimately to become Latin. We display in (8) the set of changes that have been hypothesized based on the correspondences represented in (7):

(8)

Grimm's Law

a. b → p
    d → t
    g → k
b. p → f
    t → θ
    k → x (> h)
c. bh → b
    dh → d
    gh → g

The changes in (8) are known collectively as *Grimm's Law*, because their systematic lawlike character was first stressed by Jacob Grimm (one of the Brothers Grimm, best known in the United States for their collection of German fairy tales). There is some controversy over whether Grimm should be credited for discovering this set of "laws," since the correspondences had already been published by a Dane, Erasmus Rask. Because of his emphasis on their lawlike properties, however, Grimm is usually given credit for the discovery.

The changes that occurred were indeed lawlike, in that all words containing the relevant phonemes underwent changes in accordance with the rules, and the changes that occurred applied to natural classes of phonemes, in the sense discussed in chapter 4. For example, the class of phonemes that underwent the changes in (8b) is the class of *voiceless stops*. Thus, after the Germanic languages split off from the other languages, they were subject to a rule that changed all voiceless stops into fricatives (with some minor restrictions that are not important here). This rule is expressed in the following form:

(9)
$$\begin{bmatrix} + \text{consonant} \\ - \text{voice} \end{bmatrix} \rightarrow [+ \text{continuant}]$$

After rule (9) had applied, words that formerly had *p, t*, and *k* then had *f, θ*, and *h*, respectively. For Germanic-speaking children acquiring their language after rule (9) had changed the consonants, there would be no evidence for the earlier *p*'s, *t*'s, and *k*'s, and they would simply learn the new consonants. Thus, without evidence from other languages, it would be impossible to tell that Germanic *f, θ*, and $x(>h)$ were derived from *p, t, k*. To summarize the thrust of this example, then, we can rephrase the principles in (6) as (10) and state the conditions under which languages can be said to be genetically related on the basis of their sound systems:

(10)
Principles for establishing genetic relationships
A group of languages can be shown to be genetically related if groups of words can be found in each of the languages such that:
a. They possess corresponding phonemes (phonemes in the same position in the word) that are either identical or can be shown to derive from the parent language as the result of the application of *regular (exceptionless) phonological rules* that have applied at some point in the history of each of the languages, and
b. The words that contain the corresponding phonemes have meanings that are related.

The Indo-European Language Family
The languages of the Indo-European family can be shown to be related because the conditions expressed in (10) are satisfied in sets of shared

words. To illustrate how the principles are satisfied, we can begin by considering words and stems meaning "brother" and "bear" (to carry):

(11)

English	*Sanskrit*	*Greek*	*Latin*
brother	bhrátar	phrātēr	frāter
bear	bhar-	pher-	fer-

Based on forms such as these, among others, scholars have *reconstructed* the original Indo-European (IE) forms for "brother" and "to bear" to be *bhráter* and *bher*, respectively. Reconstructed forms such as *bhráter* are frequently referred to as *proto-forms*. Likewise, a reconstructed "parent" language is often referred to as a *proto-language*. A reconstructed form is the most plausible hypothetical source from which all of the forms in all the descendent (daughter) languages can be derived. Thus, starting from reconstructed IE forms such as *bhráter* and *bher*, each of the daughter languages has undergone its own separate and regular changes. Some of these changes are given in figure 8.1. It is important to stress that, when certain conditions are met, *all* IE *bh*'s changed to *ph* in Greek and *b* in Germanic; that is, these changes are the result of rules of the sort we considered in chapters 3 and 4. Thus, it is the consistency (or regularity) of the correspondences among the daughter languages of the Indo-European language family (due to rule-governed phonological change) that is

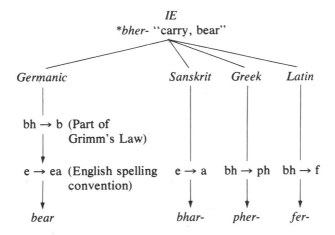

Figure 8.1
The descendent forms from a reconstructed (hypothesized) Indo-European *bher-* "carry, bear." Each of the "daughter" languages has changed from the "parent" form in a different way, and thus their common ancestry has been obscured.

decisive in establishing their historical relatedness. Note that none of the descendent languages preserves all of the phonetic features of the hypothesized (parent) proto-language for the words under consideration. That is, none of the daughter languages is identical to the proto-language. Sanskrit turns out to be more conservative in terms of preserving the original consonants, whereas the other three languages have undergone changes in the consonants but have maintained the original *e* vowel.

The considerations that lead to positing original **e* instead of **a* in forms such as **bher* go beyond the scope of this introductory text, but the reference list at the end of this chapter includes several books on historical linguistics in which such issues are discussed.

Language reconstruction and the establishment of language relatedness involve many additional complications beyond those discussed here, and as a result of techniques used in those fields, much has been learned about the IE language family in the nearly two centuries of research that has been devoted to them. Most of the languages in Europe, for example, have been shown to be related to each other historically. Many of these languages are displayed in figure 8.2. Languages on the same "branch" of the tree in the figure share certain features (or changes) not shared by languages on the other branches of the tree. For example, all the Indic languages underwent the change of short *e* and *o* to *a*, and all the Germanic languages shared the Grimm's Law changes in their consonants. Hence, figure 8.2 reflects a classification system similar to ones used by biologists for plants and animals.

Using techniques of reconstruction such as those discussed here, linguists have worked out a fair idea of the original IE language. Many questions remain, however, concerning the original homeland of the IE speakers. Until recently the consensus was that the Indo-European homeland was in the steppes of Russia, north of the Black Sea, and that the Indo-Europeans were associated with the Kurgan people (Gimbutas 1970). This theory is supported by archeological as well as linguistic evidence. From this centrally located homeland, some of the Indo-Europeans would have migrated east to India and others would have migrated west toward mainland Europe. Recently an alternative hypothesis has been proposed (Renfrew 1989), placing the Indo-European homeland in what is today Turkey. The expansion of the Indo-Europeans into the surrounding areas was due to development of agriculture and the need for new farmland. Whereas earlier theories portrayed the Indo-Europeans as mounted conquerors entering new territory, the most recent theory envisions the offspring from one generation of farmers moving onto adjacent, unused

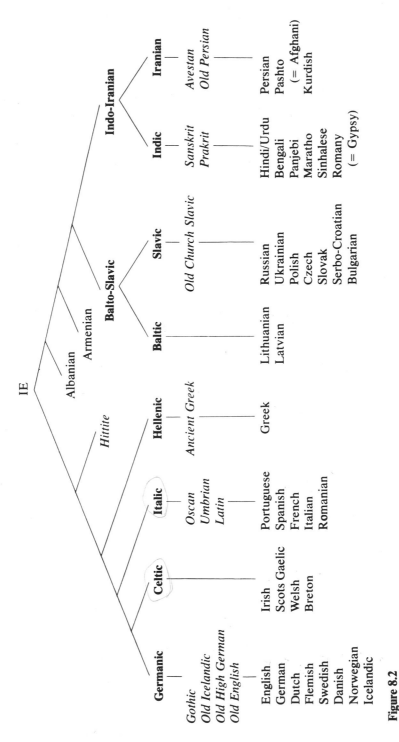

Figure 8.2
The Indo-European language family. Families are listed in boldface type. The oldest attested forms of each family are given in italics, and currently spoken languages are listed in plain roman type at the end of each vertical branch.

farmland, thus continuing a repeating sequence that applied until all arable land was settled.

Whatever the pattern of settlement of the Indo-Europeans, the migrations occurred a long time ago. The Indo-European community of speakers had already split into very different languages more than 4,500 years ago, so the original language could not have been a single language (or group of dialects) less than 5,000 to 6,000 years ago. To answer the question of whether this earlier language was more primitive than the languages that descended from it, we can state confidently that there is no evidence that Indo-European was in any sense more primitive than its daughters. Ironically, when the details of Indo-European were first being worked out, it was commonly believed that the daughter languages were "decayed" versions of the pristine original language. The quotation from Sir William Jones at the beginning of this section shows traces of this prejudice. However, it simply does not appear that we can gain any important information about the origin of language from the analytical techniques of reconstructing earlier forms of a language. All reconstructed languages are full-fledged human languages, and there is no evidence that languages have become more expressive or have "improved" in some sense during the past 10,000 years, the most remote time to which we can reconstruct language.

Languages of the World

Although we cannot answer the question of the ultimate origin of human language through analytical techniques such as the comparative method, we can learn about the more recent origins of the world's languages in that we can show that many languages can be grouped together as members of a larger family. As noted earlier, most of the languages of Europe are members of the Indo-European language family. Among those that are not members are Finnish, Estonian, and Hungarian, members of the Finno-Ugric family. The Basque language has not been shown to be conclusively related to any other language and is thus termed an *isolate*.

The grouping of other languages of the world—and even of their number—is much less clear. Part of the problem lies in the differing definitions of dialect, which have a political basis just as often as a linguistic one, as we saw in chapter 7. Though estimates of the number of different languages vary greatly, from 3,000 to 10,000, a commonly cited range is 4,000 to 5,000, with half of the world's population speaking Indo-European languages. The large number of speakers of Indo-European languages is due in part to the European settlement of the New World. The individual language with the most native speakers is Mandarin Chinese. The most common second language—that is, the language learned most frequently as a foreign language—is currently English. For example, a Japanese pilot landing in Paris communicates with a Russian pilot and the French control tower in English.

Very few of the world's languages are unrelated to other languages; most can be grouped into families. Some linguists are becoming quite bold in the grouping of languages. Joseph Greenberg (1987, 1989; but see Campbell 1988) has proposed that the Native American languages of the New World can be grouped into three families, a rather striking proposal when one considers that more than a thousand languages are involved, covering North, Central, and South America. It has been proposed that Japanese and Korean are descendents of a common ancestor (Martin 1966), and work continues on proving this hypothesis. It might appear that we are moving toward collapsing all the world's languages into a single family. Given our present state of knowledge, however, it appears unlikely that all languages will be shown to be descendents of a single ancestor. In table 8.1 we list some of the world's non-Indo-European languages, grouped according to families, giving an approximate number of speakers for each.

Why Languages Change and How Language Change Spreads

Having answered our first question, concerning how to establish historical relationships among languages, we now turn to the second—namely, what are the causes and mechanisms of language change?

Surprisingly perhaps, linguists currently have little understanding of the exact causes of language change. For purposes of discussion, we may divide the topic of language change into two areas: individual and community. By individual change we refer to a spontaneous change in a language on the part of a single speaker. Community change we may define as the transmission and ultimate sharing of changes among speakers in a linguistic community.

Individual Change

One type of individual change that spontaneously occurs is *grammar simplification*. Modern English has a small class of exceptional nouns in which the final voiceless fricative must be voiced in the plural form (for example, *leaf* versus *leaves*). With respect to the regular Plural Rule of English, this change to a voiced fricative is an exception and represents a *complication* of the regular process of plural formation. Many speakers of

Table 8.1
Some non-Indo-European languages of the world

Family	Language	Principal Area Where Spoken	No. of Speakers in Millions
Afro-Asiatic	Hausa	West Africa	23
	Amharic	East Africa	10
	Arabic	North Africa	155
	Hebrew	Israel	3
Altaic	(Khalkha) Mongolian	Mongolia	2
	Turkish	Turkey	45
Austro-Asiatic	Vietnamese	Vietnam	45
Austronesian	Indonesian-Malay	Indonesia, Malaysia	115
Caucasian	Georgian	Caucasus (South-eastern USSR)	3
Dravidian	Kannada	India	32
	Malayalam	India	31
	Tamil	India, Sri Lanka	59
	Telugu	India	60
Finno-Ugric	Finnish	Finland	5
	Hungarian	Hungary	13
Japanese	Japanese	Japan	119
Korean	Korean	Korea	60
Niger-Congo	Swahili	East Africa	32
	Igbo	West Africa	12
	Yoruba	West Africa	14
Sino-Tibetan	Cantonese	Southern China	55
	Mandarin	Northern China	726
	Burmese	Burma	26
	Tibetan	Tibet	6

English are now regularizing these forms and use plurals such as *hand-kerchiefs* and *hoofs* instead of the previously used *handkerchieves* and *hooves*. Test yourself with the following expression: Snow White and the Seven _____. Not too long ago the common pronunciation was *dwarves*, but now more and more people are using *dwarfs*, the regular form, in the plural. Also, in forming the plural of words derived from exceptional nouns like *leaf*, speakers apply the regular rule if the derived word differs significantly in meaning. For example, the National Hockey League team located in Toronto is known as the Toronto *Maple Leafs* (not *Maple Leaves*). In other words, the pressure to simplify and regularize is quite strong, and regularization leading to language change is probably carried out a great deal by children during language acquisition. Adults may also be a source of change, although very little is known at present about the possible contribution of adults to language change. We simply do not know why a rule such as Grimm's Law applied in Germanic, or why in more recent English, rules for flapped and glottal stop variants of *t* have been added (recall chapter 3). Once a group of speakers has changed their language, however, the change may then spread to other speakers.

Community Change

If a change begins in one area, it is sometimes possible to follow its progress through time and space as it moves *wavelike* through a community of speakers. Although some areas tend to be more active in innovating than others, changes often spread in an overlapping fashion. For example, a difference has been noticed (Joos 1942) in the pronunciation of the word *typewriter* in two dialects of Canadian English: /tʌyprayDər/ and /tʌyprʌyDər/. This difference can be explained in terms of the interaction of two rules, the rule for flapped D discussed in chapter 3 and the Vowel Centering rule illustrated in problem 1 of chapter 4. Vowel Centering applies in some dialects of American and Canadian English, so that the diphthongs /ay/ and /aw/ become /ʌy/ and /ʌw/ before *voiceless* consonants. The pronunciation of the word *typewriter* in the two Canadian dialects can be accounted for by an interesting interaction of the two rules:

(12)

a. *Flap Rule*

$$\begin{bmatrix} t \\ d \end{bmatrix} \rightarrow D \ / \ \acute{V} \underline{\quad} V$$

b. *Vowel Centering*

$$\begin{bmatrix} ay \\ aw \end{bmatrix} \rightarrow \begin{bmatrix} \Lambda y \\ \Lambda w \end{bmatrix} \ / \ \underline{\quad} \begin{bmatrix} \text{voiceless} \\ \text{consonant} \end{bmatrix}$$

Imagine two geographical areas, A and B. In area A, Canadian speakers have rule (12a) in their dialect, but not rule (12b). In area B, on the other hand, speakers have rule (12b), but not rule (12a). What effect might this have on speakers who are located between these two groups? How might their pronunciation be influenced by their neighbors in areas A and B? We know that speakers in one area may have an influence on neighboring speakers, so that features of language such as pronunciation (as well as vocabulary, morphology, and syntax) can be assimilated by the neighboring group. The neighboring group in turn can pass on the feature of pronunciation (which we write as a rule) to further neighbors, so that the rule appears to move "wavelike" through successive groups of speakers. Given this observation, two rules could originate in different areas, but

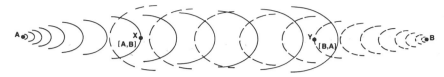

Figure 8.3
Geographic spread of two intersecting rules

gradually spread. They would eventually "meet" and "cross," creating areas where their effects overlap, as shown in figure 8.3.

Figure 8.3 represents an idealized geographic spread of two rules. At point X, which is close to area A, rule (12a) "arrives" first; since X is farther away from area B, rule (12b) "arrives" later. In contrast, point Y is closer to area B, the area of rule (12b), and thus rule (12b) "arrives" at Y *before* rule (12a) does. This difference in the order of arrival of the rules yields the difference in the pronunciation of the word *typewriter* in the two Canadian dialects, as shown in (13):

(13)

	X-dialect		Y-dialect
	taypraytər		taypraytər
First rule (12a):	tayprayDər	First rule (12b):	tʌyprʌytər
Next rule (12b):	tʌyprayDər	Next rule (12a):	tʌyprʌyDər

This example gives a good indication of how a change in pronunciation can "move" among dialects. The Flap Rule, which is not found in British English, has spread among most speakers of American English, although there still are some who pronounce *water* with a *t*. The same type of spreading also occurs with lexical, morphological, and syntactic change, and thus radical language change is possible. If one group of speakers becomes isolated or sufficiently separated from another group of speakers of the same language, each group may undergo its own changes and spreading may not take place between the two groups. Under these conditions new, mutually unintelligible languages will eventually arise.

Spread of Changes among Different Languages

An interesting feature of language change is that grammatical properties, especially phonological ones, can spread between adjacent but *different* languages. For example, the *uvular-r* (an *r*-like sound pronounced in the uvular region of the vocal tract; see figure 3.3) has been replacing the tongue-tip-*r* in many of the languages of Europe. Uvular-*r* is characteristic of French, but it is now common in many dialects of German as well; it is also replacing the tongue-tip-*r* in dialects of southern Sweden and northern Italy. As might be expected, there is much dispute about where the change started.

One of the more remarkable cases of the spread of a phonological change is found in the Native American languages of the northwestern United States. In Washington State, three distinct language groups were geographically adjacent (or in close social contact) before the contact with the Europeans. These groups are represented by Makah (a language of the Wakashan family), Quileute (a language of the Chemakuan family), and several members of the Salish language family. The relative geographic locations of these languages are indicated in figure 8.4, in which A is the Makah region, B is the Quileute region, and C is the Salish language region.

What is remarkable about these different languages is that they *all* lost their nasal consonants by changing them to voiced stops: *m* became *b*, *n* became *d*, and *ŋ* became *g*. Although it is not possible to establish in which language the change began, it is noteworthy that this far-reaching change (indicated by shading in figure 8.4) spread throughout these mutually unintelligible, distinct languages. Almost all of the world's languages have nasal consonants, but these languages are among the few that do not. Notice that the name *Makah* has a nasal consonant—thus appearing to contradict the claim that these languages have no nasals. Also, one of the Puget Sound Salish languages, *Snohomish*, another nasalless language, has *two* nasals in its name. The solution to this apparent contradiction is that the names *Makah* and *Snohomish* represent the pronunciations of the

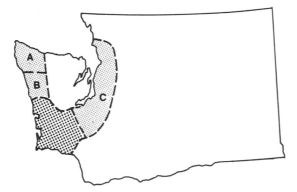

Figure 8.4
Geographical proximity of three distinct language families in the northwestern United States

names of these peoples by neighboring groups that do have nasals in their languages. The Snohomish actually call themselves *sdəhóbš*, in which *d* corresponds to *n* and *b* corresponds to *m*, according to the regular changes mentioned above.

Language Change: Decay or Improvement?

We now turn to the third question that was posed earlier: does language change lead to a gain or loss in expressiveness?

In the past, language change has been viewed variously as decay and as progress, but at present neither of these views seems appropriate or true. Languages seem to maintain a balance in expressiveness and grammatical complexity over time. If a particular grammatical feature is lost (say, because of a phonological change), some feature may be added in another portion of the grammar (say, in the syntax). For example, when English lost most of its inflectional endings (see the next section)—due, it is often claimed, to the deletion of unstressed final syllables as an effect of phonological rules—it was no longer possible to identify the functional role (subject or object) of nouns by their inflectional endings. However, the functional notions of subject and object are now indicated by the syntactic position of nouns, that is, by their position in the linear order of words. In the next section we will also discuss the loss of a morphological rule that created causative verbs from adjectives. But speakers of English did not lose the notion of causation when this word-building rule was lost. In fact, we can still say "to cause to be blue," even though we cannot say *bluen* (compare *redden, whiten, blacken*). Thus, the expressive possibilities of a language are not limited by the lack of an overt grammatical structure that carries a particular notion. For example, Chinese has no overt past tense marker, but this does not mean that the Chinese do not have a notion of past time. The idea of past time can be quite clear either from context or from the presence of an adverb that refers to past time.

In the next section we study the changes that have occurred in English during the past fourteen hundred years. The language has changed radically, but there is not a shred of evidence that it has lost any of its powers of expression.

8.3 THE LINGUISTIC HISTORY OF ENGLISH

The English language has undergone extensive changes between the Old and Modern English periods, although speakers of Modern English are still able to recognize Old English as a relative of Modern English. An example will illustrate this point:

(14)

a. *Old English*

In þām tūne wǣron þæt hūs and þæt būr þæs eorles.

b. *Modern English*

In the town were the house and the chamber of-the chief (earl).

In (14b), a word-for-word Modern English translation of (14a), many of the words show a strong similarity to the Old English words. Nevertheless, changes in grammar and vocabulary have made Old English no longer understandable to the speaker of Modern English.

As noted earlier, the English language is part of the Germanic family of languages and is thus historically related to Modern German, Dutch, Swedish, Norwegian, Danish, and Icelandic. English began its own separate development in the middle of the fifth century A.D. after a series of invasions of England by Germanic-speaking tribes from what is now northwestern Europe. The invading groups included Saxons, Angles, and Frisians, among others. The invaders fought against Celtic-speaking inhabitants, who, after fierce battles, were overcome. These were not the first Europeans to invade England and do battle with the Celts, however. The Romans had colonized England during the first century A.D., before the migrations of the Angles and Saxons began. As the Roman Empire began to collapse, however, the Roman legions withdrew, making possible the conquest of the British Isles by the Germanic tribes. The Celtic tribes who were in the north spoke Scottish, and the remaining Celtic speakers were confined to Wales (Welsh) and Cornwall (Cornish). Welsh is still spoken by a small number of people in Wales, and Cornish became extinct in the eighteenth century. The original Celtic language of Scotland became extinct, although Gaelic speakers from Ireland moved to Scotland in the fifteenth century and there developed their own dialect, Scots Gaelic, which is still spoken by a small population. The Irish Gaelic language is also still spoken in Ireland, but only by a minority of its inhabitants.

During the sixth century, the Germanic invasions ended and England entered a period of relative political stability. The island became covered with a patchwork of kingdoms, and during this period of political stability several dialect areas arose. The major dialects were West Saxon, Kentish, Mercian, and Northumbrian, the West Saxon dialect eventually becoming the most important. The differences among these dialects, which mainly involved pronunciation, were similar to differences among dialects in the present-day United States. The language of this period, called Old English (or Anglo-Saxon), was in many ways grammatically similar to Modern German. For instance, the nouns, adjectives, and verbs were highly inflected, as the examples in (15) show.

(15)
Typical Old English nouns, adjectives, and verbs
a. Noun: *cyning* "king"

Singular	Nominative	cyning
	Accusative	cyning
	Genitive	cyninges
	Dative/Instrumental	cyninge
Plural	Nominative	cyningas
	Accusative	cyningas
	Genitive	cyninga
	Dative/Instrumental	cyningum

b. Adjective: *gōd* "good" (weak declension)

		Masculine	Feminine	Neuter
Singular	Nominative	gōda	gōde	gōde
	Accusative	gōdan	gōdan	gōde
	Genitive	gōdan	gōdan	gōdan
	Dative/Instrumental	gōdan	gōdan	gōdan
Plural	(Same plural endings in all genders)			
	Nominative	gōdan		
	Accusative	gōdan		
	Genitive	gōdra		
	Dative/Instrumental	gōdum		

c. Verb: infinitive *dēman* "judge" (compare Modern English *deem*, *doom*)

Present Tense	Singular	1	dēme
		2	dēmst, dēmest
		3	dēmþ, dēmeþ
	Plural	1,2,3	dēmaþ
Past Tense	Singular	1	dēmde
		2	dēmdest
		3	dēmde
	Plural	1,2,3	dēmdon

The words in (15) consist of two parts, a base and one of a set of inflectional suffixes. The inflectional morphology of Old English was in fact much more complicated than (15) indicates. The noun *cyning* is an example of a so-called *masculine* noun, but there were two other genders, *feminine* and *neuter*, both of which had different endings. Each of the three nominal genders had, in turn, different subclasses, and each subclass had its own set of inflectional endings. There were, then, about two dozen different types of inflectional endings that could be added to nouns alone.

The adjectives and verbs were also divided into classes that required different endings, so that there were altogether dozens of different classes of inflectional endings that were added to nouns, adjectives, and verbs. One of the major changes between Old English and Modern English, then, was obviously the loss of almost all of these nominal, adjectival, and verbal endings—for the language has very few such suffixes today (recall the discussion of English morphology in chapter 2). In the nouns, only the regular genitive ending -s/-es (now the possessive) and the plural ending -s/-es have survived. Flurals such as *children* carry on an earlier -*en* plural ending, and plurals such as *geese* also reflect an earlier class of inflectional ending. (We will discuss the origin of the stem alternation between *goose* and *geese* later.) The adjective endings have also been completely lost, although archaic spellings and phrases such as *ye olde shoppe* or *in the olden days* are relics from this earlier period.

Another indicator of English language history is found in modern words with an initial *sk-* sequence. Old English words containing this sequence underwent a rule that changed a *sk* sequence into a *sh* /š/ sound. Sound changes being exceptionless (recall principle (10)), Modern English *sk-* initial words cannot be descendents of Old English *sk*-initial words. It turns out that the *sk* sequence found in words such as *sky* and *skirt* is the result of borrowings from the Scandinavian languages. (The Danes in fact controlled northeastern England in the ninth and tenth centuries.) An interesting pair of words is *ship* and *skiff*. The word *ship*, which has come down to us from Old English, would have originally begun with a *sk* sequence that later underwent the change to *sh* (/š/). The word *skiff*, which refers to a small boat, retains the initial *sk* sequence, signaling that it is a borrowing from Scandinavian.

By far the greatest influence on English came from a Continental language—French. The influence of French is of course due to the Norman Conquest of England by William the Conqueror in 1066. The Normans brought with them the French language, and French remained the language of the ruling class for a considerable period. Under its influence the English language changed in terms of vocabulary, phonology, and morphology, as we will see.

Although the changes from Old English to Modern English were continuous and gradual, linguists traditionally distinguish three major periods in this development: the Old English period (fifth to eleventh centuries), the Middle English period (eleventh to fifteenth centuries), and the Modern

English period (fifteenth century to the present). Scholars studying the history of English are fortunate in that there are written documents spanning more than 1,200 years that enable them to trace many of the changes that English has undergone during this time. In discussing them, we will concentrate on the three structural components of language—phonology, morphology, and syntax—as well as on vocabulary changes that have occurred between Old and Modern English. Each of these four components can undergo three major types of change: addition, loss, and change in structure.

Lexical Change

Addition

From Old English times to the present, new words have continuously been added to the English language. Surprisingly, only a few Celtic words have found their way into English, in spite of the fact that English speakers have been continuously in contact with Celtic speakers in Wales, Ireland, and Scotland. Personal names such as *Lloyd* and its variant *Floyd* are Celtic borrowings.

By far the greatest number of new words came from French as a result of the Norman invasion. These French words did not always replace Old English words but in many instances expanded an already existing vocabulary. For example, the words *pork, beef, veal, mutton*, and *venison* are all derived from French words referring respectively to the edible meat of the *swine, cow, calf, sheep*, and *deer*, the latter being Old English words. Formerly, the Anglo-Saxon words were used to refer to both the meat and the animals. Interestingly, the words *beef* and *cow* are both descendents of the same Indo-European word *$g^{wh}ow$-, which, because of the different historical changes in the Germanic and Romance families, has given rise to quite different-sounding words.

Although English has borrowed most heavily from French, other languages have also contributed words. During the Renaissance, for example, a large number of so-called learned words from Latin and Greek became part of English (*reverberate* from Latin and *polygon* from Greek are typical examples). From Spanish we have words such as *mesa, lariat*, and *taco*. Russian words such as *perestroika* and *glasnost* are still identified as Russian but may someday join words such as *vodka* and *czar* (think of William Bennett, the "drug czar") as words borrowed into English. From German we have words such as *kindergarten, hamburger*, and *gesundheit*. *Woodchuck* is ultimately an Algonquian word, and *tomato* comes to us from

Aztec (via Spanish). English has thus borrowed freely from other languages, a habit that partially accounts for its enormous vocabulary.

In chapter 2 we also noted the many ways that new words can be introduced into English via abbreviations and word formation rules, producing such words as *TV*, *finalize*, and *laser*. Consequently, the number of words that can be added to our language—by borrowing or otherwise—is in principle unbounded.

Loss

Conversely, many words have been lost since the Old English period, though a surprising number of the lost words are still present in compounds. One example is OE *wer* "man." This word is historically related to the Latin word *vir*, also meaning "man," forms of which (for example, *virile*) have been borrowed into English. The form *wer*, even though lost as an independent word, still exists in *werewolf*, which originally meant "man-wolf" or "wolfman." The OE word *rice* "realm, kingdom" has a similar history. This word, which was originally borrowed from a Celtic language, has been lost in the modern language. In contrast, the German language, which also borrowed this word, has preserved it in the word *Reich*. The only relic of this word in Modern English is in the compound word *bishopric*, which originally meant "bishop's realm," a sense close to its present-day meaning.

Change

Many examples of meaning change have already been discussed in chapter 2, which focused on narrowing, broadening, and metaphorical extension of meaning. Another example of semantic narrowing that occurred between Old English and Modern English is seen in the word *hound* (OE *hund*). This word once referred to any kind of dog, whereas in Modern English the meaning has been narrowed to a particular breed. The word *dog* (OE *docga*), on the other hand, referred in Old English to the mastiff breed; its meaning now has been broadened to include any dog. The meaning of *dog* has also been extended metaphorically in modern casual speech (slang) to refer to a particularly unattractive person.

Semantic Change and Semantic Fields

We have seen examples of individual words undergoing a meaning change. But semantic change at the word level is not limited to single words—rather, entire groups of words can undergo parallel semantic changes. In her study of semantic fields, Lehrer (1974) has noted that words belonging to the same semantic field undergo similar semantic changes. To take an example (Lehrer and Battan 1983), consider the following set of words, drawn from the semantic field of bird names: *goose*, *cuckoo*, *pigeon*, *coot*, *turkey*. In addition to its literal meaning, each of these words has a metaphorical use indicating "foolishness." According to the *Oxford English Dictionary*, the words *goose*, *cuckoo*, and *pigeon* were the first of this set to be used in the metaphorical sense in question, and all three acquired their metaphorical meaning at roughly the same time (the first recorded instances dating from the mid-sixteenth century). This could be due to coincidence; but it seems plausible to assume that the simultaneous metaphorical extension of the three words was based on their membership in the same semantic class. Later, the words *coot* and *turkey* came to have the same metaphorical use, again underscoring the idea that words in the same semantic field can undergo similar semantic changes. The word *pigeon*, incidentally, had a metaphorical use indicating "cowardice" in Shakespeare's time—recall *pigeon-livered*—but this use later became obsolete. What bird has taken over this metaphorical meaning of cowardice in Modern English?

It is also the case that the structure of a semantic field plays a role in semantic change. For example, the words *hot* and *cold* are antonyms that describe physical temperature. With pairs of antonyms, if one member undergoes a metaphorical extension, the other tends to change in a parallel fashion. Thus, just as *hot* and *cold* are opposites in describing temperature, so they are also opposites in their metaphorical extension in phrases such as *hot news* (news that is just breaking) versus *cold news* (news that is old). In colloquial style, we can speak of a *hot car* (stolen car); hence, we would not be surprised if speakers began using the phrase *cold car* (one that is not stolen), on the grounds that semantic change tends to affect entire semantic fields in a parallel fashion, and not just single members of the field (for discussion, see Lehrer 1974).

Phonological Change

Rule Addition

There have been many phonological changes between Old English and Modern English, and the rules discussed in chapter 3 (for example, the rules governing flapped and glottal stop variants of *t*) have been *added* to American English relatively recently. Of course, rules that are added to a language can later be lost as living rules, and only certain effects of the

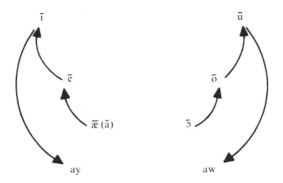

Figure 8.5
The Great Vowel Shift

rules remain. For example, an important set of extensive sound changes affecting the tense (long) vowels occurred at the end of the Middle English period, and these changes are the cause of one of the major discrepancies between the spelling of Modern English and its current pronunciation. Known as the *Great Vowel Shift*, this change had the effects shown in figure 8.5, where the arrows indicate the direction of the changes.

Both of the tense (or long) mid vowel phonemes of Middle English, which we can represent by /ē/ and /ō/ (where the *macron* over the vowel indicates length), were raised and diphthongized to yield the current high vowels /iy/ and /uw/, respectively. The earlier pronunciation of these tense mid vowels is still reflected in the spelling of words such as *feet* (once pronounced /fēt/, now pronounced /fiyt/) and *mood* (once pronounced /mōd/, now pronounced /muwd/). The high vowels of Middle English, in turn, became diphthongs, the first part of the vowel "moving down" to become a low vowel. As part of the Great Vowel Shift, then, /ī/ became /ay/ and /ū/ became /aw/. The current orthography still reflects the former pronunciation in spellings such as *five* (once pronounced /fīv/, now pronounced /fayv/). Note also the spelling of OE *tūne* for "town" in (14), the vowel having been pronounced /ū/ before the diphthong /aw/ was created.

Two of the tense low vowel phonemes, /æ/ and /ɔ/, were also raised to yield a new set of mid vowels, /ey/ and /ow/, respectively. Thus, Modern English *mate* /meyt/ was formerly pronounced /mæt/, and the word *goat* /gowt/ was formerly pronounced /gɔt/. The addition of these phonological rules, then, caused a significant change in the pronunciation of English words, and even though the Great Vowel Shift has now been lost from English as a purely phonological rule, its effects are still revealed in the discrepancy between the pronunciation of Modern English and its spelling system.

Rule Loss

Early in the history of English a rule called *i-Mutation* (or *i-Umlaut*) existed that turned back vowels into front vowels when an /i/ or /y/ followed in the next syllable. For example, in a certain class of nouns in the ancestor of Old English, the plural was formed not by adding /s/ but by adding /i/. Thus, the plural of /gōs/ "goose" was /gōsi/ "geese." Later, when the *i*-Mutation rule was added, the *i*-ending of the plural conditioned the change of /gōsi/ to /gœsi/. The /œ/ phoneme is a combination of the /o/ and /e/ phonemes; it is a mid front vowel like /e/ but has lip rounding like /o/. Hence, the effect of *i*-Mutation was to cause back vowels to move forward, but the newly fronted vowels kept the rounding that they had when they were back vowels. Still later, the lip rounding was lost, and the plural of /gōs/ became /gēs(e)/. When /gos/ and /ges/ finally underwent the Great Vowel Shift, the current pronunciations /guws/ and /giys/ resulted. Thus, *i*-Mutation is an example of a rule that was once present in Old English but has since dropped out of the language, and thanks to the Great Vowel Shift even the effects of *i*-Mutation have been altered.

Change in Rule Applicability

In Old English, fricatives became voiced when they occurred between voiced sounds (that is $f \to v$, $\theta \to \eth$, $s \to z$). Since the most common plural ending was formerly *-as*, all nouns ending in fricatives underwent this rule in the plural. The rule causing this voicing is no longer present in Modern English, but its effects can still be observed in pairs such as singular *wife* /wayf/ and plural *wives* /wayvz/. This change of the stem in the plural is still the result of a rule, but the form of the rule is quite different from the form that it had in Old English. In Old English the rule was *phonological*: it applied whenever fricatives occurred between voiced sounds. In contrast, the alternation between voiced and voiceless fricatives in Modern English is not phonological, but *morphological*: the voicing rule applies only to certain words and not to others. Thus, a particular (and now exceptional) class of nouns must undergo voicing of the final voiceless fricative when used in the plural (for example, *wife/wives*, *knife/knives*, *hoof/hooves*). Other nouns, however, do not undergo this process (for example, *proof/proofs*). The fricative voicing rule of Old English has changed from a phonological rule to a morphological rule in Modern English.

Differences in Phonemic Inventory

Addition of Phonemes

The phonemic system of Old English was similar to that of Modern English, although several differences can be noted. For example, the voiced labiodental fricative [v] was not an independent phoneme in Old English. The [v]'s that did occur were voiced allophonic variants of the phoneme /f/. As a result of subsequent changes between Old English and Middle English, /v/ has become an independent phoneme.

Loss of Phonemes

As noted in the previous section, the mutated (or umlauted) vowels /œ/ and /y/ (front rounded vowels) lost their rounding during the Old English period. The word *thimble*, for example, probably was originally pronounced as [θymbɪl] in very early Old English. Later /y/ became unrounded to /ɪ/. (Knowing that the suffix *-il* was used to form nouns with diminutive meaning from other nouns, what can you surmise about the origin of the word *thimble*?)

Morphological Change

Rule Addition

The *-able* rule discussed in chapter 2 is an example of a rule that has been added to English since the Old English period. As a result of the influx of a large number of *-able* words from French into English, English speakers were able to extract a rule from these words that is still productive in the language. Words such as *doable* and *washable* have been formed by adding *-able* to the Germanic roots *do* and *wash*.

Rule Loss

An example of a morphological rule that has been lost is the Causative Verb Formation rule of Old English. In Old English causative verbs could be formed by adding the suffix *-yan* to adjectives. The modern verb *redden* meaning "to cause to be or make red" is a carry-over from the time when the Causative Verb Formation rule was present in English, in that the final *-en* of *redden* is a reflex of the earlier *-yan* causative suffix. However, the rule adding a suffix such as *-en* to adjectives to form new verbs has been lost, and thus we can no longer form new causative verbs such as **green-en* "to make green" or *blue-en* "to make blue." (Do you see now how *awake* and *awaken* are related to each other?)

Rule Change

New nouns could be formed in Old English by adding *-ing* not only to verbs, as in Modern English (*sing* + *ing* = *singing*), but also to a large class of nouns. For example, the word *viking* was formed by adding *-ing* to the noun *wic* "bay." (Why might the word for "bay" be used to describe the Vikings?) It turns out that the *-ing* suffix can still be added to a highly restricted class of nouns, carrying the meaning "material used for," as in *roofing, carpeting*, and *flooring*. Thus, the rule for creating new nouns with the *-ing* suffix has changed by becoming more *restricted* in its application, so that a much smaller class of nouns can still have *-ing* attached.

Syntactic Change

Rule Addition

A syntactic rule that has been added to English since the Old English period is the Particle Movement rule discussed in chapter 5. Thus, sentence pairs of the type *John threw out the fish* and *John threw the fish out* did not occur in Old English.

Rule Loss

A syntactic rule that has been lost from English is the morphosyntactic rule of Adjective Agreement. At one time adjectives required endings that had to agree with the head noun in case, number, and gender (see (15)). This rule is no longer found in English, since most of the inflectional endings of English have been lost.

Syntactic Change: Auxiliary Verbs versus Main Verbs

Recall from chapter 5 that contemporary English makes a distinction between auxiliary verbs and main verbs, a distinction reflected in questions (only auxiliary verbs can be fronted in questions, as in *Can you leave?*), negative sentences (only auxiliary verbs can take the contracted negative *n't*, as in *You can't leave*), and tag questions (only auxiliary verbs can appear in tags, as in *You can leave, can't you?*). Focusing now only on so-called modal verbs (*can, must*), it is interesting to note that prior to the sixteenth century these syntactic distinctions between main verbs and auxiliary verbs did not exist.

At that time it was possible for main verbs to take *not*, and examples such as the following can be found in Shakespeare's writings:

(16)

a. I deny it *not*. ("I don't deny it.")

b. Forbid him *not*. ("Do not forbid him.")

Similarly, main verbs could be fronted in forming questions:

(17)

a. Revolt our subjects? ("Do our subjects revolt?")

b. Gives not the hawthorn-bush a sweeter shade? ("Does the hawthorn-bush not give a sweeter shade?")

However, by Shakespeare's time such patterns were already beginning to disappear as a series of grammatical changes was taking place in the mid-1500s (see Lightfoot 1979 for a summary and discussion). After the sixteenth century the grammar of English had changed so that auxiliary verbs—and never main verbs—had to be used in negation, questions, and other patterns we have noted.

The changes that took place between Old English and Modern English are typical of the kinds of changes that all human languages undergo over time, and after enough years have passed the descendent language (or languages) can be very different from its (their) ancestor language. Moreover, language change offers important indirect evidence about the nature of human language—namely, that it is rule-governed. We have seen that the major changes that the English language underwent between the Old English and Modern English periods are best viewed as changes in the *sets of rules* characterizing the two stages of English. Over time, grammatical rules can be added, lost, or changed; so language has always changed, and given the complexity of language and the way that humans use it creatively, change is also part of the nature of human language and perhaps humans themselves.

Study Questions

1. Discuss the various theories for the origin of human language.

2. What is the Indo-European language family?

3. What is one way to establish that languages are descendents of a common ancestor for which no written records exist?

4. What is Grimm's Law? Illustrate its effect with some comparisons between English and Latin or Greek words.

5. What does it mean to say that some language changes move "wavelike" through a community of speakers?

6. What was the Great Vowel Shift? What consequences did this sound change have on contemporary English? Give examples in your answer. *{spelling pronounciation}*

tense/long vowels raised + dipthongizeds but still spelled the same way.

Exercises

feet, five, town.

1. How can knowledge of Grimm's Law help one remember that a *podiatrist* is a *foot doctor*?

2. The Indo-European word **ghostis* corresponds to the Latin word *hostis* "enemy" and to the English word *guest*. What is a plausible meaning that **ghostis* could have had that would account for the different meanings in Latin and English?

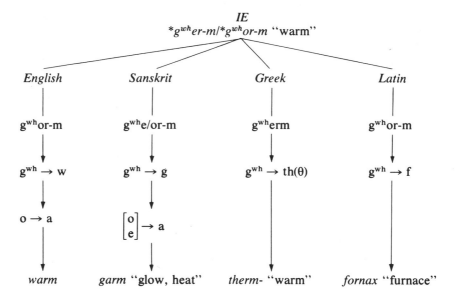

Chart (Exercise 3)

Changes that original IE **g^{wh}erm–*g^{wh}orm* underwent in several daughter languages. The *n* found in Latin *fornax* is not from IE **m* but instead is a different suffix that was added to the stem **g^{wh}or-*.

3. Using the accompanying chart, explain the relationships among the italicized words in the following English sentence: I turned up the *thermostat* on my *furnace* to get *warm*.

4. Each of the Indo-European words in the following list has a cognate (a word inherited from an earlier form of the language or a word shared by two daughter languages) in English. You can determine what the words are by (1) applying Grimm's Law to the Indo-European forms and (2) using the meaning of the

corresponding Latin, Greek, or Sanskrit borrowing as a clue. (Hint: Don't worry about finding regular changes in the vowels for this exercise.)

Indo-European	Word borrowed from classical languages into English
a. *$g^hw\bar{e}n$	a. *gynecologist* (from Greek)
b. *dekm̥	b. *decimate* (from Latin)
c. *gnō-	c. *agnostic* (from Greek)
d. *medhyos-	d. *medium* (from Latin)
e. *yug(om)	e. *yoga* (from Sanskrit, means "work")

Bibliography and Further Reading

Bloomfield, L. (1933). *Language*. New York: Holt, Rinehart and Winston.

Bynon, T. (1977). *Historical linguistics*. Cambridge: Cambridge University Press.

Campbell, L. (1988). Review article on *Language in the Americas*. *Language* 64, 591–615.

Cardona, G., H. M. Hoenigswald, and A. Senn, eds. (1970). *Indo-European and Indo-Europeans*. Philadelphia: University of Pennsylvania Press.

Fell, B. (1977). *America B.C.: Ancient settlers in the New World*. New York: New York Times Book Company.

Gimbutas, M. (1970). Proto-Indo-European culture: The Kurgan culture during the fifth, fourth, and third millenia, B.C. In Cardona, Hoenigswald, and Senn 1970.

Greenberg, J. (1987). *Language in the Americas*. Stanford, Calif.: Stanford University Press.

Greenberg, J. (1989). Classification of American Indian languages: A reply to Campbell. *Language* 65, 107–114.

Harnad, S., H. Steklis, and J. Lancaster (1976). *Origins and evolution of language and speech*. Annals of the New York Academy of Science, vol. 280. New York.

Hewes, G. (1976). The current status of the gestural theory of language origins. In Harnad, Steklis, and Lancaster 1976.

Joos, M. (1942). A phonological dilemma in Canadian English. *Language* 18, 141–144.

Lehmann, W. (1967). *A reader in nineteenth-century historical linguistics*. Bloomington, Ind.: Indiana University Press.

Lehrer, A. (1974). *Semantic fields and lexical structure*. Amsterdam: North Holland.

Lehrer, A., and P. Battan (1983). Semantic fields and semantic change. In *Coyote papers* 4. Department of Linguistics, University of Arizona, Tucson.

Lenneberg, E. (1964). A biological perspective of language. In E. Lenneberg, ed., *New directions in the study of language*. Cambridge, Mass.: MIT Press.

Lieberman, P. (1975). *On the origins of language: An introduction to the evolution of human speech*. New York: Macmillan.

Lightfoot, D. (1979). *Principles of diachronic syntax*. New York: Cambridge University Press.

Martin, S. (1966). Lexical evidence relating Korean to Japanese. *Language* 46, 185–251.

Miller, G. (1981). *Language and speech*. San Francisco: W. H. Freeman.

Molony, C. (1988). The truth about the Tasaday. *Sciences* 28, 12–20.

Moore, S., and T. Knott (1963). *The elements of Old English*. Ann Arbor, Mich.: George Wahr Publishing Co.

National Geographic Magazine (1989). Did Neanderthals speak? New bone of contention. October 1989.

Renfrew, C. (1989). The origins of the Indo-European languages. *Scientific American* 261.4, 106–114.

Sloat, C., S. Taylor, and J. Hoard (1978). *Introduction to phonology*. Englewood Cliffs, N.J.: Prentice-Hall.

Traugott, E. (1972). *A history of English syntax*. New York: Holt, Rinehart and Winston.

Part II

COMMUNICATION AND COGNITIVE SCIENCE

INTRODUCTION

In the previous chapters we have explored human language as an abstract system with numerous structural (morphological, phonetic, phonological, syntactic, and semantic) properties. We have seen that human language can be fruitfully analyzed in terms of various units of representation (features, phonemes, morphemes, words, phrases, clauses, sentences, concepts, and so on), along with rules and principles that capture regularities and generalizations among these units. Thus, various "levels" in the description of a language (the morphological, phonetic, phonological, syntactic, and semantic levels) represent regularities in the behavior of the units at that level, and such levels in linguistics are like the levels in other sciences. For instance, chemists describe substances in terms of elements and their principles of combination: water is two parts hydrogen and one part oxygen, combined in a certain way. A physicist might then describe oxygen and hydrogen in terms of their atomic structure, atomic weight, and principles of atomic interaction. Furthermore, it is an important fact about human languages that they are susceptible to variation and change (we do not view the principles that govern the world of physics as varying or changing, though our knowledge of them surely will), and we have seen that often such variation and change is itself principled in interesting ways.

It is now time to remind ourselves, theoretically, of the importance of the fact that languages are *used* and *learned* by human beings (and many would say *only* by human beings). How could a language change or vary if it were not? Thinking of languages as being used and learned by humans raises still more questions, such as, How do people use language to communicate? How is this knowledge represented in and utilized by the mind/brain? How is it learned?

In chapter 9 we explore the nature of pragmatics, the study of language use in relation to language structure and context of use. As such, the study of pragmatics straddles the boundary between language and the world. Speaking a language involves producing sounds for others to hear, understand, and act upon. How is it possible for a speaker to put thoughts into words and for a hearer to understand them? This, it turns out, is not a trivial or simple accomplishment: a rich and subtle system of principles underlies this apparently facile skill.

It is an important fact about human beings that virtually all of them learn to speak (or sign) a language. Placed in a minimal linguistic environment, all human children with normal brain function will quickly and apparently effortlessly acquire the language spoken (or signed) around them. Thus, we should expect that human language and its use will be interestingly related to human cognition. So far this has proved to be true, and a richly diverse new field called *cognitive science* has developed, incorporating aspects of linguistics, philosophy, psychology, neuroscience, and computer science. The basic idea behind cognitive science is that the study of cognition (perception, memory, thought, and action) should be a unified subject of research, drawing on the expertise of many traditional disciplines. For instance, in computer science one learns how to write programs that can perform certain tasks. One also learns how machines can be built that will execute these programs and actually exhibit the capacity written into them. Cognitive science draws on these activities of computer science, using them as an analogy that helps to unify our picture of the human mind. What if the human mind is like a mental "program" and neurons are our "hardware"? Knowing how programs and hardware are related in computer science might help us better understand, by analogy, how our knowledge and our thoughts might be related to the neural structure of our brains. In particular, we might better understand how our knowledge of language and our ability to speak and understand might be related to the structure of our brain. Recent work on "connectionist" models shows that we must not restrict our conception of computers and programming them to just the architectures that happen to be available and commercially viable.

One of the most active areas of psychology is the study of linguistic knowledge, how it is acquired, and how it is used in the production and comprehension of speech. In chapters 10 and 11 we investigate some significant results in the *psychology of language* (also called *psycholinguistics*).

Chapter 10 is devoted to exploring issues in the production and comprehension of speech. Here we consider how linguistic knowledge might be represented in the mind and how this information can be put to use in speaking and understanding. Following the flow of information from speaker to hearer, we will both review broad theoretical options and report interesting experimental results.

Chapter 11 is devoted to the study of the acquisition of language. Here we examine the character of normal language development in the (human) child, and the implications this process might have for better understanding human biological endowment. For instance, are human beings preprogrammed to learn (or create) the kind of language system described here? Can the young of another species (such as primates) acquire human language, and if so do they acquire it in the same way? To begin to answer these questions, we first explore the normal course of human language development. We then survey some controversial attempts to teach American Sign Language to chimpanzees. Do they learn as human children do, or are there important differences?

Given that human language is clearly unique among communication systems in its richness and complexity, and given the natural disposition children have for mastering it, it is quite reasonable to suppose that there is something special about the human brain, either in capacity or in its structural organization, that makes this distinctively human achievement possible. In spite of the splendid work in the last few decades of a highly dedicated group of neuroscientists, we are still quite ignorant about the structure and functioning of the human brain with respect to such basic cognitive functions as language. In fact, the study of the brain has often been described as the next intellectual frontier. It is certainly true that we understand the rest of the human body a great deal better than we understand the brain. Chapter 12 is devoted to some of the central ideas and controversies to come out of *neurolinguistics*, the study of the neural basis of language. Since it is hardly feasible to perform experiments on the neuroanatomy of speakers' brains, a crucial source of data about how language might be represented and used by the brain is the experience of patients suffering some loss of speech or comprehension due to brain injuries.

All in all, it seems that linguists will gain a deeper perspective on their subject matter by seeing exactly how it is related to the neighboring concerns of psychology, neuroscience, and biology. Likewise, these neighboring areas of research can gain something from linguistics; language constitutes the richest and most rigorously described domain of human expertise yet. The structures and regularities discovered by linguists in their analyses of human languages pose a unique challenge to psychological, neurological, and biological theories of human capacities.

Chapter 9

PRAGMATICS: THE STUDY OF LANGUAGE USE AND COMMUNICATION

9.1 LINGUISTIC COMMUNICATION: SOME BACKGROUND CONCEPTS

Probably the most pervasive characteristic of human social interaction, so pervasive that we hardly find it remarkable, is that we talk. Sometimes we talk to particular persons, sometimes to anyone who will listen; and when we cannot find anyone to listen, we even talk to ourselves. Although human language fulfills a large variety of functions, from waking someone up in the morning with a cheery *Wake up!* to christening a ship with a solemn *I hereby christen this ship "H.M.S. Britannia,"* we will be focusing here on those uses of language that are instrumental for human communication. Fluent speakers of English, for instance, know facts such as these:

(1)
a. *Hello* is used to greet.
b. *Goodbye* is used to bid farewell.
c. The phrase *that desk* can be correctly used by a speaker on a given occasion to refer to some particular desk.
d. The phrase *is a desk* can be correctly used on a given occasion to characterize any number of desks.
e. *Pass the salt, please* is used to request some salt.
f. *How old are you?* is used to ask someone's age.
g. *It's raining* is used to state that it is raining.
h. *I promise I will be there* is used to promise.

From this list we get a glimpse of the wide variety of possible uses of language, but before we survey these various uses, we must first distinguish between using language *to do* something and using language *in doing* something. It is certainly a very important fact about human beings that we use language *in* much of our thought. It is likely that we could not think some of the thoughts we think, especially abstract thoughts, if we did not have language at our disposal. Central as this fact may be to our cognitive life, it is not central to the pragmatic notion of language use, the use of language to *do* things. When we focus on what people use language to do, we focus on what a person is doing with words in particular situations; we focus on the intentions, purposes, beliefs, and desires that a speaker has in speaking.

When Charles Morris proposed his famous trichotomy of syntax, semantics, and pragmatics, he defined the last as "the study of the relation of signs to interpreters" (1938, 6), but he soon generalized this to "the relation of signs to their users" (1938, 29). One year later Rudolf Carnap proposed to "call *pragmatics* the field of all those investigations which take into consideration . . . the action, state, and environment of a man who speaks or hears [a linguistic sign]" (1939, 4). This tradition continues; both linguists and philosophers (see Gazdar 1979, Bach and Harnish 1979) have taken the term *pragmatics* to cover the study of language use in relation to context, and in particular the study of linguistic communication.

As common and effortless as it is to talk, using language successfully is a very complex enterprise, as anyone knows who has tried as an adult to master a second language. Moreover, much goes into using a language besides knowing it and being able to produce and recognize sentences in it. Communication is also a social affair, usually taking place within the context of a fairly well defined social situation. In such a context we rely on one another to share our conception of what the situation is. With people we know, rather than spell everything out, we rely on shared understandings to facilitate the problem of communicating.

The Problem

What sort of process is this? Linguistic communication is easily accomplished but, as it turns out, not so easily explained; any theory of linguistic communication worth the title must attempt to answer the following question:

(2)
How does successful communication work? For example, suppose that a speaker has an *intention* to report to a hearer that conditions on the road are icy. What makes it possible for the speaker to communicate this to the hearer?

Strangely enough, this question has not received intensive consideration in the literature of any major discipline. Linguistics, focusing on structural properties of language, has tended to view communicative phenomena as outside its official domain. Likewise, it seems possible to pursue philosophical concerns about meaning, truth, and reference without investigating the details of communication. Traditional psychology has focused on the processing of sentences, but without much concern for the specifics of communicative phenomena. Finally, some sociologists and anthropologists have begun to concern themselves with conversations, but have bypassed (or assumed an answer to) the question of the nature of communication itself. Thus, what is needed is an integrated approach to communication, where the question of its nature is the focus of investigation. Only recently has the general shape of an adequate theory of communication begun to emerge, and more time and research will be required to explore it in detail.

The Message Model of Linguistic Communication

For the last thirty years the most common and popular conception of human linguistic communication has been what we will term the *Message Model*, illustrated in figure 9.1.

This model accounts for certain commonsense features of talk-exchanges: it predicts that communication is successful when the hearer decodes the same message that the speaker encodes; and as a corollary it predicts that communication breaks down if the decoded message is different from the encoded message. Likewise, it portrays language as a bridge between speaker and hearer whereby "private" ideas are communicated by "public" sounds, which thereby function as the vehicle for communicating the relevant message.

Though it has a modern ring, the Message Model goes back at least three centuries to the philosopher John Locke, who wrote in 1691 that

Man, therefore, had by nature his organs so fashioned, as to be fit to frame articulate sounds, which we call words. But this was not enough to produce language; for parrots, and several other birds, will be taught to make articulate sounds distinct enough, which yet by no means are capable of language.

Besides articulate sounds, therefore, it was further necessary that he should be able to use these sounds as signs of internal conceptions; and to make them stand as marks for the ideas within his own mind, whereby they might be made known to others and the thoughts of men's minds be conveyed from one to another.

The comfort and advantage of society not being to be had without communication of thoughts, it was necessary that man should find out

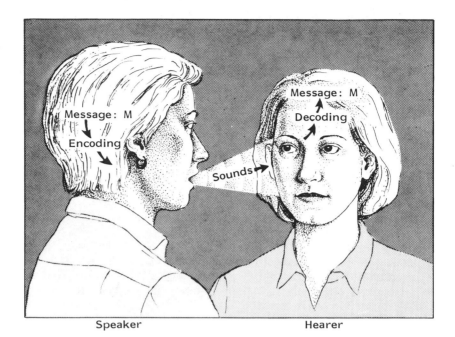

Speaker   Hearer

Figure 9.1
The Message Model of talk-exchanges. A speaker has some message in mind that
she wants to communicate to a hearer. The speaker then produces some expression
from the language that encodes the message as its meaning. Upon hearing the
beginning of the expression, the hearer begins a decoding process that sequentially
identifies the incoming sounds, syntactic categories, and meanings, then composes
these meanings in the form of the successfully decoded message.

some external sensible signs, whereof those invisible ideas, which his
thoughts are made up of, might be made known to others.

There are, moreover, many contemporary statements of essentially this
same idea:

The speaker, for reasons that are linguistically irrelevant, chooses some
message he wants to convey to his listeners: some thought he wants them
to receive or some command he wants to give them or some question he
wants to ask. This message is encoded in the form of a phonetic representation of an utterance by means of the system of linguistic rules with which
the speaker is equipped. This encoding then becomes a signal to the
speaker's articulatory organs, and he vocalizes an utterance of the proper
phonetic shape. This, in turn, is picked up by the hearer's auditory organs.
The speech sounds that stimulate these organs are then converted into a
neural signal from which a phonetic representation equivalent to the one
into which the speaker encoded his message is obtained. This representa-

tion is decoded into a representation of the same message that the speaker originally chose to convey by the hearer's equivalent system of linguistic rules. Hence, because the hearer employs the same system of rules to decode that the speaker employs to encode, an instance of successful linguistic communication occurs. (Katz 1966, 103–104)

There can be little doubt that this model has fascinated many who are interested in human communication, and it is entrenched, to some extent, in our language. For example, Reddy (1979, 311–316) lists some 80 metaphors built on the idea of language as a "conduit for ideas," among which are the following:

(3)

a. Try to *get* your thoughts *across* better.
b. You still haven't *given* me any idea of what you mean.
c. Try to *pack* more thoughts into fewer words.
d. The sentence was *filled* with emotion.
e. Let me know if you *find* any good ideas *in* this essay.

According to Reddy (1979, 290), the major ideas structuring this metaphor are:

(1) language functions like a conduit, transferring thoughts bodily from one person to another; (2) in writing and speaking, people insert their thoughts or feelings in the words; (3) words accomplish the transfer by containing the thoughts or feelings and conveying them to others; and (4) in listening or reading, people extract the thoughts and feelings once again from the words.

These are clear analogues of the major tenets of the Message Model, and this suggests that our language has come to reflect this conception of communication.

Problems with the Message Model

In order to determine the meaning of expressions, the hearer must be able to mentally process sentences that reflect complex structural properties of human language (such as structural ambiguity and discontinuous dependencies). The decoding of the meaning(s) of a sentence is certainly a crucial part of linguistic communication, but the communicative process does not end with processing structural properties and decoding meaning. Indeed, there is considerably more to the process, and it is here that the Message Model encounters a number of problems. We will briefly outline six typical problems faced by the Message Model, and in so doing we hope to give an idea of how complex the communication process is.

First, since many expressions are linguistically ambiguous, the hearer must determine which of the possible meanings of an expression is the one the speaker intended as operative on that occasion. Thus, as far as the Message Model is concerned, disambiguation is a process that is not governed by any principles, and the Message Model certainly does not supply any such principles. But in actuality, disambiguation is not un-principled and random; rather, it is usually quite predictable. Although humorous cases of misunderstanding do arise from time to time, in general we do a good job of picking the appropriate reading of an ambiguous expression. To overcome ambiguity, the hearer presumes the speaker's remarks to be *contextually appropriate*. For example, at an airport zoning meeting the sentence *Flying planes can be dangerous* would naturally be taken as a remark about the danger of planes flying overhead; but at a meeting of the Pilot's Insurance Board it would naturally be taken as a reminder of occupational risk. To take another example, imagine the following conversation:

(4)
A: We lived in Illinois, but we got Milwaukee's weather.
B: Which was worse

Notice that without some extra optional cue (such as exaggerated intonation), A does not know whether B was making an assertion or asking a question:

(5)
Assertion: It was worse getting Milwaukee's weather!
Question: Which weather was it worse to get?

Hence, the Message Model must be supplemented by principles of contextual appropriateness to compensate for the pervasive ambiguity of natural language.

Second, the Message Model does not account for the fact that the message often contains information about particular things being referred to, and reference is rarely uniquely determined by the meaning of expressions. For example, the phrase *the shrewd politician won the election* can be used on different occasions to refer to different people such as Winston Churchill, Richard Nixon, and Franklin D. Roosevelt. Yet the phrase always means one thing ("politician who is shrewd"). A hearer who thinks of Richard Nixon when the speaker's intended referent is Franklin Roosevelt will not have understood the message correctly. So the Message Model must be supplemented by mechanisms for successfully recognizing the intention to refer.

Third, the Message Model represents successful communication as simply producing, hearing, and understanding meaningful expressions. But this is not all there is to communication. What is missing in the model so far is an account of the speaker's *communicative intention*, which is not, in general, uniquely determined by the meaning of the expression uttered. For example, *I'll be there tonight* might be a prediction, a promise, or even a threat, depending upon the speaker's intentions in the appropriate circumstances. Despite these various intentions on the part of the speaker, the sentence has only one relevant meaning.

One of the most interesting facts about communicative intentions is that they are intended to be recognized. When speakers intend to communicate something, they intend to be recognized as trying to communicate it, and communication is successful only if the hearer recognizes that intention. Thus, if a speaker utters the sentence *I'll be there tonight*, intending it as a threat, and if the hearer fails to recognize the speaker's intention and takes the utterance as a simple prediction, then communication has broken down.

Fourth, the Message Model does not account for the fact that we often speak *nonliterally*; that is, we may not mean what our words mean. Common cases of this are irony, sarcasm, and figurative uses of language such as metaphor. Thus, a speaker who says *Oh, that's just great* can, in the appropriate context, be taken to mean the opposite of what the words mean. (Think of discovering a flat tire on your way to class in the morning.) Nonliteral cases are especially difficult for the Message Model to accommodate, since in nonliteral communication the message conveyed by the speaker does not incorporate the literal meaning at all. Rather, the hearer is intended to *use* the literal meaning in figuring out what the speaker actually intends to communicate.

Fifth, the Message Model does not account for the fact that we sometimes mean to communicate more than what our sentences mean. We sometimes speak *indirectly*; that is, we sometimes intend to perform one communicative act by means of performing another communicative act. For example, it would be quite natural to say *My car has a flat tire* to a gas station attendant, with the intention that he repair the tire: in this case we are *requesting* the hearer to *do* something. But how can the speaker mean that the hearer is to do something if the sentence he utters merely reports on the state of his car? The answer is that in uttering the sentence the speaker is (literally and) *directly* reporting a state of affairs presumed to be unsatisfactory and is *indirectly* requesting the hearer to rectify the situation. How does a hearer know if a speaker is speaking indirectly as well as directly? Again, the answer is contextual appropriateness. In the above case, it would be contextually inappropriate to be only reporting a flat tire at a gas station. In contrast, if a police officer asks why a motorist's car is illegally parked, a simple report of a flat tire would be a contextually appropriate response. In the latter circumstance, the hearer (the police officer) would certainly not take the speaker's words as a request to fix the tire. Again, we see the surprisingly pervasive role that presumptions of contextual appropriateness play in successful communication. A speaker can use the very same sentence to convey quite different messages depending on the context.

The final problem with the Message Model is that communicating a message is not always the purpose of our remarks, and this model does not connect at all with these other uses. For example, there are "institutional" acts such as firing or baptizing someone, whose function is to change the institutional status of that person. There are also "institutional" speech acts such as calling a base runner out or finding a defendant guilty, which involve judgments of truth with institutional and social consequences. Communicative success is not the point of such "ritual" utterances since the runner is out, the employee is fired, and the baby is baptized, whether or not they recognize it at the time. Thus, it is not necessary to recognize any communicative intention for these acts to succeed. Likewise, there are speech acts (called *perlocutionary acts*) involving the causing of an effect in a hearer. For instance, a speaker might say things with an intent to persuade, impress, or deceive an audience, but the members of the audience may well not be persuaded, impressed, or deceived if they happen to recognize the speaker's intention to do these things. In contrast, communicative intentions are always intended to be recognized.

To summarize, the Message Model would answer question (2) as follows:

(6)

Linguistic communication is as successful as it is because messages have been conventionalized as the meaning of expressions, and by sharing knowledge of the meaning of an expression, the hearer can recognize a speaker's message—the speaker's communicative intention.

We have seen that this answer to the central question of communication is seriously defective, in that it does not accommodate most of the common cases of successful linguistic communication. For instance, the Message Model of communication must assume that (1) the language is unambiguous, (2) what the speaker is referring to is determined by the meaning of the referring expressions uttered, (3) the communicative intention is determined by the meaning of the sentence, (4) speakers only speak literally, and (5) speakers only speak directly; and it suggests that (6) speakers use words only to communicate.

The six problem areas discussed above show why the simple Message Model of talk-exchanges does not even begin to be adequate to account for the full richness of normal human language use. Clearly, more than just a common language is required to enable the hearer to identify the speaker's communicative intentions on the basis of the speaker's utterances. A *shared system of beliefs and inferences* must be operating, which function in effect as communicative strategies.

9.2 AN INFERENTIAL APPROACH TO COMMUNICATION

If the connection between a speaker's communicative intention (message) and a sentence is *not* one of conventional coding of the message into the sentence via its meaning, then what is it? What is the connection between sounds and communicative intentions that makes communication in all its forms possible?

Basically, the connection is *inferential*. According to the theory of communication to be presented here (see Grice 1957, Bach and Harnish 1979), linguistic communication is successful when the hearer, upon hearing an expression, recognizes the speaker's communicative intention. Thus, we propose the following answer to question (2):

(7)
Linguistic communication is possible because the speaker and hearer share a system of inferential strategies leading from the utterances of an expression to the hearer's recognition of the speaker's communicative intent.

If this is the correct approach to take to communication, then we need to know more about the system of inferential strategies; we want to know how such a system can account for successful communication, while avoiding the limitations of the Message Model. In particular, we want to know how it (1) incorporates the notion of communicative intentions, (2) does not make these communicative intentions uniquely determined by the meaning of the expression uttered, and (3) accounts for literal, nonliteral, direct, and indirect ways of communicating. We take up these matters in the next three sections.

Direct and Literal Communication

The Message Model of linguistic communication applies, if at all, only to a highly idealized form of communication—which may not ever actually take place! However, if one tries to construct a theory of actual, normal communication, then the idea that *rules* or *conventions* of language connect sounds with messages (see (6)) is replaced by the idea that systems of *intended inference* and *shared beliefs* are at work, and that therefore the real job of the communicative part of pragmatics is to investigate these systems.

In what follows we will do just that. The basic idea is quite simple: linguistic communication is a kind of problem solving. The speaker faces the problem of getting the hearer to recognize certain communicative intentions; so the speaker must choose an expression that will facilitate such recognition, given the context of utterance. From the hearer's point of view the problem is to successfully recognize the speaker's communicative intent on the basis of the words the speaker has chosen and the context of utterance.

The *Inferential Model* of communication proposes that in the course of learning to speak our language we also learn how to communicate in that language, and learning this involves acquiring a variety of shared beliefs or *presumptions*, as well as a system of inferential *strategies*. The presumptions allow us to presume certain helpful things about potential hearers (or speakers) and the inference strategies provide communicants with short, effective patterns of inference from what someone utters to what that person might be trying to communicate. Taken together, the presumptions and strategies provide the basis for an account of successful linguistic communication.

Presumptions

Linguistic Presumption (LP)
The hearer is presumed capable of determining the meaning and the referents of the expression uttered.

Communicative Presumption (CP)
Unless there is evidence to the contrary, a speaker is assumed to be speaking with some identifiable communicative intent.

Presumption of Literalness (PL)
Unless there is evidence to the contrary, the speaker is assumed to be speaking literally.

Conversational Presumptions (ConPs)

Relevance: The speaker's remarks are relevant to the conversation.

Sincerity: The speaker is being sincere.

Truthfulness: The speaker is attempting to say something true.

Quantity: The speaker contributes the appropriate amount of information.

Quality: The speaker has adequate evidence for what she says.

If a speaker and hearer share the above presumptions on a given occasion, then the problem of successful communication is easier to solve, since the hearer already has a fairly specific set of conversational expectations. Moreover, we will propose that the speaker and hearer also share a system of inference strategies, each of which handles one of the inadequacies in the Message Model. Thus, there will be strategies not only for direct and literal communication but also for indirect and nonliteral communication. We can "flowchart" these strategies as shown in figure 9.2.

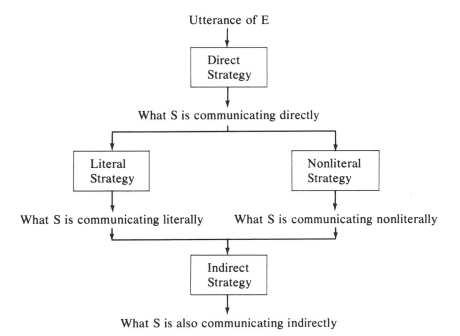

Figure 9.2
The system of inferential strategies. S = speaker, E = expression.

Strategies for Literal and Direct Communication

We have been advocating the idea that even the "simplest" forms of linguistic communication are complicated affairs, and that once we drop the idealizations that the Message Model imposes, we can see that we need more than just rules of language. Rather, we need notions like *intended inference, shared contextual beliefs*, and various *presumptions* to explicate the connection between sounds and communicative intents.

We now want to put these ingredients together into inferential *strategies* for literal and direct communication. That is, we want to represent the patterns of inference, presumption, and shared beliefs that go into this form of communication.

Our first strategy, the *Direct Strategy*, will enable the hearer to infer from what he hears the speaker utter to what the speaker is directly communicating.

Any alternative to the Message Model of linguistic communication must represent any information the hearer is intended to make use of in order to understand the speaker, in spite of ambiguity. It may seem trivial, but clearly one of the most basic pieces of information the hearer needs for communication to be successful is to know what expression the speaker uttered. If the hearer misses the words, it is unlikely the message will be understood. So the first step in successful communication is for the hearer to recognize the speaker's utterance:

(Step 1)
Utterance act
The hearer recognizes what expression the speaker has uttered.

Recall that the first failure of the Message Model involves ambiguity. The Message Model makes no allowance for the fact that the expression uttered may be ambiguous and that the hearer will usually be expected (by the speaker) to realize which meaning was intended to be operative on that occasion. Often, one meaning is contextually inappropriate, and the speaker will be assumed to mean only the appropriate one. For instance, the sentence *Give me a cheap gas can* has the potential for meaning either *Give me a can for cheap gas* or *Give me a gas can which is cheap*. We normally take it to mean only the latter because we use the same cans for cheap and expensive gas. However, it is possible that cheap gas could require a different kind of can. Thus, once the expression is heard, the hearer must decide which meaning of the expression is the relevant intended one. This process is still not well understood, so we will simply represent the hearer's success as step 2:

(Step 2)
Operative meaning
The hearer recognizes which meaning of the expression is intended to be operative on this occasion.

However, even after the hearer has disambiguated the expression in the context, another task usually remains before it is possible to determine what communicative act has been performed. As noted before, this involves determining what, if anything, the speaker is referring to. This is a problem because reference is rarely determined solely by the meaning of the utterance. This is clearer if we remember that a message is often about particular objects in the world, but the *meaning* of an expression in the language rarely, if ever, determines *which* objects. Even "singular" referring expressions like *John, he*, and *the book I left at your house* can be used to refer to endless different objects without changing their meaning. In normal communication we presume that the hearer can use the operative meaning of the expression as well as the context to determine our references. Thus, the next step of the hearer's inference will be to identify what it is that the speaker is referring to:

(Step 3)
Speaker reference
The hearer recognizes what the speaker is referring to.

The third problem for the Message Model involves the "message." Just because a speaker produces some sounds (an *utterance*) does not guarantee that something is being communicated, since it is possible to utter words without communicating anything: we can talk in our sleep, give examples of grammatical sentences, practice our pronunciation, or just recite a pleasant-sounding phrase. Moreover, we do not expect hearers to figure out that we are intending to communicate each time we say something; rather, we rely on the Communicative Presumption to alert the hearer to the possible presence of a communicative intent.

One of the most interesting facts about communicative intentions is that they are intended to be recognized. When speakers try to communicate something, they intend to be understood as trying to communicate, and they are successful in communicating when the hearer recognizes that intention. Thus, for a speaker to request hearers to do something and be successful in the communication, hearers must understand not only *what* is being requested but also *that* they are being requested. To take our earlier example, if a speaker utters the sentence *I'll be there tonight*, then if it is a promise, the hearer must recognize the utterance *as* a promise in order for communication to be successful. If the speaker instead intends the utterance to be a threat, then the hearer must take it *as* a threat for communication to be successful. Communication breaks down if the speaker intends the utterance one way and the hearer takes it another way.

Given this, it is easy to see that in successful communication the hearer can use the Communicative Presumption as well as contextual information and the Operative Meaning to infer what it is that the speaker might be *doing*—what *communicative act* the speaker might be performing. If the inference is correct, the speaker's communicative intention will be recognized and communication will be successful:

(Step 4)
Direct
The hearer recognizes what the speaker is intending to communicate directly.

The *Direct Strategy* is therefore simply this: from step 1, infer steps 2, 3, and 4. We diagram this strategy in figure 9.3.

The next strategy, the *Literal Strategy*, will enable the hearer to infer from what the speaker would be directly communicating, if speaking literally, to what the speaker is literally (and directly) communicating. Recall that the fourth failure of the Message Model involves the nature of the connection between the message and the meaning of the expression uttered. The fact is that we do not always mean (to communicate) just what our words mean. The Message Model of communication has no way of handling cases requiring the message to be distinct from the meaning of the expression uttered. To accommodate nonliteral utterances, we must elaborate the above communicative step, since the hearer really has a choice to make upon hearing an utterance: is the speaker speaking literally (and if not, what *is* she trying to communicate)? Thus, the next step in the

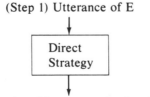

(Step 1) Utterance of E

Direct
Strategy

(Step 4) What S is communicating directly

Figure 9.3
The Direct Strategy

hearer's communicative inference would be to recognize the fact that it would be contextually appropriate for the speaker to be speaking literally:

(Step 5)
Contextual appropriateness
The hearer recognizes that it would be contextually appropriate for the speaker to be speaking literally.

However, we do not seem to always be in a quandary about how to take people's words. According to the Presumption of Literalness, literal utterances seem to have a certain communicative priority in that we presume a person to be speaking literally unless there is some reason to suppose the contrary (for some psychological evidence, see chapter 10). Given this presumption, the hearer can infer what the speaker is communicating literally:

(Step 6)
Literal
The hearer recognizes what the speaker is intending to communicate literally (and directly).

The hearer who reasons to step 6 will take the speaker to be speaking literally simply on the basis that there is nothing contextually inappropriate in doing so. But what is it to be contextually appropriate? Many things can contribute to this, but among the most important are certain shared beliefs about the nature, stage, and direction of the talk-exchange. We can call these kinds of beliefs *Conversational Presumptions* (see Grice 1975). For example, there is a presumption of *Relevance* to the effect that the speaker's contribution to the talk-exchange is relevant at that point. There is a presumption of *Sincerity* to the effect that speakers believe what they say, want what they ask for, intend to do what they commit themselves to, and so on. Moreover, there is a presumption of *Truthfulness* to the effect that speakers attempt to say what is true, and presumptions concerning the *Quantity* (speakers say not too much, not too little) and *Quality* (speakers have adequate evidence for what they say) of information that is offered. There are also Conversational Presumptions that speakers will speak clearly, politely, and ethically. The violation of any of these presumptions, when they are thought to be in effect, can constitute a case of contextual inappropriateness.

In conclusion, the *Literal Strategy* is simply this: from step 4 of the Direct Strategy, infer steps 5 and 6, given the Presumption of Literalness and the Conversational Presumptions. We diagram this strategy in figure 9.4,

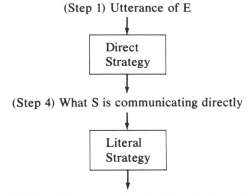

(Step 1) Utterance of E

Direct
Strategy

(Step 4) What S is communicating directly

Literal
Strategy

(Step 6) What S is communicating literally (and directly)

Figure 9.4
The Direct and Literal Strategies

adding it to the previously illustrated Direct Strategy. A hearer who follows
these strategies can infer what the speaker is literally and directly communicating, from what the hearer hears the speaker utter. If the hearer is correct
in this inference, communication will have been successful; but if the hearer
fails, so will communication.

Nonliteral Communication

Sometimes when we speak, we do mean something other than what our
words mean. When what we mean to communicate is not compatible with
what our expression literally means, then we are speaking nonliterally.
Here are some typical expressions that are sometimes uttered nonliterally:

Overstatement

(8)
a. No one understands me. (Not enough people understand me.)
b. A pig wouldn't eat this food. (A person, given a choice, wouldn't eat it.)
c. Her eyes opened as wide as saucers. (Her eyes opened very wide.)
d. I can't make a shot today. (I'm making very few.)

(9)
That was the worst food I've ever had. (It was very bad.)

(10)
a. Paul Newman *is* Jesse James. (Paul Newman plays the part
convincingly, or with conviction.)

b. We do it all for you. (We look after your interests.)

c. When you say "Bud," you've said it all. (All that needs to be said about beer.)

d. If it's not Schlitz, it's not beer. (Not the way beer should be.)

e. The future is now. (You should prepare now for the future.)

Irony, sarcasm

(11)

a. Boy, this food is terrific! (terrible)

b. That argument is a real winner. (loser)

Figures of speech

(12)

a. I've got three *hands* (workers) here to help.

b. Look at the *TV Guide* and see what's on the *tube* (TV)!

c. Down in Texas, cattle are only $200 a *head* (animal).

If one thing bears a very close association to another, the utterance is sometimes classified as a case of *metonymy*:

(13)

a. The White House (the president or staff) said so.

b. The Crown (the monarch or staff) said so.

c. I have read all of Chomsky (Chomsky's works).

If the connection is some kind of similarity or comparison, then the utterance is sometimes classified as a *metaphor*:

(14)

a. He punted the idea away. (He totally rejected the idea.)

b. Kim is a block of ice. (Kim is cold and unresponsive.)

c. She's a ball of fire. (She's got a lot of energy.)

d. Time is money. (Time is valuable.)

Note that these examples differ in one crucial respect: some are rare or novel or in some way have to be figured out (for example, (14a)), whereas others are often heard and verge on being cliches (for example, (14b–d)). The crucial difference is that in the novel cases we must not only reason from various cues and context that the utterance is in fact nonliteral, but also use these cues and contextual information to figure out *what the speaker means*. We will say that these forms of communication are *non-standardized*. Owing to prior exposure, precedence, or training, however, the other forms are *standardized* for a particular nonliteral interpretation (or a narrow range of such interpretations). With standardized forms, such as (11a–b) uttered with that distinctive bratty and sarcastic intonation, or (14c), it is only necessary to know from context *that* the speaker is speaking nonliterally—the hearer then automatically knows what the speaker is communicating because that form is standardized for that alternative message. In general, standardized forms are often on their way to getting *new meanings*, but they have not yet lost all vestiges of their origins and still require some rudimentary reasoning (see Bach and Harnish 1979, chaps. 9, 10, Morgan 1978).

In the case of (mainly nonstandardized) nonliteral communication, the hearer must figure out what the speaker is trying to communicate, given that the speaker is speaking nonliterally. Why should the hearer suppose that the speaker is not speaking literally—that is, meaning what the expression means? A glance back at examples (8)–(14) will reveal that utterances of these (and similar) expressions would, if taken literally, violate Conversational Presumptions that are supposed to be in effect. For instance, if the speaker were being sincere and truthful, and generally had beliefs similar to ours, then she could not *literally* mean

(10a)
Paul Newman is Jesse James.

(10e)
The future is now.

(14a)
He punted the idea away.

In these cases there is conflict between the literal meaning of the expression and the Conversational Presumptions, *if* the speaker is speaking literally. Since the hearer has no reason to suppose that the speaker is still not abiding by the presumptions, the hearer will infer that the speaker is speaking *nonliterally*. In short, contextual inappropriateness can lead the hearer to take the speaker nonliterally. So instead of step 5, which records contextual appropriateness, we have alternative step 5', which records contextual *in*appropriateness:

(Step 5')
Contextual inappropriateness
The hearer recognizes that it would be contextually inappropriate for the speaker to be speaking literally.

Once the hearer realizes that the speaker cannot plausibly mean what she says, there is the problem of figuring out what *was* meant. At this point the hearer must make an intelligent guess as to what the speaker's communicative intent might be, based on shared background information as well as the literal meaning of the expression uttered.

The literal meaning of the expression helps the hearer in a number of different ways. From examples (8)–(14) we can infer some very general shared principles that can help the hearer make this inference:

(P1)
Sarcasm, irony
The opposite of what is said

(P2)
Metaphor
Some relation of salient similarity

(P3)
Exaggeration
The next evaluation toward the midpoint of the relevant scale

Notice how a normal hearer might use (P1)–(P3) to interpret the examples of nonliteral communication given earlier. Suppose that the speaker and the hearer have just seen a movie and they share the belief that it was terrible. Under these circumstances it would be contextually inappropriate for the speaker to say *That was a real winner* and mean it literally. So the hearer will conclude that it is nonliteral, and that (P1) is the appropriate principle connecting what the speaker said literally with what the speaker meant nonliterally. If the hearer does this correctly, he will conclude that the speaker was intending to communicate *That was a real loser*, which is just the message we wanted to account for.

Thus, the information a hearer must recognize in order to make nonliteral communication possible is that the speaker does not mean what she has said, but rather means something related to it:

(Step 6′)
Nonliteral
The hearer recognizes what the speaker is communicating nonliterally (and directly).

When a hearer reaches step 6′ correctly, nonliteral communication is successful.

Strategies for Nonliteral Communication

As with literal and direct communication, in order to account for a common type of talk-exchange we have had to supplement considerably the

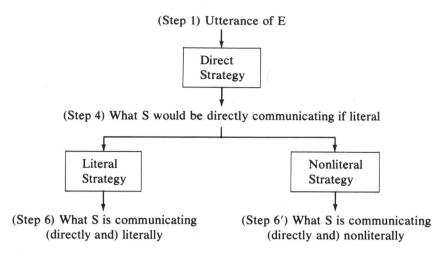

Figure 9.5
The Literal and Nonliteral Direct Strategies

resources of the Message Model. We will now add to our previous strategies the *Nonliteral Strategy*: from step 4 of the Direct Strategy, infer steps 5' and 6'. Our system of strategies is summarized in figure 9.5.

Indirect Communication

Sometimes when we speak we are not only performing some direct form of communication but also speaking indirectly—we mean something *more* than what we mean directly. For instance:

(15)
a. The door is over there. (used to request someone to leave)
b. I want 10 gallons of regular. (used to request 10 gallons of regular)
c. I'm sure the cat likes having its tail pulled. (used to request the hearer to stop pulling the cat's tail)
d. You're the boss. (used to agree to do what the hearer says)
e. I should never have done that. (used to apologize)
f. Did you bring any tennis balls? (used to inform the hearer that the speaker did not bring any)
g. It's getting late. (used to request the hearer to hurry)

Notice that indirect acts can be performed by means of either literal or nonliteral direct acts. Examples (15a) and (15b) are cases of indirect acts being performed by means of literal direct acts—the speaker really does mean what is said, but also means *more*. In case (15c) this is not so; the speaker does not, presumably, really mean that the cat likes having its tail pulled. Instead, the speaker is being sarcastic—she means directly, but nonliterally, that the cat does *not* like having its tail pulled, and she wants the hearer to conclude that he should stop it.

How does the hearer know that the speaker is not speaking merely directly? How does he know to seek an indirect use of language as well as a direct one? Mainly, again, by virtue of contextual inappropriateness. For instance, it would be strange if, on driving into a gas station, the speaker of (15b) had only been reporting her wants and was not also making a polite request for some gas. A mere report of what one now wants is relevant to the taking of a poll, perhaps, but is not contextually appropriate at a gas station. Thus, the same sorts of contextual information and presumptions used in recognizing previous communicative intentions and acts are also used with indirect acts.

The hearer is also able to use context and the Conversational Presumptions to *find* the speaker's indirect communicative intent. Once the hearer identifies why the speaker cannot merely be speaking directly, he is able to use this information to aid in recognizing her indirect intent. Thus, reporting a desire for a tank of gas at a service station would be contextually inappropriate if that were all the speaker was doing. Since requesting expresses the desire that the hearer do something, it would be natural in the circumstances for the hearer to conclude that in reporting this desire the speaker was also requesting the gas, since requesting would be the contextually appropriate thing to do.

Once we are aware of such forms of communication, it becomes obvious how often we talk indirectly. (In fact, we do it so often that certain forms have become standardized for their *indirect* use. Such forms as "Could you lend me five dollars?" and "Why don't you try the other key?" are rarely used literally and directly in normal circumstances.) To account for the possibility of indirect communication, we must supplement our (literal and nonliteral) direct strategies with *indirect* strategies. To see how (non-standardized) indirect communication works on an inferential model, we will examine one of the examples given earlier.

Suppose that the speaker utters (15a) *The door is over there* to the hearer, thereby indirectly requesting the hearer to leave. How might the hearer reason? The first thing he must notice is that it would be contextually inappropriate for the speaker to be merely reporting the location of the door, assuming that they both already know the location of the door, and this is not relevant to the conversation. Thus, step 7 of the Inferential Model will be relevant to initiating a search for the indirect messate; the hearer will note the following information:

(Step 7)
Contextual inappropriateness
The hearer recognizes that it would be contextually inappropriate for the speaker to be speaking merely directly.

As with nonliteral communication, the hearer now faces a problem-solving situation: if the speaker means something *more* than what is directly communicated, what is it? In the above example we might suppose that the speaker and the hearer were having a dispute, and in that case it would be clear that the speaker was requesting the hearer to leave. Unfortunately, little is known at present about the actual reasoning processes that take place during indirect communication, so we will represent only the result of an indirect inference:

(Step 8)
Indirect
The hearer recognizes what the speaker is also communicating indirectly.

In example (15a) the communication has both a direct and an indirect component. Moreover, the direct component is literal—the speaker does really mean that the door is over there, though this is not all that she means.

Strategies for Indirect Communication

We can now supplement the existing direct strategies with strategies for indirect communication. The *Indirect Strategy* says: from step 6 or 6′, infer steps 7 and 8. The augmented system of strategies is shown in figure 9.6.

Looking back at (15c), we see an example of communication that has both a direct and an indirect component. The direct component in this case is *non*literal, however, in that the speaker does not really mean that the cat likes having its tail pulled. In this case communication is successful only if the hearer first applies the Direct Strategy and the Nonliteral Strategy, then the Indirect Strategy. That is, the hearer must first reach step 6′:

(Step 6′)
Nonliteral
The hearer recognizes what the speaker is communicating nonliterally and

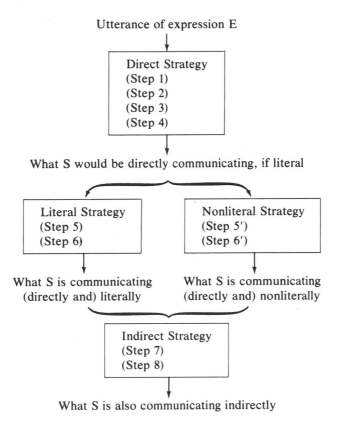

Figure 9.6
Strategies for direct and indirect communication

directly—in particular, that the speaker is nonliterally and directly claiming that the cat does not like having its tail pulled.

However, since the direct act would be conversationally inappropriate if it was the only communicative act being performed, the hearer infers step 7:

(Step 7)
Contextual inappropriateness
The hearer recognizes that it would be contextually inappropriate for the speaker to be speaking merely directly—in particular, merely claiming that the cat does not like having its tail pulled.

The hearer must recognize the indirect communicative intent as well and will therefore go on to step 8:

(Step 8)
Indirect
The hearer recognizes what the speaker is also communicating indirectly—
in particular, that she is requesting him to quit pulling the cat's tail.

When the hearer reaches step 8, communication is complete and successful.

Conclusion: Inferential Theories versus the Message Model

The crucial defect of the Message Model of linguistic communication is
that it equates the message a speaker intends to communicate with the
meaning of some expression in the language. As we have seen, this leads
to six specific defects: the Message Model cannot account for (1) the use
of ambiguous expressions, (2) real world reference, (3) communicative
intentions, (4) nonliteral communication, (5) indirect communication, and
(6) noncommunicative uses of language.

To account for these sorts of facts, an Inferential Model is called for—
that is, a model that connects the message with the meaning of the uttered
expression by a sequence of inferences. This model involves a series of
inference strategies that, if followed, take the hearer from hearing the
expression uttered to the speaker's communicative intent. Moreover, each
major step in the inference accounts for some failure of the Message Model.
For instance, to infer step 2 is to infer the operative meaning, which is to
contextually disambiguate the utterance and so avoid the first objection to
the Message Model. The Inferential Model also includes referential, nonliteral, and indirect strategies, thereby avoiding the second, fourth, and
fifth objections; and it provides an account of communicative intentions
and noncommunicative uses of language, thereby avoiding problems three
and six.

If the Inferential Model is correct, communicative competence consists,
in part, of the mastery of certain pragmatic strategies, including the ones
given above. Each strategy contains a pattern of inference and an appeal
to various presumptions or shared contextual beliefs. These are the real
building blocks of a theory of language use and communication. It is up
to psychology to discover the actual principles of inference; linguistics and
philosophy can only constrain the correct answer.

9.3 DISCOURSE AND CONVERSATION

Even a casual survey of normal linguistic communication will reveal an
important fact: the unit of communication is rarely a single complete

sentence. Often we speak in single words, phrases, and fragments of sentences:

(16)
A: Want to see a movie tonight?
B: Uh, well, uh . . .
A: You don't want to, do you?

At other times we speak in units of two or more connected sentences:

(17)
A: Let me tell you about my ski accident. You see, I was . . .

Broadly speaking, the study of *discourse* is the study of units of language and language use consisting of more than a single sentence, but connected by some system of related topics. The study of discourse is sometimes more narrowly construed as the study of connected sequences of sentences (or sentence fragments) produced by a single speaker. In what follows we will construe the term *discourse* narrowly, and when more than one person is involved, we will speak of a *talk-exchange*. There are many forms of discourse and many forms of talk-exchange. Letters, jokes, stories, lectures, sermons, speeches, and so on, are all categories of discourse; arguments, interviews, business dealings, instruction, and conversations are categories of talk-exchanges.

Conversations (and talk-exchanges in general) are usually structured sequences of expressions by more than a single speaker. This structure is rarely consciously apparent to speakers. However, we need only recall a conversation that has "gone wrong" in some sense, in order to become aware of the conversational principles we have mastered. Although the structure of conversations (and other talk-exchanges) has not been exhaustively described, being presently under intense investigation, we can summarize some of their major properties here. First, any reasonable number of people can participate, and there are principles that govern how and when people can take a turn. Second, there are principles that make certain aspects of the conversation socially obligatory, such as saying hello and goodbye. Third, as we have already seen, there are principles making contributions to conversations relevant to each other, such as answering questions or justifying refusals.

We will first illustrate some cases where English provides devices that are sensitive to communicative contexts and are therefore useful in the study of both discourse in general and conversation in particular. We will then look at some of the salient features of conversational openings, turn taking, and closings.

Language and Context

Our contributions to conversations both *reflect* and *affect* the linguistic and nonlinguistic context of utterance.

Our comments can *reflect* features of the context of utterance in that we often "watch our language" by avoiding certain words or phrases. More subtly, our language also has structural devices that allow us to merge more easily into the flow of conversation. Compare the following simple conversations:

(18)
Conversation 1
A: Who shot the bear?
B: John. John shot him. John shot the bear.
B′: *It was a bear *that* John shot.
B″: *What John shot *was* a bear.

(19)
Conversation 2
A: I don't see how the country is going to pull out of this economic slump.
B: *Speaking of* economics, ...
B′: *Speaking of Bush's economic advisors, ...
B″: **Speaking of North America*, ...

The italicized devices are all sensitive to the speaker's beliefs and intentions concerning the communication situation; that is, to utter expressions containing these devices and be contextually appropriate requires certain beliefs and intentions on the part of the speaker. Thus, a speaker who does not believe that Bush's economic advisors were spoken of in conversation 2 should not say "Speaking of Bush's..." Likewise, in conversation 1, speaker A is focusing on John, but answers B′ and B″ focus on the bear; this disruption in continuity of topic makes these contributions subtly inappropriate.

Our comments also can *affect* the context by making it appropriate for the same speaker to go on and say one sort of thing rather than another. For instance, it would be appropriate for the speaker to follow (20a) with a joke and (20b) with a story, but not vice versa:

(20)
a. I heard a good joke yesterday. How many...
b. Here is the story, ...

Or one speaker's remark might make it appropriate for another speaker to say one thing rather than another:

(21)
a. Tell me what you did in Paris!
b. Who remembers the plot of *King Lear*?

So language structure can both reflect and affect the course of a talk-exchange. In the sections that follow we will focus on a different kind of structure—the structure of conversations over time.

Openings

There are many ways of beginning a conversation or other talk-exchange. One is to start out with no preliminaries whatsoever: "Something's wrong with the xerox machine." Another is to preface our remarks with an *opening*. For instance, there are a number of attention-getters (called *vocatives*) used at the beginning of a conversation, such as "Hey," "Hey, John," "Excuse me," "Say, ..." Once we have the hearer's attention, we might then use a conversational parenthetical such as "You know," "Listen," "Know what?" But probably the most common opening in casual conversations is the *greeting*. Basically, a greeting is an expression of pleasure at meeting someone. But these expressions can vary enormously in complexity and formality. Consider, for instance, the following sample:

(22)
Casual
Hello! Good morning! Ahoy!
How are you? How have you been?
Look who just walked in! What a pleasant surprise!

(23)
Informal
Howdy! Hi! Greetings!
How y'doing? What's up?
Go ahead, don't say hello! (ironic) Long time no see!

(24)
Formal
Good day, Mrs. Smith.
To what do I owe this lucky meeting?

Greetings tend to be highly ritualized in form, in that we generally use a small number of them over and over again. They serve mostly to give everyone in the conversation a turn at saying something (notice that it would be odd if, halfway through the introductions, someone were to launch into a long narration on some topic). However, after a round of greetings it is normally quite proper for someone to take the floor and either begin the substance of the talk-exchange or initiate closings.

Turn Taking

The person who starts speaking after the greetings are over in fact initiates the substance of the conversation by taking the next turn. How did that person get the conversational baton, and how is it passed on? One influential analysis (Sacks, Schegloff, and Jefferson 1974) has proposed that turn taking is controlled by three principles:

(P1)
The speaker "selects" the next speaker.

(P2)
The first to talk becomes the speaker.

(P3)
The speaker continues her own remarks.

Current speakers "select" the next speaker in various ways, one of which, of course, is to ask someone a question. Generally the person being asked has the next turn, though someone else could, in accordance with (P2), simply break in and start talking. Clearly, unless these remarks were urgent in some way, we would consider such an act rude. The same is true if the speaker asks someone a question and then keeps on talking, in accordance with (P3). These observations suggest that (P1) overrides (P2) and (P3) in the sense that (P1) has conversational priority. A speaker who wants to violate that principle needs to have a good reason, on pain of being considered rude, ignorant, or insensitive. This in itself suggests that we have the sort of expectations about conversations that these principles describe.

Why do we have such principles governing conversations? One reason is that for information to get through, everyone cannot be talking at once, and sequencing principles help minimize the chances of disruptive overlap. When disruptive overlap does happen for any length of time, the result is usually embarrassing to other members of the conversation.

Closings

Just as conversations rarely begin with their central topic, so they rarely come to an abrupt end. Participants don't simply quit talking—as when beginning conversations, they have a highly ritualized way of bringing normal conversations to an end. Schegloff and Sacks (1973) propose that the end of normal conversations consists of a *pre-closing* sequence, where the participants more or less agree to close, followed by a *closing section*, where they actually do close. These two stages have some characteristic ways of being communicated. Consider the following examples:

(25)
Pre-closing
We-ell, it's been nice talking to you...
Say hello to Joan for me...
Closing
See you.
Goodbye. Bye bye. Bye. Cheerio. Ciao.

Except for special circumstances, such as forgetting something important, once the closing phase has been reached, the conversation should be brought to a conclusion. A speaker can do this either collectively with one remark or a glance at everybody, or separately with appropriate closings to each person or group of persons.

Conclusion

Normal conversations have a discernible structure. They tend to begin and end in certain ritualistic ways. The change of speakers tends to be orderly and based on principles of turn taking. There tend to be recognizable levels of formality, informality, and familiarity in such interchanges. Moreover, the language seems to make available devices for smoothly integrating one's remarks into the flow of words. It should not be surprising that conversations reflect both social and linguistic principles; they are, after all, both social and linguistic events.

9.4 SPECIAL TOPICS

Speaker Reference

In chapter 6 we distinguished between speaker reference and denotation, only to put speaker reference aside. We now focus our attention on these

acts of referring to things in the world. Although speakers can (in some sense) refer in speaking to themselves, or to nobody in particular, normally we refer communicatively; we refer to objects and intend our audience to recognize our reference to those very things.

Linguists tend to work with a *broad* conception of speaker reference where the speaker has some particular thing in mind and utters something that will enable the hearer to also have that thing in mind. Under the broad usage, sentence (26) could be used, in part, to refer to a particular beer:

(26)
There's a beer in the refrigerator.

Notice that there is nothing in the sentence that denotes a single beer. Philosophers tend to work with a *narrow* conception of speaker reference where the speaker has some particular thing in mind and uses a singular term to refer to that thing:

(27)
The *Bohemia* in the refrigerator is cold.

Let's concentrate on the narrow conception and see how literal, nonliteral, and indirect reference works with the singular terms we investigated in chapter 6: indexicals, definite descriptions, and proper names.

Literal Singular Reference

To use a singular term literally is to refer to something that the term denotes. For example:

(28)
He is tired.
a. A particular *male* is being referred to.
b. *He* denotes *males*.

(29)
The first man on the moon is right-handed.
a. A particular person who is *the first man on the moon* is being referred to.
b. *The first man on the moon* denotes Neil Armstrong.

(30)
Neil Armstrong is right-handed.
a. A particular person named *Neil Armstrong* is being referred to.
b. *Neil Armstrong* denotes all people named *Neil Armstrong*.

In each case the speaker uses the singular term literally to refer the hearer to the particular person or thing the speaker has in mind, which is a part

of the denotation of the singular term. By referring literally, the speaker makes communication easier because the hearer need only find the particular thing from among the objects in the denotation of the singular term.

Nonliteral Singular Reference

In the case of nonliteral singular reference the speaker intends to refer to some particular thing that the singular term does *not* denote. This can make communication more difficult because the hearer cannot use the denotation to cut down the class of potential referents. Instead, the hearer must use the meaning of the singular term as a clue to what the speaker has in mind, then use contextual information to determine the referent. For example, someone might use *he* to refer to a masculine woman, or *Napoleon* to refer to a diminutive megalomaniac, or *the world's most famous linguist* to refer to a presumptuous colleague.

Indirect Singular Reference

In the case of indirect singular reference the speaker refers to one thing by first referring the hearer to another. For instance, pointing to a dot on a map of Australia, a speaker might say,

(31)
Here is the town we should stay in when we visit the Uluru.

By referring the hearer directly to a point on the map (with, say, the name *Curtain Springs*), the speaker could be referring indirectly to the town of Curtain Springs. Indirect reference can even become ritualized when the identity of the indirect referent is not as important as the direct referent. Thus, a waiter might turn in an order by saying,

(32)
The fillet of sole [the person who ordered it] at table four wants a glass of Chablis.

What Determines Reference?

At present there are two major competing theories of what determines reference: the Description Theory and the Historical Chain Theory. The basic idea behind the Description Theory is that an expression refers to its reference because it describes the referent, either uniquely or uniquely enough in the context to be identified. For instance, the phrase *the first person to walk on our moon* refers to Neil Armstrong by virtue of the fact that the description fits him uniquely. What about other kinds of singular terms, such as the pronouns *he, she, that*, or proper names such as *Charles de Gaulle, America*, Fido? These do not seem to describe anything uniquely, so how does the Description Theory handle them? It says that people using these expressions have *in mind* some description of the thing they intend to refer to. A speaker might say *Close the window*, intending the hearer to pick out the open window as the relevant window. If there are two open and closable windows, then the hearer can reasonably ask which one.

The Historical Chain Theory says, in effect, that an expression refers to its referent by virtue of there being a certain historical relation between the words uttered and some initial dubbing or christening of the object with that name. For instance, when a speaker uses the name *Charles de Gaulle*, it refers, in this view, to the person christened by that name, provided there is a chain of uses linking the current speaker's reference with the original christening. This view proposes no unique description to pick out the proper referent; rather, it proposes that referential uses are handed down from speaker to speaker, generation to generation, from the original dubbing or christening. As Kripke (1980, 96), one of the originators of this theory, put it,

An initial 'baptism' takes place. Here the object may be named by ostension, or the reference of the name may be fixed by a description. When the name is 'passed from link to link', the receiver of the name must, I think, intend when he learns to use it with the same reference as the man from whom he heard it.

Both theories of reference have strengths and weaknesses. The Description Theory works best for definite descriptions, and perhaps also for common nouns and adjectives, whereas the Historical Chain Theory works best for the kinds of referring expressions that function as names, which can be given to persons, places, and things. Perhaps some mixture of these theories can be extended to account for indexicals.

Performatives and Speech Acts

Austin (1961, 220) introduced *performative* as a "new and ugly word" into philosophy and linguistics. Here is part of what he said:

I want to discuss a kind of utterance which looks like a statement . . . and yet is not true or false . . . in the first person singular present indicative active . . . if a person makes an utterance of this sort we would say that he is *doing* something rather than merely *saying* something.

What kind of utterance does Austin have in mind? He continues,

When I say *I do* (take this woman to be my lawful wedded wife), I am not reporting on a marriage, I am indulging in it.

Typical examples of performatives include the following:

(33)
a. I (hereby) promise to be there.
b. I (hereby) apologize for that.
c. I (hereby) advise you to leave.
d. I (hereby) declare this meeting adjourned.

Austin soon came to realize that performatives were not so distinctive. They can take other forms:

(34)
a. Passengers are warned to cross the tracks by the bridge.
b. You are hereby authorized to conduct negotiations for us.

Some performatives also can be viewed as true or false:

(35)
a. I state once and for all that I am innocent.
b. I deny your claim that you are innocent.

And finally, performatives seem to be both sayings *and* doings. These and other observations led Austin (1962) to propose a general theory of uses of language or *speech acts* in which the category of performatives plays no special role.

Types of Speech Acts

Speech act theorists found no appropriate terminology already available for labeling types of speech acts, so they had to invent one. The terminology used here comes, in large part, from the work of Austin (1962) and Searle (1969). According to the theory they have developed, there are four important categories of speech acts, illustrated in figure 9.7.

Utterance acts are simply acts *of* uttering sounds, syllables, words, phrases, and sentences from a language. From a speech act point of view, these are not very interesting acts because an utterance act per se is not communicative; it can be performed by a parrot, tape recorder, or voice synthesizer. The main interest of utterance acts derives from the fact that in performing an utterance act, we usually perform either an *illocutionary act* (an act performed *in* uttering something) or a *perlocutionary act* (an act performed *by* uttering something—an act that produces an *effect* on the hearer). It is illocutionary acts that interest speech act theorists most.

Austin (1962) characterized the *illocutionary act* as an act performed *in* saying something. For instance, in saying *Graf can beat Evert*, one might

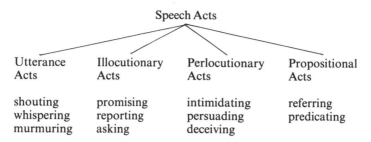

Figure 9.7
Types of speech acts

perform the act of asserting that Graf can beat Evert. Some other examples
of illocutionary acts are these:

(36)

promising	threatening
reporting	requesting
stating	suggesting
asking	ordering
telling	proposing

What are some of the important characteristics of illocutionary (as opposed to perlocutionary) acts? First, illocutionary acts can often be successfully performed simply by uttering the right *explicit performative* sentence,
with the right intentions and beliefs, and under the right circumstances.
For instance, the utterance acts of producing sentences (37a–c) can be
performances of the illocutionary acts of ordering, promising, and appoint-
ing, respectively:

(37)
a. I (hereby) order you to leave.
b. I (hereby) promise to pay.
c. I (hereby) appoint you chairman.

Second, illocutionary acts (unlike perlocutionary acts) are central to
linguistic communication. Our normal conversations are composed in
large part of statements, suggestions, requests, proposals, greetings, and
the like. When we do perform perlocutionary acts such as persuading or
intimidating, we do so by performing illocutionary acts such as stating or
threatening.

Third, and most important, unlike perlocutionary acts, most illocutionary acts used to communicate have the feature that one performs them
successfully simply by getting one's illocutionary intentions recognized.

For example, if A says *Graf can beat Evert* and if B recognizes A's intention to tell B that Graf can beat Evert, then A will have succeeded in telling B, and B will have understood A. But if A is attempting to persuade B that Graf can beat Evert, it is not sufficient for B just to recognize A's intention to persuade B; B must also believe what A said. If Graf says to A, *I can beat Evert*, A will recognize her intention to tell or inform A that she can beat Evert, but A will not necessarily be persuaded that she can beat Evert. To be persuaded of it, A must believe it; and that will probably require watching her play, not just hearing her talk.

Austin (1962) characterizes *perlocutionary acts* as acts performed *by* saying something. For instance, suppose John believes everything Bud Collins says; then by saying *Graf can beat Evert*, Collins could convince John that Graf can beat Evert. Some typical examples of perlocutionary acts are these:

(38)

inspiring	persuading
impressing	deceiving
embarrassing	misleading
intimidating	irritating

What are some important characteristics of perlocutionary acts? First, perlocutionary acts (unlike illocutionary acts) are not performed by uttering explicit performative sentences. We do not perform the perlocutionary act of convincing someone that Graf can beat Evert by uttering (39):

(39)
I (hereby) convince you that Graf can beat Evert.

Second, perlocutionary acts seem to involve the *effects* of utterance acts and illocutionary acts on the thoughts, feelings, and actions of the hearer, whereas illocutionary acts do not. Thus, perlocutionary acts can be represented as an illocutionary act of the speaker (S) plus its effects on the hearer (H):

(40)
a. S tells + H believes ... = S persuades H that ...
b. S tells + H intends ... = S persuades H to ...

Illocutionary acts are therefore means to perlocutionary acts, and not the converse. Perlocutionary acts have not been investigated to the extent that illocutionary acts have been, partly because they are not as intimately related to linguistic structure, semantics, and communication as are illocutionary acts. We mention them here mainly to set them aside.

Looking again at illocutionary acts such as asserting, questioning, requesting, and promising, note that there can be an overlap in *what* is asserted, questioned, requested, and promised. For instance, suppose a speaker utters the following sentences and thereby performs the indicated acts:

(41)
a. Becker beat Lendl. (statement)
b. Becker beat Lendl? (question)
c. Becker, beat Lendl! (request, demand)

All of these illocutionary acts are concerned with Becker's beating Lendl, which is called the *propositional content* of the illocutionary act. As (41) illustrates, different types of illocutionary acts can have the same propositional content. Furthermore, each type of illocutionary act can have different propositional contents. For example, the illocutionary act of stating can have a wide variety of propositional contents in that a wide variety of propositions can be stated:

(42)
a. Becker beat Lendl. ⎫
                 ⎬ (statements)
b. Cash beat Becker. ⎭

The simplest type of propositional content is expressed by means of acts of *referring* and *predicating*, wherein a speaker refers to something and then characterizes it. Suppose that a speaker utters the sentence *Becker is tired* and thereby asserts that Becker is tired. In making this assertion, the speaker also performs the *propositional acts* of referring to Becker with the name *Becker* and of characterizing him with the predicate *is tired*.

We have now delineated four major types of speech acts: utterance acts, illocutionary acts, perlocutionary acts, and propositional acts—the latter including the subacts of referring and predicating. Although a speaker's purposes in talking may require the performance of any one or more of these types of acts, communication seems centrally bound up with illocutionary acts and propositional acts, and we have given these acts the major portion of our attention (see Harnish 1990 for a brief survey).

Communicating with Performatives

How can hearers recognize speakers' communicative intentions and how can speakers expect them to? One suggestion when speaking with performatives is that such acts are governed by pragmatic rules, and by sharing such rules, speaker and hearer are able to communicate (see Searle 1969).

This proposal has the virtue of extending our picture of language as rule-governed beyond the study of structure to the study of function and use. If such a theory could be made to mesh with the present components of a grammar (phonology, syntax, semantics), it would be a valuable addition to our ability to explain the creative aspect of language use.

Recall that the simplest and most straightforward sort of speech act is performed literally and directly. By being literal and direct, a speaker imposes a minimal load on the hearer in understanding the speaker. With nonliteral and indirect acts, more inferring is required on the part of the hearer; breakdowns and misunderstanding can result whenever these extra inferences are required. Thus, the simplest kind of case is the literal and direct act.

The major problem with treating sentences such as (33) as literally and directly used to perform the acts named in the sentences themselves is that the performative verb does not have its normal meaning and does not make its normal contribution to the meaning of the sentence it occurs in. For instance, if the word *promise* in (33a) conventionally indicates that the speaker is promising in uttering it, then why isn't the speaker promising in uttering (43a) and (43b)?

(43)
a. I promised that I would be there.
b. I promise too much to too many.

In these cases the speaker is reporting a promise, not indulging in one. In order to be adequate, a theory of performatives must treat sentences such as (33) and (43) as having a compositionally determined meaning. Yet we still need an account of how (33a) and not (43) can be used to promise.

In the face of these difficulties some theorists (see Bach and Harnish 1979, Recanati 1987) have proposed that performatives such as (33) are not *directly* used to promise, apologize, and so on, but rather are directly used to do what declarative sentences normally do—declare or state. They are only *indirectly* used to promise, apologize, and so on. Recall our earlier discussion of indirect speech acts, where (44) might be used to request the hearer to move:

(44)
You're standing on my foot.

We analyze this request as *indirect* by saying that *directly* the speaker uses (44) to state that the hearer is standing on the speaker's foot. Likewise (33a), on this account, is used directly to state or declare that the speaker is promising, and *indirectly* it is used to promise that the speaker will be there. How might the hearer be expected to recognize the speaker's intention to promise in stating that she is promising? Given the pragmatic presumptions and especially the Presumption of Truthfulness, the hearer might be expected to reason as follows:

1. The speaker is stating that she is promising to be there.
2. If her statement is true, then she must be promising to be there.
3. Presumably the speaker is being truthful.
4. So the speaker must be promising to be there in saying *I promise that I'll be there*.

The chief advantage of this approach is that since the performative sentence is directly used to state, not to promise, the word *promise* can mean the same thing in performative as well as in nonperformative sentences, and there is no problem of compositionality either below or above the level of the phrase.

Implicature, Presupposition, and Invited Inference

So far we have noted two ways in which what is communicated goes beyond what is said: nonliteral and indirect communication. Various authors have proposed other ways. A special and interesting class has been explored by Grice under the label of *conversational implicatures*, so called because they are implied (or as Grice prefers to say, implicated) by virtue of the fact that the speaker and hearer are cooperatively contributing to a conversation. According to Grice (1975), such conversations are governed by a cooperative principle:

(45)
Cooperative Principle (CP)
Make your conversational contribution such as is required, at the stage at which it occurs, by the accepted purpose or direction of the talk-exchange in which you are engaged.

But what does cooperating amount to? Grice suggests that for stretches of conversation involving mainly transfer of information, cooperating amounts to obeying (if only implicitly) certain *conversational maxims* such as those given in (46):

(46)
Quantity-1
Make your contribution as informative as is required (for the current purposes of the conversation).

Quantity-2
Do not make your contribution more informative than is required.
Quality-1
Do not say what you believe to be false.
Quality-2
Do not say that for which you lack adequate evidence.
Relevance
Be relevant.
Manner
Be perspicuous:
a. Avoid obscurity of expression.
b. Avoid unnecessary ambiguity.
c. Be brief (avoid unnecessary prolixity).
d. Be orderly.

These inspired our conversational presumptions. Grice proposes that conversations are cooperative endeavors where participants may be expected (unless they indicate otherwise) to comply with general principles of cooperation, such as making the appropriate contribution to the conversation. Now, imagine the following interchange between friends:

(47)
a. Questioner: Where is your husband?
b. Speaker: He is in the living room or the kitchen.
c. Implication: The speaker does not know which room he is in.

In this case the speaker in saying (47b) implies that (47c) is true, though she does not say that it is. This implication arises because, since the speaker has not indicated noncooperation, she may be assumed to be cooperating and so to be giving all of the relevant and requested information. Since the speaker has said (47b) and may be presumed to be cooperative, she has implied (47c). Of course, the speaker may know exactly where her husband is; in that case she would be misleading the hearer in that she is pretending to cooperate in the conversation but is not really doing so.

In the everyday sense of *presuppose*, to presuppose something is to assume something, or to take it for granted in advance, but not to say it. Since assuming something is normally considered not an act but a state, presupposing is best viewed as a state and not an act. Related to (pragmatic) presupposing is (pragmatic) *presupposition*: that which is assumed or taken for granted. Clearly, presuppositions are not acts, though they are related to them. This characterization is pretty vague, but the phenomena cited in current linguistics under the label of (pragmatic) presupposition are quite varied, and our characterization has at least the virtue of reflecting a common denominator among many different kinds of cases. To simplify matters, we will identify three main types of phenomena that go by the label of (pragmatic) presupposition in current discussions.

According to one conception, *presupposition*₁, a speaker's assumptions (beliefs) about the speech context are presuppositions. As one author (Lakoff 1970, 175) writes,

Natural language is used for communication in a context, and every time a speaker uses a sentence of his language ... he is making certain assumptions about that context.

Some typical examples of (pragmatic) presupposition₁ are the following:

(48)
a. Sam realizes that Irv is a Martian.
b. Sam does not realize that Irv is a Martian.
c. Irv is a Martian.

(49)
a. Sam has stopped kissing his wife.
b. Sam has not stopped kissing his wife.
c. Sam was kissing his wife.

In (48) and (49), the (a) and (b) sentences are said to presuppose the truth of the (c) sentence. Notice that on this pragmatic conception of presupposition, as with the semantic notion of presupposition, both a sentence and its negation have the same presupposition.

A more restrictive notion, (pragmatic) *presupposition₂*, is this: the (pragmatic) presupposition₂ of a sentence is the set of conditions that have to be satisfied in order for the intended speech act to be appropriate in the circumstances, or to be felicitous. As one author (Keenan 1971, 49) writes,

Many sentences require that certain culturally defined conditions or contexts be satisfied in order for an utterance of a sentence to be understood ... these conditions are naturally called presuppositions of the sentence.... An utterance of a sentence pragmatically presupposes that its context is appropriate.

This view is echoed by another linguist (Fillmore 1971, 276):

By the presuppositional aspects of a speech communication situation, I mean those conditions which must be satisfied in order for a particular illocutionary act to be effectively performed in saying particular sentences.

Some typical examples of presupposition$_2$ are these:

(50)

a. John accused Harry of writing the letter.

b. John did not accuse Harry of writing the letter.

c. There was something blameworthy about writing the letter.

(51)

a. John criticized Harry for writing the letter.

b. John did not criticize Harry for writing the letter.

c. Harry wrote the letter.

(52)

a. Tu es dégoûtant. ("You are disgusting.")

b. Tu n'est pas dégoûtant. ("You are not disgusting.")

c. The addressee is an animal or child, is socially inferior to the speaker, or is personally intimate with the speaker.

Again, in each of (50)–(52) it is claimed that the (c) sentence is presupposed by both the (a) sentence and the (b) sentence.

A final notion, (pragmatic) *presupposition$_3$*, is that of shared background information, which one author (Jackendoff 1972, 230) characterizes as follows:

We will use ... "presupposition of a sentence" to denote the information in the sentence that is assumed by the speaker to be shared by him and the hearer.

The following sentences are typical examples of presupposition$_3$:

(53)

a. Was it Margaret that Paul married?

b. Wasn't it Margaret that Paul married?

c. Paul married someone.

(54)

a. Betty remembered to take her medicine.

b. Betty did not remember to take her medicine.

c. Betty was supposed to take her medicine.

(55)

a. That Sioux Indian he befriended represented the chief.

b. That Sioux Indian he befriended did not represent the chief.

c. He had befriended a Sioux Indian.

Again, in (53)–(55), the (a) and (b) sentences are said to presuppose the (c) sentence in that the conditions mentioned in (c) must be shared information. It may be disputed whether or not it is useful to apply the term *presupposition* to all of the phenomena just listed, but it cannot be disputed that these data must be explained (or explained away) by an adequate pragmatic theory.

It is sometimes held that certain sentences *invite an inference*, on the part of the hearer, to other sentences, even though the first sentence does not entail the second sentence (see Geis and Zwicky 1971). For example, the (a) sentences in (56) and (57) invite an inference to the (b) sentences:

(56)
a. If you *mow* the lawn, I *will* give you five dollars.
b. If you *don't mow* the lawn, I *won't* give you five dollars.

(57)
a. If young girls *or* young boys can compete, it will be a success.
b. If young girls *and* young boys can compete, it will be a success.

It is often proposed that a pragmatic theory must account for cases of invited inference.

Conclusion

We have briefly surveyed three special topics in pragmatics: reference, performatives, and implicature. Any adequate general pragmatic theory will have to incorporate an account of these phenomena. The exciting thing about pragmatics at present is that there is broad consensus on the general shape of a pragmatic theory, and much interesting and hard work to be done within that theory (see Horn 1988 for a survey).

Study Questions

1. What is the problem of linguistic communication as formulated in the text?

2. What is the Message Model of linguistic communication?

3. What six problems does the Message Model have?

4. Does a speaker need to be intending to linguistically communicate anything to a hearer in firing, sentencing, or awakening that person? Discuss.

5. What are the four major types of communication?

6. How has each type been characterized?

7. State the strategy for direct and literal communication.

8. State the strategy for nonliteral communication.

9. State the strategy for indirect communication.

10. What is the broad notion of discourse? What is the narrow notion of discourse?

11. What is a greeting?

12. State three principles of turn taking.

13. What are the two major steps in closing a conversation?

14. What is the difference between denotation and speaker reference?

15. What is the difference between the broad and the narrow conception of speaker reference?

16. What are literal, nonliteral, and indirect reference?

17. What are the two major theories about what determines reference?

18. What are four basic categories of speech acts?

19. What three factors distinguish illocutionary from perlocutionary acts?

20. What is the main problem with treating performatives as *directly* used to perform the acts they denote?

21. What is the indirect analysis of performatives?

22. What are conversational implicature and Grice's maxims?

23. What are three notions of presupposition?

Exercises

1. Find some examples of humor that turn on one or more of the inadequacies of the Message Model.

2. The text gives no specific principles for inferring a direct and literal message from an utterance. In part this is because context can influence which inferences the hearer is intended to make (recall problem three of the Message Model). To see this, consider the following sentences and state what some of the most common literal and direct communicative acts performed in uttering them might be:

a. It's getting late.
b. Who won the battle of Waterloo?
c. Leave by the back door!

3. What are some literal and direct communicative acts commonly performed in the utterance of (a) declarative, (b) imperative, (c) interrogative sentences? What sorts of linguistic devices are used to mark sentences in these three categories? Discuss. (Look again at section 6.3.)

4. If a speaker were to utter the following sentences, what might that speaker commonly be taken as intending to communicate? Discuss.

a. Move and I'll shoot!
b. Move or I'll shoot!

c. You've been drinking again, have you!
d. You've been drinking again, haven't you?
e. Marry my daughter, will you!
f. Marry my daughter, will you?
g. What, me worry?

5. Consider the following sentences, then state what you take the speaker's intended meaning to be.

a. I'm all thumbs today!
b. He's plowing his profits back into the business.
c. Cat got your tongue today?
d. That movie was a real turkey!
e. You took the words right out of my mouth.
f. She's got something on her mind.

6. Which, if any, of the above sentences involve lexical or syntactic ambiguity? Identify the nonliteral word or phrase. Defend your answer.

7. Can the sentence *I promise I will call the police if you don't quiet down* be literally and directly used to promise, or only to warn? Or both? Defend your answer.

8. Sometimes the absurdity of taking a nonliteral remark literally can best be brought out by a drawing. Try your hand at drawing an absurd literal interpretation for one of the above sentences, or for an example of your own.

9. Find five everyday, commonplace examples of nonliteral language use. Try to include an imperative and an interrogative example in your list. Paraphrase the intended nonliteral interpretation as best you can.

10. Consider the following proverbs:

a. A rolling stone gathers no moss.
b. Look before you leap.
c. A stitch in time saves nine.

How would you paraphrase the intended message behind each of them? What kinds of communicative uses of language do proverbs exemplify?

11. In what sense, if any, are proverbs *nonliteral*? Defend your answer.

12. Think of ten more common proverbs and then paraphrase their intended message.

13. Using the results of the previous exercise, try to state how proverbs work; for instance, do they differ from *metaphors*? Discuss. (Note that we do not normally call proverbs metaphors, nor do we call metaphors proverbs.)

14. Find five typical, commonplace cases of speaking *indirectly* that are not given in the text. Say what the direct communicative message is (is it literal or nonliteral?) and also say what the indirect message is. Try to include an example from each major mood of English: declarative, imperative, and interrogative.

15. Is *I promise to be there* literally and directly a promise, or is it literally and directly a statement that you will be there, and only indirectly a promise? Defend your answer.

16. Show how the Inferential Model tries to overcome each of the inadequacies of the Message Model. Discuss.

17. Some forms of words do not receive their proper interpretation in any regular way; they are in effect *idiomatic* and must be learned case by case. Here are some typical examples; try to think of more:

Declarative form
a. That just goes to show (you).

Imperative form
a. Take it easy! (meaning: Calm down!)
b. Buzz off! (meaning: Leave!)
c. (Go) Fly a kite! Take a hike! Get lost! (meaning: Leave!)
d. Never mind! Forget it! (meaning: Don't bother doing it!)

Interrogative form
a. Where does he get off saying that?
b. What do you say we leave?
c. What's things?
d. What's up?
e. What's the matter?
f. How about lunch?
g. How about that?

18. Try to paraphrase the declarative and interrogative examples above. Why might these cases be so difficult?

19. When is it normal not to open a talk-exchange with a greeting? Discuss.

20. Can you think of any modifications or additions that might be made to the three principles of turn taking discussed in the text? Elaborate.

21. We sometimes use *she* to refer to countries, boats, guns, and so on. Are these uses nonliteral? Discuss.

22. Consider some of our earlier examples of figures of speech:

a. The White House (the president or staff) said so.
b. I've read all of Chomsky (Chomsky's works).

Are these also cases of (nonliteral) indirect reference? Discuss.

23. Give three new examples each of nonliteral and indirect (singular speaker) reference; use a definite description, pronoun, and proper name.

24. Try to give an explicit definition of a *performative sentence*, keeping all of Austin's examples in mind.

25. Compare and contrast the direct versus indirect analysis of how we communicate with performatives.

26. What is the relation between conversational implicature, presupposition, and invited inference? Are they different? The same? Discuss.

27. What is the relation between conversational implicature, nonliterality, and indirection? Discuss.

Bibliography and Further Reading

Akmajian, A., R. Demers, and R. Harnish (1980). Overcoming inadequacies in the "Message-Model" of linguistic communication. *Communication and Cognition* 13, 317–336.

Austin, J. (1961). Performative utterances. In *Philosophical papers*. Oxford: Oxford University Press.

Austin, J. (1962). *How to do things with words*. Oxford: Oxford University Press.

Bach, K. (1988). *Thought and reference*. Oxford: Oxford University Press.

Bach, K., and R. Harnish (1979). *Linguistic communication and speech acts*. Cambridge, Mass.: MIT Press.

Blakemore, D. (1988). The organization of discourse. In Newmeyer 1988.

Brown, G., and G. Yule (1983). *Discourse analysis*. Cambridge: Cambridge University Press.

Carnap, R. (1939). *Foundations of logic and mathematics*. Chicago: University of Chicago Press.

Cole, P., ed. (1978). *Syntax and semantics 9: Speech acts*. New York: Academic Press.

Cole, P., and J. Morgan, eds. (1975). *Syntax and semantics 3: Pragmatics*. New York: Academic Press.

Coulthard, M. (1977). *An introduction to discourse analysis*. London: Longman.

Fillmore, C. (1971). Verbs of judging. In C. Fillmore and D. T. Langendoen, eds., *Studies in linguistic semantics*. New York: Holt, Rinehart and Winston.

Gazdar, G. (1979). *Pragmatics: Implicature, presupposition and logical form*. New York: Academic Press.

Geis, M., and A. Zwicky (1971). On invited inferences. *Linguistic Inquiry* 2, 561–565.

Green, G. (1989). *Pragmatics and natural language understanding*. Hillsdale, N.J.: L. Erlbaum Associates.

Grice, H. P. (1957). Meaning. *Philosophical Review* 66, 377–388.

Grice, H. P. (1975). Logic and conversation. In Cole and Morgan 1975.

Harnish, R. (1983). Pragmatic derivations. *Synthese* 54, 325–373.

Harnish, R. (1990). Theories of speech acts. In W. Bright, ed., *Oxford international encyclopedia of linguistics*. New York: Oxford University Press.

Holdcroft, D. (1978). *Words and deeds*. Oxford: Oxford University Press.

Horn, L. (1988). Pragmatic theory. In Newmeyer 1988.

Jackendoff, R. (1972). *Semantic interpretation in generative grammar*. Cambridge, Mass.: MIT Press.

Katz, J. (1966). *The philosophy of language*. New York: Harper and Row.

Katz, J. (1980). *Propositional structure and illocutionary force*. Cambridge, Mass.: Harvard University Press.

Keenan, E. (1971). Two kinds of presupposition in natural language. In C. Fillmore and D. T. Langendoen, eds., *Studies in linguistic semantics*. New York: Holt, Rinehart and Winston.

Kripke, S. (1980). *Naming and necessity*. Cambridge, Mass.: Harvard University Press.

Lakoff, G. (1970). Linguistics and natural logic. *Synthese* 22, 151–271.

Levinson, S. (1983). *Pragmatics*. Cambridge: Cambridge University Press.

Locke, J. (1691). *An essay concerning human understanding*. New York: Dover Publications (1959).

Morgan, J. (1978). Two types of convention in indirect speech acts. In Cole 1978.

Morris, C. (1938). *Foundations of the theory of signs*. Chicago: University of Chicago Press.

Newmeyer, F., ed. (1988). *Linguistics: The Cambridge survey*, vol. 4. Cambridge: Cambridge University Press.

Nunberg, G. (1978). *The pragmatics of reference*. Bloomington, Ind.: Indiana University Linguistics Club.

Ortony, A., ed. (1979). *Metaphor and thought*. New York: Cambridge University Press.

Recanati, F. (1987). *Meaning and force: The pragmatics of performative utterances*. Cambridge: Cambridge University Press.

Reddy, M. (1979). The conduit metaphor: A case of frame conflict in our language about language. In Ortony 1979.

Sacks, H., E. Schegloff, and G. Jefferson (1974). A simplest systematics for the organization of turn-taking for conversation. Reprinted in Schenkein 1978.

Sadock, J. (1974). *Toward a linguistic theory of speech acts*. New York: Academic Press.

Schegloff, E., and H. Sacks (1973). Opening up closing. *Semiotica* 8, 289–327.

Schenkein, J., ed. (1978). *Studies in the organization of conversational interaction*. New York: Academic Press.

Schiffrin, D. (1988). Conversation analysis. In Newmeyer 1988.

Searle, J. (1969). *Speech acts*. Cambridge: Cambridge University Press.

Searle, J. (1975). Indirect speech acts. Reprinted in Searle 1979b.

Searle, J. (1979a). Metaphor. Reprinted in Searle 1979b.

Searle, J. (1979b). *Expression and meaning*. Cambridge: Cambridge University Press.

Smith, N., ed. (1982). *Mutual knowledge*. New York: Academic Press.

Sperber, D., and D. Wilson (1986). *Relevance*. Cambridge, Mass.: Harvard University Press.

Stubbs, M. (1983). *Discourse analysis*. Chicago: University of Chicago Press.

PSYCHOLOGY OF
LANGUAGE: SPEECH
PRODUCTION AND
COMPREHENSION

10.1 COMPETENCE AND PERFORMANCE

We have seen that it is possible to analyze a natural language at a number of different levels: sounds (phonology), words (morphology), sentence structure (syntax), meaning (semantics), and use (pragmatics). The task of linguistics is in part to discover the appropriate units of analysis at each level and to state generalizations in terms of these units that capture the regularities inherent in the language itself.

But languages are not just abstract structured systems. They are also used in thought and communication, and it is the task of *psycholinguistics* (or *psychology of language*) to discover how knowledge of language is represented in the mind/brain of a fluent speaker, how this information is utilized in the production and understanding of expressions, and how speakers acquire these abilities.

Chomsky (1972) proposes that we construct three models. The first model reflects what a fluent speaker knows (what information is stored) about the sound-meaning relations in the language—the speaker's linguistic competence (figure 10.1). This is to be distinguished from a *performance model*, which reflects the actual processes that go into producing and understanding speech (and language) (figure 10.2). Finally, a language *acquisition model* (or device) reflects the changes in the competence and performance of a child during the acquisition period and thus provides a model of the child's language-learning achievements (figure 10.3). In the remainder of this chapter we will explore some of the central issues surrounding current attempts to build a *performance* model. In section 10.2 we will look at some empirical constraints on the production side of a performance model, and in section 10.3 at constraints on the comprehension side. In the next chapter we will investigate language acquisition.

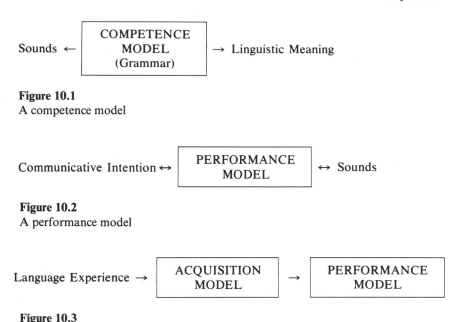

Figure 10.1
A competence model

Figure 10.2
A performance model

Figure 10.3
An acquisition model

10.2 SPEECH PRODUCTION

The easiest way of thinking about theories of speech production is to imagine building a device that will simulate the flow of information from message to sounds—in other words, a model of the phenomenon of a speaker expressing a message to a hearer: the speaker thinks of a message, plans how to express it, and finally articulates the expression with the vocal tract.

Conceiving the Message

A speaker brings to the communication situation a wide variety of general beliefs about the world, about the past, present, and future course of the conversation, and about the hearer's beliefs about these things. Accompanying these beliefs are the speaker's desires, hopes, intentions, and so forth. In the course of the conversation many of these beliefs, desires, and intentions not only affect what is said (see Gazdar 1981) but themselves change as a result of what is said. We will organize our discussion of speech production around the idea that these mental states form the *cognitive background* for normal conversation:

(1)
Cognitive background
The speaker has a variety of beliefs and desires concerning such factors as
a. the nature and direction of the conversation,
b. the social and physical context of the utterance,
c. the hearer's beliefs in general, beliefs pertinent to the speaker's impending remark in particular, and whatever contextual beliefs the hearer shares with the speaker.

Given these cognitive states, the speaker next must formulate the beginnings of the message to be communicated, as well as the manner in which it is to be communicated. Following the usage in chapter 9, we will refer to these as *pragmatic intentions*:

(2)
Pragmatic intentions
On the basis of the cognitive background, the speaker begins to form pragmatic intentions to
a. refer to something (referential intent),
b. perform some communicative act(s) (communicative intent),
c. perform these acts literally, nonliterally, directly, or indirectly,
d. have various effects on the hearer (perlocutionary intent).

We know very little at present about the psychological mechanisms underlying the storage of background information and the formation of pragmatic intentions, in part because there are serious methodological problems with studying speech production.

The standard methodology in psycholinguistics is to test for regular relationships between what subjects perceive and how they respond to it. Studying comprehension, the experimenter can manipulate characteristics of the input (such as the rate of the speech coming in) and look for regularities in the subjects' responses (such as the kinds of errors they make), but with speech production there is no good way of controlling the input, since the input is the subjects' *thoughts*. Psychologists know of no effective and ethically permissible way of controlling thoughts for experimental purposes, and so researchers in speech production must rely on very different kinds of phenomena, such as the analysis of hesitations, speech errors (both spontaneous and induced), and language disorders.

Planning the Expression: Speech Errors

Having begun to formulate at least some of the above pragmatic intentions, how does the speaker put them into words? What sort of process is this?

The Message Model suggests one possibility: that expression is basically a word-by-word encoding of the message from beginning to end. For instance, as the concept THE PLUMBER... comes into the message, the words of an English speaker "The plumber..." might begin to come out. Furthermore, when a word itself requires planning, the procedure is the same: build it up from left to right out of phonemes and syllables.

However, there is considerable evidence against this picture of speech planning, some of which comes from the study of speech errors. Speech errors have been the subject of both casual and scientific interest for centuries, partly due to their relative infrequency, given the complexity of the task (see the discussion of articulation). It has been estimated that there is one error in about every 1,000 spoken words (Bock and Loebell 1988).

Probably the most famous speech error maker of all time was the Reverend William A. Spooner (1844–1930) of Oxford University, who lent his name (spoonerisms) to such classics as:

(3)
a. "Work is the curse of the drinking class" for "Drink is the curse of the working class"
b. "Noble tons of soil" for "Noble sons of toil"
c. "You have hissed all my mystery lectures. I saw you fight a liar in the back quad; in fact, you have tasted the whole worm" (try your own hand at paraphrasing this one)

From a casual inspection of these errors, one might conclude that they are unsystematic, that errors are virtually a random phenomenon. But students of the subject agree that only certain types of errors predominate; in fact, the kinds of errors that predominate are those that involve *linguistic constituents* in some way. (Klima and Bellugi (1979, chap. 5) show that the same is true for "slips of the hand" in American Sign Language.) Although there is a wide variety of subtle types of error, a small number of types predominate. These include:

(4)
a. *Exchange errors*
   h̲issed all my m̲ystery lectures
b. *Anticipation errors*
   a l̲eading l̲ist (reading list)

c. *Perseveration errors*
    a phonological fool (phonological rule)
d. *Blends*
    moinly (mostly, mainly), impostinator (imposter, impersonator)
e. *Shifts*
    Mermaid— moves (mermaids move) their legs together.
f. *Substitutions*
    sympathy for symphony (form), finger for toe (meaning)

We have illustrated these types of error with mainly phonological segments, but they happen with all sorts of linguistic units, though rarely with nonunits. Consider, for instance, the following samples:

(5)
a. *Phonetic features (voicing)*
    glear plue sky (clear blue sky)
    pig and vat (big and fat)
b. *Stress*
    Stop beating your brìck against a head wall. (Stop beating your héad against a brick wall.)
c. *Syntactic features*
    (Indefinite) a meeting —arathon (an eating marathon)
    (Past tense) Rosa always date shranks. (dated shrinks)
d. *Stem and affix*
    He favors pushing busters. (busting pushers)
e. *Negation*
    I disregard this as precise. (I regard this as imprecise.)

These examples illustrate important features of speech errors as evidence for the speech planning process. First, errors usually involve the alteration of some linguistic unit. Rarely are the speech error data completely random, and this suggests that *the speech planning process uses linguistic units in its planning operations.* Second, the errors reveal that the planning system must be looking ahead. A system that did not look ahead could hardly make the errors shown in (5a); the voicing feature appears to have moved backward in the first example and forward in the second.

Consider next example (5b). The words *brick* and *head* were interchanged, but notice that the stress (indicated with ´) did not move with the originally intended stressed word (*head*). Instead, it stayed in its original location, suggesting that there must be a level of representation for stress that is abstract and detached from the words themselves.

The syntactic feature examples are particularly interesting. In the case of the indefinite article the speaker had intended to say *an eating marathon*, but when the /m/ moved forward and was attached to *eating*, the indefinite article changed from *an* to *a* to accommodate the error: the subject did not say *an meeting arathon*. This means that during the planning process there was a stage where the /m/ could move forward and a later stage where the indefinite article /a/ could adjust to the next vowel by the deletion of /n/. Again, the error indicates that the processor has planned ahead.

The examples involving negation and the past tense emphasize the point that the processor works in stages and is able to anticipate, using information about what is coming three or four words ahead. Consider (5e), *I disregard this as precise*: not only was negation anticipated by three words, but the form of the negation was adjusted to conform to morphological constraints as well; the subject did not say *I imregard this as precise*. Finally, the past tense example is interesting in that the tense feature moved onto a word that is homophonic with a verb (*to shrink*) but is in this occurrence a noun (*a shrink* "psychiatrist"). However, the speech planning system apparently could not use this information at this stage; it treated the word as a verb in the past tense, producing *shrank*. The challenge for theories of speech production is not only to account for these errors but also to account for these *patterns* of errors.

One influential proposal is that of Garrett (1975, 1980), who noticed certain patterns in his error data that could be accounted for if the production system contains at least two important levels of planning activity: what he calls the *functional* level and the *positional* level (see figure 10.4). Functional level planning deals with multiphrasal representations of the functional roles of words—their semantic values and syntactic relations. Positional level planning deals with single phrase representations of the sound structure and serial ordering of the elements of the sentence. The patterns of error can be summarized as follows:

1. *Word* exchange errors are predominantly *between* phrases, and in fact between words of the same syntactic category (say, noun).
2. *Sound* exchange errors are predominantly *within* phrases and do not respect syntactic categories.
3. *Morpheme* exchange errors are of both types. If they occur between phrases, then the morphemes are from words of the same category. If they occur within phrases, then the morphemes are rarely from words of the same category.
4. *Exchange* errors for words, morphemes, and sounds are restricted mainly to major (open, content) categories such as noun, verb, adjective.

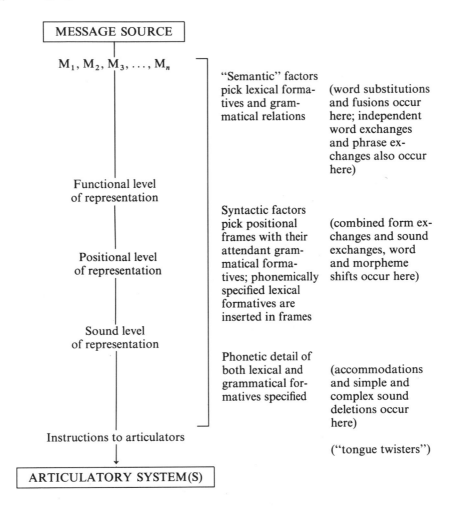

Figure 10.4
Garrett's model of levels of speech production. (From Garrett 1975.)

5. *Shift* errors are restricted mainly to minor (closed, function) categories.
6. *Substitution* errors are either form-related or meaning-related.

These regularities can be accounted for if the planning process involves the two levels just described; the idea is that items can get scrambled *at a level* because information about them is simultaneously available, but items cannot become scrambled *between* levels because information about items at these two levels is not simultaneously available. Thus, words can exchange across phrasal boundaries at the functional level, but sounds can only exchange within a phrase at the positional level, and so on for the other error regularities (see Dell and Reich 1981, for another analysis).

Speech error studies have some distinctive methodological pitfalls that must be avoided if the data are to be reliable. One interesting class of mistakes has been called *slips of the ear*. Cutler (1982, 12) reports examples such as these:

(6)
a. Do you know about reflexes?
    Perceived: Do you know about Reith lectures?
b. Because they can answer inferential questions.
    Perceived: Because they can answer in French.
c. If you think you have any clips of the type shown ...
    Perceived: If you think you have an eclipse ...

Clearly, if such examples were to enter a body of data as "speech" errors, rather than hearing errors, they could substantially distort theory construction in this area. Researchers take a number of precautions to guard against this possibility, such as requiring witnesses or tape recordings. Clearly, also, these errors can be the source of communication breakdowns, as noted in chapter 9.

10.3 COMPREHENSION

The study of the processes of comprehension, from signal to understanding, does not suffer from the problems of identifying and manipulating the input. If anything it is the output, understanding, that is the problem in this case. On reflection it is not so clear what we really mean when we say that a hearer understood what a speaker said, or what a speaker meant (to communicate). For the time being we will leave the issue of the nature of understanding open and begin our review with the input to speech comprehension, the speech signal itself. The entire process of comprehension is summarized in figure 10.5.

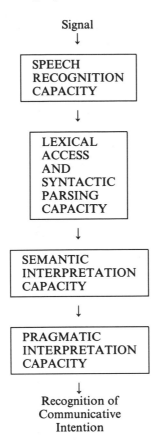

Figure 10.5
Functional analysis of comprehension into subcapacities

It is generally assumed that the speech recognition capacity identifies as much about the speech sounds as it can from the sound wave. The syntactic parsing capacity identifies the words by their sounds and analyzes the structure of the sentence, and the semantic interpretation capacity puts the meaning of the words together in accordance with these syntactic relations. The pragmatic interpretation capacity selects a particular speech act or communicative intent as the most likely. If the hearer is right, communication is successful; if not, there has been a breakdown.

It should not be assumed that these different capacities are carried out either by different "areas of the brain" or necessarily one after the other. Many of these processes can overlap both in time and in brain activity. The question of the neurological realization of these linguistic capacities is the province of the field of neurolinguistics, which is the subject of chapter 12.

Modularity

When the "cognitive" perspective replaced behaviorism in the 1960s, it brought with it a conception of mental functioning as mental computation (Neisser 1967). The most pervasive example of computational devices at the time was the standard stored program von Neumann machine. This traditional model represents minds as constructed out of two principal components—input (sensory data) and output (motor) response processors—and a central processing unit. All higher-level cognitive functions were thought to be explainable by a single set of principles. On this model, incoming stimuli are first processed by sensory systems such as the retina or tympanic membrane, then these raw data are turned over to the central cognitive processor. There is no place for special perceptual processing *between* sensory input and central cognitive processing.

More recently another cognitive architecture utilizing special-purpose perceptual processors has been proposed (see Fodor 1983). These processors are called *modules*, and systems containing modules are said to be *modular*. We can expect differences between perceptual systems and cognition when we consider that the purpose of perceptual systems is to track the ever-changing environment, whereas the purpose of central cognitive systems is to make considered judgments. Because of these differences in purpose there are important differences in the way these systems function. Consider perceptual systems. First, such special-purpose computational systems are *fast*. Typically, perceptual processes are completed within a few tenths of a second. Second, there seems to be *special neural circuitry* devoted to the various perceptual processes. Third, perceptual systems are sensitive to *specific domains* of information. The language system responds to language input but not to sneezes, and the face recognition system responds to upright faces but not to inverted faces (or to photographic negatives of faces). Fourth, perceptual systems are *mandatory*: once they begin processing, they cannot be turned off by knowledge or decision. Fifth, perceptual systems are *informationally encapsulated*: they can utilize only certain information and do not make use of all the information available to the person as a whole. Consider illusions. Knowing that the line segments in figure 10.6 are actually the same length (measure them) does not cause the illusion of difference to go away. Finally, the inner workings of perceptual systems are *not available to introspection*.

These features make perceptual systems like special-purpose computers, well suited for tracking the environment—they are fast and relatively reliable. Central processes, on the other hand, trade off speed for accuracy. They are relatively slow (think about the processes of deciding where to go to college or what to major in), but they allow us to consider lots of available information, from a wide variety of domains. Central processes typically involve processes of deductive and probabilistic reasoning (but see Harman 1986).

Is the language processor a module? Fodor (1983) and others contend that language processing is indeed modular, like (other) perceptual systems (but see Marslen-Wilson and Tyler 1987). Language functions to *pick up information about the environment*; it is not infallible in this, but neither are other perceptual systems. Also, the language processor seems *specific to language* input, regardless of the sensory modality (see the discussion of the curious "McGurk effect" in section 10.4). It is *fast* enough that we can recognize syllables and even activate semantic information within three-tenths of a second, and it is *mandatory* or *automatic* in that we cannot just decide to turn it off once it has started. Language processing is *not accessible to introspection*, and there is considerable evidence (see chapter 12) that

Figure 10.6
The Müller-Lyer illustion

language is processed directly on *specific neural circuits* in the brain. When these areas are damaged, specific language capacities can be affected. The most controversial claim of modularity is *information encapsulation*. After surveying some central topics, we will return to this issue.

Within the general framework of the modularity hypothesis, various claims concerning the structure of the comprehension process (see figure 10.5 again) must be distinguished. First, there is the strong "autonomy" claim (Forster 1979) that each component of the language processor functions like a little module, working autonomously on its input. Second, there is the claim that components *within* the language faculty can interact with one another, but there can be no influences on the language module from central systems. Since this second position allows for interaction inside the language module, it is important where such a theory draws the line between language processing and general cognition. Some, such as proponents of *cohort theory* (see Marslen-Wilson 1987), draw the line quite early and include only lexical access—the process of contacting lexical information in memory. Others (Fodor 1983) suggest that basic mechanisms of parsing (and semantic interpretation) are also a part of the language module. Contrasting with these positions are highly *interactive* theories such as the artificial intelligence model HEARSAY II (see Lesser et al. 1977) and current connectionist models (see section 10.4).

Speech Perception

The hearer, having heard an expression uttered by the speaker, must now recover its meaning(s). For a fluent speaker of a given language this might seem like a trivial task. After all, what is there to understanding sentences of our native language aside from knowing the individual words of the language plus a few simple word order rules for forming word sequences that "make sense"?

A serious problem with this view is that in actual speech, sentences are, physically, continuous streams of sound, not broken down into the convenient discrete units that we call words. A good illustration of this is the experience of a traveler in a foreign land who does not know the local native language. The traveler does not hear neatly arranged sequences of individual words—the sentences and phrases of the language all sound like streams of unintelligible noise. The idea that we *do* hear such sequences as discrete, linearly ordered units is only an illusion resulting from the fact that in knowing a language we perceptually analyze a physical continuum into individual sounds (as well as words and phrases). A striking aspect of this perceptual analysis of sounds was demonstrated in a set of experiments by Schatz (1954). Tape recordings of various consonant-vowel combinations were made, then cut and respliced to create new consonant-vowel combinations. In one case, the word *ski* was cut between the *k* and the *i*, and the initial *sk* was then combined with other sounds to form the new consonant-vowel sequences. When the *sk* from *ski* was combined with a new sequence *ar* and played to English speakers, the subjects did not hear the word *scar*, as we might expect. Instead, they reported hearing the word *star* 96 percent of the time. Further, when the *sk* from *ski* was combined with the sequence *ool*, the word *spool* was heard 87 percent of the time, rather than the expected *school*. Thus, the acoustic signal corresponding to the *k* in the word *ski* can be perceived as a *k* (as in *ski*), *t* (as in *star*), or *p* (as in *spool*), depending on the following vowel. These cases show that a single acoustic signal can be perceived as different consonants, which cannot be identified until the following vowel is known.

A particularly striking example of context effects in speech perception is the *phoneme restoration effect* discovered by Warren (1970). Subjects were presented with the word *legislature*, but with the /ǰ/-sound removed and replaced by a noise such as a cough. Interestingly, they did not hear something like /le-cough-islature/; rather, they heard the word *legislature* with a cough in the background. This works with a variety of other noises such as tones and buzzes, but if silence is presented in place of the /ǰ/-sound, then the /ǰ/ is not restored.

Another illustration of the nonlinearity of speech processing comes from an experiment by Pollack and Pickett (1963). Speech sequences were created by excising portions of conversations via an electronic gate of controllable width. Individual words that were excised from the tape were rarely intelligible when the gate was so narrow that the preceding and following words were not included. However, as the gate was widened after the original word to allow more and more of the original utterance, the entire sequence eventually became intelligible. As reported by Lieberman (1966), the excised portion does not become gradually more intelligible as the gate width increases; rather, the signal remains unintelligible until a particular gate width is reached. At this point, the entire sequence suddenly becomes intelligible. More recent work (see Grosjean and Gee 1987) extends this idea to prosodic information. The implication is that word-by-word models of speech perception may apply only to some speech phenomena.

Although there has been an enormous amount of interesting work on speech perception in the last 25 years, the fundamental problem of saying how the speech signal is converted into meaningful units remains unsolved (for a survey, see Pisoni and Luce 1987).

Lexical Access and Syntactic Analysis

The output of the speech recognition capacity is a representation of as much information as it can obtain about the speech sounds of the utterance, based on the sound wave alone. In most cases information about some of the segments will be missing, as will information concerning aspects of intonation and word or phrase boundaries. It is the job of the syntactic analysis capacity to identify the relevant words and relate them syntactically. It is the job of the semantic interpretation capacity to produce a representation of the meaning of the sentence (or other expressions). We will follow this process from words to sentence to meaning as best we can, though current research shows that very little is known about many of these operations.

Lexical Access

If we are to understand what speakers are trying to say, we must understand the sentences they utter; and to do this we must recognize (at least some of) the words that make up these sentences. The psycholinguistic literature often distinguishes two processes here: *lexical access*, in which the language processor unconsciously "accesses" or makes contact with the information stored at an address in the mental lexicon, and *word recognition*, in which one of the accessed words (and its meaning) is selected and made available to introspection. There are at least two prominent experimental techniques for investigating lexical access and word recognition. *Lexical decision* requires subjects to decide whether or not a displayed series of letters constitutes a word. *Naming* requires subjects to pronounce the displayed series of letters. By presenting words and nonwords to subjects and timing their responses in these tasks, researchers can test different aspects of models of word recognition. Since these two tasks are sensitive to different aspects of this process, results that generalize across both tasks are probably more reliable.

Given the speed at which comprehension is possible (over 4 words per second), it is clear that the time it takes to identify words need not be very long at all, perhaps an average of about $\frac{1}{5}$ second (Rohrman and Gough 1967). Thus, it would be implausible to suppose that a hearer looks randomly through a mental dictionary (lexicon) of 50,000 words to find which word (with its syntactic and semantic properties) is associated with what sounds. In fact, it appears that accessing the mental lexicon is systematic.

First, the mental lexicon appears to some extent to be *ordered by sounds*—much as a normal dictionary is ordered by the alphabet (Fay and Cutler 1977). Second, lexical access also seems sensitive to how frequently one has heard the word (Forster and Chambers 1973) or how recently one has heard the word (Scarborough, Cortese, and Scarborough 1977). If frequent or recent words are more easily accessed, then the more likely a word is to occur in one's experience, the more likely it is to be accessed easily. This is the *frequency* (or *recency*) *effect*. Third, as we will see shortly (see also section 10.4), various kinds of prior context can favorably influence the speed and accuracy of lexical access (*priming*): repeated words prime themselves, *doctor* primes *nurse*, *banjo* primes *harp*, and even *bribe* primes *tribe* (orthographic priming) (Meyer and Schvaneveldt 1971). Fourth, an interesting side effect of lexical access involves the *word superiority effect*: letters are more quickly and accurately recognized in the context of words than they are by themselves or in the context of nonwords (Reicher 1969). This suggests that lexical access is implicated in letter recognition of the very letters that make up the word being recognized. How could this be so? Finally, possible but nonactual words such as *optle* are rejected more slowly (about 650 milliseconds) than clear nonwords such as *xnit*, which are rejected in about the same amount of time as it takes to recognize actual words (500 milliseconds).

As a theory of word recognition, Forster (1978) proposed the influential *search model*, which resembles the search method for finding a book in a library: get a reference to a book; go to the card catalogue; find the card for the book (the cards being organized in different ways—by author, title, subject); from the card, get the number that points to the book's location in the stacks. According to Forster's model (see figure 10.7), when a word is first perceived, it activates the appropriate *access code*, which is orthographic if the word is read, phonological if it is heard. (The syntactic/ semantic code is used primarily for finding words to speak, and we ignore it for now.) The system next begins searching the relevant access file, which is arranged so that the most frequent/recent items are compared first. If the perceived word is sufficiently close to an item in the access file, the search will stop and the system will follow the pointer to the location in the master lexicon where the full entry for the word is given. The system then does a *postaccess check* to verify all information.

This model neatly explains some of the basic findings. For instance, it explains why frequent/recent words are recognized faster than infrequent

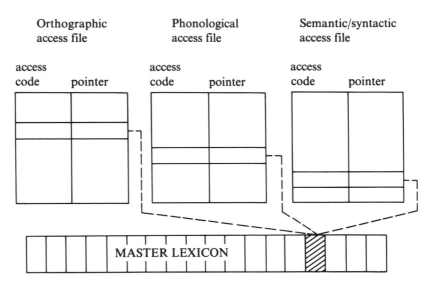

Figure 10.7
Organization of peripheral access files and master lexicon. (From Forster 1978.)

words, since frequent words are searched first. The model also predicts that nonwords should take longer to reject than actual words do to be accepted, because the system will continue to look for a nonword until the file (or some bins in the file) has been exhausted, whereas the search will terminate whenever a word is found. Nonwords that are similar to words will trick the system momentarily (perhaps until the postaccess check) and so will take even longer to reject. (See Marslen-Wilson 1987, for a critical discussion and an alternative "cohort" model.)

Ambiguity and Disambiguation

Let's suppose that a word has been recognized—how about its meaning(s)? Not only are most of the words in English ambiguous; probably most of the words in each speaker's idiolect are ambiguous as well. This poses an interesting problem for the speech understander—should it note all of the meanings of each word, or only some (normally one), and if so which one? (Note that it does seem that we normally hit on the right or appropriate meaning most of the time.) Since this process is so fast, we should not expect introspection to answer this question.

Recent work suggests that more processing is going on than introspection may reveal. One early sequence of studies (Bever, Garrett, and Hurtig 1973) found evidence that hearers typically represent *all* of the meanings (that they know) of the clauses they hear; by the end of a clause, the most plausible meaning is selected and the processing continues. If this should turn out to be the wrong choice, as in so-called garden path sentences such as (7), then the processor must go back and try again.

(7)
He gave the girl the ring impressed the watch. (put *whom* after *girl*)

It is still not clear exactly what causes a meaning to be selected: is it memory limitations, or time limitations, or the arrival of some structural unit (such as the end of the clause)? One study (Tanenhaus, Leiman, and Seidenberg 1979) found that up to about $\frac{1}{4}$ second, both meanings of ambiguous noun-verb words (such as *watch*) were activated, but after that period of time one reading was selected. A related study (Swinney 1979) found that by three syllables after an ambiguous word, a decision had been made on the appropriate meaning. Seidenberg et al. (1982) found that the language processor will activate the "flower" meaning of *rose* not only in the context of (8a) but also, surprisingly, in the context of (8b):

(8)
a. He handed her a *rose*.
b. The balloon *rose* into the clouds.

All of this suggests that when we process sentences, all known meanings of the word are first automatically activated, then some as yet poorly understood process selects the most appropriate one based on various cues.

In some cases the speaker can help the hearer out. In one study (Lehiste 1973) subjects were asked to listen to ambiguous sentences such as (9) where the speaker had a particular meaning in mind:

(9)
The steward (*greeted* [*the girl*) with a smile].

It was found that when hearers disambiguated the sentence correctly and got the intended smiling-girl meaning, the speakers had taken more time (as much as $\frac{1}{6}$ second) in pronouncing the crucial words (italicized above), thus giving the hearers a cue to what was meant.

Syntactic Strategies

Imagine that the speech comprehension capacity has determined which words it is presently hearing and has looked up their idiosyncratic syntactic and semantic characteristics. What does it do now? Recall that one goal is to figure out the meaning(s) of the whole sentence on the basis of the meaning(s) of its words and their syntactic relations. So it must begin to determine those relations.

One very influential proposal about how this is done was made by Bever (1970). He proposed that part of this system consists of perceptual *strategies*. These principles tell the system how to make decisions about syntactic structures in the face of uncertainty and incomplete information. For instance, given the speed of speech comprehension it is unlikely that *all* possibilities are investigated at every level of analysis; rather, hearers use strategies as rules of thumb to make intelligent guesses. Of course, if these principles are only strategies, and not exhaustive searches, then it should be possible for the speech comprehension capacity to err—we should be able to trick it. And trick it we can. Consider one of Bever's strategies:

(10)
Main Clause Strategy (MCS)
The first NP + V + (NP) sequence is the main clause of the sentence, unless the verb is marked as subordinate.

Such a strategy works well for sentences such as (11a), but it is tricked by sentences such as (11b), which should be read as (11c):

(11)
a. The horse raced the car, and won.
b. The horse raced past the barn fell.
c. The horse which (was) raced past the barn fell.

Thus, it would seem that something like the MCS is operating in understanding. But might the MCS be simply a special case of some more general processes? In fact, it has been proposed (Frazier and Fodor 1978) that parsing capacity involves two stages. The first stage, because of (short-term) memory limitations, looks at about six words of the sentence at a time, attempting to categorize the words as nouns, verbs, and so on, and to group as many of them together in a phrase as its limited capacity allows. The second stage takes these structured phrasal "packages" and attempts to build a coherent syntactic structure for the whole sentence. On this view, many errors can be accounted for by the operating characteristics of the two stages. In particular, these errors can, in many cases, be attributed to the "shortsightedness" of stage one; it will follow the principle of Minimal Attachment:

(12)
Minimal Attachment (MA)
Try to group the latest words received together under existing category nodes; otherwise, build a new category.

This parsing strategy explains many intuitive and experimental results. Frazier (1979) reports a sequence of experiments in which such sentences were presented to subjects visually one word at a time (at the rate of about 3 words per second) and the subjects were asked to judge their grammaticality. If comprehension tends to follow the principles of the two-stage model, then sentences like (13b) will take longer to process than sentences like (13a). (The extra embedded pair of brackets indicates the new node that is required. MA = minimal attachment; NMA = nonminimal attachment.)

(13)

a. (MA) We gave [the man the grant proposal we wrote] because he had written a similar proposal last year.

b. (NMA) We gave [the man [the grant proposal was written by last year]] a copy of this year's proposal.

The model (and intuition) predicts (13b) to be more difficult to process because *the man* is not minimally attached. The experiment confirmed this; on average, it took over twice as long to process sentences like (13b) than sentences like (13a). This result was confirmed by Rayner, Carlson, and Frazier (1983) by tracking eye movements of subjects reading sentences such as (14a) and (14b):

(14)

a. (MA) The kids [played all the albums *on the stereo*] before they went to bed.

b. (NMA) The kids played all [the albums [*on the shelf*]] before they went to bed.

Even though general knowledge makes it clear that *on the shelf* modifies *albums* and not *play* in (14b), the difficulty normally associated with nonminimal attachment was in fact observed in eye-movement patterns; relevant world knowledge was not consulted during the parse.

Constituent structure of sentences is not merely an artifact of syntactic theory; there is reason to think that gross constituent structure in fact has reality in the minds of speakers. In various experiments that have come to be known as the *click experiments*, Fodor, Bever, and Garrett (1974) tried to show that test subjects utilize major constituent boundaries in their perception of sentences. Subjects wearing headphones heard a tape-recorded sentence in one ear, while in the other ear they heard a "click" noise simultaneously superimposed on some part of the sentence. They were asked to write down each sentence they had heard and to indicate where in the sentence they had heard the click sound. A typical sentence in this experiment was (15), where the dots underneath words indicate the various locations of the superimposed click noises:

(15)

That the girl was happy | was evident from the way she laughed.

The major constituent break in this sentence occurs between *happy* and *was*, and clicks were superimposed both before this major break and after it. The subjects in the experiment showed a definite tendency to "mis-hear" the location of the click: when the click actually occurred *before* the major break, subjects reported hearing it *later* (closer to the major break); when the click actually occurred *after* the major break, subjects reported hearing it *earlier* (again closer to the major break). When the click was located in the major break itself, the tendency to "mis-hear" its location was much lower.

This experiment has been interpreted as showing that hearers process sentences in terms of major *clauses* of a sentence and that these major constituents *resist interruption*. Hence, when a click was placed within a major clause (say, at the word *was* in (15)), hearers tended to report it as occurring in the break, and not in the clause itself, suggesting that on a perceptual level major clauses are integrated units that resist being broken up. The results of the click experiments are by no means uncontroversial (see Fodor, Bever, and Garrett 1974 and Clark and Clark 1977 for a review of much of this work, and of the problems and controversy that surround it). If these results hold up, then it appears that major constituent structure is both a theoretical device used by linguists to explain syntactic phenomena and a psychologically real unit of perception on the part of hearers.

The picture of parsing that emerges from these and other studies is that as words are heard and identified, their meanings are activated and the comprehension device begins to try to put them together into phrases. As comprehension proceeds, the device runs out of immediate memory and must group the words together as best it can. As words come in, this process continues, but the comprehension device also tries to connect these phrases into a total coherent sentential structure. The details of this process are the topic of much current research.

Context/Interaction Effects and Modularity

As we have seen, the modularity of lexical access is heavily supported by the fact that even in the face of biasing sentential contexts, more than one meaning of a word is briefly activated (recall the *rose* example). This suggests that highly interactive models are wrong in predicting that context guides the processor away from contextually inappropriate meanings. There is even evidence that *hearing* a word activates information about its *spelling*, even though this could not be relevant in the context. Seidenberg and Tanenhaus (1979) found that in an auditory rhyme detection task, similarly spelled words (*tie, pie*) were detected faster than dissimilarly spelled words (*rye, pie*).

Putting highly interactive theories temporarily aside, how are we to decide among the strong "autonomy" conception, "cohort" theory, and Fodor's modular input system conception of language processing? This proves quite difficult since each type of theory can accommodate a wide number of effects (see Norris 1986); but let us at least sample the findings relevant to this issue.

Word Recognition and Contextual Plausibility

Fishler and Bloom (1979) found that subjects in a lexical decision task respond more quickly to *teeth* than to *tree* or *truth* in contexts such as these:

(16)
a. John brushed his teeth.
b. John brushed his tree.
c. John brushed his truth.

A modularity theorist must account for this without supposing that our general knowledge that one brushes teeth more often than trees is affecting lexical access.

Garden Path Sentences

If the language module extends beyond lexical access to parsing, then the assignment of structure ought to be mandatory and encapsulated; we have already seen evidence from eye-movement studies of reading that this is so. Crain and Steedman (1985) argue that such sentences indicate encapsulation only because they are being studied in isolation. Normally, they claim, a pragmatic principle is at work:

(17)
Principle of Referential Success (PRS)
If there is a reading that succeeds in referring to an entity already established in the hearer's mental model of the domain of discourse, then it is favored over one that is not.

Crain and Steedman argue that if there is a relevant set of horses in the hearer's discourse model, then (11b) will not be misanalyzed; the hearer will not be led down the garden path. They found that on a sentence classification task, subjects could be influenced by prior context as well as by the nature of the lexical items in the sentence. For instance, (18a) was misclassified as ungrammatical more frequently than (18b):

(18)
a. The teachers taught by the Berlitz method passed the test.
b. The children taught by the Berlitz method passed the test.

How could this be, if the parser treats these as structurally identical? The first answer comes from the fact that *teacher* and *children* differ in their semantics, and semantic information is in principle available to the syntax on Fodor's version of modularity (though not on the autonomy version). The second comes from an experiment that tested the PRS (Clifton and Ferreira 1987). Subjects were given the following types of sentences, in contexts that established discourse referents and so should have facilitated processing:

(19)
a. (NMA) [The editor [played the tape]] agreed the story was big.
b. (MA) [The editor played the tape] and agreed the story was big. (control sentence)

Here, the nonminimally attached structure should have been computed first, as it is for (19b). If, however, hearers follow the Minimal Attachment principle *regardless* of context, then they should have had trouble with (19a), compared to (19b). This is the result reported, indicating that although the PRS was available to guide the parser (subjects used it to answer true/false questions about these senetences), the parser was incapable of utilizing this information—in short, it is informationally encapsulated.

Semantic Interpretation: Mental Representation of Meaning

How does the mind represent the meaning of words or morphemes, and how does it combine these to represent the meaning of phrases and sentences? These are the central questions of this area of research and although much interesting work has been done, investigators are only beginning to glimpse what the answers might look like.

Word and Phrase Meaning

The problem of word meaning for psychology is finding a psychological state that could plausibly be the state of knowing the meaning of a word. We saw in chapter 6 that images are not the answer, at least not the whole answer. The most popular and influential theory in psychology at present is that the mental representation of meaning involves *concepts*. But how are we to think of concepts? One way to think of them is in terms of their *role* in thought; another is in terms of their *internal structure*.

Probably the most pervasive role for concepts to play in thought is *categorization*. Concepts allow us to group things that are similar in some respect into classes. We are able to abstract away from irrelevant details to the properties that are important for thought or action. The stability of our everyday mental life depends to a great extent on our capacity to categorize and conceptualize particular objects and events.

Concepts also combine to form *complex concepts* and *complete thoughts*. For example, we might have the concepts MISCHIEVOUS and BOYS, and form the complex concept MISCHIEVOUS BOYS. Or we might form the thought that BOYS ARE MISCHIEVOUS, the wish that BOYS NOT BE MISCHIEVOUS, and so on. From the point of view of semantics, some concepts are taken to be the mental representation of the meaning of *words* (following Fodor 1981, we call these *lexical concepts*), some concepts are taken to be the mental representation of the meaning of *phrases* (*phrasal concepts*), and thoughts are taken to be the mental representation of the meaning of *sentences*. How may we describe the internal structure of concepts, especially the internal structure of lexical concepts? In exploring this issue, we will look at the traditional view of concepts, some criticisms of this view, and an alternative view that has recently become popular.

Concepts: The Traditional View   The traditional view of the mental representation of the meaning of words, dating from the seventeenth-century British Empiricists, holds that there are two sorts of concepts: simple and complex. Simple concepts, such as RED, are thought to be the result of innate sensory and perceptual processes. Complex concepts, on the other hand, are generally learned and are the result of combining simple concepts in accordance with various principles, such as *conjunction*. For instance, the concept TRIANGLE might be constructed by conjoining the concepts PLANE, CLOSED, FIGURE, WITH, THREE, STRAIGHT, SIDES. Moreover, the traditional view holds that if a complex concept is the meaning of a word, then its constituent concepts *define* that word. This view, then, can be summarized as follows:

(20)
a. The meaning of words involves simple or complex (lexical) concepts.
b. Simple concepts are innate and derived from sensation or perception.

c. Complex concepts are learned and composed ultimately out of simple concepts, using such devices as conjunction and negation.

d. Understanding a word involves activating the associated lexical concept.

e. Such lexical concepts are associated in memory with the word as its definition, and the defining concepts are each necessary and jointly sufficient.

f. Understanding a phrase or sentence involves activating the associated concepts.

Problems with the Traditional View: Decomposition and Typicality Effects
The traditional view has been under serious attack for the last two decades. First, it is very implausible that *all* complex concepts can be analyzed eventually into innately determined perceptual properties. Consider the concept of a CHAIR or a HAT. Clearly, chairs and hats have certain structural characteristics that can be represented perceptually. However, they also have certain important *functions* or *uses*, and these are not perceptual properties, since we do not see "sitability" or "wearability." Even worse, think of BACHELOR: what is the *perceptual* property of being UNMARRIED? There is also evidence from the acquisition of perceptual language by blind children that more than sensation must form the basis of word meaning (see Landau and Gleitman 1985).

Second, there is experimental evidence against the idea that understanding words, phrases, and sentences involves activating the kinds of complex defining concepts that the traditional view requires. For instance, Fodor, Fodor, and Garrett (1975) asked subjects to evaluate the validity of arguments such as the following:

(21)
a. If practically all of the men in the room are *not married*, then few of the men in the room have wives.

b. If practically all of the men in the room are *bachelors*, then few of the men in the room have wives.

Notice that (21b) contains *bachelors*, which is commonly thought to be definable in terms of NOT MARRIED. Since experiments have shown that negation adds significantly to comprehension time, we would expect that if *bachelor* is in fact decomposed into the concepts including NOT MARRIED, (21b) should take at least as much time on the average to process as (21a). However, subjects processed sentences like (21b) significantly *faster* than sentences like (21a), suggesting that the definitional decomposition posited by the traditional view was not taking place.

A more elaborate study (Fodor et al. 1980) has provided further evidence against definitional decomposition. First it was established that subjects are experimentally sensitive to differences or "shifts" between surface grammatical relations and deeper grammatical relations. For example, consider (22a) and (22b):

(22)
a. John expected Mary to write a poem.
b. John persuaded Mary to write a poem.

These sentences have the same surface structure, but they differ in their underlying grammatical relations in that *Mary* is both the object of *persuade* and the subject of *write* in (22b), but only the subject of *write* in (22a). To see this, contrast the meaning of the following passives:

(23)
a. John expected a poem to be written by Mary.
b. ?John persuaded a poem to be written by Mary.

Given that these differences are experimentally detectable, Fodor et al. gave subjects sentences like (24a) and (24b):

(24)
a. John saw the glass.
b. John broke the glass.

On the traditional view, these should have very different conceptual structures. In (24a) *the glass* is the object of *saw*, but in (24b) *the glass* is really the subject, not the object, of *break*. According to the traditional view, (24b) is *really* stored as something like (25):

(25)
John caused the glass to break.

This "shift" should be detectable with the tests just described, but it was not, thereby providing further evidence against the traditional view.

Third, there is experimental evidence that the internal structure of many lexical concepts does not resemble that of definitions (that is, of equally necessary and sufficient conditions). In an influential series of papers Rosch and her associates (1973, 1975) provide evidence that the categorization process exhibits "typicality effects," suggesting that concepts possess an internal structure favoring typical members over less typical ones. Let us look at two of these effects.

First, people are quite consistent in rating certain kinds of objects as more or less typical of a kind. For instance, in one experiment Rosch (1973,

Table 10.1
Judgments of "goodness of category membership." (From Rosch 1973.)

Category	Member	B & M[a] Frequency	"Exemplariness" Rank	Category	Member	B & M[a] Frequency	"Exemplariness" Rank
Fruit	Apple	429	1.3	Vehicle	Car	407	1.0
	Plum	167	2.3		Boat	145	2.7
	Pineapple	98	2.3		Scooter	99	2.5
	Strawberry	58	2.3		Tricycle	43	3.5
	Fig	16	4.7		Horse	14	5.9
	Olive	3	6.2		Skis	3	5.7
Science	Chemistry	367	1.0	Crime	Murder	387	1.0
	Botany	242	1.7		Assault	132	1.4
	Geology	76	2.6		Stealing	95	1.3
	Sociology	46	4.6		Embezzling	40	1.8
	Anatomy	19	1.7		Blackmail	16	1.7
	History	3	5.9		Vagrancy	3	5.3
Sport	Football	396	1.2	Disease	Cancer	316	1.2
	Hockey	130	1.8		Measles	168	2.8
	Wrestling	87	3.0		Cold	90	4.7
	Archery	49	3.9		Malaria	54	1.4
	Gymnastics	16	2.6		Muscular dystrophy	15	1.9
	Weight lifting	3	4.7		Rheumatism	3	3.5
Bird	Robin	377	1.1	Vegetable	Carrot	316	1.1
	Eagle	161	1.2		Asparagus	138	1.3
	Wren	83	1.4		Celery	96	1.7
	Chicken	40	3.8		Onion	47	2.7
	Ostrich	17	3.3		Parsley	15	3.8
	Bat	3	5.8		Pickle	2	4.4

[a]Frequency with which the member was listed in response to the category name from Battig and Montague 1969.

experiment 3) asked over 100 subjects to rank members of eight assorted categories with regard to typicality or exemplariness. Table 10.1 gives these categories, their members, and their ranking.

On the basis of these results and similar ones from other experiments, it is possible to see whether "typical" members of a category behave differently in thought from "atypical" members. For instance, Rosch (1973, experiment 4) constructed sentences such as (26a) and (26b) from the list in table 10.2:

(26)

a. A *doll* is a *toy*. (typical)

b. A *skate* is a *toy*. (atypical)

Subjects took significantly less time to judge a "typical" sentence true than an "atypical" sentence—they could decide that a doll is a toy faster than that a skate is a toy. This was found to be true not only for adults but also

Table 10.2
Categories and members used in reaction time experiment. (From Rosch 1973.)

Category	Member	
	Central	Peripheral
Toy	Doll	Skates
	Ball	Swing
Bird	Robin	Chicken
	Sparrow	Duck
Fruit	Pear	Strawberry
	Banana	Prune
Sickness	Cancer	Rheumatism
	Measles	Rickets
Relative	Aunt	Wife
	Uncle	Daughter
Metal	Copper	Magnesium
	Aluminum	Platinum
Crime	Rape	Treason
	Robbery	Fraud
Sport	Baseball	Fishing
	Basketball	Diving
Vehicle	Car	Tank
	Bus	Carriage
Science	Chemistry	Medicine
	Physics	Engineering
Vegetable	Carrot	Onion
	Spinach	Mushroom
Part of the body	Arm	Lips
	Leg	Skin

Table 10.3
Feature listings for 12 concepts. (Adapted from Smith and Medin 1981.)

| Features | Bird | | | | |
	Bluebird	Chicken	Falcon	Flamingo	Owl
Eats fish	0	0	0	0	0
Flies	12	0	7	0	0
Ugly	0	0	0	0	0
Eats insects	9	0	0	0	0
Eats dead	0	0	0	0	0
Is food	0	17	0	0	0
Pink	0	0	0	23	0
Stands on one leg	0	0	0	13	0
Says "who"	0	0	0	0	24
Tuxedo	0	0	0	0	0

for children. Moreover, these results have proved quite reliable in many such experiments using a wide variety of materials.

Typical versus atypical members of a class tend to be (1) more likely categorized correctly, (2) learned first by children, (3) recalled first from memory, (4) more likely to serve as cognitive reference points (for instance, an ellipse is judged "almost" a circle, rather than a circle being judged "almost an ellipse"), and (5) likely to share more characteristics and so have a high "family resemblance." These results (see Smith and Medin 1981 for a good survey) are generally thought to imply that concepts are structured in ways incompatible with the traditional view. In particular, on the traditional view component concepts are *equally* and *exhaustively defining*. Thus, the component concepts that define BIRD are all necessary for something to be correctly categorized BIRD. And if something is correctly represented as falling under all of the defining concepts, then it is correctly categorized BIRD. Yet when features of concepts for various birds are actually evoked from subjects (see table 10.3), it is clear that a trivial feature such as "says 'who'" can be sufficient to pick out one bird (an owl), and that no feature is necessary for all birds.

New Theories: Prototypes and Fuzzy Concepts   These experimental findings have evoked a variety of responses. Some theorists (see Miller and Johnson-Laird 1976) have attempted to revise the traditional view by distinguishing a conceptual *core* of defining concepts from an *identification procedure* sensitive to typicality characteristics.

Other theorists (Smith, Shoben, and Rips 1974) have moved to a *probabilistic* model of concepts. On this view, component concepts are given a

Bird						
Penguin	Robin	Sandpiper	Seagull	Starling	Swallow	Vulture
11	0	0	18	0	0	0
0	9	5	9	6	7	2
0	0	0	0	0	0	15
0	20	8	0	4	5	0
0	0	0	0	0	0	22
0	0	0	0	0	0	0
0	0	0	0	0	0	0
0	0	0	0	0	0	0
0	0	0	0	0	0	0
11	0	0	0	0	0	0

Table 10.4
The probabilistic view: Featural approach. (See Smith and Medin 1981.)

Robin	Chicken	Bird	Animal
1.0 moves	1.0 moves	1.0 moves	1.0 moves
1.0 winged	1.0 winged	1.0 winged	.7 walks
1.0 feathered	1.0 feathered	1.0 feathered	.5 large size
1.0 flies	1.0 walks	.8 flies	
.9 sings	.7 medium size	.6 sings	
.7 small size		.5 small size	

certain probability of applying correctly, as shown in table 10.4. An object is categorized as (for instance) a robin rather than a chicken if it reaches some critical sum of probabilities.

Still others (Rosch and Mervis 1975) have proposed a *prototype* or *exemplar* model of concepts, wherein concepts are structured around descriptions or images of typical/focal instances of the concept. As Rosch and Mervis (1975, 112) put it, "Categories are composed of a 'core meaning' which consists of the 'clearest cases' (best examples) of the category, 'surrounded' by other category members of decreasing similarity to that core meaning."

None of these theories has been worked out to the point where it can be evaluated in detail, though all can handle the typicality effects. Unfortunately, each new theory has difficulties at present. Of particular interest and concern is the apparent failure of probabilistic and exemplar models to provide a general account of *phrasal* concepts. What, for instance, is the exemplar for the concept GRANDMOTHER LIVING IN A LARGE AMERICAN CITY or PET FISH? Without such an exemplar

we do not have a concept and without a concept, no meaning. But surely the associated phrases do have meaning, and we do have such concepts (see Fodor 1981).

Versions of the prototype theory have encountered both experimental and theoretical problems. Armstrong, Gleitman, and Gleitman (1983) ran a series of "typicality" experiments that seem to show that subjects respond to such well-defined concepts as "even number," "odd number," and "plane geometry figure" with the same graded responses that Rosch found for notions like "sport" and "bird." A sample of their results is shown in table 10.5. Clearly, it makes no sense to structure the concept of an *even number* around the number 2 rather than 6, because there is no numerical difference in their "evenness." If some numbers were "more even than others," then balancing a checkbook would be a lot harder than it already is. (How would you add, subtract, and divide by both very even numbers and not-so-even numbers?) As Armstrong, Gleitman, and Gleitman comment, "What they [these results] do suggest is that we are back at square one in discovering the structure of everyday categories *experimentally...* the study of conceptual structure has not been put on an experimental footing, and the structure of those concepts studied by current techniques remains unknown."

Furthermore, Osherson and Smith (1981) have shown that prototype models yield counterintuitive conceptual and semantic results when combined with *fuzzy set* theories. In fuzzy set theory (Zadeh 1965), objects belong to a set *to a certain extent*, and the notion of set membership is a *graded* notion. Thus, Rover's membership in the class of dogs might be .85, and his membership in the class of females might be .10 (he might have some female characteristics).

The problem for conceptual combination arises when we look at the principles for combining fuzzy sets. For instance, the rule for conjunction (intersection) says that the membership of the resulting conjoined set is equal to the *lower* membership rating of the component sets or classes C_1 and C_2:

(27)
Rule for &
Membership of $(C_1 \ \& \ C_2)$ = lower of C_1, C_2.

Thus, Rover's membership rating in the combined class of FEMALE DOGS is .10, since his membership in FEMALE is .10, and that is the lower of the two.

Table 10.5
Categories, category exemplars, and exemplariness ratings for prototype and well-defined categories. Under each category label, category exemplars and mean exemplariness ratings are displayed (N = 32). (Adapted from Armstrong, Gleitman, and Gleitman 1983.)

Category	Exemplar	Exemplariness Rating	Category	Exemplar	Exemplariness Rating
Even number			Female		
Group A	4	1.1	Group A	Mother	1.7
	8	1.5		Housewife	2.4
	10	1.7		Princess	3.0
	18	2.6		Waitress	3.2
	34	3.4		Policewoman	3.9
	106	3.9		Comedienne	4.5
Group B	2	1.0	Group B	Sister	1.8
	6	1.7		Ballerina	2.0
	42	2.6		Actress	2.1
	1000	2.8		Hostess	2.7
	34	3.1		Chairwoman	3.4
	806	3.9		Cowgirl	4.5
Odd number			Plane geometry figure		
Group A	3	1.6	Group A	Square	1.3
	7	1.9		Triangle	1.5
	23	2.4		Rectangle	1.9
	57	2.6		Circle	2.1
	501	3.5		Trapezoid	3.1
	447	3.7		Ellipse	3.4
Group B	7	1.4	Group B	Square	1.5
	11	1.7		Triangle	1.4
	13	1.8		Rectangle	1.6
	9	1.9		Circle	1.3
	57	3.4		Trapezoid	2.9
	91	3.7		Ellipse	3.5

But this rule for conjunction is problematic with any concept whose intuitive prototype rating is *greater* for the conjoined concepts than for the minimal one. Thus, a guppy is low on typicality for fish and low on typicality for pets, but it is relatively high on typicality for the conjoined concept PET FISH, thus contradicting the rule for conjoining fuzzy sets. Similar examples can be found for other rules of fuzzy set theory as well. In the words of Osherson and Smith (1981, 55):

Amalgamation of any of a number of current versions of prototype theory with Zadeh's. . .fuzzy set theory will not handle strong intuitions about the way concepts combine to form complex concepts and propositions. This is an important failing because the ability to construct thoughts and complex concepts out of some basic stock of concepts seems to lie near the heart of human mentation.

More recently Smith and Osherson (1984) have proposed an alternative account of conceptual combination with prototype concepts that conforms to experimental results on typicality judgments of conjoined concepts.

We have concentrated on the representation of lexical meaning because in general that is currently an area of intense study. But as can be seen from our discussion, much work needs to be done before we have a theory of concepts that is adequate as an account of word meaning. In particular, such an account must (1) relate to categorization, typicality effects, and so forth, (2) relate to how words apply to objects and events in the world, and (3) relate to how words and concepts can combine to form more complex expressions, concepts, and thoughts.

Sentence Meaning

In chapter 6 we saw that at the sentence level, there seem to be two main types of semantic information: information regarding the *communicative force* of literal utterances of the sentence (assertion, question, command, and so on), and information regarding the *conditions that satisfy* the sentence, make it true, answered, obeyed, and so on. We also explored various semantic relations, such as entailment, contradiction, and presupposition. There have been a number of studies on particular aspects of sentence-level processing, but there is still no single theory of phenomena at this level. In what follows we will just sample some relevant recent work.

Presupposition and Given-New Information   We noted in chapter 9 that it may be helpful for a speaker to distinguish information that is presupposed, unfocused, or *given*, from information that is asserted, focused, or *new*. Languages make available a number of different devices that can be used to mark this distinction. English speakers often use the definite article (*the*), passive voice, repeating adverbs (*again*), cleft constructions, and various topicalization constructions to make the focus of their thoughts clear:

(28)

a. *The* boy came for the money.

b. A boy came for the money.

(29)

a. Sam *was* met at the airport *by* a friend of ours.

b. A friend of ours met Sam at the airport.

(30)

a. This Christmas Eugene got drunk *again*.

b. This Christmas Eugene got drunk.

(31)

a. *It was* Eugene *who* got drunk at Christmas.

b. *What* Eugene *did was to* get drunk at Christmas.

c. *As for* Eugene, *he* got drunk at Christmas.

d. Eugene got drunk at Christmas.

Thus, in (28a) the speaker may take the identity of the boy as known. In (29a) Sam is already the focus or a topic of conversation. In (30a) it is assumed that Eugene has been drunk at Christmas before. In (31a) it is assumed that someone got drunk at Christmas. In (31b) it is assumed that Eugene did something. And in (31c) Eugene is the focus or a topic of conversation.

On the basis of such examples, Haviland and Clark (1974) have proposed that speakers and hearers share the Given-New Strategy:

(32)

Given-New Strategy

(GN1)

Divide the sentence into given and new information.

(GN2)

Match the given information in memory.

(GN3)

Integrate new information into memory.

Experimental evidence in fact exists for something like the Given-New Strategy. For instance, Haviland and Clark (1974) report a sequence of experiments designed to test step (GN2). Subjects were given sentences such as (33)–(35):

(33)

a. Last Christmas Eugene became absolutely smashed.

b. This Christmas he got very drunk again. (984 milliseconds)

(34)

a. Last Christmas Eugene went to a lot of parties.

b. This Christmas he got very drunk again. (1040 milliseconds)

(35)

a. Last Christmas Eugene couldn't stay sober.

b. This Christmas he got very drunk again. (1063 milliseconds)

In the first example, the context sentence (33a) provides an appropriate antecedent for *again* in sentence (33b), and the match at step (GN2) should be quite direct. In the second example, the context sentence (34a) provides only the basis for an inference to an appropriate match, so step (GN2) should be less directly or immediately carried out. In example (35), the context sentence specifies the appropriate condition negatively; an inference involving negation is required and thus (35) is also less direct than (33). The average amount of time that elapsed between the subjects' beginning to read the second sentence and their understanding it is given in parentheses for each case. These figures confirm the plausibility of step (GN2) of the strategy.

Nonliteral Communication   Research on the development of linguistic abilities suggests that children up to the age of about 10 have considerable difficulty giving the figurative meaning of even the most common proverbs (Richardson and Church 1959). Since these children obviously have their literal linguistic abilities, we might suppose that understanding novel non-literality is an additional layer of processing and as such takes additional time, even in adults.

Unfortunately, the situation is very unclear at the moment. Brewer, Harris, and Brewer (1974, 3) did find evidence that "unfamiliar proverbs are understood in two sequentially ordered steps, with comprehension of the literal level of meaning preceding comprehension of the figurative level." On the other hand, Gibbs (1986, 3) found evidence that "people do not need to process the literal meaning of sarcastic expressions ... before deriving their nonliteral sarcastic interpretations." In one experiment subjects were given sentences such as *You're a big help* at the end of passages that would lead one to interpret them either just literally or sarcastically, and it took them about the same amount of time to identify each. In another experiment, subjects' memory for sarcastic occurrences of the same expressions used in the first study was superior to their memory for literal occurrences. These results are suggestive, but because the tasks the subjects were asked to perform in these experiments were so distantly related to the processes of comprehension they are supposed to inform us about, we must be hesitant about drawing processing conclusions here.

Indirection and Politeness As noted in chapter 9, when we speak indirectly, we mean more than we say, and we expect our audience to infer what we mean on the basis of what we have said plus contextual information. Is there any experimental evidence for such processes?

Some evidence for inferential strategies in comprehension comes from work on politeness. After all, one of the main reasons for indirection is either to be polite, to avoid being rude, or to show deference and respect. Unfortunately, the notion of politeness is not all that clear, and to use it as an experimental tool requires that it be made precise. Clark and Schunk (1980) proposed to treat requests as polite to the extent that the *cost* to the hearer of complying with the request goes *down* and/or the *benefits* to the hearer go *up*. On the hearer's side, Clark and Schunk suggest the Attentiveness Hypothesis:

(36)
Attentiveness Hypothesis
The more attentive the hearer is to all aspects of the speaker's remark, within limits, the more polite it is.

Subjects were asked in a pair of experiments to rate various indirect requests, such as (37a–c), and various possible replies, such as (38a–c), for politeness:

(37)
a. May I ask you where Jordan Hall is?
b. Do you know where Jordan Hall is?
c. Do you want to tell me where Jordan Hall is?

(38)
a. Certainly, it's around the corner.
b. It's around the corner.
c. No.

It was found that the Attentiveness Hypothesis could account for a significant amount of the correlation in these rankings, and to that extent these experiments support the view that the literal meaning is being processed in such cases.

Of course, a hearer need not always wait until the end of a sentence to figure out that it is being used indirectly. Prior context can bias the hearer in favor of *expecting* indirect communication. In a pair of experiments, Gibbs (1979) gave subjects sentences such as *Must you open the window?* embedded in two different contexts—one that biased the interpretation toward the literal meaning, and one that biased the interpretation toward the indirect message:

(39)

Literal context: Mrs. Smith was watering her garden one afternoon. She saw that the housepainter was pushing a window open. She didn't understand why he needed to have it open. A bit worried, she went over and politely asked, "Must you open the window?"
Paraphrase: "Need you open the window?"

(40)

Indirect context: One morning John felt too sick to go to school. The night before he and his friends had gotten very drunk. Then they had gone surfing without their wetsuits. Because of this he caught a bad cold. He was lying in bed when his mother stormed in. When she started to open the window, John groaned, "Must you open the window?"
Paraphrase: "Do not open the window."

Subjects were to judge whether the paraphrase was true or false. It was found that subjects took less or equal time to judge the indirect interpretations in context compared to the time they took to judge the literal ones. How could this be if the literal meaning is computed first?

Conclusion

This completes our brief survey of some of the main areas of current work on the psychology of language. We have followed the flow of information from thoughts to sounds (see Levelt 1989 for a comprehensive survey), from sounds to words, phrases, and sentences, and from sentences to the communicative intentions of speakers. Along the way we have found not only different ideas about the right answers to crucial questions but also huge gaps in current understanding of them. The psychology of language has all the signs of being a vital and active area of scientific research.

10.4 SPECIAL TOPICS

The following topics do not fit naturally into the preceding survey of psycholinguistics, but they are interesting areas of research and have important consequences for the field.

The McGurk Effect

In 1976 McGurk and McDonald reported a short but striking experiment on the sort of stimuli that can switch on the language processor. In this experiment a videotape was made of a woman uttering various syllables such as *ba-ba* and *ga-ga*. The sound track was then spliced onto the visual track so that, for each syllable, viewers saw the woman saying one syllable, but they heard her saying a different one. These tapes were then shown to 21 preschool children (3–4 years), 28 elementary school children (7–8 years), and 54 adults (18–40 years). The subjects heard the sound track by itself, saw and heard the audiovisual combination, and in each case were asked to repeat what they heard.

Subjects were quite accurate when listening to the sound track alone: preschool children 91 percent, elementary school children 97 percent, and adults 99 percent. But for the audiovisual combination the error rate was high, and the interaction of the audio and the visual components was quite interesting. The left-hand columns of table 10.6 list the various possible auditory and visual stimuli, and the right-hand columns list the various responses subjects gave to what they thought they heard. The percentages of these responses for the different age groups are given in table 10.7. Of particular interest are the "fused" responses, where the subject hears a speech sound that is not on the audio portion of the tape. The experienced

Table 10.6
Stimulus conditions and definition of response categories from auditory-visual condition. (From McGurk and McDonald 1976.)

Stimuli Auditory component	Visual component	Response categories Auditory	Visual	Fused	Combination	Other
ba-ba	ga-ga	ba-ba	ga-ga	da-da	—	—
ga-ga	ba-ba	ga-ga	ba-ba	da-da	gabga bagba baga gaba	dabda gagla etc.
pa-pa	ka-ka	pa-pa	ka-ka	ta-ta	—	tapa pta kafta etc.
ka-ka	pa-pa	ka-ka	pa-pa	—	kapka pakpa paka kapa	kat kafa kakpat etc.

Table 10.7
Percentage of responses in each category in the auditory-visual condition. (From McGurk and McDonald 1976.)

Stimuli			Responses				
Auditory	Visual	Subjects	Auditory	Visual	Fused	Combination	Other
ba-ba	ga-ga	3–5 yr (n = 21)	19	0	81	0	0
		7–8 yr (n = 28)	36	0	64	0	0
		18–40 yr (n = 54)	2	0	98	0	0
ga-ga	ba-ba	3–5 yr (n = 21)	57	10	0	19	14
		7–8 yr (n = 28)	36	21	11	32	0
		18–40 yr (n = 54)	11	31	0	54	4
pa-pa	ka-ka	3–5 yr (n = 21)	24	0	52	0	24
		7–8 yr (n = 28)	50	0	50	0	0
		18–40 yr (n = 54)	6	7	81	0	6
ka-ka	pa-pa	3–5 yr (n = 21)	62	9	0	5	24
		7–8 yr (n = 28)	68	0	0	32	0
		18–40 yr (n = 54)	13	37	0	44	6

sound seems to arise from the interaction of the visual and auditory systems. As anyone who has experienced the "McGurk effect" will testify, it is quite disorienting to change what you hear by opening and closing your eyes—to watch a tape of someone speaking a familiar sound, close your eyes and hear a different sound, then open your eyes and hear the original sound again! And these effects do not disappear even after the subject has seen and heard hundreds of tapes. It is also interesting that adults tend to be more influenced by the visual input than younger subjects. Subsequent work has broadened researchers' knowledge of these effects and how they are produced, but many aspects of the McGurk effect are still not understood (see Summerfield 1987 for a survey).

Open and Closed Class Items

Many processes we have been discussing seem to be sensitive to the distinction drawn in chapter 2 between two kinds of words and morphemes: open class items and closed class items:

(41)

Open class items	*Closed class items*
(content words)	(function words)
Major Categories	Minor Categories
nouns	auxiliaries
verbs	pronouns
adjectives	conjunctions
	determiners
	pronouns
	prepositions

Open and closed class items differ in several ways. (1) As noted in chapter 2, open class items are typically words belonging to categories that can and are frequently added to over time (hence "open"), whereas closed class items belong to categories that are rarely added to (hence relatively "closed" over time). (2) Open class items have explicit *descriptive* content, whereas closed class items help define the syntactic *structure* of the expressions they are a part of. This makes the distinction potentially important to any process that is sensitive to such structure. (3) Educated speakers of English know about 75,000 open class items, but there are only about 200 closed class items. (4) Closed class items have fewer syntactic category ambiguities (such as the noun-verb ambiguity of *jump*) than open class items. (5) Closed class items average much higher frequencies of occurrence than open class items. (6) Closed class items take contrastive, but not sentential, stress.

As we might expect, these differences have certain consequences for processing; we will look at two of them. First, the processing consequences of the open class/closed class distinction show up in speech errors. In general, open class items occur often in exchange errors but rarely in shift errors, whereas closed class items occur rarely in exchanges but often in shift errors. It is interesting and important to note that inflectional affixes pattern like closed class items. Thus, exchanges have been observed in which endings are stranded as in (42a), but not as in (42b):

(42)
a.   She's already <u>trunk</u>ed two <u>pack</u>s.
b.   *She's already <u>pack</u>s two <u>trunk</u>ed.

Second, recall that the time needed to recognize a word decreases sharply as its frequency of occurrence increases. However, this does not seem to hold for closed class items (see Bradley, Garrett, and Zurif 1982; but see also Gordon and Caramazza 1982).

These results extend to another finding. A nonword beginning with an open class word (such as *glasset*) is recognized as a nonword more slowly than a comparable item beginning with a sequence that is not a word (such as *slasset*). However, if the word occurs at the end of the nonword (such as *teglass*), then recognition time is the same as that for nonwords. The recognition system works from left to right; when it hits a part of a nonword that is a word, it is fooled momentarily into thinking it has found a word, and it needs extra time to recover from this interference. Interestingly, none of this seems to be true of closed class items. Nonwords with closed class initial segments (such as *inslet*) are not significantly harder to recognize than nonwords with initial segments that are also nonwords (such as *enslet*). This indicates that sentence processing seems to be sensitive in various surprising ways to the open versus closed class distinction, a distinction drawn in morphology on linguistic grounds.

The Psychological Reality of Empty Categories

Certain experimental work indicates that linguistic categories might be psychologically real. To understand the following experiment, recall that a word like *doctor* primes recognition of a word like *nurse*. This technique of activating one item by means of previously activating semantically related items is called *semantic priming*. Recall that there are other varieties of priming as well. For instance, *APPLE* primes *apple* (font), *hair* primes *bare* (sound), *bribe* primes *tribe* (spelling), and a word primes itself (repetition priming).

We can now describe the experiment on empty categories using priming. In a sentence such as (43), what is the object of the verb *control*? (The expression [e] will be explained shortly.)

(43)
The astute lawyer was hard for the judge to control [e] during the very long trial.

Who was hard for the judge to control during the trial? Clearly it was *the astute lawyer*. But how could that phrase be the object of *control* in (43)? It is not even in object position—it is at the beginning of the sentence, separated from *control* by intervening words. Various current theories claim that there really *is* a syntactic object after *control*; however, this element is not pronounced and is therefore phonologically "empty." Hence, it constitutes an *empty category*, symbolized in some cases as [*e*] and in others as [PRO] (see Chomsky 1981). Here the empty category is the object of *control*. This category, in its location after *control*, is also semantically linked to the meaning of *the astute lawyer*. Bever and McElree (1988) argue that if the semantic information is there, then the location after *control* should show priming effects for semantically related words, and it does. In Bever and McElree's experiments subjects first read sentences such as these:

(44)
The astute lawyer who faced the female judge hated the long speech during the trial. (nonanaphor construction)

(45)
The astute lawyer who faced the female judge hoped he would speak during the trial. (pronoun construction)

Probe: *astute*

At the end of each sentence there was a probe word (such as *astute*). The subject had to decide whether it occurred in the sentence or not. The amount of time subjects took was measured, as well as the number of errors they made. The results, displayed in table 10.8, suggest that the task was sensitive to the presence of the anaphoric pronoun *he* in (45). The technique was then extended to sentences without explicit pronouns, but with gaps and empty categories that access their antecedents in the same way:

Table 10.8
Response times (seconds) to recognize that the probe word was in the preceding
sentence (error response times are not included in the mean reaction times). %
error rates are in (parentheses); % subjects with at least 1 error on a given
construction are in [brackets]. (From Bever and McElree 1988.)

Experiment	1		
Nonanaphor (type [(44)])	1.05	(12)	[43]
Pronoun (type [(45)])	0.93	(6)	[33]
PRO (type [(46)])	0.96	(15)	[50]
NP-raising (type [(47)])	0.92	(7)	[27]
Tough-movement (type [(48)])	0.87	(7)	[27]

(46)
The astute lawyer who faced the female judge strongly hoped [PRO] to
argue during the trial. (PRO construction)

(47)
The astute lawyer who faced the female judge was certain [e] to argue
during the trial. (NP-raising construction)

(48)
The astute lawyer was hard for the judge to control [e] during the very long
trial. (*tough*-movement construction)

Again, the results indicate that these elements are processed just as overt
pronouns are. Decision times and error rates are both significantly better
than for the control sentence (44). Thus, the linguistic evidence and the psycholinguistic evidence converge on the same analysis of these sentences.

Connectionist Models of Lexical Access and Letter Recognition

The idea that cognition is computation has suggested to some that we are
cognitively organized like a normal production line computer. Neuroscience, on the other hand, seems to suggest a rather different organization.
In recent years this second, *connectionist* trend has been gaining popularity
as a framework within which to pursue a wide variety of psychological
studies, including work on language processing (see Rumelhart, McClelland, and the PDP Research Group 1986). The reason for this increase in
popularity is twofold: dissatisfaction with traditional models, and discovery of the virtues of the new models (see Churchland and Sejnowski
1989).

One of the striking facts about current attempts to program computers
to do "intelligent" tasks (tasks we would say require intelligence in a

Table 10.9
People versus computers: strengths and weaknesses

	Well	Badly
Computer	extended logical and arithmetic reasoning	pattern recognition (language, vision) motor coordination spontaneous generalization learning
People	pattern recognition (language and vision) motor coordination spontaneous generalization learning	extended logical and arithmetic reasoning

human) is the complementarity between what computers do well or badly and what brains do well or badly (see table 10.9). Why such a disparity? Partisans of traditional views on artificial intelligence claim that bigger, faster machines and better programming techniques will eventually erase the difference. Critics think the problem runs deeper: that the brain's architecture is simply different from that of standard computers. After all, unlike technological computation, biological computation has been around for millions of years and has evolved its architecture to deal with problems posed by our environment. Perhaps it is this difference in architecture that accounts for the complementary differences in abilities. Connectionists often describe their models as brainlike, but there is no claim that they exactly model the known behavior of networks of neurons (see Smolensky 1988, 1989).

Connectionist Models

At its simplest a connectionist model consists of a collection of *units* or *nodes* that can have varying degrees of *activation*, say between 0 and 1. These units are *connected* to other units in a *network*. Each connection has a certain *weight* or *strength*. When a node is activated, it *passes activation* to the nodes it is connected to according to the strength of those connections. This activation can be either *excitatory* (causes other nodes to become more active) or *inhibitory* (causes other nodes to become less active). Connectionist networks can *learn* by changing the strength of the connections between different nodes.

There are a wide variety of possibilities in assembling a network. How highly activated must a node be to fire? Which nodes are connected to which nodes? Are they excitatory or inhibitory? How does the system represent its environment? How is its output to be interpreted? How does the system learn from experience? We will look first at a sample connectionist network and then at the virtues of such networks and the problems that they pose.

In a pair of influential papers McClelland and Rumelhart proposed a connectionist model of letter recognition in four-letter words and defended its psychological plausibility (see McClelland and Rumelhart 1981, Rumelhart and McClelland 1982). By investigating its structure and operation in some detail, we can get a feel for how connectionist models work in general. Consider the fragment of the network shown in figure 10.8. This device operates at three levels: the feature level, at which nodes represent parts of letters; the letter level, at which nodes represent parts of words (that is, letters); and the word level, at which nodes represent words. The feature level can excite or inhibit letters at the letter level, and these can in turn excite or inhibit words at the word level—and be excited or inhibited by them.

Suppose we present the letter T to the network. T is made up of the features ⎯ and |, so it will activate the first two feature detectors. Notice that *these and only these* feature-detecting nodes excite the T-node at the

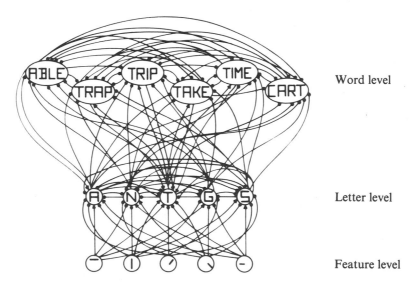

Figure 10.8
A connectionist model of letter recognition. Excitatory connections are symbolized by arrowheads and inhibitory connections by dots. (From McClelland and Rumelhart 1981.)

letter level. The remaining features *inhibit* the other letter nodes. Thus, only the T-node is activated by a *T*. Activating the T-node also partially excites the words beginning with a *T*, such as TAKE, but it inhibits other words (remember this is just a fragment of the network). The system *recognizes* a letter (or word) when (1) it settles down into a stable pattern and (2) a particular node is activated above the proper threshold.

McClelland and Rumelhart were able to show that the behavior of this model conforms to many experimental results in word recognition. Consider the so-called word superiority effect reviewed earlier: letters are recognized faster and more reliably in the context of words than alone or in nonword letter strings. The model accounts for this because as the letters for (say) TAKE are recognized, more and more activation builds up on the TAKE-node and it passes this activation back to its constituent letter nodes (look at the network again). This is a kind of priming that facilitates the recognition of these letters, resulting in the word superiority effect.

As this simple example indicates, and as summarized in table 10.10, connectionist models can have some very different properties from standard computational models. Probably the basic difference is this: standard machines compute by executing a program on symbolic structures (both stored in memory) in a serial fashion, whereas connectionist machines compute via the simultaneous interactivation of many connected nodes, each of which passes on only very limited information.

Table 10.10
A comparison of standard computer models and connectionist models

STRUCTURAL DIFFERENCES	
Standard Computer Models	Connectionist Models
Fast (billionths of a second)	Slow (hundredths of a second)
Few components	Many components ($= 10^{11}$)
Few connections in all	Many connections in all ($= 10^{15}$)
Few connections per unit ($= 10$s)	Many connections per unit ($= 10^4$)
Location-addressable memory	Content-addressable memory

FUNCTIONAL DIFFERENCES	
Standard Computer Models	Connectionist Models
Described by algorithms	Described by differential equations
Serial processing	Parallel processing
Brittle, fault-intolerant	Gracefully degrading
Sensitive to noise	Tolerant of noise
Do not learn, generalize, or extract central tendencies naturally	Learn, generalize, and extract central tendencies naturally

In spite of the obvious virtues of connectionist models, doubts and open questions abound in the literature. There are two kinds of criticism. First, concerning connectionist models in general, Fodor and Pylyshyn (1988) argue that much of cognition involves a languagelike representation system—a language of thought—and they claim that connectionism offers no way of accounting for the compositionality of thought (for a reply, see Smolensky 1987). Second, concerning specific models, especially of language, Rumelhart and McClelland (1986) argue that a connectionist model can learn the past tense of English verbs in the way children learn them, without being given or learning any linguistic rules. However, Pinker and Prince (1988) and Lachter and Bever (1988) argue that the model only appears to do this: that linguistic information was actually built in and that the training program was unnatural. By consulting the references in this section, you can decide for yourself whether connectionism is an exciting new prospect or just old associationism in new clothing.

Study Questions

1. What is the competence versus performance distinction? Discuss.

2. What methodological problems arise in the study of speech production?

3. What might researchers do to ensure that speech errors recorded in their collections are genuine?

4. What are the main properties of input systems?

5. What is the "phoneme restoration effect"? What are its implications for modularity? Discuss.

6. What is the function of input systems? Does language serve this function? Discuss.

7. What are two main experimental tasks used in lexical access studies?

8. What are five basic findings in the study of lexical access?

9. Describe Forster's "search model" of word recognition. How might it account for the five basic findings? Discuss.

10. What evidence is there that hearers normally process (subconsciously) all of the meanings of an expression that they know? How does this relate to modularity? Discuss.

11. What are some experimental results that might pose a problem for modularity? Discuss.

12. What is the traditional doctrine of concepts?

13. What problems does the traditional doctrine have? Discuss.

14. What new theory has developed concerning the structure of concepts? How does it deal with the problems of the traditional theory? Discuss.

15. What are some problems with this new view of concepts? Discuss.

16. What are the major conclusions concerning the psychological mechanisms underlying successful nonliteral and indirect communication? Discuss.

17. What is the McGurk effect? What implications does it have for modularity? Discuss.

18. What is the distinction between open and closed class items? What implications does this distinction have for language processing?

19. What evidence is there that unspoken words or phrases may still be constituents of a sentence, in some sense?

20. Can the connectionist letter recognition model as presented in the text account for how (for example) *doctor* might semantically prime *nurse*? Discuss.

21. What are the strengths and weaknesses of traditional models of mental capacities and connectionist models of mental capacities?

Bibliography and Further Reading

Armstrong, S., L. Gleitman, and H. Gleitman (1983). On what some concepts might not be. *Cognition* 13, 263–308.

Battig, W., and W. Montague (1969). Category norms for verbal items in 56 categories: A replication and extension of the Connecticut category norms. *Journal of Experimental Psychology* 80 (Monograph Supplement 3, Part 2).

Bever, T. (1970). The cognitive basis for linguistic structures. In J. Hayes, ed., *Cognition and the development of language*. New York: Wiley.

Bever, T., M. Garrett, and R. Hurtig (1973). The interaction of perceptual processes and ambiguous sentences. *Memory and Cognition* 1, 277–286.

Bever, T., and B. McElree (1988). Empty categories access their antecedents during comprehension. *Linguistic Inquiry* 19, 35–43.

Bock, K., and H. Loebell (1988). Framing sentences. Ms., Michigan State University.

Bradley, D., M. Garrett, and E. Zurif (1982). Syntactic deficits in Broca's aphasia. In D. Caplan, ed., *Biological studies of mental processes*. Cambridge, Mass.: MIT Press.

Brewer, W., R. Harris, and E. Brewer (1974). Comprehension of literal and figurative meaning. Paper presented at the meeting of the Midwestern Psychological Association.

Brown, F., and S. Levinson (1978). Universals in language usage: Politeness phenomena. In E. Goody, ed., *Questions and politeness*. Cambridge: Cambridge University Press.

Butterworth, B., ed. (1980). *Language production*, vol. 1. New York: Academic Press.

Chomsky, N. (1965). *Aspects of the theory of syntax*. Cambridge, Mass.: MIT Press.

Chomsky, N. (1972). *Language and mind*. Enlarged edition. New York: Harcourt Brace Jovanovich.

Chomsky, N. (1981). *Lectures on government and binding*. Dordrecht, Holland: Foris.

Churchland, P. S., and T. Sejnowski (1989). Neural representation and neural computation. In Nadel et al. 1989.

Clark, H., and E. Clark (1977). *Psychology and language*. New York: Harcourt Brace Jovanovich.

Clark, H., and D. Schunk (1980). Polite responses to polite requests. *Cognition* 8, 111–143.

Clifton, C., and F. Ferreira (1987). Modularity in sentence comprehension. In Garfield 1987.

Cooper, W., and E. Walker (1979). *Sentence processing: Psycholinguistic studies presented to Merrill Garrett*. Hillsdale, N.J.: L. Erlbaum Associates.

Crain, S., and M. S. Steedman (1985). On not being led up the garden path: The use of context of the psychological syntax parser. In D. Dowty, L. Karttunen, and A. Zwicky, eds., *Natural language parsing*. Cambridge: Cambridge University Press.

Cutler, A. (1982). The reliability of speech error data. In A. Cutler, ed., *Slips of the tongue*. The Hague: Mouton.

Dell, G., and P. Reich (1981). Stages in sentence production: An analysis of speech error data. *Journal of Verbal Learning and Verbal Behavior* 20, 611–629.

Fay, D., and A. Cutler (1977). Malapropisms and the structure of the mental lexicon. *Linguistic Inquiry* 8, 505–520.

Fishler, I., and P. Bloom (1979). Automatic and attentional processes in the effects of sentence contexts on word recognition. *Journal of Verbal Learning and Verbal Behavior* 18, 1–20.

Fodor, J. A. (1981). Current status of the innateness controversy. In *Representations*. Cambridge, Mass.: MIT Press.

Fodor, J. A. (1983). *The modularity of mind*. Cambridge, Mass.: MIT Press.

Fodor, J. A., T. Bever, and M. Garrett (1974). *The psychology of language*. New York: McGraw-Hill.

Fodor, J. A., M. Garrett, E. Walker, and C. Parkes (1980). Against definitions. *Cognition* 8, 263–367.

Fodor, J. A., and Z. Pylyshyn (1988). Connectionism and cognitive architecture. In Pinker and Mehler 1988.

Fodor, J. D., J. A. Fodor, and M. Garrett (1975). The psychological unreality of semantic representation. *Linguistic Inquiry* 6, 515–531.

Forster, K. (1978). Accessing the mental lexicon. In E. Walker, ed., *Explorations in the biology of language*. Cambridge, Mass.: MIT Press.

Forster, K. (1979). Levels of processing and the structure of the language processor. In Cooper and Walker 1979.

Forster, K. (1990). Lexical processing. In Osherson and Lasnik 1990.

Forster, K., and S. Chambers (1973). Lexical access and naming time. *Journal of Verbal Learning and Verbal Behavior* 12, 627–635.

Foss, D. (1969). Decision processes during sentence comprehension: Effects of lexical item difficulty and position upon decision times. *Journal of Verbal Learning and Verbal Behavior* 8, 457–462.

Foss, D., and D. Hakes (1978). *Psycholinguistics*. Englewood Cliffs, N.J.: Prentice-Hall.

Frauenfelder, U., and L. Tyler, eds. (1987). *Spoken word recognition*. Cambridge, Mass.: MIT Press.

Frazier, L. (1979). *On comprehending sentences*. Bloomington, Ind.: Indiana University Linguistics Club.

Frazier, L., and J. D. Fodor (1978). The sausage machine: A new two-stage parsing model. *Cognition* 6, 291–325.

Fromkin, V. (1973a). Slips of the tongue. *Scientific American*, 110–116.

Fromkin, V., ed. (1973b). *Speech errors as linguistic evidence*. The Hague: Mouton.

Garfield, J., ed. (1987). *Modularity in knowledge representation and natural language understanding*. Cambridge, Mass.: MIT Press.

Garnham, A. (1985). *Psycholinguistics: Central topics*. New York: Methuen.

Garrett, M. (1975). The analysis of sentence production. In G. Bower, ed., *The psychology of learning and motivation*. New York: Academic Press.

Garrett, M. (1980). Levels of processing in sentence production. In Butterworth 1980.

Garrett, M. (1990). Sentence processing. In Osherson and Lasnik 1990.

Gazdar, G. (1981). Speech act assignment. In A. Joshi et al., eds., *Elements of discourse understanding*. Cambridge: Cambridge University Press.

Gibbs, R. (1979). Contextual effects in understanding indirect requests. *Discourse Processes* 2, 1–10.

Gibbs, R. (1986). On the psycholinguistics of sarcasm. *Journal of Experimental Psychology: General* 115, 3–15.

Gordon, B., and A. Caramazza (1982). Lexical decision for open and closed class: Failure to replicate differential frequency sensitivity. *Brain and Language* 15, 143–160.

Grosjean, F., and J. Gee (1987). Prosodic structure and spoken word recognition. In Frauenfelder and Tyler 1987.

Harman, G. (1986). *Change in view*. Cambridge, Mass.: MIT Press.

Haviland, S., and H. Clark (1974). What's new? Acquiring new information as a process in comprehension. *Journal of Verbal Learning and Verbal Behavior* 13, 512–521.

Klima, E., and U. Bellugi (1979). *The signs of language*. Cambridge, Mass.: Harvard University Press.

Lachter, J., and T. Bever (1988). The relation between linguistic structure and associative theories of language acquisition: A constructive critique of some connectionist learning models. In Pinker and Mehler 1988.

Landau, B., and L. Gleitman (1985). *Language and experience: Evidence from the blind child*. Cambridge, Mass.: Harvard University Press.

Lehiste, I. (1973). Phonetic disambiguation of syntactic ambiguity. *Glossa* 7, 107–122.

Lesser, V., R. Fennel, L. Erman, and R. Reddy (1977). Organization of the Hearsay II speech understanding system. *IEEE Transactions*. ASSP 23, 11–23.

Levelt, W. (1989). *Speaking: From intention to articulation*. Cambridge, Mass.: MIT Press.

Liberman, A. M. (1970). The grammars of speech and language. *Cognitive Psychology* 1, 301–323.

Lieberman, P. (1966). *Intonation, perception, and language*. Cambridge, Mass.: MIT Press.

McClelland, J., and D. Rumelhart (1981). An interactive activation model of context effects in letter perception: Part 1. An account of basic findings. *Psychological Review* 88, 375–407.

McGurk, H., and J. McDonald (1976). Hearing lips and seeing voices. *Nature* 264, 746–748.

Marslen-Wilson, W. (1987). Functional parallelism in spoken word-recognition. In Frauenfelder and Tyler 1987.

Marslen-Wilson, W., and L. Tyler (1987). Against modularity. In Garfield 1987.

Meyer, D., and R. Schvaneveldt (1971). Facilitation in recognizing pairs of words: Evidence of a dependence between retrieval operations. *Journal of Experimental Psychology* 90, 227–234.

Miller, G., and P. Johnson-Laird (1976). *Language and perception*. Cambridge, Mass.: Harvard University Press.

Munro, A. (1979). Indirect speech acts are not strictly conventional. *Linguistic Inquiry* 10, 353–356.

Nadel, L., L. Cooper, P. Culicover, and R. Harnish, eds. (1989). *Neural connections, mental computation*. Cambridge, Mass.: MIT Press.

Neisser, U. (1967). *Cognitive psychology*. New York: Appleton-Century-Crofts.

Norris, D. (1986). Word recognition: Context effects without priming. *Cognition* 22, 93–136.

Osherson, D., and H. Lasnik, eds. (1990). *Language: An invitation to cognitive science, volume 1*. Cambridge, Mass.: MIT Press.

Osherson, D., and E. Smith (1981). On the adequacy of prototype theory as a theory of concepts. *Cognition* 9, 35–58.

Pinker, S., and J. Mehler, eds. (1988). *Connections and symbols*. Cambridge, Mass.: MIT Press.

Pinker, S., and A. Prince (1988). On language and connectionism: Analysis of a parallel distributed processing model of language acquisition. In Pinker and Mehler 1988.

Pisoni, D., and P. Luce (1987). Acoustic-phonetic representation in word recognition. In Frauenfelder and Tyler 1987.

Pollack, I., and J. Pickett (1963). The intelligibility of excerpts from conversation. *Language and Speech* 6, 165–171.

Rayner, K., M. Carlson, and L. Frazier (1983). The interaction of syntax and semantics during sentence processing: Eye movements in the analysis of semantically based sentences. *Journal of Verbal Learning and Verbal Behavior* 22, 358–374.

Reicher, G. (1969). Perceptual recognition as a function of the meaningfulness of the stimulus material. *Journal of Experimental Psychology* 81, 275–280.

Richardson, C., and J. Church (1959). A developmental analysis of proverb interpretations. *Journal of Genetic Psychology* 94, 169–179.

Rohrman, N., and P. Gough (1967). Forewarning, meaning and semantic decision latency. *Psychonomic Science* 9, 217–218.

Rosch, E. (1973). On the internal structure of perceptual and semantic categories. In T. Moore, ed., *Cognitive development and the acquisition of language*. New York: Academic Press.

Rosch, E., and C. Mervis (1975). Family resemblance studies in the internal structure of categories. *Cognitive Psychology* 7, 575–605.

Rumelhart, D., and J. McClelland (1982). An interactive activation model of context effects in letter perception: Part 2. The contextual enhancement effect and some tests and extensions of the model. *Psychological Review* 89, 60–94.

Rumelhart, D., and J. McClelland (1986). On learning the past tenses of English verbs. In Rumelhart, McClelland, and the PDP Research Group 1986.

Rumelhart, D., J. McClelland, and the PDP Research Group (1986). *Parallel distributed processing*. 2 vols. Cambridge, Mass.: MIT Press.

Scarborough, D. L., C. Cortese, and H. S. Scarborough (1977). Frequency and repetition effects in lexical memory. *Journal of Experimental Psychology: Human Perception and Performance* 3, 1–17.

Schatz, C. (1954). The role of context in the perception of stops. *Language* 30, 47–56.

Seidenberg, M., and M. Tanenhaus (1979). Orthographic effects on rhyme monitoring. *Journal of Experimental Psychology: Human Learning and Memory* 5, 546–554.

Seidenberg, M., and M. Tanenhaus (1986). Modularity and lexical access. In I. Gopnik and M. Gopnik, eds., *From models to modules*. Norwood, N.J.: Ablex.

Seidenberg, M., M. Tanenhaus, J. Leiman, and M. Bienkowski (1982). Automatic access of the meanings of ambiguous words in context. *Cognitive Psychology* 14, 489–537.

Shattuck-Hufnagel, S. (1979). Speech errors as evidence for a serial-ordering mechanism in sentence production. In Cooper and Walker 1979.

Smith, E., and D. Medin (1981). *Categories and concepts*. Cambridge, Mass.: Harvard University Press.

Smith, E., and D. Osherson (1984). Conceptual combination with prototype concepts. *Cognitive Science* 8, 337–361.

Smith, E., E. Shoben, and L. Rips (1974). Structure and process in semantic memory: A featural model for semantic decisions. *Psychological Review* 81, 214–241.

Smolensky, P. (1987). The constituent structure of connectionist mental states: A reply to Fodor and Pylyshyn. In T. Horgan and J. Tienson, eds., *Connectionism and the philosophy of mind*. Department of Philosophy, Memphis State University.

Smolensky, P. (1988). On the proper treatment of connectionism. *The Behavioral and Brain Sciences* 11, 1–74.

Smolensky, P. (1989). Connectionist modeling: Neural computation/mental connections. In Nadel et al. 1989.

Summerfield, Q. (1987). Some preliminaries to a comprehensive account of audiovisual speech perception. In B. Dodd and R. Campbell, eds., *Hearing by eye*. Hillsdale, N.J.: L. Erlbaum Associates.

Swinney, D. (1979). Lexical access during sentence comprehension: (Re)consideration of context effects. *Journal of Verbal Learning and Verbal Behavior* 18, 645–659.

Tanenhaus, M., J. Leiman, and M. Seidenberg (1979). Evidence for multiple stages in the processing of ambiguous words in syntactic contexts. *Journal of Verbal Learning and Verbal Behavior* 18, 427–440.

Wanner, E., and M. Maratsos (1978). An ATN approach to comprehension. In M. Halle, J. Bresnan, and G. Miller, eds., *Linguistic theory and psychological reality*. Cambridge, Mass.: MIT Press.

Warren, R. (1970). Perceptual restorations of missing speech sounds. *Science* 167, 392–393.

Zadeh, L. (1965). Fuzzy sets. *Information and Control* 8, 338–353.

LANGUAGE ACQUISITION IN CHILD AND CHIMP

Anyone concerned with the study of human nature and human capacities must somehow come to grips with the fact that all normal humans acquire language, whereas acquisition of even its barest rudiments is quite beyond the capacities of an otherwise intelligent ape.
—N. Chomsky, *Language and Mind*

The view expressed by Noam Chomsky reflects a traditional idea about human beings, namely, that they are distinct from all other animal species in possessing language. Indeed, if we examine the natural communication systems of animals and humans—natural in the sense that these systems develop spontaneously in a normal linguistic environment—we see a wide gulf between the relatively simple animal communication systems and human language. For example, if we compare monkey calls used in the wild with the elaborately structured sentences of human languages, it is evident that the two systems are strikingly different in complexity. Given the available evidence, it is reasonable to hypothesize that humans have a species-specific capacity to develop a "set of complex linguistic principles" typical of human language. In this sense humans can be said to have a biological (genetic) endowment that predisposes them to acquire and use human language. Thus, humans can be said to have a unique cognitive basis for language.

11.1 LANGUAGE ACQUISITION IN CHILDREN

Biological Innateness of the Linguistic Capacity and the Role of Instruction and Imitation in Child Language Development

One need only study a foreign language, or take a course in linguistics, to begin to appreciate the enormous complexity of human language. At every level—phonological, morphological, syntactic, semantic, and pragmatic—human language is an intricate system of abstract units, structures, and rules, used in a powerful system of communication. Once we appreciate the nature of language and the true depth of its complexity, we can also appreciate the remarkable, and in many ways fascinating, feat that children accomplish in mastering it so easily.

First of all, language development occurs in all children with normal brain function, regardless of race, culture, or general intelligence. In other words, the capacity to develop language is a capacity of the human species as a whole. Even though different groups of people speak different languages, all human languages have a similar level of detail and complexity, and all languages share general abstract properties; for example, all human languages can be analyzed as systems consisting of discrete structural units, with rules for combining those units in various ways. Even though languages differ superficially, they all reflect general properties of a common linguistic system typical of the human species.

Second, language development in children occurs spontaneously and does not require conscious instruction or reinforcement on the part of adults. In a very short period of time (a span of four to five years) children are able to develop very complex linguistic systems, moving from a one-word stage to multiword stages, on the basis of limited and often fragmentary data. Although adults often imagine that they are "teaching" their children how to speak, there is no convincing evidence that children need such instruction. Indeed, as many a parent has discovered, the attempt to instruct children in language can produce frustrating results:

(1)
Child: I taked a cookie.
Parent: Oh, you mean you *took* a cookie.
Child: Yes, that's right, I taked it.

It may be that a certain amount of conscious instruction on the part of parents and peers has some effect on the language of the child, but the available evidence indicates that such tutoring plays a minor role at best. The child, simply by exposure to a language, is able to master its linguistic features.

Another mechanism that seems to play little or no role in the child's mastery of language is the process of imitation (see Ervin 1964, Bloom, Hood, and Lightbown 1974). Indeed, children show enormous creativity in their use of language. They utter words, phrases, and sentences they have never heard before; they also understand utterances they have never heard before. Anyone who has studied child language, or has observed children, can recount examples such as the following:

(2)
Parent: Did you like the doctor?
Child: No, he took a needle and shotted my arm.

The child (a 6-year-old girl) has spontaneously created a new verb in this context, one that makes perfect sense, and one that she could not have learned by imitating adult speakers. This is not to say that imitation plays no role whatsoever in learning one's native language—for example, it may be a factor in learning some vocabulary—but the point, again, is that imitation, like overt teaching, plays at best a very minor role in the child's mastery of language.

Finally, language development takes place during a very specific maturational stage of human development. Sometime during the second year of life (at roughly anywhere from 12 to 18 months), children begin uttering their first words. During the following four to five years, linguistic development occurs quite rapidly. By the time children enter school, they have mastered the major structural features of their language. Refinements of the major features continue to appear, and the ability to learn language (one's native language or foreign languages) continues to be strong until the onset of puberty. At this point, for reasons that are not fully understood, the "knack for languages" begins to decline, to a greater or lesser extent depending on the individual. The optimal period of time for language acquisition (2 years to puberty) is sometimes referred to as the *critical period*.

Evidence that maturation plays a role in a child's ability to acquire language can be drawn from the experience of "Genie." Genie (not her real name) was kept in total isolation by her parents until she was discovered by the outside world at the age of 13 years 7 months. Her father had not permitted anyone to speak to her (or around her, for that matter). When Genie was found, she gave no evidence of having any linguistic capabilities whatsoever. A central question was, To what extent could Genie be rehabilitated? Was she beyond the critical period for acquiring language? Interestingly, within seven months she was able to count (to five), she knew some color terms as well as a couple of verbs, and she was able to name most objects in her surroundings. However, she had considerable trouble with syntax. Curtiss (1977, 31) reports:

There were attempts to teach her...rituals, for example, to ask specific questions. This attempt failed. Genie could not memorize a well-formed

WH-question. She would respond to "What do you say?" demands with ungrammatical, bizarre phrases that included WH-question words, but she was unable to come up with a phrase she had been trained to say. For example, instead of saying the requested "Where are the graham crackers?" she would say "I where is graham cracker," or "I where is graham cracker on top shelf." In addition, under pressure to use WH-question words, she came out with sentences such as:

Where is tomorrow Mrs L.?
Where is stop spitting?
Where is May I have ten pennies?
When is stop spitting?

These problems are significant, for they illustrate, as Curtiss points out, "that Genie, like normal children, was unable to imitate or even retain in memory, syntactic structures which were not in keeping with her grammatical development."

The properties of language development that we have cited—a spontaneous maturational development typical of the human species as a whole—strongly suggest that the linguistic capacity is part of the genetic endowment of human beings. The hypothesis of biological innateness of the language faculty has been most vigorously advanced by Noam Chomsky, who has put it this way (1986, 4):

Consider . . . the idea that there is a language faculty, a component of the mind/brain that yields knowledge of language given presented experience. It is not at issue that humans attain knowledge of English, Japanese, and so forth, while rocks, birds, or apes do not under the same (or indeed any) conditions. There is, then, some property of the mind/brain that differentiates humans from rocks, birds, or apes. Is this a distinct "language faculty" with specific structure and properties, or, as some believe, is it the case that humans acquire language merely by applying generalized learning mechanisms of some sort, perhaps with greater efficiency or scope than other organisms? These are not topics for speculation or *a priori* reasoning but for empirical inquiry, and it is clear enough how to proceed: namely, by facing the questions of (1) [What constitutes knowledge of language? How is knowledge of language acquired? and How is knowledge of language put to use?]. We try to determine what is the system of knowledge that has been attained and what properties must be attributed to the initial state of the mind/brain to account for its attainment. Insofar as these properties are language-specific, either individually or in the way they are organized and composed, there is a distinct language faculty.

From this point of view, then, the development of language in children is guided by a set of "innate ideas and principles," that is, a genetically determined linguistic capacity that all humans are endowed with at birth. From this point of view, all children are biologically programmed with the capacity to develop language—namely, the language(s) they are significantly exposed to during the appropriate maturational stage. Language development can thus be regarded as analogous to other biological developments in human growth and maturation. In this way, the traditional view that language is unique to human beings may in fact have a sound biological basis. Just as other biological characteristics can be unique to a certain species (such as the shape of the body or the structure of internal organs), so too the capacity for language and other properties of human mental functioning may well be a unique part of the genetic endowment of human beings.

The Rule-Governed Nature of Child Language and Language Development

Given that children have an innate capacity to acquire language, and given that conscious instruction or imitation is not required for this development, exactly how do children go about learning a particular language? There is very good evidence that children do not merely internalize individual expressions of a language, but in fact develop *rules* for forming these expressions.

Consider the fact that all native speakers of English have learned how to interpret expressions such as the following:

(3)
a. the child
b. the child who is reading the book
c. the child who is reading the book which was written by Dr. Seuss

As noted in the discussion of recursion in chapter 5, phrases such as these can be iterated indefinitely—there is no upper bound on the length they can attain. The syntactic rules of English allow us to add modifiers to nouns as shown in (3), and no matter how long such phrases were to become, at no point could we say that the rules of English syntax had been violated (even if such phrases were stylistically awkward or difficult to comprehend due to performance factors). Such examples show that it is impossible *in principle* to memorize all the expressions of a language. Clearly, we have mastered *rules* or *principles*—not simply individual expressions—that allow us to associate sound and meaning for a potentially infinite set of expressions.

In the realm of morphology, as well, there is evidence that children develop creative principles—in this case for word formation. A commonly cited piece of evidence for this is the phenomenon of *overgeneralization*, in which the child extends a rule-governed pattern to forms that do not follow the rule (see Ervin 1964, Slobin 1971). For example, the regular past tense in English is formed by adding the suffix -ed to the verb stem: *talk–talked*. However, there are numerous verbs in English with irregular past tenses, such as *take–took*. A child who says *taked* is overgeneralizing the rule for the regular past tense by using the regular past ending with an irregular verb. One explanation for the "error" is that the child has mastered a rule for forming the regular past tense.

In this regard, the form *shotted*, cited in (2b), provides a particularly interesting example. Here, the child has created a new verb (presumably the verb *to shot*, which is probably a denominal verb based on *shot*—a noun meaning "hypodermic injection"; the verb *to shoot* already existed in the child's vocabulary and was used exclusively in situations involving toy guns and playing dead). However, having created a new verb stem, the child nevertheless assimilated it into the regular morphology of English and provided it with the regular -ed past tense ending.

In a well-known experiment involving English morphology, Berko (1958) presented nonsense words to children of ages 4–7 and asked them to give a variation of the nonsense word reflecting certain morphological properties, such as the plural morpheme. For example, children were presented with test frames like the following:

(4)

This is a wug. (accompanied by a picture of imaginary birdlike animal)

Now there is another one.

There are two of them. (accompanied by picture of two of the imaginary animals)

There are two ____.

The idea is to provide the plural form of the nonsense word *wug*. If children have mastered a rule for forming plurals, they should be able to answer *wugs*. As Berko put it,

If knowledge of English consisted of no more than the storing up of many memorized words, the child might be expected to refuse to answer our questions on the grounds that he had never before heard of a *wug*, for instance, and could not possibly give us the plural form since no one had ever told him what it was. This was decidedly not the case. The children answered the questions; in some instances they pronounced the inflectional endings they had added with exaggerated care, so that it was obvious they understood the problem and wanted no mistake made about their solution. (1958, 164)

Stages in the Development of Language

Studies of linguistic development have revealed that children pass through a series of recognizable stages as they master their native language. Although the age at which children pass through a given stage can vary significantly from child to child, the particular sequence of stages seems to be the same for all children acquiring a given language. Here we will review some of the better-known stages of language development for children learning English (see the references at the end of the chapter for more detailed summaries).

Babbling

Prior to the development of language, all children, regardless of the language they will ultimately learn, pass through a stage referred to as *babbling*. In this stage, which begins at around 5 to 6 months, the child utters sounds and sound sequences (syllables such as *ba*, *ma*, *ga*) that are as yet meaningless but nevertheless recognizable as being more languagelike than earlier infant cries. Indeed, a number of sounds and syllables of the babbling stage will occur later as the child develops language. It has also been noted that certain sounds that occur in babbling appear to be lost when the child begins to use language (see Jakobson 1968) but appear again at a later stage. As Clark and Clark (1977, 390) note:

...when children start to use their first words, they no longer seem able to produce some of the very sounds they used when babbling. One striking example can be found in their use of *l* and *r*: although these are very frequent in babbling, they rarely appear in children's first words and are among the latest sounds that children master.

It seems, then, that in the babbling stage children produce languagelike sounds quite freely, but as they develop their native language they must master a systematic set of rules and patterns and they must, in effect, learn how to fit given sounds into those patterns. It has been argued, however, that babbling is not unrelated to the development of linguistic abilities (see Sachs 1985 and references cited there).

The fact that *all* children (including the congenitally deaf) go through a babbling stage, regardless of language and culture, and make very similar kinds of sounds at this time suggests that humans are biologically predisposed to go through this phase.

The One-Word Stage

The babbling phase, which lasts for some six to eight months, gradually gives way to the earliest recognizable stage of language, often called the *one-word stage*. At some point in the late part of the first year of life or the early part of the second year, the child begins using recognizable words of the native language. These words are usually the names of familiar people, animals, and objects in the child's environment (*mama, dada, kitty, doggie, ball, bottle, cup*) and words indicating certain actions and demands (*More!, No!*). Viewed from the perspective of adult grammar, the kinds of words that occur at this stage include simple nouns and verbs; there are as yet very few so-called function words (prepositions, articles, auxiliary verbs, interrogative words) in the child's language (see Brown 1973).

In evaluating children's language at the one-word stage, one must be extremely cautious about comparisons between the child's language and the adult language. For example, it is not clear that a given word uttered by a child at this stage has the same use that it would have in the adult language. Children's use of words sometimes shows an *overextension* or *underextension* of reference (see Leopold 1970, Bowerman 1976). For example, a certain child might use the word *doggie* to refer not just to dogs but to all common animals in the environment (an example of overextension). In contrast, a child might use the word *doggie* to refer not to all dogs (that is, all animals that could properly be referred to by the word *doggie*) but only to certain specific dogs (an example of underextension). It is not clear exactly what children's early words mean to them. For example, what do *mommy* and *baby* mean to a child who uses these words to refer to inanimate objects? For obvious reasons we cannot interview a young child to find out. The fact that adults (especially parents) claim to understand these early utterances should not be taken as evidence that children's utterances mean what adult utterances mean. Adults have a strong ability to interpret utterances in terms of the nonlinguistic context of the utterance (the time, place, situation, and participants involved), and based on this nonlinguistic context a child's utterances can be assigned an appropriate meaning by the adult. This method of *rich interpretation*, as it has sometimes been called, allows the adult to arrive at a certain understanding of the child's utterances, but this, in and of itself, does not reveal what the child might actually have in mind, nor does it reveal what the expression means to the child. For such reasons, it is difficult to determine whether an individual word uttered by the child is to be understood as *holophrastic* (as standing for an entire sentence or proposition), or whether it is to be taken as simply expressing a concept that is somehow relevant to the particular context of the utterance.

Multiword Stages

At some point during the second year of life, the child's utterances gradually become longer, and the one-word stage gives way to multiword stages. As noted earlier, the exact age at which children pass through a given stage varies significantly from child to child. For example, one child might enter the two-word stage at 20 months of age, and another might enter the same stage at 27 months. In general, the multiword stages we will describe here begin roughly in the second half of the child's second year and extend roughly to the child's fifth year. Although age varies, the particular sequence of stages described below is quite similar for all children.

As shown in table 11.1, during the early multiword stage—at roughly the two-word stage—children begin to express a variety of grammatical and conceptual relations. It is during this stage that children learning English begin to use word order to indicate certain relations—for example, Possessor followed by Possessed, or Subject followed by Predicate (again see table 11.1). In addition, the child's language begins to reflect the distinction between sentence types, such as negative sentences, imperatives, and questions. In this stage of linguistic development, we see the beginnings of a structured language (for example, subject + predicate structure), and it is clear that the child is beginning to master the broader grammatical features of the language. As the length of the child's utterances increases beyond the two-word stage, the major grammatical constructions of the native language begin to develop in more detail. Two constructions of English that have been studied from the point of view of their development in child language are negative sentences and questions. This development is summarized in table 11.2. Beginning first with negative sentences, we see that at the one-word stage negation is simply expressed by single words with negative meaning, such as *no* or *allgone*. In the early multiword stage, these negative words occur at the beginning (or, more rarely, at the end) of expressions—for example, *no eat, allgone milk* (see also table 11.1, section 8). At this stage the negative word does not intervene between other words; that is, it does not occur "internally" within an expression. However, in later multiword stages, the negative word begins to occur within expressions, between subject and predicate (*Mommy no play*).

Recall from the discussion of questions in chapter 5 that English draws a distinction between auxiliary verbs and main verbs. For example, in the adult grammar, the negative *not* (or the contracted *n't*) occurs with auxiliary verbs such as *do, does, did, is, am, are, have, has, can, could, may, might, shall, should, will, would, must*, and a few others. Thus, Modern English has no sentences of the form **I drink not*, but instead has sentences

Table 11.1
Common types of utterances found in the early multiword stage. (From Foss and Hakes 1978.)

Semantic Characterization	Syntactic Characterization	Forms	Examples
1. Nomination (naming, noticing)	Existential	$\left.\begin{array}{l}\text{here it}\\ \text{there 's}\\ \text{this see}\\ \text{that hi}\end{array}\right\}$ + Noun	there book that car see doggie hi spoon
2. Possession	Noun Phrase	$\left.\begin{array}{l}\text{Noun}\\ \text{Pronoun}\end{array}\right\}$ + Noun	my stool baby book Mommy sock
3. Attribution	Noun Phrase or Predicate Adjective	Adjective + Noun $\left.\begin{array}{l}\text{Noun}\\ \text{Pronoun}\end{array}\right\}$ + Adjective	pretty boat party hat big step carriage broken that dirty Mommy tired
4. Plurality	Noun Phrase	Quantifier + Noun	two cup all cars
5. Actor-Action	a. Subject + Predicate	Noun + Verb	Bambi go Mommy push (Kathryn) airplane by
	b. Subject + Predicate	Noun + Noun	Mommy (wash) jacket Lois (play) baby record
	c. Predicate	Verb + Noun	pick glove pull hat helping Mommy

		Examples
6. Location		
a. object location	Subject + Prepositional Phrase	sweater chair lady home baby room
b. action toward location	Verb + Prepositional Phrase	sat wall walk street
7. Requests and Imperatives	a. Verb + Object	want milk gimme ball
	b. Quantifier + Object	$\begin{Bmatrix}\text{more}\\\text{'nother}\end{Bmatrix}$ + Noun — more nut 'nother milk
8. Negation		
a. nonexistence	Neg + Sentence	Neg + $\begin{Bmatrix}\text{Noun}\\\text{Verb}\\\text{Adjective}\end{Bmatrix}$ — allgone milk no hot nomore light any more play
b. rejection	Neg + Sentence	Neg + $\begin{Bmatrix}\text{Verb}\\\text{Noun}\end{Bmatrix}$ — no dirty soap no meat no go outside
c. denial	Neg + Sentence	Neg + $\begin{Bmatrix}\text{Noun}\\\text{Verb}\\\text{Adjective}\end{Bmatrix}$ — no morning (it was afternoon) no Daddy hungry no truck
9. Questions		
a. requests and imperatives	Yes/No Question	Same word order as statements and imperatives; signaled only by rising intonation
b. information requests	Wh- Question	Fixed forms with wh- — What dat? What (NP) do? Where (NP) go?

Table 11.2
Development of negative sentences and questions in child language. (Adapted from Foss and Hakes 1978 and Clark and Clark 1977.)

Stage	Negative Sentences	Questions	
		Yes/No Questions	*Wh*-Questions
One-word stage	Negation expressed by single negative word: no allgone	Questioning indicated by intonation and/or context	
Early multiword stage	Negative word occurs at beginning of expression; does not occur between other words: No eat No sit down Allgone milk No hot No mommy go	Auxiliaries have not developed; no inversion of word order; only intonation is used: That mine? See baby? Drink baba?	Very limited; *where* and *what* are predominant forms, used at beginning of expressions: Where doggie? Where Daddy go? What dat?
Later multiword stage	Negative word occurs inside expression, between subject and predicate; negative auxiliaries *can't* and *don't* appear: There no milk He not big Mommy no play I can't do that I don't know him	Continued use of intonation; no inversion of word order; auxiliaries do not yet occur in positive sentences: You can't fix it? She no play? See doggie? Dolly go boom?	Additional *wh*-words develop to include *why*; no inversion of word order: Why mommy go? What dolly do? Why kitty sleep?

Wider range of negative auxiliaries appears; auxiliaries begin to appear in positive as well as negative sentences:

I didn't do it
He doesn't like it
I'm not a baby
I won't read the book
Mommy can't find dolly

Auxiliaries begin to appear in positive sentences; inversion of auxiliary appears:

Can't you get it?
Will you help me?
Did you see him?

Additional *wh*-words develop to include *how*; still no inversion of word order:

What she did?
Why doggy run?
What he can do?
How she can do that?

of the form *I don't drink*, *I won't drink*, *I mustn't drink*, and so on. In mastering English, then, children must become aware that a special class of auxiliary verbs functions both to "carry" the negative and to invert with the subject to form questions. At the stage where the negative word begins to appear internally in expressions (as in *Mommy no play*) we find the first negative auxiliary verbs in the child's language, usually the auxiliaries *can't* and *don't* (as in *I can't do that*, *I don't know him*). At this stage auxiliaries do not yet occur in the positive form. That is, although we find *can't* and *don't*, we do not yet find *can*, *does*, or *did*.

In the following stages, a wider range of negative auxiliaries begins to appear, and auxiliaries finally begin to appear in positive sentences as well as negative sentences. Thus, it seems that mastery of the system of negation in English is dependent upon, or at least tightly connected with, the mastery of auxiliary verbs.

The same connection is found in the development of questions, for auxiliary verbs play an important role here as well. Beginning with the one-word stage (see table 11.2), questioning is indicated solely by intonation and/or nonlinguistic cues in the context of utterance. As the child proceeds to an early multiword stage, auxiliary verbs have not yet developed, and yes/no questions (questions that can be answered "yes" or "no") are indicated by rising intonation at the end of the expression. So-called *wh*-questions (questions that begin with one of the "*wh*-words," such as *who, what, when, where, why*, and *how*) are quite limited at this early multiword stage (*Where doggie?*, *What dat?*).

As children enter later multiword stages, additional *wh*-words (such as *why, who*) begin to enter their language. Yes/no questions continue to be indicated by intonation until the stage is reached where auxiliary verbs develop in positive sentences as well as negative sentences. With the development of auxiliary verbs, inversion of subject and auxiliary begins to appear in children's yes/no questions (*Can't you get it?*, *Will you help me?*). However, even at this stage the inversion of word order has not yet begun to occur in *wh*-questions, which continue to be marked by *wh*-words at the beginning of expressions (as in *What she did?*, *What he can do?*, and so on). The inversion of auxiliaries in *wh*-questions (*What did she do?*, *What can he do?*) develops at a stage later than the stage where inversion of auxiliaries occurs in yes/no questions.

The above examples, though brief, illustrate the fact that children develop their native language in a sequence of identifiable stages. Further, we see that specific constructions of a language develop in an interrelated way:

the development of negative sentences and questions in English is intimately connected with the development of the auxiliary verb system.

Acquisition of Phonological Principles

As exemplified below, small children are unable to produce all the sounds of their native language with equal facility. (We display all children's expressions in square brackets to remain consistent with the conventions of the child language researchers cited here. We also preserve their transcription systems.)

Father: "Say 'jump'"
Son: [ḍʌp]
Father: "No, 'jump'"
Son: [ḍʌp]
Father: "No, 'jump'"
Son: [uːli: ḍɛdi: gæn ḍe: ḍʌp]
(Only Daddy can say "jump.")   (Smith 1973, 10)

The collective results of Olmsted (1971), Templin (1957), and Wellman et al. (1931), as cited by Owens (1984), reveal that sounds classed by manner of articulation are acquired roughly in the following order: nasals, glides, stops, liquids, fricatives, and finally affricates. Sounds classed by point of articulation are acquired in the order: labials, velars, alveolars, dentals, palatals (Owens 1984, 179). Therefore, /m/, which is a labial nasal, is expected to be among the first consonants acquired, and the affricate /ǰ/ is expected to be one of the last.

Individual case studies of children's pronunciation of words (see, for example, Smith 1973) reveal many examples of *substitution*. That is, a child often substitutes one sound in a word for another. For example, *Ken* is pronounced [tɛn] instead of [kɛn] (fronting); *light* is pronounced [yait] (replacing a liquid with a glide); *this* becomes [dɪs] (fricative is replaced by a stop); *glove* becomes [gwʌm] (/m/ is substituted for /v/, maintaining the labial feature).

A child may also change a sound in anticipation of another sound (*anticipatory assimilation*). Smith (1973, 20) cites the examples in (5), in which an initial sound becomes labial in anticipation of a following labial:

(5)

knife	→	[maip]
nipple	→	[mibu]
stop	→	[bɔp]
table	→	[ḅeːbu]
room	→	[wum]

rubber   →   [b̥ʌbə]
shopping   →   [wɔbin]
zebra   →   [wiːbə]

Menn (1985, 82) notes that her subject (Daniel) replaced initial labial stops with [g] when the word ended with a velar stop:

(6)
bug   →   [gʌg]
big   →   [gɪg]
book   →   [gʊk]
bike   →   [gajk]
pig   →   [gɪg]

Other examples that we have noticed (with our own children) are *popcorn* → [kakorn], *octopus* → [apəpʊs]. Assimilation may go the other way as well: *cooperate* → [kakakrey], *zebra* → [zizra], *popsicle* → [papsipo].

Syllable structure starts out quite simply CV. When confronted with a word with CVC syllable structure, the child may delete the final consonant (*ball* → [ba]) or insert a vowel (*good* → [gʊdə]). Either strategy serves to "open up" the syllable. Then a word is particularly long, syllables may be deleted, though the stressed syllable is always retained (*hippopotamus* → [hɪpánɪs], *Jennifer* → [défɹ̩], *elephant* → [ɛ́fan], *Nicholas* → [níkəs]). Consonant clusters tend to be eliminated (*jump* → [d̥ʌp]. Smith (1973, 166) notes that there are certain universal tendencies:

The most clear-cut tendency is where one member of the cluster is a stop and the other is not, in which case the cluster is almost invariably reduced to the stop alone. This seems to obtain whether the stop is the first or second element concerned.

He offers the following examples (p. 166):

(7)
stop   →   [d̥ɔp]
play   →   [b̥ei]
tree   →   [d̥iː]
piano   →   [pænəu]
clean   →   [ġiːn]
queen   →   [kiːm]
milk   →   [mik]

These data reveal that children do not substitute randomly in pronouncing words that are hard for them. Rather, their substitutions appear to be sensitive to properties of the syllable as well as to properties of the segments in the word.

Smith (1973) discusses several arguments from language acquisition that support the reality of distinctive features. One argument involves *metathesis* (transposition). Examples of metathesis involving segments are *desk* → [dɛks], *animal* → [aminal]. An example involving the metathesis of a feature is *difficult* → [gipətul] (Smith 1973, 187). In *difficult* the first and third consonants are targeted: /d/ → /g/ and /k/ → /t/. However, this is not a segment-for-segment exchange; rather, certain features are exchanged, and others remain in their original position. Voicing, for instance, remains in place (/d/ and /g/ are both voiced and /k/ and /t/ are both voiceless). What metathesizes is backness and coronality ([+back, −coronal] → [−back, +coronal] and [−back, +coronal] → [+back, −coronal]). Smith notes (p. 187) "...that [it would appear] these metatheses can only be satisfactorily explained in terms of the feature composition of the segments involved and not merely in terms of the segments as such."

Conclusion

Our discussion of language development in children has focused on two important and intimately interconnected properties of human language use. First, it is *rule-governed*; that is, humans master and follow rules for forming and using expressions of their native language. (For a challenge to this view, see, for example, Rumelhart and McClelland 1986; and for a recent defense, see Pinker and Prince 1988.) Second, it is *creative* (that is, humans spontaneously produce and understand expressions they have never encountered before in their linguistic experience). These are both properties that have been stressed in putting forth the claim that the human linguistic capacity is unique.

11.2 IS THE HUMAN LINGUISTIC CAPACITY UNIQUE: CHILDREN AND PRIMATES COMPARED

In recent years, in a fascinating set of experiments, the traditional idea that language is unique to the human species has been challenged. Psychologists, working in teams, have attempted to teach primates various communication systems (for example, sign language) that are thought to reflect certain essential properties of human language. Such projects have raised an intriguing possibility: even if a primate species (such as the chimpanzee) has a very rudimentary natural communication system in the wild, perhaps a member of this species could be taught a communication system not natural to the species, with complex properties on a par with certain properties of human spoken language.

Are primates in fact able to acquire and use language in a way similar to the way humans do? Primates have often been compared with children with respect to the acquisition of language, yet the contrast between the two is striking. Young children acquire complicated linguistic systems apparently effortlessly, whereas primates have required massive training efforts to master quite rudimentary communication systems. From one point of view—the traditional one referred to above—this would hardly be surprising. Humans, after all, are predisposed to learn language, whereas chimpanzees and gorillas are not. From this perspective, comparing children and chimpanzees with respect to language development is quite instructive, and the contrast between the two serves to clarify the nature of the task that all children carry out in mastering their native language.

In asking whether any other species can be shown to use a communicative system in a way similar to the way humans use language, we will need to pay particular attention to the two just-mentioned properties of human language use that supposedly set it apart from other animal communication systems. Can these properties be shown to exist in the communication systems that have been taught to primates? To put it another way, are primates and children comparable in their acquisition and use of language? To answer this, we will now turn our attention to some of the chimpanzee and gorilla projects that have attracted notice in recent years.

Washoe

In June 1966, Alan and Beatrice Gardner began a project that was to have immediate popular appeal, if not immediate academic acceptance. Their project was to teach a young (approximately 1-year-old) female chimpanzee to communicate in American Sign Language (ASL). Although their avowed purpose was to probe "the extent to which another species might be able to use human language" (Gardner and Gardner 1969, 664), it is evident that they were challenging claims such as the one that opened this chapter. As might well be expected, the success of the project quickly became a hotly debated issue. The popular press concluded almost immediately that Washoe was able to converse in ASL, and articles began appearing with titles such as "First Message from the Planet of the Apes." This kind of reaction put the skeptic in a position comparable, in the public mind, with that of seventeenth-century defenders of the uniqueness of man, who argued that "brutes" (animals), unlike man, have no souls. It is unfortunate that the skeptic was placed in this position, because the Gardners' project is interesting and important enough to deserve serious intellectual consideration, and such consideration requires that we carefully scrutinize all claims about the linguistic proficiency of chimps. We will review Washoe's basic accomplishments, inviting you to consider for yourself some of the central questions raised by these studies (see the exercises at the end of the chapter).

The problem of teaching a member of another species a human language presents the investigator with two fundamental preliminary decisions: what species to pick, and what language to use. The Gardners' choice in these matters was inspired. First and foremost, chimpanzees are among the most intelligent creatures of the animal world. Combining this with the fact that they are notoriously imitative and quite sociable with their human cousins, one gets a promising picture of a prospective language learner. Chimps have other important characteristics as well. They are manually adept, are sociable with members of their own species, and grow to a convenient size through a sequence of phases that are comparable to those in human development. These latter characteristics are important in that they allow the possibility of investigating communication among members of the species as well as allowing comparison of the chimp's acquisition of language with that of a normal child.

Why did the Gardners choose to teach Washoe ASL? Attempts to teach chimps *spoken* English have not been at all encouraging. For instance, Keith and Catherine Hayes attempted to teach spoken English to a chimp named Vicki (Hayes 1951). They raised Vicki like a human child, in an optimal home environment. Yet after six years of training, Vicki's speaking vocabulary was barely four words: *mama*, *papa*, *cup*, and *up*. The main problem seemed to be that a chimp's vocal apparatus is not suited to the production of many human speech sounds. Recalling the dexterous and imitative nature of chimps (who will occasionally gesture spontaneously to humans), the Gardners hit upon the idea of using a gestural language as the test system. A number of gestural systems of communication are available, but ASL was a natural choice for a number of reasons. Most important, it is a system used naturally by many people; it therefore affords a good basis of comparison for such factors as acquisition rate, proficiency, and comprehension. It is also a system whose structure is comparable in many ways to spoken human language. Finally, there is an iconic aspect to many signs that may be of some value at early stages of instruction. We

Table 11.3
Washoe chronology

Date	Event
1965 (c. June)	Washoe is born in the wild
1966 (June)	Is brought to Nevada and begins training
1966 (December)	Has acquired her first 4 signs
1967 (April)	Signs her first combinations
1967 (July)	Has acquired her first 13 signs
1968 (April)	Has acquired her first 34 signs
1969 (c. June)	Has acquired 85 signs; end of first three years of training
1970	Is sent to the Institute for Primate Studies in Norman, Oklahoma
1975	Is reported to have 160 signs

will see examples of this iconicity in Washoe's acquisition of the signs for *bib*.

Unlike Vicki (the Hayes's chimp), Washoe was not raised in the home like a child. She was not raised in a conventional laboratory, either. Most of her time with the Gardners was spent in a two-and-a-half room house trailer supplied with the usual trappings of human life and surrounded by a pleasant yard, 5,000 square feet in area. Washoe spent her nights alone, but during the day she was provided with an environment that was as stimulating as possible for learning ASL. She never lacked an ASL communicant, and there were abundant opportunities for conversation, play, and outings. It will be easier to follow Washoe's progress with the chronology of events provided in table 11.3.

How Washoe Learned

Since the goal of the Gardners' experiment with Washoe was to assess the extent of her ability to learn ASL, and not to test any particular theory of learning, virtually any teaching method thought to work was tried on occasion. In spite of this variation, the Gardners were able to keep track of how Washoe learned at least some of her signs.

Just as human children do a great deal of verbal babbling, so chimps do a certain amount of manual babbling, that is, natural and spontaneous gesturing. The Gardners thought that some of these natural gestures might form the basis of meaningful signs. But this hope was thwarted: probably only one of Washoe's signs was based on her natural gestures (the sign for *funny*), and this sign proved to be unstable. Babbling shades easily into invention, and it is possible to describe Washoe's acquisition of signs for *come/gimme* and *hurry* either as modified babbling or as invention. However, the Gardners describe a less controversial example of an invented sign when they write,

Sometimes we could not find an ASL equivalent for an English word in any of our manuals of ASL and no informant was available to supplement the manuals. In these cases we would adapt a sign of ASL for the purpose. The sign for *bib* was one of these cases and we chose to use the ASL sign for *napkin* or *wiper* to refer to bibs as well. This sign is made by touching the mouth region with an open hand and a wiping movement. During Month 18 Washoe had begun to use this sign appropriately for bibs, but it was still unreliable. One evening at dinner time, a human companion was holding up a bib and asking her to name it. Washoe tried *come-gimme* and *please*, but did not seem to be able to remember the *bib* sign that we had taught her. Then, she did something very interesting. With the index fingers of both hands she drew an outline of a bib on her chest—starting from behind her neck where a bib should be tied, moving her index fingers down along the outer edge of her chest, and bringing them together again just above her navel.

We could see that Washoe's invented sign for *bib* was at least as good as ours, and both were inventions. At the next meeting of the human participants in the project, we discussed the possibility of adopting Washoe's invention as an alternative to ours, but decided against it. The purpose of the project was, after all, to see if Washoe could learn a human system of two-way communication, and not to see if human beings could learn a system devised by an infant chimpanzee. We continued to insist on the *napkin-wiper* sign for bibs, until this became a reliable item in Washoe's repertoire. Five months later, when we were presenting films on Washoe's signing to fluent signers at the School for the Deaf in Berkeley, we learned that drawing an outline of a bib on the chest with both index fingers is the correct sign for *bib*. (Gardner and Gardner 1971, 39)

As a further possible case of innovation, Washoe was later reported (in Oklahoma) to have signed *water bird* for swans, though her attendant used the sign for *duck*.

Some signs—for instance, *sweet*, *flower*, *toothbrush*, and *smoke*—were acquired by imitation. On the other hand, *more* and *open* were selectively shaped from gestures that were similar in some respect to these signs.

Finally, *tickle* and many other signs were the result of guidance (also called *molding*). In these cases, Washoe's hand was formed or molded into the proper shape and then brought through the motion required for the sign.

There is some evidence that Washoe was able to generalize the use of a sign from its original referent to new cases, and thus an important feature of human language acquisition may have been present in her case. The sign for *key* is a relevant example:

A great many cupboards and doors in Washoe's quarters have been kept secure by small padlocks that can all be opened by the same simple key. Because she was immature and awkward, Washoe had great difficulty in learning to use these keys and locks. Because we wanted her to improve her manual dexterity, we let her practice with these keys until she could open the locks quite easily (then we had to hide the keys). Washoe soon transferred this skill to all manner of locks and keys, including ignition keys. At about the same time, we taught her the sign for "key," using the original padlock key as a referent. Washoe came to use this sign both to name keys that were presented to her and to ask for the keys to various locks when no key was in sight. She readily transferred the sign to all varieties of keys and locks. (Gardner and Gardner 1971, 162)

What Washoe Learned

Although it has been reported that by 1975 Washoe had a vocabulary of at least 160 signs (Fouts 1975), the most detailed report of her vocabulary is by Gardner and Gardner (1975), who describe Washoe's first 85 signs in the order of acquisition. These signs passed the test of being used spontaneously and appropriately on 15 consecutive days.

As Washoe's chronology indicates, her first combinations (such as *gimme sweet* and *come open*) were observed after about 10 months of training. Over the next 26 months she was observed to make 294 different two-sign combinations. By the spring of 1968, after about two years of training, Washoe was appropriately using four-and five-sign combinations such as *you me go out* and *you me go out hurry*. Does this mean that Washoe was spontaneously creating new combinations, the way children spontaneously create new multiword sentences? The Gardners' evidence does not establish this, and studies of other chimpanzees strongly suggest that multisign combinations used by chimpanzees are quite different in character from sentences used by children.

The Gardners have attempted to establish that in Washoe's idiolect the signs are grouped into such categories as proper names, common nouns, pronouns, modifiers, verbs, and locatives (Gardner and Gardner 1975). However, the evidence for this categorization comes mainly from comparing Washoe's question-and-answer sequences with those of young children; such comparison leaves open a number of issues that might call the conclusions into question. In particular, this procedure assumes that one can really motivate these syntactic categories in the analysis of child language, which, as we have already noted, is not obviously the case, because many of these tests are semantic and pragmatic, not syntactic.

Washoe Compared with Children

Part of the attractiveness of ASL as a language to teach Washoe was that it is a human language and thus it might be possible to compare Washoe's progress against that made by children. We know of no detailed comparison of Washoe's development and that of deaf children acquiring ASL, but the Gardners (1971) have compared her two-sign combinations with the earliest two-word utterances of hearing children, as shown in table 11.4.

As can be seen, the two schemes resemble each other closely. Curiously, though, there are no reports of Washoe spontaneously asking questions, and this distinguishes her in one important respect from the normal child.

What is one to conclude about Washoe's linguistic ability? Does she use ASL? Has she learned to communicate in a human language? These are extremely difficult questions to answer. It is important to keep in mind that chimps are quite clever, and care should be taken not to be too impressed by their ability to figure out complicated ways of getting what they want. Further, it should be noted that the Nim Chimpsky project (see Terrace 1979), carried out after the Washoe project, raised serious questions about the interpretation of data in chimpanzee projects, and at present there is little convincing evidence from the Washoe project (or others) for a linguistic ability among chimpanzees that is comparable to that of human children.

Is Language a Uniquely Human Cognitive Ability?

The chimpanzee project we have discussed in this chapter, as well as other primate projects we have not reviewed (such as the Sarah project (Premack and Premack 1972), the Nim Chimpsky project (Terrace 1979), the Lana project (Rumbaugh 1977), and the Koko project (Patterson 1981)), represent a fascinating new direction in research on interspecies communication. In less than two decades, the idea of systematic communication between humans and nonhuman species has become more than just a fanciful speculation. Promising work is currently underway with pygmy chimpanzees (Savage-Rumbaugh 1986) and dolphins (Herman, Richards, and Wolz 1984). Whether or not these projects can ever show that animals are able to use a linguistic system in the way humans do, such research has indeed shown that primates and cetaceans (whales and dolphins) can manipulate symbols and that they can learn simple communication systems that are not natural to their species. Building on these results, future research may well be able to give us an overall picture of how primate

Table 11.4
Parallel descriptive schemes for the earliest combinations by children and Washoe. (Thorpe 1974, from Gardner and Gardner 1971.)

Brown's (1970) scheme for children

Types	Examples
Attributive: Adj + N	big train, red book
Possessive: N + N	Adam checker, mommy lunch
N + V	walk street, go store
Locative: N + N	sweater chair, book table
Agent-Action: N + V	Adam put, Eve read
Action-Object: V + N	put book, hit ball
Agent-Object: N + N	mommy sock, mommy lunch

intelligence is structured, and this information in turn may provide interesting points of comparison and contrast with human intelligence.

To sum up, convincing evidence has yet to be presented that would indicate that a nonhuman species has the capacity to use a communication system in the creative and rule-governed way that humans use language. It seems that language use is indeed a uniquely human cognitive ability, and the development of language in children continues to be a cognitive development that is unparalleled in any other species.

11.3 SPECIAL TOPICS

What *I pick your nose* Means to Nicholas

As noted in the text, it is difficult for adults to know exactly what a small child means. We attempt to construct scenarios that enable a reasonable interpretation to be attributed to an utterance. Often it is quite a challenge, as we will see in connection with the sentence "I pick your nose," which was uttered by a child named Nicholas at 25 months of age.

Scheme for Washoe	
Types	Examples
Object-Attribute	drink red, comb black
Agent-Attribute	Washoe sorry, Naomi good
Agent-Object	clothes Mrs. G., you hat
Object-Attribute	baby mine, clothes yours
Action-Location	go in, look out
Action-Object	go flower, pants tickle
Object-Location	baby down, in hat
Agent-Action	Roger tickle, you drink
Action-Object	tickle Washoe, open blanket
Appeal-Action	please tickle, hug hurry
Appeal-Object	gimme flower, more fruit

Some background is necessary. The deictic pronouns *I* and *you* are very interesting from the point of view of acquisition. The child needs to figure out that when the speaker utters "I will pick you up," *I* refers to the speaker by virtue of being the speaker of the utterance and *you* refers to the hearer by virtue of being the intended addressee. Children often start out using *you* to refer to themselves; thus, "Carry you!" is a command to the hearer to carry the child, who happens to be the speaker. Interestingly, autistic children continue to have trouble with these pronouns, using *you* to refer to themselves (see Tanz 1980).

By 21 months, Nicholas had figured out that *I* refers to the speaker, and he knew that the subject of an imperative is the hearer. (He was often told, "Don't throw your truck!") However, in his grammar the possessive pronoun *your* referred to himself. So, what did he mean when he pronounced to a rather startled adult, "I pick your nose"? He meant that he was picking his own nose, not the hearer's.

Acquisition of Anaphora

Just as children need to figure out how to use deictic pronouns, they also must learn to recognize whether a speaker intends to refer to one individual or two in examples such as (8) and (9) (from Lebeaux 1988, 404):

(8) *Mickey* is afraid that *he* might fall down.

(9) *He* was glad that *Donald* got the earring.

In (8) the speaker may intend *Mickey* and *he* to be either coreferential or not. However, in (9) one would take the speaker to be referring to two different individuals. Carden (1986) demonstrates that children (age 3.5–7.0) share the same judgments as adults with respect to examples such as (8) and (9). As noted in chapter 5, linear order is not directly responsible for this judgment. Under the right structural circumstances, the pronoun can precede the noun phrase and still be used coreferentially:

(10)
Near *him*, *Wayne* found the program.

The pronoun *him* and the noun phrase *Wayne* can be used here to refer to the same individual. Again, children share this judgment. In chapter 5 we pointed out that the difference between examples such as (9) and (10) is that in (9) the pronoun *c-commands* the noun phrase. Coreference appears to be blocked in this situation.

Now consider the examples in (11):

(11)
a. Under *Mickey*, *he* found a penny.
b. Near *Barbara*, *she* dropped the earring.

Adults would assume that a speaker uttering (11a) or (11b) intends to refer to two different individuals. Lebeaux (1988), however, reports that children (age 3.5–7.0) allow coreference in such examples. According to Lebeaux, adults' and children's judgments differ not because they have different principles for interpreting pronouns and noun phrases but because adults compute a more abstract syntactic level of representation than do children. For adults, Lebeaux argues, (11a) would also be associated with a structure corresponding to the sentence in (12). Notice that the only difference between (11a) and (12) is linear order.

(12)
He found a penny under *Mickey*.

(12) is similar to (9). In both examples the pronoun c-commands the noun phrase (*Donald* and *Mickey*, respectively). The child, however, does not compute the more abstract structure (12) in which the prepositional phrase (*under Mickey*) is "put back" in its "original" position, which is to the right

of the verb and its direct object; hence, in the child's grammar the pronoun does not c-command *Mickey* (assuming *under Mickey* is not attached under the S node that immediately dominates *he*) and (12) does not play a role in interpreting whether or not *he* and *Mickey* can be used to refer to one individual.

As these examples illustrate, the task before the child learning language is complex. Children ultimately learn tens of thousands of words and thousands of rules (phonological, morphological, and syntactic) and use language creatively, understanding and producing expressions that they have never encountered before. Their acquisition takes place accurately and effortlessly, and for all of the above reasons, many linguists have proposed that the way acquisition takes place is only possible because of a rich genetic predisposition for the learning of language in the human species.

Study Questions

1. What is the evidence that children acquiring language do not simply memorize words and sentences?

2. Who is "Genie" and what linguistic issues does her case address?

3. Discuss the experiment that demonstrated that children have not memorized the plural forms of all nouns.

4. In what ways is infant babbling different from the earliest forms of "real" language that the child begins to speak?

5. What is a *holophrastic expression* in child language?

6. What is *overextension*? What is *overgeneralization*?

7. What is *anticipatory assimilation*?

8. What evidence is there that Washoe produces and understands ASL?

9. Recall, from chapter 5, four important aspects of syntactic structure. What evidence is there that Washoe's dialect has syntactic structure?

Exercises

1. Compare and contrast the sentence types found in table 11.2 (children's language) with the sentences in table 11.4 (children's language and Washoe's language).

2. Why might Washoe have called miniatures, but not pictures, *baby*? (Could *baby* also mean to Washoe "small example of"?)

3. Design an experiment (a thought experiment) that could show, to your satisfaction, whether Washoe can use ASL as a human does.

4. What semantic similarities and differences are there between Washoe's sign language and natural spoken languages? Can we attribute *meaning* to Washoe's code?

5. What are some similarities and some differences between the way Washoe was instructed in sign language and the way normal children learn their first language?

6. Suppose Washoe were to successfully pass a suitable language test. What would this tell us about the answers to such questions as:

A. Is the capacity for language acquisition innate?
B. Is the capacity for language acquisition specific to the human species?
C. Is the capacity for language acquisition innate in the human species?

Bibliography and Further Reading

Anisfeld, M. (1984). *Language development from birth to three*. Hillsdale, N. J.: L. Erlbaum Associates.

Atkinson-King, K. (1973). *Children's acquisition of phonological stress contrasts. Working Papers in Phonetics 25*. UCLA, Los Angeles, Calif.

Baker, C. L., and J. J. McCarthy, eds. (1981). *The logical problem of language acquisition*. Cambridge, Mass.: MIT Press.

Bar-Adon, A., and W. F. Leopold, eds. (1971). *Child language: A book of readings*. Englewood Cliffs, N. J.: Prentice-Hall.

Berko, J. (1958). The child's learning of English morphology. *Word* 14, 150–177.

Bloom, L. (1970). *Language development: Form and function in emerging grammar*. Cambridge, Mass.: MIT Press.

Bloom, L., L. Hood, and P. Lightbown (1974). Imitation in language development: If, when, and why. *Cognitive Psychology* 6, 380–420.

Bowerman, M. (1976). Semantic factors in the acquisition of rules for word use and sentence construction. In D. M. Morehead and A. E. Morehead, eds., *Normal and deficient child language*. Baltimore, Md.: University Park Press.

Brown, R. (1970). The first sentences of child and chimpanzee. In *Selected psycholinguistics papers*. New York: Free Press.

Brown, R. (1973). *A first language*. Cambridge, Mass.: Harvard University Press.

Carden, G. (1986). Blocked forwards coreference: Theoretical implications of the acquisition data. In B. Lust, ed., *Studies in the acquisition of anaphora*, vol. 1. Dordrecht, Holland: Reidel.

Chomsky, C. S. (1969). *The acquisition of syntax in children from 5 to 10*. Cambridge, Mass.: MIT Press.

Chomsky, N. (1986). *Knowledge of language: Its nature, origin, and use.* New York: Praeger.

Clark, H., and E. Clark (1977). *Psychology and language: An introduction to psycholinguistics.* New York: Harcourt Brace Jovanovich.

Curtiss, S. (1977). *Genie: A psycholinguistic study of a modern-day "wild child."* New York: Academic Press.

Dale, P. S. (1976). *Language development: Structure and function.* 2nd ed. New York: Holt, Rinehart and Winston.

de Villiers, J. G., and P. A. de Villiers (1978). *Language acquisition.* Cambridge, Mass.: Harvard University Press.

Ervin, S. M. (1964). Imitation and structural change in children's language. In E. H. Lenneberg, ed., *New directions in the study of language.* Cambridge, Mass.: MIT Press.

Ferguson, C. A., and D. I. Slobin, eds. (1973). *Studies of child language development.* New York: Holt, Rinehart and Winston.

Foss, D., and D. Hakes (1978). *Psycholinguistics.* Englewood Cliffs, N. J.: Prentice-Hall.

Fouts, R. (1972). The use of guidance in teaching sign language to a chimpanzee. *Journal of Comparative and Physiological Psychology* 80, 515–522.

Fouts, R. (1973). Acquisition and testing of gestural signs in four young chimpanzees. *Science* 180, 978–980.

Fouts, R. (1974). Language: Origins, definition and chimpanzees. *Journal of Human Evolution* 3, 475–482.

Fouts, R. (1975). Capacity for language in great apes. In R. Tuttle, ed., *Socioecology and psychology of primates.* The Hague: Mouton.

Gardner, R., and B. Gardner (1969). Teaching sign language to a chimpanzee. *Science* 165, 664–672.

Gardner, B., and R. Gardner (1971). Two way communication with an infant chimpanzee. In A. Schrier, H. Harlow, and F. Stollnitz, eds., *Behavior of non-human primates.* New York: Academic Press.

Gardner, R., and B. Gardner (1975). Evidence for sentence constituents in early utterances of child and chimpanzee. *Journal of Experimental Psychology* 104, 244–267.

Gleason, J. B., ed. (1985). *The development of language.* Columbus, Ohio: Charles E. Merrill Publishing Co.

Hayes, C. (1951). *The ape in our house.* New York: Harper and Row.

Herman, L., D. Richards, and J. Wolz (1984). Comprehension of sentences by bottlenosed dolphins. *Cognition* 16, 129–219.

Jakobson, R. (1968). *Child language, aphasia, and phonological universals.* The Hague: Mouton. (Originally published in German, 1941.)

Klima, E., and U. Bellugi (1978). *The signs of language.* Cambridge, Mass.: Harvard University Press.

Lebeaux, D. (1988). Language acquisition and the form of the grammar. Doctoral dissertation, University of Massachusetts, Amherst.

Leopold, W. F. (1970). *Speech development of a bilingual child: A linguist's record.* Vol. 3: *Grammar and general problems in the first two years.* New York: AMS Press. (Originally published 1949.)

Linden, E. (1976). *Apes, men and language.* Baltimore, Md.: Pelican Books.

Menn, L. (1985). Phonological development: Learning sounds and sound patterns. In Gleason 1985.

Olmsted, D. (1971). *Out of the mouth of babes.* The Hague: Mouton.

Owens, R. E. (1984). *Language development: An introduction.* Columbus, Ohio: Charles E. Merrill Publishing Co.

Patterson, F. (1981). *The education of Koko.* New York: Holt, Rinehart and Winston.

Pinker, S., and J. Mehler, eds. (1988). *Connections and symbols.* Cambridge, Mass.: MIT Press.

Pinker, S., and A. Prince (1988). On language and connectionism: Analysis of a parallel distributed processing model of language acquisition. In Pinker and Mehler 1988.

Premack, A., and D. Premack (1972). Teaching language to an ape. *Scientific American* 227, 92–99.

Rumbaugh, D. (1977). *Language learning by a chimpanzee: The Lana project.* New York: Academic Press.

Rumelhart, D. E., and J. L. McClelland (1986). On learning the past tenses of English verbs. In J. L. McClelland, D. E. Rumelhart, and the PDP Research Group, *Parallel distributed processing: Explorations in the microstructure of cognition.* Vol. 2: *Psychological and biological models.* Cambridge, Mass.: MIT Press.

Sachs, J. (1985). Prelinguistic development. In Gleason 1985.

Savage-Rumbaugh, S. (1986). Spontaneous symbol acquisition and communicative use by pygmy chimpanzees (*Pan paniscus*). *Journal of Experimental Psychology* 115, 211–235.

Slobin, D. (1971). On the learning of morphological rules: A reply to Palermo and Eberhart. In D. I. Slobin, ed., *The ontogenesis of grammar: A theoretical symposium.* New York: Academic Press.

Smith, N. V. (1973). *The acquisition of phonology.* Cambridge: Cambridge University Press.

Tanz, C. (1980). *Studies in the acquisition of deictic terms.* Cambridge: Cambridge University Press.

Templin, M. (1957). *Certain language skills in children.* Minneapolis, Minn.: University of Minnesota Press.

Terrace, H. S. (1979). *Nim.* New York: Alfred A. Knopf.

Thorpe, W. H. (1974). *Animal nature and human nature.* Garden City, N.Y.: Doubleday.

Wanner, E., and L. R. Gleitman (1982). *Language acquisition: The state of the art.* New York: Cambridge University Press.

Wellman, B., I. Case, I. Mengert, and D. Bradbury (1931). Speech sounds of young children. University of Iowa Studies in Child Welfare 1931, 5.

Chapter 12

LANGUAGE AND THE BRAIN

The biological side of language is the subject of increasing research, and advances are possible because of the growing sophistication of available experimental techniques and equipment. It is somewhat ironic that until recently, progress in our understanding of brain functions has come not from the study of normal individuals but largely from the study of individuals with injured brains. Whenever disease or injury affects the left side of the brain, some aspect of the ability to perceive, process, or produce language may be disturbed. Individuals with such brain disease or injury are said to be *aphasic*, and their brain disturbances can give us insight into how the human brain carries out its language-related tasks.

Aphasia is a broad term encompassing numerous syndromes of communicative impairment. Some aphasics labor to speak a single word, whereas others effortlessly produce long but meaningless utterances. By studying the effect of brain damage on speech and comprehension, researchers have obtained invaluable clues to the organization of speech and language in the human nervous system. *Neurolinguists* are interested in the correlation between brain damage and speech and language deficits. These language and brain specialists believe that the study of language form and use will reveal principles of brain function, and that the study of brain function may support or refute specific linguistic theories.

Of the many questions of interest to neurolinguists, three are fundamental: (1) Where in the brain are speech and language localized? (2) How does the nervous system function to encode and decode speech and language? and (3) Are the components of language—phonology, syntax, semantics—neuroanatomically distinct and therefore vulnerable to separate impairment?

Sections 12.1, 12.2, and 12.3 were written by Kathryn Bayles, Department of Speech and Hearing Sciences, University of Arizona.

12.1 WHERE IS LANGUAGE LOCALIZED IN THE BRAIN?

Language: A Left Hemisphere Phenomenon

For over a century scholars have debated the question of speech and language localization within the brain. In the 1860s, scientists known as localizationists speculated that the functioning of specific regions in the brain was responsible for language. Antilocalizationists argued that speech and language were the consequence of the brain functioning as a whole.

In 1861, Paul Broca, a French surgeon and anatomist, described to the Société d'Anthropologie in Paris a patient who in life had had extreme difficulty in producing speech. Later, at autopsy, the patient was found to have damage in the posterior inferior part of the *frontal lobe* in the left cerebral hemisphere, now known as Broca's area (see figure 12.1). With the publication of this report Broca became the first individual to substantiate the claim that damage to a specific area of the brain results in a speech deficit. In 1865, Broca extended his claim about speech localization by reporting that damage to sites in the left cerebral hemisphere produced aphasia, whereas destruction of corresponding sites in the right hemisphere left linguistic capacities intact.

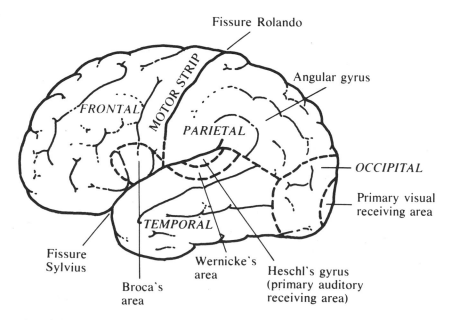

Figure 12.1
Landmarks of the left cerebral hemisphere

In 1874, Carl Wernicke, a young German physician, published a monograph describing patients with speech comprehension deficits who had damage (lesions) outside Broca's area, in the left posterior temporal lobe. Wernicke's work strengthened Broca's claim that left hemispheric structures are essential for speech and generated intense interest in the hypothesis that different areas within the left hemisphere fulfill different linguistic functions.

Today scientists agree that specific neuroanatomic structures, generally of the left hemisphere, are vital for speech and language, but debate continues as to which structures are committed to the various linguistic capacities. For most individuals the left cerebral hemisphere is dominant for language, regardless of handedness. Approximately 70 percent of all individuals with damage to the left hemisphere will experience some type of aphasia, as compared with only 1 percent of those with right hemispheric lesions.

Confirmation of left cerebral language dominance has come from many research techniques, one of which was introduced by J. Wada in 1949. Wada reported that the injection of sodium amytal into the main (carotid) artery on the language-dominant side of the brain induces a temporary aphasia. Physicians have subsequently used this technique as a means of determining cerebral dominance in patients facing neurosurgery; in this way, they can avoid damaging the language centers during surgery.

Substantially adding to our knowledge of the neurology was a report published in 1959 by Wilder Penfield and LaMar Roberts, neurosurgeons at the Montreal Neurological Institute. Penfield and Roberts had been studying the brain as well as treating its infirmities. To provide relief from intractable seizures in patients with epilepsy, Penfield and Roberts surgically removed portions of the brain. Because of the threat of producing aphasia by removing regions subserving speech and language, they used electrical stimulation to map the functions of the exposed brains of their patients.

Electrical current applied to a spot on the brain can sometimes activate involuntary expression of the function associated with that brain site. Stimulation may also interfere with a function being performed by the conscious patient. For example, electrical stimulation applied to areas on one side of the brain associated with motor function can produce limb twitching, numbness, and movement on the opposite side of the body. Penfield and Roberts discovered that when electrical current was applied to a brain area involved in speech, one of two things occurred: the patient either had trouble talking or uttered a vowellike cry. However, no patient ever produced an intelligible word as a result of electrical stimulation.

Through the cooperation of hundreds of courageous patients, who remained conscious during surgery, Penfield and Roberts were able to conclude that three areas of the left hemisphere are vital to speech and language: *Broca's area*, *Wernicke's area*, and *the supplemental motor area* (see figure 12.2).

As evidence accumulated verifying left cerebral speech dominance, researchers sought to discover whether the left hemisphere speech areas were structurally unique. Geschwind and Levitsky (1968) were the first to report that a region in the left temporal lobe was larger than the same area on the right in 65 percent of the brains they studied. This area, called the *planum temporal*, has also been found to be larger even in fetal brains, a finding that suggests the readiness of the left hemisphere for language dominance at birth (Wada, Clarke, and Hamm 1975, Witelson and Pallie 1973).

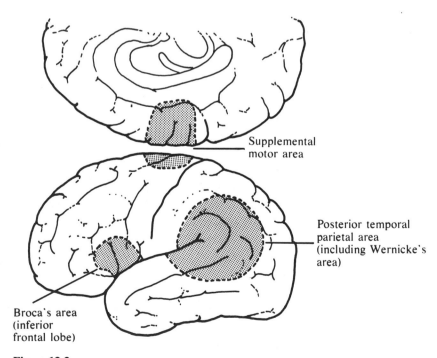

Figure 12.2
Primary cortical areas involved in speech and language function. (After Penfield and Roberts 1959.)

In order to understand the details of localization theory, it is first necessary to become familiar with some basic concepts about the structure and function of the nervous system.

The Nervous System

The central and peripheral nervous systems form an intricate communication network through which the behavior of the body is governed. The brain and spinal cord constitute the *central nervous system* (CNS) and are linked to the *peripheral nervous system* by bundles of nerve fibers that extend to all parts of the body. Impulses received from peripheral receptors are sorted, interpreted, and responded to by the CNS.

The basic cellular unit of the nervous system is the *neuron*, of which there are an estimated 12 billion. Each neuron is structurally distinct and composed of (1) a *cell body*, (2) receptors known as *dendrites*, and (3) a conductive mechanism, or *axon*. The dendrites receive input from other neurons and transmit *away from* the cell body. Some nerve fibers transmit sensory information to the CNS, others carry information from the CNS to the limbs and body parts, and still others form communicative links between the different parts of the nervous system.

Levels of the Central Nervous System

The central nervous system is hierarchically organized, higher structures being more complex than lower ones (see figure 12.3). At the lowest level is the spinal cord, which acts as a cable through which streams of neuronal messages between the body and the brain are transmitted. Above the spinal cord is the brain stem, the regulator of such things as breathing, muscle tone, posture, sleep, and body temperature. Lower nervous system structures, such as the spinal cord and lower brain stem, are primarily reflexive and controlled by higher centers. At the highest level of the nervous system are the cerebral hemispheres, responsible for voluntary activity.

The cerebral hemispheres emerge from the higher brain stem and are covered with a convoluted sheath of gray matter, called the *cortex*, which is approximately one-fourth of an inch thick. Within the cortex are approximately 10 billion neurons arranged in at least six layers. The degree of connectivity in this three-dimensional cellular network is almost beyond comprehension. Sholl (1956), a noted neuroanatomist, writes that the cortex contains fields of neurons where a single axon may influence up to 4,000 other neurons.

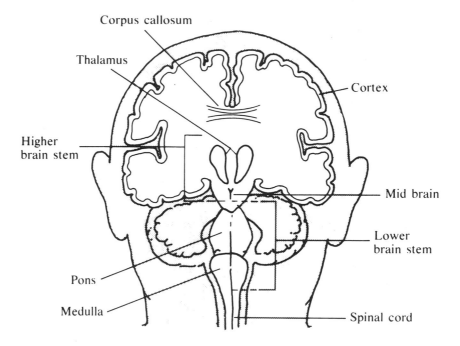

Figure 12.3
Hierarchical arrangement of the central nervous system

The Cerebral Cortex: General Characteristics

In outward appearance the two cerebral hemispheres are roughly similar, being composed of convolutions, called *gyri*, and depressions or fissures, known as *sulci*. Certain gyri and sulci serve as landmarks helping to differentiate the boundaries of the four lobes of each hemisphere. The structures are illustrated in figure 12.1.

The *fissure of Sylvius* separates the frontal lobe from the temporal; the *fissure of Rolando* separates the frontal lobe from the parietal. No fissure separates the parietal and occipital lobes; these two lobes can be distinguished only by microscopic examination of cell structures. Located in the parietal lobe, at the upper end of the fissure of Sylvius, is the cortical area known as the *angular gyrus*, in which functions necessary to speech, reading, and writing are interrelated.

Within each hemisphere are areas known to serve specific functions. In front of, and running parallel to, the fissure of Rolando is a strip of cortex, known as the *motor strip*, which controls fine, highly skilled, voluntary motor movements. Sections of the motor strip are related to voluntary movements in particular parts of the body; for example, the facial and laryngeal muscles are represented in the lower end, in close proximity to Broca's area.

Next to Wernicke's area, in the temporal lobe, is *Heschl's gyrus*, known also as the primary auditory cortex. When auditory impulses arrive at Heschl's gyrus, a noise is perceived, but meaningful interpretation must be made by the adjacent auditory association area (Wernicke's area). This pattern of cortical organization, consisting of interpretive regions of the cortex lying adjacent to sensory receiving areas, is repeated in the visual cortical system as well as in the system receiving sensations from the body.

Cortical Conduction

The bulk of the cerebral hemispheres, beneath the outer layer of gray matter, is composed of three basic types of nerve fiber tracts that form a neural communication network of astonishing complexity. Association nerve fibers connect different portions of the same hemisphere. Projection fibers connect the cortex with lower portions of the brain and spinal cord, and transverse fibers interconnect the cerebral hemispheres.

Of particular importance to speech and language function is the massive transverse fiber tract called the *corpus callosum* (see figure 12.3). By means of the corpus callosum the two hemispheres are able to communicate with each other in the form of electrical impulses. Eccles (1972) estimated that if one assumes that each of the approximately 200 million nerve fibers constituting the corpus callosum has an average firing capacity of 20 impulses per second, then the corpus callosum can carry the astronomical number of 4 billion impulses per second.

You may wonder why, if speech is localized in the left hemisphere, it is necessary for the cerebral hemispheres to communicate with each other for speech to function normally. The reason is that sensations from the right and left halves of the body go primarily to the *contralateral* (opposite) hemisphere. If, for example, an object is held in the left hand, impulses travel from the left side of the body to the *right* hemisphere, and although the right hemisphere would recognize the object, verbalizing the name of the object would require involvement of the speech center in the left hemisphere.

The importance of the corpus callosum has been made strikingly clear through split-brain research. Gazzaniga and associates studied the effect of disruption of communication between the hemispheres in patients who had had them disconnected surgically by severing the corpus callosum, an operation that is performed to reduce the frequency and severity of incapacitating seizures. Once the cerebral hemispheres are disconnected, there are techniques whereby stimuli can be visually presented to a single hemisphere. When Gazzaniga and Sperry (1967) presented stimuli in the form of written words, letters, and numbers to the left hemisphere alone, patients were able to describe them orally. But information perceived exclusively by the right hemisphere could not be verbalized, either orally or in writing. The right hemisphere was mute.

To investigate the possibility that even though split-brain subjects could not describe visual stimuli presented to their right hemispheres, they nevertheless comprehended them, Gazzaniga and Sperry gave the patients a nonverbal means of responding. For instance, subjects were asked to match a written word with its referent by pointing to the object when it was displayed as one item in a group of assorted items. Under these conditions the right hemisphere was found to be capable of recognizing letters, short words, and numbers.

To discover whether the right hemisphere could also comprehend spoken words, Gazzaniga and Sperry asked patients to identify words presented auditorily. Because auditory stimuli are received by both sides of the brain, Sperry and Gazzaniga limited the available answers to the right hemisphere. Subjects were instructed to push a button when they saw that one of a set of nouns projected serially to the left visual field (the right hemisphere) matched one previously spoken. Results with split-brain patients showed that the right hemisphere can understand oral (as well as written) language, although the limits of its comprehension have yet to be determined.

Recent research suggests that the right hemisphere may be limited in its linguistic competence. Split-brain subjects have been observed to have difficulty responding appropriately to verbal commands, simple active and passive subject-verb-object sentences, and word sequences when they were presented visually to the right hemisphere.

Thus, although the right hemisphere is generally unimpaired in grasping the meaning of single words, it performs poorly with phrases. Perhaps only certain kinds of linguistic stimuli can be comprehended by the right hemisphere. More research is needed to explore its decoding capacities.

12.2 HOW DOES THE BRAIN ENCODE AND DECODE SPEECH AND LANGUAGE?

Speech and Language: A Cortical and Subcortical System

What the silence of the isolated right hemisphere has dramatized is that speech is not solely a cortical function. Subcortical fiber tracts as well as gray matter areas deep within the brain—particularly the *thalamus*—also participate in speech and language.

The thalamus can be conceived of as a great relay station, receiving nerve fiber projections from the cortex and lower nervous system structures and radiating fibers to all parts of the cortex (see figure 12.4).

Emerging as especially important to speech and language function is the left thalamus. Damage to portions of this structure produces involuntary repetition of words and disturbs the patient's ability to name objects. The thalamus is thought to be involved in the focusing of attention by temporarily heightening the receptivity of certain cortical sensory areas. Ojemann and Ward (1971) observed that information presented to patients during left thalamic stimulation was more easily retrieved, both during and after stimulation, than information that had been presented prior to stimulation. They speculated that the thalamus may provide an interaction between language and memory mechanisms.

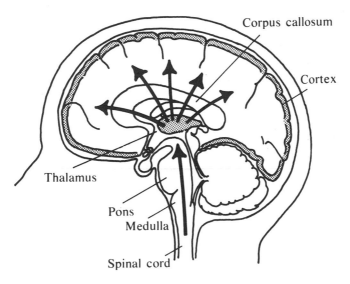

Figure 12.4
Fiber radiations from the thalamus to the cortex

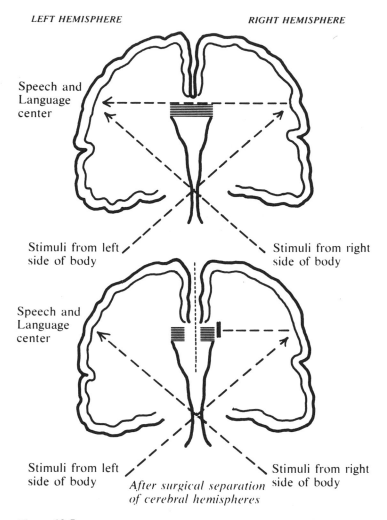

Figure 12.5
Callosal connection

Neurolinguists are far from being certain which neuroanatomical structures are essential to the encoding and decoding of linguistic stimuli, but they agree that speech results from an integrated cortical and subcortical system. An awareness that the neural sensory, motor, and associative mechanisms are interconnected is basic to understanding how the brain functions to encode and decode language.

A simple model can represent our knowledge of the transmission of signals to the language mechanism. In figure 12.5, the dark band between the semicircles (which represent coronal sections of the cerebral hemispheres) represents the hemispheric connection. Notice that impulses coming from the right side of the body have direct access to the dominant speech center, whereas those from the left must touch base with the right hemisphere before passing over the corpus callosum for processing. The left hemisphere is not dominant, however, for the processing of *all* auditory signals. Nonspeech environmental sounds do not have to be passed on to the left hemisphere but are processed primarily in the right hemisphere. How do we know this?

Evidence from Dichotic Listening Research

By means of a research technique called *dichotic listening*, we can analyze the characteristics of incoming stimuli processed by the individual hemispheres. During a dichotic listening task two different stimuli are presented simultaneously, through earphones, to the left and right ears. For example, the right ear may be given the word *base* and the left ear *ball*. The listeners are instructed to say what they hear. Interestingly, certain types of stimuli delivered to a particular ear will be more accurately reported by the listener. This is because the nervous system is capable of scanning incoming stimuli and routing them to that area of the brain specialized for their interpretation. Kimura (1961) was the first to observe that when two digits were presented simultaneously, one to each ear, the listener more accurately identified those presented to the right ear. However, when the listener was known to have the less common right hemispheric dominance for speech, Kimura observed a left ear advantage. In other words, the ear having more direct access to the language center had an advantage. Although there is some auditory input to each cortex from the ear on the same side of the body, these uncrossed, or *ipsilateral*, inputs are thought to be suppressed.

The right ear advantage (REA) was originally thought to exist only for linguistically meaningful stimuli, but the same advantage has been found for nonsense syllables, speech played backward, consonant-vowel syllables, and even small units of speech such as fricatives. Intrigued by these findings, investigators have sought to discover those features of speech likely to trigger left hemisphere processing. One hypothesis was that an REA would be found for any sound produced by the vocal tract musculature. Research results have disconfirmed this explanation, for REAs have been found for synthetic speech and Morse code, but not for laughing and coughing.

The REA associated with Morse code stimuli suggests that the left hemisphere may be dominant for more than the phonetic structure of language. In fact, the left hemisphere may be dominant for a number of nonlinguistic functions. For example, several investigators have noted that the ability to perform fine judgments of temporal order is a function of the left hemisphere: aphasics perform poorly, compared with controls and subjects with right hemisphere damage, on nonlinguistic tasks requiring temporal order judgments (Brookshire 1972, Swisher and Hirsh 1972). Lackner and Teuber (1973) have proposed that the left hemisphere has an advantage in temporal acuity and, as a consequence, language processing may have been drawn to the left hemisphere since speech is temporally ordered.

Much evidence implies that left hemisphere damage also impairs the ability to program complex motor sequences such as playing a violin. A disorder known as *oral nonverbal apraxia* is commonly associated with left hemisphere damage. DeRenzi, Pieczuro, and Vignolo (1966, 51) defined the disorder as "the inability to perform voluntary movements with the muscles of the larynx, pharynx, tongue, lips, and cheeks, although automatic movements of the same muscles are preserved." Patients have trouble voluntarily performing simple gestures such as whistling, blowing, clearing the throat, or sticking out the tongue. It has been argued that if the left hemisphere is dominant for programming motor sequences, it is logical that this special ability would be used to program the extremely complex motor sequences associated with speech, which, as pointed out in chapter 3, requires the simultaneous coordination of at least 100 muscles.

Besides having a superior capacity for processing temporally ordered stimuli and programming complex motor sequences, the left hemisphere is believed to be specialized for associative thought. Two notable studies support this hypothesis. DeRenzi, Scotti, and Spinnler (1969) observed that patients with left hemisphere damage performed more poorly than right-lesioned patients in an object-matching task. Patients were handed an object and required to match it to one of ten on display in front of them; the held object differed in form and color from its displayed match. The left hemisphere was found to be superior at recognizing the same object in a different form. In the second study, by Faglioni, Spinnler, and Vignolo (1969), subjects with left hemisphere damage exhibited significantly greater difficulty than both right-damaged individuals and controls in matching a sound, such as a bell, with a picture of its source.

It may be the case, as some investigators theorize, that speech and language function is not cognitively unique but is imposed in the left hemisphere because speech and language functions require the special nonlinguistic capacities of this hemisphere.

Complementary Specialization of the Cerebral Hemispheres

For some time the view prevailed that the left hemisphere was superior, overall, to the right; but this misconception has recently been corrected. The research techniques providing insight into speech and language function have unveiled functions for which the right hemisphere is dominant, particularly those functions requiring spatial ability.

Injury to the right hemisphere can result in visuospatial impairment. An affected individual may have trouble getting from one place to another, drawing objects, assembling puzzles, or recognizing faces. Such an individual may disregard anything on the left side of the body, even to the extent that when asked to draw the face of a clock, the patient may squeeze all the numbers in on the right side of the face.

Psychological research suggests that the two hemispheres differ in the manner in which they treat incoming stimuli, the right hemisphere processing stimuli holistically (as wholes) and the left analytically (by parts). For example, Kimura (1966) exposed three to ten dots to each visual half-field for 80 milliseconds. Subjects exhibited a left visual field superiority in guessing the number of dots. The brevity of the exposure time prevented subjects from counting the dots, lending support to the notion that the right hemisphere (associated with the left visual field) is superior at grasping the whole without a complete analysis of its parts.

Some musical skills are thought to be right hemisphere dependent. Although musical deficits are likely to exist after damage to the language-dominant (left) hemisphere, people with right hemisphere damage show deficits in discriminating complex sounds, timbres, and melodies. In a dichotic listening task, Kimura (1973) played a different melody to each ear simultaneously. Subjects were then asked to pick out these two melodies from among four melodies, each of which was played, individually, to both ears. Normal subjects were able to pick out the melody that had been

presented to the left ear (right hemisphere) better than the one presented
to the right ear.

Bever (1975) discussed Kimura's findings and suggested that to musically naive subjects the perception of melody is a holistic phenomenon,
thereby generating a left ear advantage for those subjects. In his own
experiments, however, Bever discovered that musically sophisticated subjects experienced a musical sequence better in the right ear (left hemisphere), because, he argued, they approached the task analytically.

Inasmuch as each cerebral hemisphere has unique functional superi-
orities (summarized in figure 12.6), it seems inappropriate to refer to the
language-dominant left hemisphere as the major one. It is more accurate
to conceive of the hemispheres as complementarily specialized. The degree
of hemispheric specialization, however, varies among individuals. Right-
handed individuals who have a family history of right-handedness show
the greatest hemispheric specialization. Least likely to show hemispheric
specialization are left-handed individuals with a family history of left-
handedness. Some of these individuals are thought to have bilateral representation of basic skills. The possibility of bilateral representation is

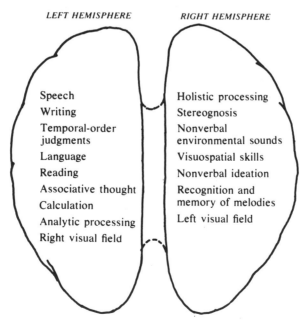

Figure 12.6
Complementary specialization of cerebral hemispheres

not surprising when we remember that each hemisphere has the capacity to replicate functions of the other; indeed, one hemisphere may take over for the other when it is injured or removed.

Right hemisphere language dominance is not uncommon in adults who sustained injury to the left hemisphere early in life. The literature is replete with documented cases of the development of language by the right hemisphere after injury to the left. Nonetheless, the adaptability of the nervous system decreases with age and when left hemisphere injury occurs after puberty, the danger of permanent aphasia is great.

Do the Hemispheres Equally Support the Development of Speech and Language?

Although speech and language function can be taken over by the right hemisphere if necessary, there is evidence that the right hemisphere does not have the same potential for speech and language specialization as the left has.

Dennis and Whitaker (1976) monitored the development of three children in whom one hemisphere of the brain was surgically removed during infancy (hemispherectomy) to arrest seizures associated with Sturge-Weber-Dimitri syndrome. Of the three children, two (SM and CA) had only the right hemisphere and one (MW) only the left. At the age of ten these children were given psychological and psycholinguistic tests. Intelligence was found to be comparable among the three, as shown in table 12.1. However, other differences emerged. When given a variety of complex verbal commands varying in information and syntactic complexity, only MW, the child with the left hemisphere, was able to maintain proficient performance. Syntactic rather than semantic complexity appeared to impair the performance of SM and CA. By contrast, as might be expected, the isolated left hemisphere (MW) performed more poorly on visuospatial tasks.

Table 12.1
IQ scores of children in the Dennis and Whitaker study (1976)

IQ Test	MW	SM	CA
Verbal	96	94	91
Performance	92	87	108
Full Scale	93	90	99

Functional asymmetry of the cerebral hemispheres is economical, enabling brain tissue to perform a wider variety of functions than would be
possible if each hemisphere were a replica of the other. On the other hand,
the potential of each hemisphere to replicate the functions of the other, in
a developing nervous system, provides a prudent backup system. As we
conclude the discussion of how the brain functions to encode and decode
speech and language, it seems appropriate to pose the question of whether
the areas within the left hemisphere speech and language system are func-
tionally divisible in phonological, semantic, and syntactic subsystems. This
is the topic of the next section.

12.3 ARE THE COMPONENTS OF LANGUAGE NEUROANATOMICALLY DISTINCT?

Within the left hemisphere there is neither uniform nor equal representation of linguistic functions. Damage to a small area in the hemisphere does
not result in the impairment of *all* linguistic capabilities. On the contrary,
lesions in different areas of the hemisphere lead to qualitatively distinct
aphasia syndromes. A review of the language and speech behaviors associated with the different aphasia syndromes will suggest a crude definition
of the boundaries of the various linguistic domains.

Aphasiologists have no uniform criteria for classifying types of aphasia,
the consequence of which is considerable terminological diversity. Widely
accepted, however, as distinct aphasia syndromes are the following:
Broca's aphasia, Wernicke's aphasia, conduction aphasia, and anomia.

Broca's Aphasia

Broca's aphasia, named for Paul Broca, who first described its symptoms,
is known also as *expressive* or *motor aphasia*. It follows from a lesion in
the posterior part of the inferior front gyrus, or Broca's area (see figure
12.1). However, according to Mohr (1976) the cluster of symptoms traditionally associated with Broca's aphasia results from a more extensive
lesion than the one described by Broca. Ironically, even Broca's own
patient had a more diffuse lesion, but Broca focused on the more circum-
scribed area in the inferior frontal region because of the view of his
contemporaries that large strokes always begin as a smaller focus.

The symptoms of Broca's aphasia will seem logical if we note the
proximity of Broca's area to the cortical region of the brain controlling the
muscles of speech (see figure 12.1). The foremost symptom is the inability

of the affected individual to speak fluently. Great effort is required to utter short halting phrases, described as telegraphic because of the absence of function words (words such as *the*, *by*, *but*). Literal *paraphasias*—substitutions, omissions, or distortions of sounds—are both frequent and inconsistent, and when the aphasic is permitted several repetitions of misarticulated phrases, articulation usually improves.

Bound morphemes such as tense, plural, and comparative markers are frequently missing. Surface word order is usually appropriate, however, and the verbal output makes sense. The characteristics of the spoken speech are mirrored in the patient's reading and writing. Although comprehension of language may not be normal, it is usually good enough for these individuals to grasp the meaning of what they hear. In fact, most of Broca's aphasics are painfully aware of their own mistakes. As you read the following samples of utterances produced by Broca's aphasics, remember that there is no way to reproduce in print the intense effort these persons must make to produce even a few words.

Examiner: Tell me, what did you do before you retired?
Aphasic: Uh, uh, uh, puh, par, partender, no.
Examiner: Carpenter?
Aphasic: (shaking head yes) Carpenter, tuh, tuh tenty [20] year.
Examiner: Tell me about this picture.
Aphasic: Boy...cook...cookie...took...cookie.

Neurolinguists agree that Broca's aphasics have suffered impairment to the phonological system but debate whether the syntactic component of language is impaired. Linguistic observations of aphasic language have a rather recent history compared with clinical studies. More research will be required to settle the issue of whether phonological theory can account for all of the linguistic aberrations displayed by Broca's aphasics when the lesion is confined to the frontal lobe.

Wernicke's Aphasia

Wernicke's aphasia, known also as *sensory aphasia* or *receptive aphasia*, is the consequence of a lesion in the auditory association cortex of the temporal lobe (see figure 12.1). This area is adjacent to the region that receives auditory stimuli. Predictably, the primary characteristic of this type of aphasia is impairment in the ability to understand spoken and written language. Wernicke's aphasics may suffer a severe loss of understanding even though their hearing is normal. Great variation in symptoms occurs in Wernicke's aphasia.

Fluency is usually not a problem, although interruptions in the flow of speech occur when the patient cannot retrieve a specific word. Often patients speak very rapidly, the content of what they say ranging from mildly inappropriate to complete nonsense, as in the following examples:

Examiner: Do you like it here in Kansas City?
Aphasic: Yes, I am.
Examiner: I'd like to have you tell me something about your problem.
Aphasic: Yes, I ugh can't hill all of my way. I can't talk all of the things I do, and part of the part I can go alright, but I can't tell from the other people. I usually most of my things. I know what can I talk and know what they are but I can't always come back even though I know they should be in, and I know should something eely I should know what I'm doing...

Circumlocutions are numerous: Wernicke's aphasics talk in circles about objects they are unable to name, as when a patient says *what you drink* for *water*. Patients with word retrieval deficits overuse empty words like *thing* and *one*. Language alterations in the form of word substitutions may be numerous. At times the substitution bears a relation to the intended word, as when someone says *slipper* for *shoe* or *corn flakes* for *cereal*. At other times there is no apparent connection between the intended and substituted words. In extreme cases, patients use unrecognizable words called neologisms.

For patients with severe comprehension deficits the prognosis for recovery is poorer than for Broca's aphasics, who have better comprehension. Aphasiologists speculate that Wernicke's aphasics have damaged feedback systems, limiting their ability to monitor what they say and thus limiting their ability to correct themselves.

Whereas Broca's aphasia is primarily a deficit in the phonological component of language, Wernicke's aphasia affects the semantic and syntactic components. The Sylvian fissure separating Broca's and Wernicke's areas may represent a neuroanatomical boundary separating the phonological from the syntactic and semantic components at the cortical level. It must be pointed out, however, that Broca's and Wernicke's areas are connected subcortically by a bundle of nerve fibers called the *arcuate fasciculus*. This may serve as a transmission line carrying signals received in the auditory reception cortex to the auditory association cortex for interpretation and, subsequently, to the speech production cortex for verbalization. Should the arcuate fasciculus be damaged, the affected individual would be expected to have difficulty repeating auditory information. And that is exactly what happens in conduction aphasia.

Conduction Aphasia

Conduction aphasia follows from localized lesions in the temporoparietal regions that serve to synthesize meaning and form. All avenues of expression are affected. Spontaneous speech is fluent but circumlocutory and inadequately structured. Similar defects are found in spontaneous writing. Reading aloud is difficult, and repeating is severely disturbed. Comprehension of oral and written material is normal or only mildly affected.

Conduction aphasics can be differentiated from Broca's aphasics by their fluent spontaneous speech; Broca's aphasics find spontaneous speech harder than repetition. Conduction aphasics are like Wernicke's aphasics in that they are fluent, but unlike Wernicke's they have good speech comprehension. Conduction aphasia is not a problem of receptive or expressive mechanisms as much as it is a problem of the transmission between the two.

Anomia

In classic *anomia* the patient has difficulty finding words, both during the flow of speech and in naming on confrontation. That is, when presented with a stimulus object, the individual is unable to retrieve its name. Yet when these individuals are offered the correct name of the stimulus item, they instantly recognize it. Further, they can usually select the correct name from a group of names.

Comprehension and repetition of speech are normal, and speech is fluent although filled with circumlocutions. The following selected responses made by anomic aphasics aptly illustrate word-finding difficulties:

Examiner: Who is the president of the United States?

Aphasic: I can't say his name. I know the man, but I can't come out and say ... I'm very sorry, I just can't come out and say. I just can't write it to me now.

Examiner: Can you tell me a girl's name?

Aphasic: Of a girl's name, by mean, by which weight, I mean how old or young?

Examiner: On what do we sleep?

Aphasic: Of the week, er, of the night, oh from about 10:00, about 11:00 o'clock at night until about uh 7:00 in the morning.

The brain lesions associated with classical anomia involve the dominant angular gyrus (see figure 12.1), that area of the brain thought to be necessary for the formation of association between the sensory modalities.

To sum up, the different forms of aphasia show that representation of linguistic functions in the left hemisphere is by no means uniform or equal. We have seen that lesions in different areas of the left hemisphere lead to distinct aphasia syndromes. Future research on these distinctions is certain to be both interesting and important.

12.4 SPECIAL TOPICS

PET Scans and Their Role in Mapping Brain Activity

By means of a new technique known as *positron emission tomography* (PET), researchers can study visual displays of the locations in the brain that are active during a variety of tasks, including those tasks involved in language use. A substance such as blood or glucose is tagged with a radioactive marker and then injected into the bloodstream. The radioactive marker gives off positrons (positively charged electrons), and when a positron collides with an electron in the body, the two particles annihilate each other, producing gamma rays. It is these gamma rays that are detected and provide information concerning the location and strength of the blood flow.

Once the radioactively tagged substance has been injected into the subject's arm, it reaches the brain within just a few seconds. This experimental technique depends crucially on the fact that more blood is delivered to the parts of the brain that are active than to the parts that are relatively inactive. The extra blood produces an increase in the number of collisions between positrons and electrons, which in turn produce increased gamma radiation, measured by detectors surrounding the head. The parts of the brain that play a role in a particular activity can then be displayed on a computer screen.

Figure 12.7 shows a cross section of a brain with superimposed PET scans, revealing locations that are active during different language tasks. The most forward location shows the part of the brain that is active when the subject is asked to think about the meaning of a word. The location at the top shows the part of the brain that is active when the subject pronounces a word. Finally, the location at the back shows the part of the brain that is active when the subject reads a word.

In order to determine which parts of the brain are active during a particular task, the researcher first obtains a brain activity baseline by having the subject, who is lying down, quietly gaze at a mark on an

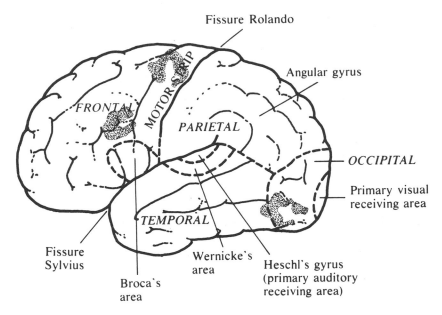

Figure 12.7
Representation of the spots (shaded areas) that are generated by positron emission tomography (PET). The spot at the back appears during reading. The upper spot appears during speech. The more forward spot appears when a subject is asked to think about what a word means. (Figure based on Montgomery 1989, 59.)

overhead computer screen. If the researcher is studying brain activity during silent reading, for instance, the subject is next asked to read silently a word that appears on the screen. A computer program then subtracts the data from the first activity (silent gazing) from the data from the second activity (silent reading). Since reading words and looking at a mark on a computer screen require different cortical activity, the result of the subtraction highlights the additional brain activities that occur in silent reading.

If the subject is next asked to pronounce words as they are presented by earphone, the places where the auditory signal is processed and where the articulation is controlled also exhibit increased gamma radiation. Proceeding in this way, experimenters can map the areas of the brain that are active in various isolatable tasks. Significantly, these experiments support the position that there are centers or local areas that are active in the control and processing of language.

One important new result of PET research is that language information of a visual nature can be transferred from the occipital lobe directly to

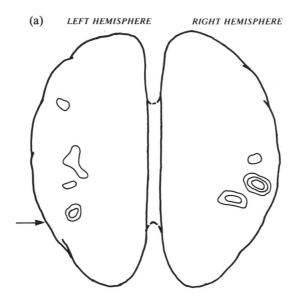

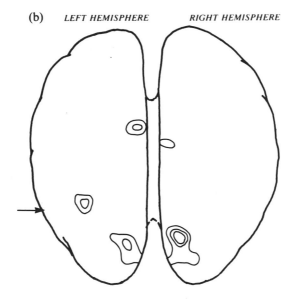

Figure 12.8
Part (a) represents the parts of the brain that are activated when we hear words.
Part (b) shows what parts light up when a subject is asked whether two written
words rhyme. Note that the part of the brain indicated by the arrow, the word
sound area, lights up in (b), even though no speaking is taking place. This area
does not light up, in fact, when adults read familiar words. (Figure based on
Montgomery 1989, 64.)

anterior portions of the brain for semantic processing without necessarily passing through the auditory association components (Petersen et al. 1988). At one time it was thought that the reading of a word required that visual information first be passed forward through Heschl's gyrus, where it would receive an auditory interpretation. From the auditory area it would pass to Broca's area, where it would receive a phonetic interpretation, and to other centers for semantic processing. In reading short and common words, it appears that the information can be received in the visual area and then directly transferred to the more forward comprehension areas, bypassing the intervening auditory areas. This is shown by the fact that during silent reading gamma radiation shows up in the posterior visual area and the more forward comprehension areas, but not in Broca's area. As figure 12.8 illustrate, when subjects are given a word visually and then asked to determien its rhyming properties, the auditory centers do "light up" as well as the centers seen in figure 12.7 that are active in silent reading. Researchers hypothesize that as children learn to read, their "sounding out" of the pronunciation always involves both the auditory area and Broca's area (Petersen et al. 1988). Later, the visual information is able to be passed directly forward to the comprehension areas, hypassing the auditory area. There are thus at least two paths from the visual cortex to the more forward comprehension areas.

Japanese Orthography and Graphic Aphasia

The Japanese language is primarily written with two types of symbols (ignoring romanji, the roman alphabet based script): *kanji* and *kana*. The kanji script uses borrowed Chinese characters (about 3,000 of them), which are associated arbitrarily with their sound. In other words, the logographic writing characteristic of Chinese is carried over into Japanese (see the Appendix). The kana script is a phonetic script (based on the syllable) for which there is a regular sound/symbol correlation. For examples of both scripts, see figure 12.9. Japanese writing consists of a mixture of these two systems, although the language could be written entirely in kana since the sound associated with any kanji character can be represented in writing with the kana syllables. These two different writing systems permit two different types of graphic aphasia to appear. If damage occurs to Broca's area, the patient loses the ability to process the kana (phonetic) script, although the ability to read and write kanji may remain intact. If part of

Kanji	Kana
一月	いちがつ
二月	にがつ
三月	さんがつ
四月	しがつ
五月	ごがつ
六月	ろくがつ
七月	しちがつ
八月	はちがつ
九月	くがつ
十月	じゅうがつ
十一月	じゅういちがつ
十二月	じゅうにがつ

Figure 12.9
The kanji characters of Japanese (borrowed from Chinese) on the left can all be
written in the kana script on the right. Represented are the names of the months.

Table 12.2

Two types of agraphia in Japanese. Japanese aphasics display some characteristics rarely found in Western patients because of the unique writing system used in Japan. There are two separate forms of such writing. One is kana, which is syllabic. The other is kanji, which is ideographic. Kana words are articulated syllable by syllable and are not easily identified at a glance, whereas each kanji character simultaneously represents both a sound and a meaning. A patient with Broca's aphasia, studied by Tsuneo Imura and his colleagues at the Nihon University College of Medicine, was able to write a dictated word correctly in kanji but not in kana (top left). When the patient was asked to write the word *ink*, even though there is no kanji character for the word, his first effort was the kanji character "sumi," which means "india ink." When required to write in kana, the symbols he produced were correct but the word was wrong. Another patient who had Wernicke's aphasia wrote kanji quickly and without hesitation. He was completely unaware that he was producing meaningless ideograms, as are patients who exhibit paraphasias in speech. Only two of the characters had meaning (top right). (From N. Geschwind, "Language and the Brain." Copyright © 1972 by Scientific American, Inc. All rights reserved.)

MEANING	BROCA'S APHASIA				WERNICKE'S APHASIA
	KANA		KANJI		
	PATIENT'S	CORRECT	PATIENT'S	CORRECT	
INK	キンス (KINSU)	インキ (INKI)	墨 (SUMI)	墨	鳥 字
UNIVERSITY	タイ (TAI)	ダイガク (DAIGAKU)	大学	大学 (GREAT LEARNING)	符 日 (LONG TIME) 久
TOKYO	トウ (TOU)	トウキョウ (TOKYO)	東京	東京 (EAST CAPITAL)	失 笑 (SOLDIER)

Wernicke's area is injured, the ability to write kanji script may be preserved, but the expressions are meaningless. Some experimental data concerning these two kinds of aphasia are shown in table 12.2.

Progress continues to be made with respect to understanding how language is stored and processed by the brain. PET scans have greatly increased our ability to look inside the working brain, but as sophisticated as this technique is, it is merely measuring blood flow. One of the guiding principles for future research will be to learn *how* the brain takes, stores, and processes information (knowledge). It may well be that questions about the storing and processing of human language will provide the most accessible features for studying the structure and functioning of the human brain.

Study Questions

1. Many technical terms appeared in this chapter. Compose a definition for each of the following:

a. aphasia   g. Wernicke's area
b. neurolinguistics   h. dichotic listening
c. corpus callosum   i. ipsilateral
d. temporal lobe   j. arcuate fasciculus
e. neuron   k. anomia
f. Broca's area   l. cortex

2. In what cortical regions are speech and language thought to be localized?

3. What is the corpus callosum, and how is it relevant to speech and language function?

4. Compare and contrast research techniques that have provided neurolinguists with information about where speech and language are located in the brain.

5. Suppose you were holding a pencil in your left hand and you wished to describe it. Discuss the chain of events occurring in the nervous system that would enable you to describe the pencil.

6. Discuss the complementary specialization of the cerebral hemispheres.

7. Why is it thought that speech and language function may not be cognitively unique?

8. Discuss how the ability to read and write kanji symbols may be preserved, whereas the ability to read the kana script is lost in some Japanese stroke victims.

9. "Lip movement" does occur when some people read. Discuss how this may occur using what you have learned in this chapter.

Bibliography and Further Reading

Bever, T. (1975). Cerebral asymmetries in humans due to differentiation of two incompatible processes: Holistic and analytic. In D. Aaronson and R. Rieber, eds., *Developmental psycholinguistics and communication disorders*. New York Academy of Sciences, vol. 263, p. 251.

Brookshire, R. (1972). Visual and auditory sequencing by aphasic subjects. *Journal of Communication Disorders* 5, 259–269.

Dennis, M., and H. Whitaker (1976). Hemispheric equipotentiality and language acquisition. In *Language development and neurological theory*. Brock University Conference, May 1975. New York: Academic Press.

DeRenzi, E., A. Pieczuro, and L. Vignolo (1966). Oral apraxia and aphasia. *Cortex* 2, 50–73.

DeRenzi, E., G. Scotti, and H. Spinnler (1969). Perceptual and associative disorders and visual recognition. *Neurology* 19, 634–642.

Eccles, J. (1972). *The understanding of the brain*. New York: McGraw-Hill.

Faglioni, P., H. Spinnler, and L. Vignolo (1969). Contrasting behavior of right and left hemisphere-damaged patients on a discriminative and a semantic task of auditory recognition. *Cortex* 5, 366–389.

Gazzaniga, M., J. Bogen, and R. Sperry (1963). Laterality effects in somesthesis following cerebral commissurotomy in man. *Neuropsychologia* 1, 209–215.

Gazzaniga, M., and R. Sperry (1967). Language after section of the cerebral commissures. *Brain* 90, 131–148.

Geschwind, N. (1972). Language and the brain. *Scientific American* 226.4, 76–83.

Geschwind, N., and W. Levitsky (1968). Human brain: Left-right asymmetries in temporal speech region. *Science* 161, 186–187.

Kean, M.-L. (1988). Brain structures and linguistic capacity. In F. Newmeyer, ed., *Linguistics: The Cambridge survey*, vol. 2. Cambridge: Cambridge University Press.

Kertesz, A., S. Blank, M. Polk, and J. Howell (1986). Cerebral asymmetries on magnetic resonance imaging. *Cortex* 22, 117–127.

Kimura, D. (1961). Cerebral dominance and the perception of verbal stimuli. *Canadian Journal of Psychology* 15, 166–171.

Kimura, D. (1966). Dual functional asymmetry of the brain in visual perception. *Neuropsychologia* 4, 275–285.

Kimura, D. (1973). The asymmetry of the human brain. *Scientific American*, March, 70–78.

Lackner, J., and H. Teuber (1973). Alterations in auditory fusion thresholds after cerebral injury in man. *Neuropsychologica* 11, 409–415.

Levy, R. (1976). The question of electrophysiological asymmetries preceding speech. In H. Whitaker and H. Whitaker, eds., *Studies in neurolinguistics and psycholinguistics*. New York: Academic Press.

McAdam, D., and L. H. Whitaker (1971a). Language production: Electroencephalographic localization in the normal human brain. *Science* 172, 499–502.

McAdam, D., and L. H. Whitaker (1971b). Electrocortical localization of language production. *Science* 174, 1359–1360.

Mohr, J. (1976). Broca's area and Broca's aphasia. In H. Whitaker and H. Whitaker, eds., *Studies in neurolinguistics and psycholinguistics*. New York: Academic Press.

Montgomery, G. (1989). The mind in motion. *Discover* 10.3, 58–68.

Ojemann, G., and A. Ward, Jr. (1971). Speech representation in ventrolateral thalamus. *Brain* 94, 669–680.

Penfield, W., and L. Roberts (1959). *Speech and brain mechanisms*. Princeton, N.J.: Princeton University Press.

Petersen, S., et al. (1988). Positron emission tomographic studies of the cortical anatomy of single word processing. *Nature* 331, 585–589.

Sholl, D. (1956). *The organization of the cerebral cortex*. New York: Wiley.

Swisher, L., and I. Hirsh (1972). Brain damage and the ordering of two temporally successive stimuli. *Neuropsychologia* 10, 137–152.

Wada, J. (1949). A new method for the determination of the side of cerebral speech dominance: A preliminary report on the intracarotid injections of sodium amytal in man. *Medical Biology* (Toyko) 14, 221–222.

Wada, J., R. Clarke, and A. Hamm (1975). Cerebral hemispheric asymmetry in humans. *Archives of Neurology* 32, 239–246.

Witelson, S., and W. Pallie (1973). Left hemispheric specialization for language in the newborn: Neuroanatomical evidence of asymmetry. *Brain* 96, 641–646.

THE WRITTEN REPRESENTATION OF LANGUAGE

Systematic writing developed in the Near East about 6,000 years ago and was originally *pictographic* or *ideographic*. Pictographs represent objects and are thus *iconic*, whereas ideographs represent ideas or sets of related ideas and are thus *symbolic*. For example, a circle ○ used as an ideograph might represent the sun, summer, light, heat, and so forth. What is crucial is that this type of writing system did not represent either words or the sounds making up the words. When the individual symbols come to be associated with certain words in a standardized fashion, the writing system is said to be *logographic*. A partially logographic writing system is used today in China. For the most part the Chinese characters represent a linking of a meaning concept and a phonetic syllable (see figure A1). Throughout China the phonetic representation of a particular character may vary, but the meaning remains relatively invariant. This lack of a constant sound/meaning association is advantageous in China because there exist so many different dialects of spoken Chinese. Mandarin, a form of Chinese spoken in the north, and Cantonese, a form spoken in the south, are for the most part mutually unintelligible. But since Mandarin speakers associate their Mandarin pronunciations with the individual characters and Cantonese speakers associate their Cantonese pronunciations with these same characters, and since both groups assign essentially the same meanings to the characters, Mandarin and Cantonese speakers can communicate via their common writing system (which functions as a lingua franca). European languages share some logographic symbols, the Arabic numerals being perhaps the most common example. For the numbers 3, 4, 5, for example, French speakers say *trois, quatre, cinq*, German speakers *drei, vier, fünf*, and English speakers *three, four, five*.

An extension of the logographic system occurs when a symbol that represents a word comes to be associated with the sound (pronunciation)

EXAMPLES OF THE COMPOSITION OF CHINESE CHARACTERS

kung[1] 'work'   Keys:

1. *hung*[2] 'big belly'

2. *k'ung*[1] 'impatience'   1. 'human being'

3. *k'ang*[2] 'carry on the   2. 'heart'
          shoulders'

4. *kang*[4] 'sedan chair'   3. 'hand'

5. *kiang*[1] 'river'   4. 'wood'

6. *hung*[2] 'red'   5. 'water'

7. *hung*[4] 'quarrel'   6. 'silk'

8. *hung*[3] 'quicksilver'   7. 'word'

                                  8. 'water'

Figure A1
Chinese characters, an example of logographic writing. These "compounds" have the form of a puzzle and are to be interpreted according to the following instruction: What is a word that sounds like *kung* "work" and is associated with the key word? Thus, *hung* "big belly" is a word that sounds like *kung* and can be associated with a human being. These Chinese compounds show that the Chinese writing system is not purely logographic. (From H. Pedersen, *The Discovery of Language*, 1962. Reprinted by permission of Harvard University Press.)

of that word and is used to represent other words that contain the same sound. We can illustrate this type of writing with an example from English. Noting that the symbol *4* is pronounced /fɔr/, we can use this symbol to represent the preposition *for*, as in the expression *4 me* "for me." It can even be used to form part of a longer word, as in *4-ground* "foreground." This type of writing is found in Egyptian hieroglyphics and is still used today in the type of children's puzzle called the *rebus*.

As soon as symbols became associated with sounds, new possibilities for representing language became available. A common writing system, one that many languages still use, is *syllabic writing*. The earliest writing of this type was done in *cuneiform* (from Latin *cuneus* "wedge"). The name reflects the fact that a wedge-shaped stylus was used to make marks on soft clay tablets that were dried or even baked in kilns. The cuneiform symbols (see figure A2) were derived from pictographs and ultimately came to represent combinations of sounds and in some cases single sounds. The Sumerians first developed this writing system more than 5,000 years ago, and it soon spread to other people such as the Babylonians and Akkadians, who used these symbols to write their own languages. Some early writing systems of Semitic (the language family that includes Arabic and Hebrew) were basically syllabic, but they did not represent the vowels (sch sntncs cn stll b ndrstd).

Egyptian hieroglyphics are also basically syllabic even though they appear to be ideographic or even pictographic. A Frenchman, Jean François Champollion, is credited with the earliest comprehensive decipherment of these Egyptian symbols. Using the Rosetta stone, on which a bilingual inscription in Greek and two forms of Egyptian writing, hieroglyphic and demotic, were found, Champollion discovered that the hieroglyphics represented sounds (see figure A3). *Hieroglyphics* are a very ornate writing system that eventually became limited to use in writing religious inscriptions on monuments. For common religious writing, a script called *hieratic* was developed, a simplified form of the original hieroglyphics. The hieratic script was better suited for writing quickly with pen on papyrus. The hieratic script remained in general use for religious writing, and from it an even simpler form, *demotic*, was developed for everyday use. Examples of the three writing systems are displayed in figure A4.

Another type of syllabic writing system uses a different symbol for each consonant + vowel combination. Such a system was invented by Sequoia in the nineteenth century for use in writing his native Cherokee language (see figure A5). Yet another variant of syllabic writing uses a single symbol

1.

𒐖 ...(cuneiform inscription lines 1)...

2.

...(cuneiform inscription 2)...

In transcription the inscriptions read thus (I add an interlinear translation):

1.

Dārayavahuš	*xšāyaþiya*	*vazarka*	*xšāyaþiya*	*xšāyaþiyānām*
Darius	king	great,	king	of kings,
xšāyaþiya	*dahyunām*	*Vištāspahya*	*puþra*	*Haxāmanišiya*
king	of countries,	Hystaspes's	son,	the Achæmenid,
hya	*imam*	*tačaram*	*akunauš.*	
who	this	palace	made.	

2.

Xšayārša	*xšāyaþiya*	*vazarka*	*xšāyaþiya*	*xšāyaþiyānām*
Xerxes	king	great,	king	of kings,
Dārayavahuš	*xšāyaþiyahyā*	*puþra*	*Haxāmanišiya* [1]	
Darius's	the king's	son,	the Achæmenid.	

Figure A2
Cuneiform, one of the earliest writing systems. The above transcription, dated from about 2400 b.p., is Old Persian, a language distantly related to English. What punctuation can you see in this example of cuneiform writing? (From H. Pedersen, *The Discovery of Language*, 1962. Reprinted by permission of Harvard University Press.)

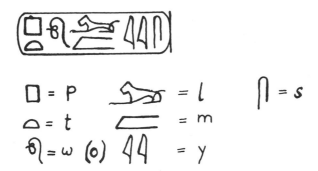

$$\square = P \qquad \text{(image)} = l \qquad \text{(image)} = s$$
$$\bigcirc = t \qquad \text{(image)} = m$$
$$\text{(image)} = \omega \ (o) \qquad \text{(image)} = y$$

Cartouche of Ptolmess and its analysis

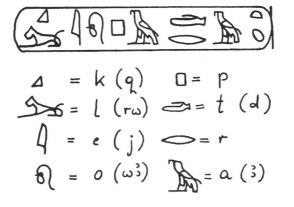

$$\triangle = k \ (q) \qquad \square = P$$
$$\text{(image)} = l \ (r\omega) \qquad \text{(image)} = t \ (d)$$
$$\text{(image)} = e \ (j) \qquad \text{(image)} = r$$
$$\text{(image)} = o \ (\omega^3) \qquad \text{(image)} = a \ (3)$$

$\bigcirc$ Feminine ending

O Determinative after feminine name

Cartouche of Cleopatra and its analysis

Figure A3
Examples of Egyptian hieroglyphic writing with accompanying sound-symbol correspondences. What does the hieroglyph for *l* look like that would help you remember this symbol? (From J. Ober, *Writing: Man's Great Invention*, 1965. Courtesy of the Peabody Library of the Johns Hopkins University.)

Figure A4
Examples of the three kinds of script used in ancient Egypt: hieroglyphic (top), hieratic (center), and demotic (bottom). Note the increasing abstractness that accompanies the evolution of Egyptian writing. (From J. Ober, *Writing: Man's Great Invention*, 1965. Courtesy of the Peabody Library of the Johns Hopkins University.)

for each consonant and a different diacritic (a mark added to the symbol) to indicate which vowel occurs with the consonant (see figure A5). An example of this type of syllabic writing is the *Devanāgarī* script that was used to write ancient Sanskrit and is still used in writing modern Indian languages. The Devanāgarī syllabary is generally believed to have descended from an early Semitic writing system.

The oldest writing system in the New World is that of the Mayans (see figure A6). This writing system, which dates from at least 700 B.C., has only recently been satisfactorily deciphered (Stuart and Houston 1989). It shares a similarity with Japanese writing in that it has both a logographic form (Japanese kanji) and a syllabic form (Japanese kana). There is no evidence, however, that the creation of this writing system was not indigenous to what is now Mexico and Central America.

The ancient Greeks were the first people to create an alphabet as we know it today—a set of symbols representing vowels as well as consonants.

Figure A5
Two examples of syllabic writing systems. The Cherokee syllabary (top) uses a different symbol for each vowel + consonant combination. The Devanāgarī system (bottom) has a single symbol for each consonant but adds diacritics (extra marks) to indicate the various vowels following the consonant. (Cherokee syllabary from Sloat, Taylor, and Hoard 1978. Devanāgarī syllabary from H. Pedersen, *The Discovery of Language*, 1962. Reprinted by permission of Harvard University Press.)

a	e	i	o	u	ʌ
D	R	T	o	u	ʌ
ga	ge	gi	go	gu	gʌ
ha	he	hi	ho	hu	hʌ
la	le	li	lo	lu	lʌ
ma	me	mi	mo	mu	
na	ne	ni	no	nu	nʌ
kwa	kwe	kwi	kwo	kwu	kwʌ
sa	se	si	so	su	sʌ
da	de	di	do	du	dʌ
dla	tle	tli	tlo	tlu	tlʌ
tsa	tse	tsi	tso	tsu	tsʌ
wa	we	wi	wo	wu	wʌ
ya	ye	yi	yo	yu	yʌ
ka	hna	nah	s	ta	ti
tla	te				

सम्मादिशत्पिता पुत्रं लिखलेखं ममाज्ञया

sa mā di śa tpi tā pu traṁ li kha lē kham ma mā jña yā

नतेनलिखितोलेखः पितुराज्ञानखण्डिता

na tē na li khi tō lē khaḥ pi tu rā jñā na kha ndi tā

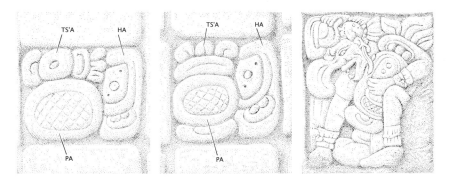

Figure A6
Graphic variation enabled Maya scribes to write each word in several ways. Shown
here are three variants of the verb *ts'apah* "was set upright." Each example includes
signs for three syllables: *ts'a*, *pa*, and *ha*. In the first (left) the signs are in conventional order. In the second (middle) the *pa* sign has been inserted into the *ts'a* sign,
which is vertical. In the third variant (right) the scribe has made use of a "full-
figure" glyph for *pa*: a seated man with a bulbous nose who cradles a *ts'a* sign.
(From D. Stuart and S. Houston, "Maya Writing." Copyright © 1989 by Scientific
American, Inc. All rights reserved.)

In fact, the word *alphabet* is formed by combining the names for the first
two letters of the Greek alphabet: *alpha* and *beta*. The Greeks adopted and
revised the writing system of the Phoenicians, Semitic people who were
sea-traders in the Mediterranean. Thus, we can trace the development from
ideographic to alphabetic writing, each step representing an increased
economy in the inventory of symbols needed. Whereas logographic writing
requires thousands of different symbols, alphabetic writing requires from
as few as 12 (for Hawaiian) to at most several dozen.

The Greek alphabet, then, is the ultimate source for all the alphabets
used today to write modern European languages, including English. There
is still controversy over what the alphabetic symbols should represent,
however. Should English be written with symbols that are phonetic? In this
case the word *democrat* /démǝkræt/ would have different vowels from the
word *democracy* /dǝmákrǝsiy/, a word to which it is closely related. Likewise, insisting that English be written with purely phonetic symbols would
require that the plural morpheme be written as either *s*, *z*, or *iz*, depending
on the nature of the final phoneme of the noun to which the plural
morpheme is attached. Another type of writing system, the *morphophonemic* system, would require the plural morpheme to be written as a single
shape. A discussion of the relative merits of these different writing systems
is beyond the scope of this text (but can be found in Reed 1970).

We conclude this appendix with the observation that writing systems do not seem to be able to halt language change. On the contrary, language change has been one of the historical causes for changes that occur in writing systems. Even though spellings such as *thru* for *through* are becoming more common, it cannot be foreseen whether the current writing system of American English will be revised in the near future. Such revisions are as much a political issue as a practical one. Language change is inexorable because of the nature of language itself. Language is extremely complicated, speakers have enormous flexibility in its use, and children must recreate the whole adult grammar when they acquire a language. We should be amazed that language stays as stable as it does and that writing systems stay in use as long as they do.

Bibliography and Further Reading

Ober, J. (1965). *Writing: Man's great invention*. Baltimore, Md.: The Peabody Institute.

Pedersen, H. (1962). *The discovery of language*. Bloomington, Ind.: Indiana University Press.

Reed, D. (1970). A theory of language, speech, and writing. In M. Lester, ed., *Readings in applied transformational grammar*. New York: Holt, Rinehart and Winston.

Sloat, C., S. Taylor, and J. Hoard (1978). *Introduction to phonology*. Englewood Cliffs, N.J.: Prentice-Hall.

Stuart, D., and S. Houston (1989). Maya writing. *Scientific American* 261.2, 82–89.

GLOSSARY

acoustic phonetics
The study of the physical properties of the speech sound waves generated by the larynx and the vocal tract.

affix
A bound morpheme that is attached to a stem and modifies its meaning in some way. Prefixes and suffixes are two common kinds of affixes.

affricate
1. A single consonant sound that consists of a stop followed by a secondary fricative release at the same point of articulation. The English words *chip* and *jump* begin with affricates. 2. A feature assigned to single phonemes that consist of a stop followed by a secondary fricative release.

algorithm
(See *effective procedure*.)

allophone
A positional or free variant of a phoneme.

alternation
The existence of two or more variant pronunciations for a given morpheme, each of which occurs under different conditions.

alveolar
Formed by means of a constriction or blockage between the tongue tip or blade and the ridge just behind the upper teeth. The English words *too*, *see*, *now*, and *lie* begin with alveolar consonants.

alveolar ridge
The bony projection located just behind the upper teeth.

alveopalatal
Formed by means of a constriction or blockage between the tongue tip or blade and the area just behind the alveolar ridge. The English words *ship* and *chip* begin with alveopalatal consonants.

ambiguity
The property of having more than one linguistic meaning.

ambisyllabic
A term used to describe consonants that occur at the border between two syllables and that can be thought of as both the coda of the first one and the onset of the second one. The /m/ in the middle of the English word *Emma* is ambisyllabic.

American Sign Language (ASL)
A system of manually produced visual

signals, analogous to words, taught to the deaf in the United States. ASL is not the same as signed English; that is, it is not a representation of the letters, sounds, words, or syntax of English but is rather a completely separate language. The signs of ASL have been analyzed into about fifty-five constituents, some involving the configuration of the hand(s), some the position of the hand(s) with respect to the rest of the body, and some the action or movement of the hand(s).

anaphora
The referential linking found between pairs of constituents in sentences such as *All people think they have a hidden talent.*

Anglo-Saxon
Another name for *Old English.*

anterior
A feature assigned to phonemes that are formed at the alveolar ridge or anywhere in front of it.

anticipatory coarticulation
A coarticulation effect in which some motion of the vocal tract needed for one sound begins during an earlier sound. Antonym: *perseverative coarticulation.*

apex
In phonetics, refers to the tip of the tongue.

aphasia
A cover term for various kinds of communicative impairment that occur as a result of brain damage.

aphasic
Suffering from a brain disease or injury that impairs communicative ability.

apical
Formed with the tip of the tongue.

argot
A variety of jargon, especially the jargon used by criminals.

articulation
The formation of a speech sound by positioning some part of the vocal tract.

articulatory phonetics
The study of how speech sounds are produced by the speech organs, in particular the vocal tract.

aspiration
The puff of air that sometimes follows the pronunciation of a stop consonant. The *p* in English *pill* is aspirated.

assimilation
A process by which the phonetic features of one sound are transferred to a neighboring sound.

back
1. Formed by placing the body of the tongue slightly behind the resting position. The English words *boot* and *boat* have back vowels. Antonym: *front.* 2. A feature assigned to vowel and consonant phonemes that are formed with the tongue body slightly in back of the resting position.

backformation
The process of creating new stems by removing some part of a word that is incorrectly analyzed as a morpheme, especially an affix.

base
1. In syntax, the part of a grammar that contains only phrase structure rules, before any transformational rules apply. 2. In morphology, another name for *stem.*

bilabial
Formed by means of a constriction between the two lips. The English words *pay*, *bay*, and *may* begin with bilabial consonants.

Black English
An informal style of English typically (though not exclusively) used by Black residents of ghettos in large urban areas of the United States.

blade
The large part of the tongue just behind the tip.

borrowing
The incorporation of words (or some other characteristic) from one language into another language.

bound morpheme
A morpheme that does not constitute an independent word, but must be combined with some other morpheme. All affixes and some stems are bound morphemes.

Broca's area
Part of the frontal lobe of the left cerebral hemisphere of the brain. Damage to this area results in a kind of aphasia characterized by lack of fluency in producing speech.

chance overlap
Accidental similarities between languages that are not genetically related.

cleft sentence
A kind of English sentence that consists of *it*, some form of the verb *to be*, a noun phrase or prepositional phrase, *that*, and a clause that modifies the noun. Examples: *It was Mary that I saw*, *It was in the park that I saw Mary*.

closed class
A group of morphemes whose membership is small and that does not readily accept new members. Function words, such as articles and conjunctions, are examples of closed classes. Antonym: *open class*.

coarticulation
The process by which some of the motions of the vocal tract needed for one sound take place during neighboring sounds.

coda
Within a syllable, the consonant or sequence of consonants that follows the nucleus.

code switching
A situation in which a speaker uses a mixture of different languages or different varieties of a single language in the same sentence or discourse.

coined word
A new word that is made up and added to the lexicon of a language.

communicative act
An act whereby a speaker succeeds in conveying a message by having his or her communicative intent recognized.

communicative intention
An intention that a speaker intends to be recognized by the hearer and that is fulfilled when it is so recognized.

comparative linguistics
The subfield of linguistics that studies related languages in order to learn about their historical development.

comparative method
A collection of analytical techniques used by linguists to reconstruct the history of two or more related languages.

competence (linguistic)
Knowledge of language; the linguistic capacity of a fluent speaker of a language. Antonym: *performance*.

complementary distribution
A relation between two speech sounds such that each occurs in one or more positions where the other one never

does. Two sounds that are phonetically similar and that are in comple-
mentary distribution are usually
allophones of the same phoneme.

complex word
A word that can be broken down into
two or more meaningful parts.

compositionality
The property by which the meaning of
a complex expression is determined by
the meaning of its constituents plus
their grammatical relations.

compound
A word that is formed by combining
two or more words or stems.

concept
A way of categorizing things, events,
and the like, into sets.

connectionism
The doctrine that connectionist models
of cognitive capacities will prove
correct. (See *connectionist model*.)

connectionist model
A model of cognitive capacity utilizing
a network of simple units with
weighted connections.

consonant
A speech sound produced with the
vocal tract relatively constricted.
Antonym: *vowel*.

consonantal
A feature assigned to phonemes that
are formed with a considerable degree
of obstruction in the vocal tract.

constituent
A word or an intuitively natural grouping of words that behaves as a unit
with respect to some grammatical rules.

constituent structure
The way in which the words of a
sentence group together into phrases
of various types.

constriction
The narrowing or closing off of some
part of the vocal tract to produce a
speech sound.

content word
A member of a large class of words to
which new items can easily be added,
for example, nouns and verbs.
Antonym: *function word*.

continuant
A feature assigned to phonemes that
are formed without a complete
blockage of the airflow in the oral
cavity. Noncontinuants are stops.

contrast
A relation between two speech sounds
such that replacing one by the other
sometimes makes a difference in the
meaning of a word. Two sounds that
are in *contrast* are allophones of
different phonemes.

conversation
Any set of connected utterances by
more than one speaker that has the
structure characterized by greetings,
turn takings, and closings.

conversational implicature
The act of implicating something via
the conversational maxims. (See
conversational maxims.)

conversational maxims
Grice's principles of Quantity, Quality,
Relevance, and Manner that govern
cooperative talk-exchanges.

coronal
A feature assigned to phonemes that
are formed by a constriction between
the tongue blade and the teeth, the
alveolar ridge, or the area just behind
the alveolar ridge.

correspondence set
A regular pattern of relationship
among similar sounds in a group of

related languages; such patterns are arrived at by comparing sets of related words.

creole
A language that developed from a pidgin by expanding its vocabulary and acquiring a more complex grammatical structure. Unlike pidgins, creoles have native speakers.

critical period
The developmental period (between infancy and puberty) during which a child can acquire language with the fluency of a native speaker (for example, without an accent).

decoding
The process of converting a signal in some communication system back into the original message. Antonym: *encoding*.

definite description
Expression of the form *the F* (for example, *the dog*).

deictic
Expression used to refer in virtue of properties of its physical production (for example, *I* refers to the utterer of the token *I*). (Same as *indexical*.)

denotation
Another name for *semantic reference*.

dental
1. Formed by means of a constriction between the tongue tip or blade and the upper teeth. 2. Can also be used to describe interdental sounds.

derivation
1. In morphology, the process by which affixes combine with words or stems to create new words or stems (as, for example, the *-able* suffix of English changes a verb into an adjective). Contrasts with *inflection*.
2. In syntax, the successive stages in the generation of a sentence that result from applying the rules of the grammar.

diachronic
Concerned with changes taking place over a period of time. Antonym: *synchronic*.

diachronic linguistics
Another name for *historical linguistics*.

dialect
A distinct form of a language (or other communication system) that differs from other forms of that language in specific linguistic features (pronunciation, vocabulary, and/or grammar), possibly associated with some regional, social, or ethnic group, but that is nevertheless mutually intelligible with them.

dichotic listening
A research technique in which two different stimuli are presented simultaneously (through earphones) to the left and right ears. This technique is used to investigate the roles of the two hemispheres of the brain.

digraph
A sequence of two letters used to spell a single sound. Two common digraphs in English are *sh* and *ng* for the final sounds of *hash* and *hang*.

diphthong
A vowel that consists of two parts, a louder vowel and either an onglide or an offglide, which together serve as the nucleus of a single syllable. The English words *buy*, *boy*, and *cow* end in diphthongs.

discontinuous dependency
The situation in which a single constituent is broken into two parts that are separated by material from outside that constituent.

discourse
Narrowly construed, any set of connected utterances by a single speaker.

distinctive
(See *contrast*.)

distinctive feature
A property that distinguishes phonemes from one another and that plays a crucial role in the statement of phonological rules. (See also *feature*.)

distributed
A feature assigned to phonemes that are formed with a relatively long area of contact or approximation between the tongue and the roof of the mouth.

domination
The relationship between a node and the material that branches down from it in a tree diagram.

effective procedure
A finite step-by-step procedure for doing something.

embedding
The occurrence of one sentence (or other grammatical construction) within another one.

encoding
The process of converting a message into a signal by means of which it can be communicated to other individuals. Antonym: *decoding*.

entailment
A relation between sentences *S* and *S'* such that if *S* is true, then *S'* must also be true.

euphemism
A polite expression used as a substitute for taboo language or to refer to some topic regarded as delicate, such as death, sex, or certain body functions.

extraposition
The process of separating a modifying clause from the noun it belongs with by moving it to the end of the sentence.

feature
Any of several articulatory characteristics into which speech sounds can be analyzed.

flap
A consonant sound formed by making a quick tap with the tip of the tongue against the roof of the mouth. In American English, the *t* in the word *better* is usually pronounced with a flap.

formal language style
A variety of a language that is used in official contexts, for example, making a speech in a courtroom. Antonym: *informal language style*.

free variation
A relation between two speech sounds such that either one can occur in a certain position, and the substitution of one for the other never makes any difference in the meaning of a word. Two sounds that are in free variation are allophones of the same phoneme.

frequency effect
The finding that high frequency words are recognized faster than low frequency words.

fricative
A consonant sound in which the airflow is channeled through a narrow opening in the vocal tract, producing turbulence. The English words *fill* and *soup* begin with fricatives.

front
Formed by placing the body of the tongue slightly forward from the resting position. The English words *beet* and *bet* have front vowels. Antonym: *back*.

function word

A member of a small class of words that does not easily permit new items to be added, for example, articles and conjunctions. Function words are usually hard to define because they indicate some grammatical relation, rather than referring to something outside of language. (See also *open class*.) Antonym: *content word*.

garden path sentence

A sentence such as *The horse raced past the barn fell* that leads the parser down a "garden path" to a (momentarily) incorrect analysis.

general term

An expression that applies to an indefinitely large group of things.

generate

In syntax, to specify the grammatical sentences of a language by applying a set of rules.

genetically related

Descended from a common ancestor language.

glide

A vowellike sound that precedes or follows a true vowel. The English words *you* and *we* begin with glides.

glottal

Formed by means of a constriction at the vocal cords. The English exclamation *oh-oh!* has a glottal stop between the two parts.

glottis

The space between the two vocal cords.

grammatical relation

The way a constituent of a sentence functions within that sentence. Two common grammatical relations for noun phrase constituents are subject and object.

Great Vowel Shift

A set of regular sound changes affecting the tense (long) vowels of English that took place around the fifteenth century. These changes account for many of the discrepancies between the pronunciation of English words and their spelling, which was established before the Great Vowel Shift took place.

Grimm's Law

A set of regular sound changes that took place in Proto-Germanic, in which Indo-European voiceless stops became voiceless fricatives, voiced stops became voiceless stops, and voiced aspirated stops became simple voiced stops.

hard palate

Another name for *palate*.

high

1. Formed by placing the body of the tongue relatively close to the roof of the mouth (said of vowels). The English words *see* and *Sue* have high vowels. 2. A feature assigned to vowel and consonant phonemes that are formed with the body of the tongue near the roof of the mouth.

historical linguistics

The subfield of linguistics that studies how languages change over time.

holophrastic speech

The utterance of a single word that expresses a thought usually expressed by an entire sentence.

hypercorrection

Overcorrection; the attempted rectification of a supposed error by introducing something that was never part of the original form, using as a model some other pattern in the language.

iconic
The relationship between an object and a representation of that object when the representation physically resembles the object in some way.

ideograph
A character in a writing system that represents some idea and is a picture of some object related to that idea.

idiolect
The variety of a language spoken by a single individual.

idiom
An expression whose meaning is non-compositional. (See *compositionality*.)

illocutionary act
1. Narrowly viewed, any utterance act that is also a communicative act. 2. Widely viewed, any utterance act that is either a communicative act or an institutional act.

implicature
The act of communicating one thing while saying another.

indexical
An expression used to refer in virtue of properties of its physical production (for instance, *I* refers to the utterer of the token *I*). (Same as *deictic*.)

indirect utterance
An utterance in which the speaker performs one illocutionary act by means of performing another (for example, *requesting* the heat to be turned up by *stating*, "It's cold in here").

Indo-European
A large group of historically related languages that includes many of the languages of northern India and Iran and most of the languages of Europe.

inflection
The process by which affixes combine with words or stems to indicate such grammatical categories as tense or plurality, for example, the *-ed* and *-s* suffixes of English. Contrasts with *derivation.*

informal language style
A variety of a language that is used in casual conversations with friends. Antonym: *formal language style.*

innate
Determined by the genetic makeup of an organism, rather than acquired by experience. Antonym: *learned.*

input system
A module for analyzing sensory and perceptual information.

institutional act
An act that consists in affecting the institutional status (social relations) of some person or thing.

interdental
Formed by placing the tongue tip between the teeth. For many English speakers, the words *thin* and *this* begin with interdental consonants.

jargon
A set of special vocabulary items used by members of some profession or specialized social group.

labeled bracketing
A linear representation of the information found in a tree diagram that uses nested brackets to show constituent groupings and subscript labels to identify categories (for example, [$_{NP}$] is a Noun Phrase constituent).

labial
A manner of articulation (or distinctive feature) that characterizes speech sounds that involve one or both lips.

labialized
Another name for *rounded*.

labiodental
Formed by means of a constriction between the lower lip and the upper teeth. The English words *fee* and *vow* begin with labiodental consonants.

laminal
Formed with the blade of the tongue.

language universal
Any property that is shared by most, if not all, human languages.

larynx
The voice box, that is, the structure of muscle and cartilage at the upper end of the windpipe that contains the vocal cords.

lateral
A feature assigned to phonemes that are formed with the tongue tip touching the roof of the mouth, but in which air passes along one or both sides of the tongue.

lax
1. Pronounced with relatively little muscular tension. Antonym: *tense*.
2. In describing English vowels, another name for *short*.

learned
Acquired by experience, rather than determined by genetic makeup. Antonym: *innate*.

lexical access
The process of contacting a word in the mental lexicon.

lexical ambiguity
The situation in which a word has two or more linguistic meanings. Contrasts with *structural ambiguity*.

lexical category
Another name for *part of speech*.

lexical decision task
The task of deciding as quickly as possible whether or not a string of letters is a word.

lexicon
A listing of all the words in a given language, each with its form, its meaning, and its part-of-speech classification.

lingua franca
Trade language; a language that is used by general agreement as the means of communication among speakers of different languages.

linguistic meaning
The meaning(s) that an expression has simply as a part of the language it belongs to.

liquid
A consonant sound in which the vocal tract is neither closed off nor constricted to a degree that produces friction. The English words *run* and *low* begin with liquids.

logical form
The representation of those aspects of a sentence that determine its logical relations.

logograph
A character in a writing system that represents a complete word. The Arabic numerals are logographs, and the Chinese writing system is heavily logographic.

long
1. In English, vowels of stressed syllables that have a relatively greater duration, have offglides to a higher vowel position, and are pronounced with relatively great muscular tension. The vowels of *feed*, *made*, and *mode* are long. Antonym: *short*. 2. A feature assigned to phonemes that have a

relatively greater duration than average.

low
1. Formed by placing the body of the tongue relatively far from the roof of the mouth (said of vowels). The English words *cat* and *cod* have low vowels. 2. A feature assigned to vowel and consonant phonemes that are formed with the body of the tongue far from the roof of the mouth and somewhat retracted.

manner of articulation
The way in which a sound is formed, usually specifying the type of constriction in the mouth. Contrasts with *place of articulation*.

matrix sentence
A sentence that contains another sentence embedded within it.

Message Model
A theory of communication in which the sender sequentially encodes the information he or she wants to communicate into a signal that travels to a receiver, who then sequentially decodes it to recover the original message.

metaphorical extension
The process of describing objects, ideas, or events from one realm by using words from a different realm (usually one that is more familiar or concrete), on the basis of some perceived similarity.

mid
Formed with the body of the tongue neither close to nor far from the roof of the mouth (said of vowels). The English words *bet* and *code* have mid vowels.

minimal pair
Two words that have different meanings and differ in form only in having different phonemes in one corresponding position. The English words *sip* and *zip* are a minimal pair; they differ in meaning and have different phonemes in initial position.

module
A special-purpose psychological capacity.

morpheme
The minimal unit of word building in a language; in other words, any part of a word that cannot be broken down further into meaningful parts.

morphology
The subfield of linguistics that studies the internal structure of words and the relationships among words.

morphophonemic
A kind of writing system in which all phonological detail that can be predicted by general rules is not symbolized.

mutual intelligibility
The situation that holds between two varieties of a language when speakers of either one are able to understand the other.

naming task
The task of pronouncing a string of letters as quickly as possible.

nasal
1. A consonant sound made by blocking the airflow in the mouth but allowing it to pass through the nose. The English word *man* begins and ends with nasals. 2. A feature assigned to vowel and consonant phonemes in which the velum is lowered, enabling the natural resonances of the nasal passages to be excited.

native speaker
A person who speaks a language fluently, typically because that person

has been brought up speaking that language as a child.

natural class
A grouping of phonemes uniquely defined by a small number of distinctive features such that that grouping plays a significant role in expressing the phonological regularities found in natural languages.

natural kind term
An expression that denotes natural kinds of things, such as *gold* or *tiger*.

neurolinguistics
The subfield of linguistics that studies the relation between language and the brain, especially the correlation between brain damage and speech and language deficits.

node
A point in a tree diagram at which lines connecting different constituents are connected.

nonliteral utterance
An utterance in which the speaker does not mean at least some of what the words uttered mean.

nonstandard language
Any variety of a language that lacks social prestige and is not considered acceptable in official contexts. Antonym: *standard language*.

nucleus
The loudest part of a syllable, usually consisting of a vowel or a diphthong.

obstruent
(See *sonorant*.)

Old English
The Germanic language spoken in Britain from the sixth to the eleventh centuries A.D. that is the ancestor of Modern English.

onset
Within a syllable, the consonant or sequence of consonants that precedes the nucleus.

open class
A group of morphemes whose membership is large and that readily accepts new members, for example, nouns, verbs, and adjectives. (See also *function word*.) Antonym: *closed class*.

operative meaning
The linguistic meaning of an utterance that the speaker expects to lead the hearer to the speaker's communicative intent.

orthography
Any writing system that is widely used by the members of a given society to write their language. Most orthographies do not represent the speech sounds of the language in a systematic way. For example, this sentence is written in English orthography.

overextension
The use of a word to refer to more than what that word properly refers to. Antonym: *underextension*.

palatal
Formed by means of a constriction between the body of the tongue and the (hard) palate. The English word *you* begins with a palatal sound.

palate
The front part of the roof of the mouth, which has bone beneath the surface.

particle
1. In English, a word that combines with a verb to create an expression with an idiomatic meaning, for example, *up* in *call up*. 2. In other languages, various kinds of affixes or function words; the class of particles

must be defined separately for each language.

part of speech
A group of words that share certain grammatical properties, such as the kinds of affixes they take and the kinds of syntactic constructions they occur in.

performance
1. What a speaker actually does in speaking or comprehending an expression. 2. The speech that is actually produced by native speakers, in which some of their linguistic capacity may be obscured by such factors as coughing, memory limitations, or inebriation. Antonym: *competence*.

performative
An expression such as *I promise to be there* that describes the act being performed in its utterance.

performative utterance
The act of sincerely uttering a performative.

perlocutionary act
An act of intentionally affecting the thought or action of the hearer by performing an utterance act. Need not be recognized to be successful.

perseverative coarticulation
A coarticulation effect in which some motion of the vocal tract needed for one sound continues on into a later sound or sounds. Antonym: *anticipatory coarticulation*.

PET scan
A PET (positron emission tomography) scan is an experimental technique that permits researchers and physicians to measure and map active areas of the brain and other organs.

phone
A speech sound. This term is generally used to avoid making any claim about

the phonemic or allophonic status of the sound.

phoneme
A speech sound that is psychologically a single unit, in contrast with other such units, but is often realized by two or more allophones that are in either complementary distribution or free variation with each other.

phoneme restoration effect
The phenomenon of hearing (and so "restoring") a phoneme in a word even though that phoneme has been removed from the signal and replaced with some other noise.

phonemic transcription
A writing system for representing speech sounds that omits some phonetic details that can be predicted by general rules.

phonetics
The study of speech sounds.

phonetic transcription
A writing system for representing speech sounds that includes much detail.

phonology
The subfield of linguistics that studies the structure and systematic patterning of sounds in human language.

phonotactics
The patterns into which phonemes and features can be arranged to form syllables and words in a given language.

phrasal category
A constituent of a tree diagram that is potentially larger than a single word. Phrasal categories are (usually) named according to the lexical categories that serve as their heads.

phrase marker representation
Another name for *tree diagram*.

phrase structure grammar
A description of the syntax of a language that contains only phrase structure rules.

phrase structure rule
A statement of an operation that expands a single symbol into two or more parts (for example, S → NP Aux VP).

pictograph
A character in a writing system that represents some object by a schematic, physical representation of that object.

pidgin
A simplified version of some language, often augmented by features from other languages. A pidgin typically arises in colonial situations and is used in the beginning primarily as a trade language.

place of articulation
The part of the mouth, throat, or larynx where the airflow meets the greatest degree of constriction in the production of speech sounds. Contrasts with *manner of articulation*.

positional variant
A phonetic form that predictably occurs in a specifiable environment. The aspirated [pʰ] that predictably occurs in *syllable-initial position* is a positional variant of the phoneme /p/ in English.

pragmatic presupposition
Something that is assumed or taken for granted in an utterance.

pragmatics
The study of language use and its relation to language structure and social context.

preglottalized
Preceded by a glottal stop or glottal constriction.

presumption
A special sort of shared belief in which speaker and hearer share the expectation that something is the case, but in which that expectation can be overridden at any time by new evidence.

program
An effective procedure written in a programming language.

programming language
A language executable directly or indirectly by a computer.

progressive assimilation
An assimilation process in which one sound affects a following sound. Antonym: *regressive assimilation*. Synonym: *perseverative coarticulation*.

propositional act
1. Widely viewed, the act of expressing a proposition. 2. Narrowly viewed, the act of referring to something and predicating something of it.

proto-form
A reconstructed word or stem that is hypothesized to be the ancestor of a set of related words or stems in daughter languages.

proto-language
A reconstructed language that is hypothesized to be the ancestor of some group of related languages.

prototype
A typical or representative instance of a concept.

prototype theory
Any theory that claims that concepts have an internal structure that reflects which members are prototypes of that concept.

psycholinguistics
A subfield of linguistics whose goal is to discover the psychological princi-

ples that underlie the human's ability to comprehend, produce, and acquire language.

reconstruction
The process of determining the probable forms of some earlier stage of a language by comparing related forms in two or more present-day languages.

recursivity
A property of grammars whereby a finite set of rules can generate an infinite set of structures.

reduced
Weakened to the point where it loses its distinctive quality (usually said of vowels in unstressed syllables). The English word *sofa* ends in a reduced vowel.

reduplication
The repetition of all or part of a word in order to modify its meaning in some way.

regressive assimilation
An assimilation process in which one sound affects a preceding sound. Antonym: *progressive assimilation.* Synonym: *anticipatory coarticulation.*

retroflexed
Formed by curling the tip of the tongue upward and backward. The English word *red* begins with a retroflexed consonant for some speakers.

rewrite rule
Another name for *phrase structure rule.*

round
A feature assigned to phonemes whose formation is accompanied by a pursing of the lips.

rounded
Formed by pursing the lips in addition to a primary constriction elsewhere in the vocal tract.

schwa
A nondistinct (mid back) vowel often found in unstressed syllables in English. The final sound of *sofa* is a schwa.

semantic decomposition
The analysis of a single word or morpheme into a set of semantic primitives that define it.

semantic field
A group of words with related meanings, for example, kinship terms or color terms.

semantic presupposition
A relation between sentences S and S' such that S would not be true *or* false unless S' were true.

semantic priming
The phenomenon whereby a word is recognized faster if a semantically related word was recognized earlier.

semantic reference/referent
The object, event, etc. that an expression applies to by virtue of the meaning of the expression. Contrasts with *speaker referent.*

semantics
The study of meaning, reference, truth, and related notions.

semivowel
Another name for *glide.*

shared beliefs
A speaker and a hearer share a belief when they both have the belief, each believes the other has the belief, and each believes the other believes they each have the belief.

short
In English, vowels of stressed syllables that have a brief duration, lack offglides, and are pronounced with relatively little muscular tension. The

vowels of *bit*, *bet*, and *bat* are short. Antonym: *long*.

simple word
A word that cannot be broken down into smaller meaningful parts.

singular term
An expression used to refer on an occasion to just one thing.

slang
A set of expressions that is characteristic of informal language style, tends to change rapidly, and often serves to indicate solidarity within a given social group.

sonorant
A feature that characterizes speech sounds whose articulation is not so narrow that the airflow across the glottis is appreciably inhibited; thus, sonorants are typically voiced. Nonsonorants are frequently referred to as *obstruents*.

speaker meaning
What the speaker means or intends to communicate in uttering an expression.

speaker reference
The speaker's act of referring to some object, event, etc. Contrasts with *semantic reference*.

speaker referent
The object, event, etc. a speaker is referring to. Contrasts with *semantic referent*.

speech comprehension model
An explicit representation of the processes leading from the hearing of speech sounds to the recognition of the speaker's communicative intent.

speech production model
An explicit representation of the processes leading from a pragmatic intent to the sounds that a speaker produces.

standard language
The variety of a language that has social prestige and is used in official contexts. Antonym: *nonstandard language*.

stem
A morpheme that serves as a base for forming new words by the addition of affixes.

stop
A consonant sound made by temporarily blocking the airflow completely. The English words *pin* and *dog* begin with stops.

strident
A feature assigned to phonemes that are characterized by high-frequency turbulent noise.

structural ambiguity
The situation in which a sentence has two or more different linguistic meanings even though none of the individual words is ambiguous. The ambiguity of such sentences resides in their different constituent structures. Contrasts with *lexical ambiguity*.

structural change
The operation carried out by a transformational rule.

structural description
A description that characterizes the analysis of a phrase marker into a sequence of constituents that serve as input to a transformational rule.

syllabic
A feature assigned to phonemes that occur as the nucleus of a syllable; such phonemes are usually vowels but are occasionally consonants.

syllable
A unit of phonological structure that usually consists of a vowel preceded and/or followed by various consonants.

symbolic
The relationship between an object and a representation of that object when there is no resemblance between the two.

synchronic
Concerned only with a single stage or time period. Antonym: *diachronic*.

syntactic parsing
The process of assigning the correct syntactic structure to a string of words by scanning it from beginning to end.

syntax
The subfield of linguistics that studies the internal structure of sentences and the relationship among their component parts.

taboo language
A set of expressions that are considered inappropriate in certain contexts. For example, profanity and obscenity are considered inappropriate in formal language contexts.

tag
Structured material added at the end of a statement; a tag contains an auxiliary verb, a pronoun that agrees with the subject of the sentence, and sometimes the word *not* or its contracted form *n't*. Example: *The infielders played well today, didn't they?*

tense
1. In phonetics, a speech sound pronounced with relatively great muscular tension. Antonym: *lax*.
2. For English vowels, another name for *long*. 3. Verbal affix indicating time.

transcription
Any system of writing used by linguists that represents the speech sounds of a language in a systematic way.

transformational grammar
A description of a language that contains both phrase structure rules and transformational rules.

transformational rule
An operation that converts an input tree structure into a different structure by adding, deleting, or rearranging material. Transformational rules consist of a structural description of the input and the structural change that they effect.

tree diagram
A graphic representation of syntactic constituent structure that uses branching lines and nodes that have category labels.

truth
A relation between a sentence and the world such that the world is the way the sentence represents it as being.

underextension
The use of a word to refer to less than what that word properly refers to. Antonym: *overextension*.

utterance act
The production of an expression from a language.

velar
Formed by means of a constriction between the body of the tongue and the velum. The English words *coo* and *go* begin with velar consonants.

velum
The back part of the roof of the mouth; there is no bone under the surface.

vocal cords
The two muscular bands of tissue that stretch from front to back within the larynx. The vocal cords vibrate periodically to produce voiced sounds.

vocal folds

Another name for the *vocal cords*.

vocal tract

The region above the vocal cords that produces speech sounds; it consists of the throat, oral cavity, and nasal cavity.

voiced

1. Accompanied by vocal cord vibration. Antonym: *voiceless*. 2. A feature assigned to phonemes that are accompanied by periodic vibration of the vocal cords.

voiceless

Not accompanied by vocal cord vibration. Antonym: *voiced*.

voicing

The sound made by the vibration of the vocal cords. This sound is heard during the production of vowels and some consonants.

vowel

A speech sound produced with a relatively open, resonating vocal tract. Antonym: *consonant*.

Wernicke's area

Part of the left posterior temporal lobe of the brain. Damage to this area results in a kind of aphasia characterized by fluent but meaningless speech and the apparent inability to comprehend language.

word formation rule

A process by which an affix is added to a word or stem to create a new word, and the meaning of the word is modified in some way.

word recognition

The process of selecting an accessed word and promoting it to consciousness.

INDEX